Assessment & Practice 4.2

Part 2 of 2

Contents

Unit 8: Probability and Data Management: Graphs 1

Unit 9: Number Sense: Fractions 23

Unit 10: Number Sense: Decimals 40

Unit 11: Patterns and Algebra: Equations 93

Unit 12: Measurement: 2-D Shapes 119

Unit 13: Measurement: Time 141

Unit 14: Geometry: 3-D Shapes 167

JUMP Math
250 The Esplanade, #408
Toronto, Ontario M5A 1J2
Canada
www.jumpmath.org

Writers: Dr. Heather Betel, Julie Lorinc
Editors: Megan Burns, Natalie Francis, Lindsay Karpenko, Daniel Polowin, Liane Tsui, Susan Bindernagel, Holly Dickinson, Jackie Dulson, Dawn Hunter
Layout and Illustrations: Klaudia Bednarczyk, Megan Blakes, Lorena González, Fely Guinasao-Fernandes, Linh Lam, Sawyer Paul, Nesba Yousef Marijke Friesen, Gabriella Kerr, Huy Lam
Cover Design: Linh Lam, based on an original design by Blakeley Words+Pictures (2014)
Cover Photograph: © Phongphan/Shutterstock

ISBN 978-1-77395-377-9

First printing June 2025

Printed and bound in Canada

To report an error or other issue in a JUMP Math resource, please visit our Corrections page at www.jumpmath.org.

A note to educators, parents, and everyone who believes that numeracy is as important as literacy for a fully functioning society

Welcome to JUMP Math

Entering the world of JUMP Math means believing that every child has the capacity to be fully numerate and to love math. Founder and mathematician John Mighton has used this premise to develop his innovative teaching method. The resulting resources isolate and describe concepts so clearly and incrementally that everyone can understand them.

JUMP Math is comprised of Teacher Resources, Digital Lesson Slides, student Assessment & Practice Books, assessment tools, outreach programs, and professional development. All of this is presented on the JUMP Math website: **www.jumpmath.org**.

The Teacher Resource is available on the website for free use. Read the introduction to the Teacher Resource before you begin using these materials. This will ensure that you understand both the philosophy and the methodology of JUMP Math. The Assessment & Practice Books are designed for use by students, with adult guidance. Each student will have unique needs and it is important to provide the student with the appropriate support and encouragement as they work through the material.

Allow students to discover the concepts by themselves as much as possible. Mathematical discoveries can be made in small, incremental steps. The discovery of a new step is like untangling the parts of a puzzle. It is exciting and rewarding.

Students will need to answer the questions marked with a  in a notebook. Grid paper notebooks should always be on hand for answering extra questions or when additional room for calculation is needed.

Contents

PART 1

Unit 1: Number Sense: Place Value

NS4-1	Skip Counting by 2s, 3s, 4s, and 5s	1
NS4-2	Using Skip Counting to Estimate Large Quantities	2

Unit 2: Number Sense: Addition and Subtraction

NS4-15	Adding Large Numbers	4
NS4-20	Estimating Sums and Differences	8

Unit 3: Measurement: Length and Mass

ME4-1	Centimetres	10
ME4-2	Millimetres	12

Unit 4: Geometry: Polygons

G4-3	Polygons	14
G4-4	Benchmark Angles	16
G6-1	Angles	19
G6-2	Measuring Angles	20
G5-4	Measuring and Constructing Angles	23
G6-3	Estimating Angles	26
G4-5	Regular and Irregular Polygons	28
G4-6	Parallel Sides	31
G4-7	Identifying and Sorting Quadrilaterals	34
G5-10	Rectangles and Rhombuses	36
G5-11	Sorting and Classifying Quadrilaterals	37
G5-7	Classifying Triangles	38
G6-5	Angles in Polygons	41
G6-6	Classifying Polygons	42
G7-11	Complementary Angles and Supplementary Angles	44

Unit 5: Patterns and Algebra: Patterns

PA4-1	Multiplication and Addition I	45
PA4-2	Arrays	47
PA4-3	Multiplying by Skip Counting	49
PA4-4	Patterns in Times Tables	50
PA4-5	Addition Sequences	53
PA4-6	Subtraction Sequences	56
PA4-7	Multiplication Sequences	59
PA4-8	Pattern Rules	61

PA5-1	Increasing and Decreasing Sequences	63
PA5-2	Rules for Sequences	66
PA5-4	Multiplying and Dividing by Skip Counting	68
PA5-5	Multiplication and Division Sequences	70
OA4-27	Advanced Patterns	72
PA4-11	Problem Solving with Patterns	73
PA6-10	Modelling Equations	74
PA6-3	Extending Patterns	77

Unit 6: Number Sense: Multiplication

NS4-21	Multiplying by Adding On	79
NS4-22	Multiplying by Tens, Hundreds, and Thousands	81
NS4-23	Multiplication and Addition II	84
NBT4-37	Multiplying 2-Digit Numbers by Multiples of 10	86
NS4-24	Doubling to Multiply	87
NS4-25	The Standard Method for Multiplication (No Regrouping)	89
NS4-26	Multiplication with Regrouping	90
NS4-27	Multiplying with the 6, 7, 8, and 9 Times Tables	91
NS4-28	Multiplying a Multi-Digit Number by a 1-Digit Number	93
NS4-29	Estimating Products	96
NS4-30	Word Problems with Multiplying	98

Unit 7: Number Sense: Division

NS4-31	Sets and Sharing	100
NS4-32	Two Ways to Share	104
NS4-33	Division, Addition, Subtraction, and Multiplication	107
NS4-34	Dividing by Skip Counting	108
NS4-35	Division and Multiplication	109
NS4-36	Multiply or Divide?	111
NS4-38	Remainders	113
NS4-39	Dividing Using Tens Blocks	115
NS4-40	Dividing Multiples of 10	116
NS4-41	Division Strategies	118
NS4-42	Estimating Quotients	121
NS4-43	The Standard Algorithm for Division	123
NBT4-45	Long Division—Multi-Digit by 1-Digit	127
NS4-44	Division Word Problems	129
NS6-18	Lowest Common Multiples (LCMs)	131
OA4-40	Factors	134
OA4-41	Finding Factors	136
OA4-42	Factor Pairs	139
OA4-43	Prime Numbers and Composite Numbers	141
NS6-21	Greatest Common Factors (GCFs)	143
NS6-23	Prime Numbers and Composite Numbers	144

PART 2

Unit 8: Probability and Data Management: Graphs

PDM4-1	Gathering Data	1
PDM4-2	Pictographs	3
PDM4-3	Creating Pictographs	5
PDM4-4	Bar Graphs	7
PDM4-5	Creating Bar Graphs	9
PDM3-10	Comparing Graphs	11
PDM3-11	Surveys	13
PDM3-2	Line Plots	16
PDM3-3	Reading Line Plots	19
PDM5-7	Primary and Secondary Data	21

Unit 9: Number Sense: Fractions

NS4-45	Naming Fractions	23
NF4-2	Comparing Fractions (Introduction)	25
NS4-46	Comparing Fractions to Benchmarks	26
NS4-47	Equivalent Fractions	28
NF5-12	Flexibility with Equivalent Fractions and Lowest Terms	31
NF4-4	Fractions on Number Lines	32
NS4-48	Comparing and Ordering Fractions	34
NS4-51	Fraction Word Problems	38

Unit 10: Number Sense: Decimals

NS4-52	Decimal Tenths and Place Value	40
NS5-50	Decimal Fractions and Place Value	43
NS4-53	Relating Fractions and Decimals—to Tenths	44
NS4-54	Decimals Greater Than 1—to Tenths	46
NF4-27	Decimals Greater Than 1	48
NS4-55	Comparing and Ordering Numbers—to Tenths	50
NS4-56	Adding and Subtracting Decimals—to Tenths	53
NS4-57	Estimating Sums and Differences—to Tenths	58
NS4-60	Combining Tenths and Hundredths	60
NS4-61	Adding and Subtracting to Hundredths	63
NS4-62	Dollar and Cent Notation	65
NS4-63	Money Math	67
NS5-57	Adding and Subtracting Money	70

NS5-60	Multiplying Decimals by Powers of 10	72
NS5-61	Multiplying and Dividing Decimals by Powers of 10	75
NS5-5	Multi-Digit Addition	77
NS5-6	Multi-Digit Subtraction	80
NS5-7	Addition and Subtraction Word Problems	83
NS4-58	Tenths and Hundredths (Fractions)	86
NS4-59	Decimal Hundredths	88
NS6-64	Percentages	90
NS6-66	Comparing Decimals, Fractions, and Percentages	92

Unit 11: Patterns and Algebra: Equations

PA4-12	Introduction to Algebra—Addition and Subtraction	93
PA4-13	Introduction to Algebra—Multiplication and Division	95
PA4-14	Totals and Equations	97
PA4-15	Differences and Equations	99
PA4-16	Addition and Subtraction Word Problems	101
PA4-17	Models and Times as Many	103
PA4-18	Problems and Equations—Multiplication and Division	107
PA6-3	Extending Patterns	109
OA5-6	Order of Operations and Brackets	111
PA5-8	Numerical Expressions	113
PA5-9	Unknown Quantities and Equations	114
PA5-10	Translating Words into Expressions	117

Unit 12: Measurement: 2-D Shapes

ME3-9	Shapes and Area	119
ME4-13	Area in Square Centimetres	122
ME4-14	Area in Square Metres	123
ME4-15	Area of Rectangles	124
ME4-16	More Area	126
ME5-15	Area and Perimeter of Rectangles	128
ME4-17	Problems with Area and Perimeter	131
ME4-18	Problems and Puzzles	133
ME4-19	Scale Drawings	134
ME4-20	Grids and Maps	136
G5-10	Rectangles and Rhombuses	138

Gathering Data

REMINDER: Data you collect yourself is called **primary** (or **first-hand**) data.
Data collected by someone else is called **secondary** (or **second-hand**) data.

1. How would you collect the primary data? Write the letter for your choice.

A. survey **B.** observation **C.** measurement

a) How does the temperature of a cup of heated water change over time? C

b) What are your classmates' favourite movies? A

c) How far can the students in your class jump? ______

d) How many students in your class have brown hair? ______

e) Do you think it will rain in the next 20 minutes? ______

2. Would you use primary or secondary data to answer the question?

a) What is the average temperature where you live? ____________________

b) How old are the students in your class? ____________________

c) How many medals has Canada won in the last five Olympics? ____________________

d) Which city gets more hours of sunlight, Calgary or Winnipeg? ____________________

e) How do most students in your class get to school? ____________________

f) How do most students in Canada get to school? ____________________

3. How is the data in Question 2 collected?

A. survey **B.** observation **C.** measurement

a) C b) A c) G d) C e) A f) A

4. Are all possible responses given? If not, add an "other" category.

a) What is your favourite sport?

☐ hockey ☐ volleyball ☐ basketball

b) What is your favourite season?

☐ spring ☐ summer ☐ fall ☐ winter

c) What is your favourite colour?

☐ blue ☐ red ☐ yellow

d) What is your favourite primary colour?

☐ blue ☐ red ☐ yellow

5. Would everyone know the answer to the question? Write "yes" or "no" to answer.

a) What's your favourite colour? ______

b) On what day of the week were you born? ______

c) When is your birthday? ______

d) What's your eyeglass prescription? ______

6. Add a category so that everyone can answer the question.

a) What is your favourite pizza topping?

☐ pepperoni ☐ pineapple ☐ mushroom ☐ ______________

b) In which season were you born?

☐ winter ☐ spring ☐ summer ☐ ______________

c) Which of these colours do you like best?

☐ red ☐ yellow ☐ blue ☐ green ☐ ______________

d) How tall are you?

☐ under 1.2 m ☐ 1.2 to 1.3 m ☐ 1.3 to 1.4 m ☐ 1.4 to 1.5 m ☐ ______________

7. a) Write a survey question to ask students in your class.

____

____

b) Write the possible responses to your question.

☐ ______________ ☐ ______________

☐ ______________ ☐ ______________

☐ ______________ ☐ ______________

8. a) Write a question that you will need secondary data to answer.

____

____

____

b) Why can't you collect the data yourself?

____

____

____

PDM4-2 Pictographs

A **scale** shows what the symbol means on a pictograph.
10 students eat lunch at home and 20 students eat lunch at school.
Both pictographs show the same data, but they use different scales.

Lunch Location

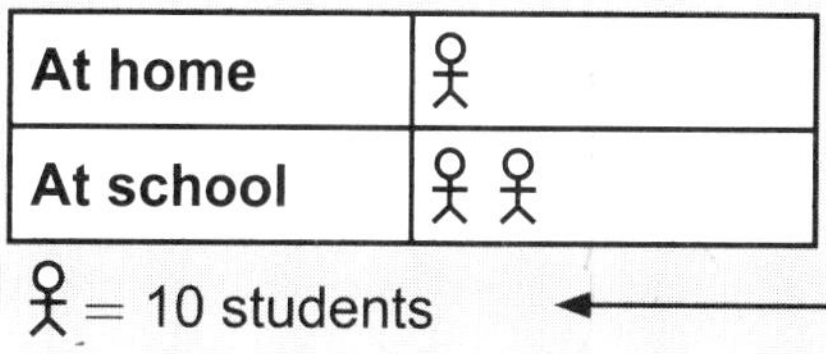
At home
At school
= 10 students

scale

Lunch Location

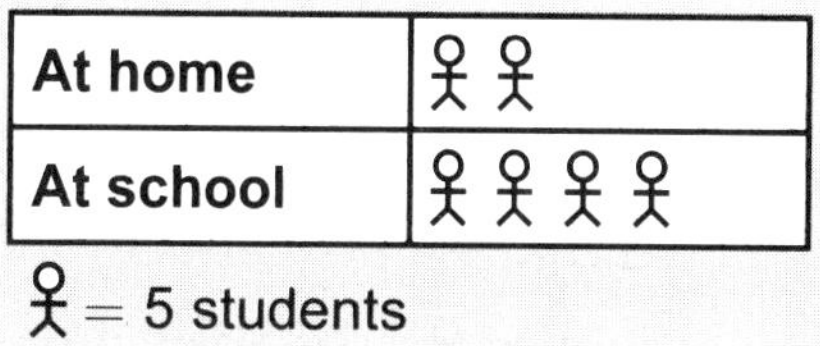
At home
At school
= 5 students

1. Look at the scale and multiply to find what the group of symbols means.

a)  = 5 people

 = 20 people

 = 7 people

b)  = 7 flowers

 = 28 flowers

 = 6 flowers

2. □ = 5 boxes. Draw symbols to show the number.

a) 15 boxes = 

b) 30 boxes = 

c) 5 boxes = 

3. a) Use the pictograph to fill in the table.

Flowers in Evan's Garden  = 5 flowers

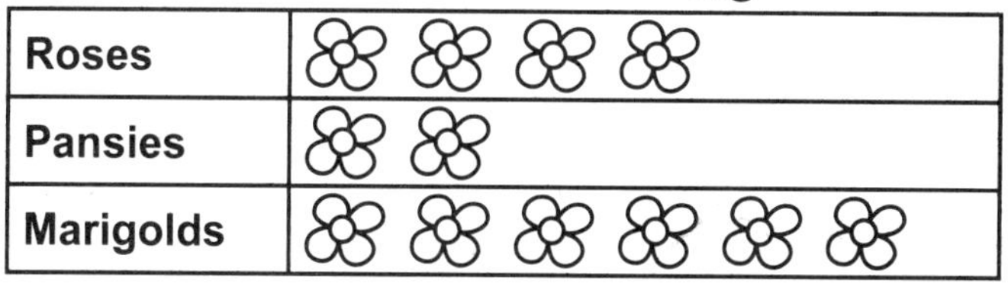
Roses
Pansies
Marigolds

Type of Flower	Number of Flowers
Roses	
Pansies	
Marigolds	

b) Use the data in part a) to draw a pictograph with the new scale.

Flowers in Evan's Garden  = 10 flowers

Roses	
Pansies	
Marigolds	

c) How many flowers does Evan have in total? ______________________

d) Evan used the flowers to plant 5 identical flower beds. How many of each type of flower does he have in each bed?

Roses: __________ Pansies: __________ Marigolds: __________

Half a symbol means half the number. Example: If  = 4, then  = 4 ÷ 2 = 2.

4. The first row shows what  means. What does  mean? Fill in the table.

	10	20	8	50	30	6	12

5. The first row shows what one symbol means. What does each group of symbols mean?

a)

	2	10	100

b)

	8	20	12

6. a) Use the pictograph to fill in the table.

How Students Get to School

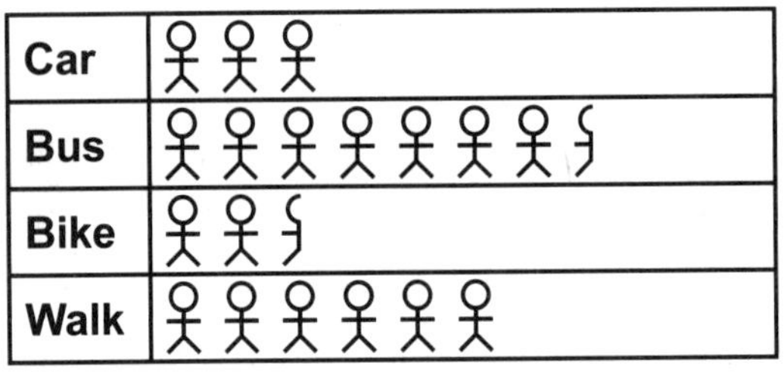

 = 10 students

Mode of Transportation	**Number of Students**
Car	
Bus	
Bike	
Walk	

b) How many students were surveyed? ______________

c) How many times as many students walk as take a car? ______

d) How many more students take the bus than walk? ______

e) Fill in the Carroll diagram with the number of students whose transportation to school is in each category.

	Has an Engine	**Does Not Have an Engine**
Has Wheels		
Does Not Have Wheels		

BONUS ▶ Name a means of transportation that has an engine but no wheels.

____

1. a) Count the tallies and draw a pictograph with the given scale.

Plant

Roses: 卌 卌 卌 卌 卌 卌 卌 卌 = ___40___ roses

Pansies: 卌 卌 卌 卌 卌 = ___25___ pansies

Dandelions: 卌 卌 = ___10___ dandelions

$8 + 81$

i) ◯ = 5 flowers

Roses	Pansies	Dandelions
◯		
◯		
◯		
◯	◯	
◯	◯	
◯	◯	
◯	◯	◯
◯	◯	◯

ii) ◯ = 10 flowers

Roses	Pansies	Dandelions
◯		
◯	◯	
◯	◯	
◯	◯	◯

b) How many times as many roses as dandelions are there? ___4___

c) Choose a title for the pictographs.

___Number of Plants___

2. The first line shows the data. Circle the scale that works best for the data.

a) 12, 4, 18, 6
♡ = ②
♡ = 3
♡ = 5
♡ = 10

b) 30, 90, 60, 105
♡ = 2
♡ = 3
♡ = 5
♡ = ⑩

c) 9, 12, 6, 27
♡ = 2
♡ = 3
♡ = 5
♡ = ⑩

d) 25, 10, 35, 15
♡ = 2
♡ = 3
♡ = ⑤
♡ = 10

3. In Question 2.b), what would be your second choice for the scale? Explain.

4. A birdwatcher made a tally of the birds she saw on her trip. Create a pictograph of the data.

a) Tally the data.

Bird

Bird	
Robins:	~~IIII~~ ~~IIII~~ ~~IIII~~ ~~IIII~~ ~~IIII~~ ~~IIII~~ ~~IIII~~ ~~IIII~~
Jays:	~~IIII~~ ~~IIII~~ ~~IIII~~ ~~IIII~~ ~~IIII~~
Sparrows:	~~IIII~~ ~~IIII~~ ~~IIII~~ ~~IIII~~ ~~IIII~~ ~~IIII~~ ~~IIII~~ ~~IIII~~ ~~IIII~~ ~~IIII~~
Finches:	~~IIII~~ ~~IIII~~ ~~IIII~~

b) Fill in the title and labels on the pictograph.

c) Choose a symbol and a scale.

d) Complete the pictograph.

Title: ______________________________

Scale: ______ = ______ birds

Bird

Robins									
Jays									
Sparrows									
Finches									

e) Order the birds from most to least common.

__________ __________ __________ __________

f) How many birds were seen in total? __________

g) Which two types of birds together make up half the birds seen? __________

h) Which type of bird was seen exactly twice as often as another type? __________

i) How many more sparrows than finches were seen? __________

j) How many more sparrows and robins were seen than jays and finches? __________

k) Make up your own question from the pictograph. Write the answer.

____

____

____

Bar Graphs

1. The bar graph shows approximately how many barrels of oil are used per person, each year, on every continent.

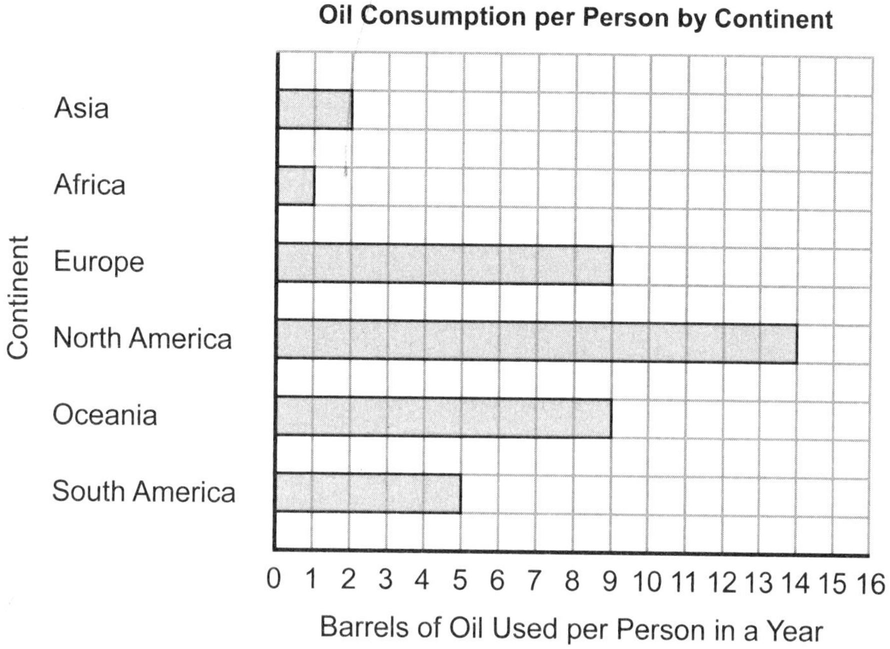

a) Which continent uses the least oil per person? ____________________

b) Which continent uses the most oil per person? ____________________

c) How many times as much oil does Asia use as Africa? ______

d) Which two continents use the same amount of oil? ____________________

e) How many barrels of oil per person per year does Europe use? ______

2. Rick asked his classmates if they liked travelling by car, plane, or train the most. He showed the answers in a bar graph.

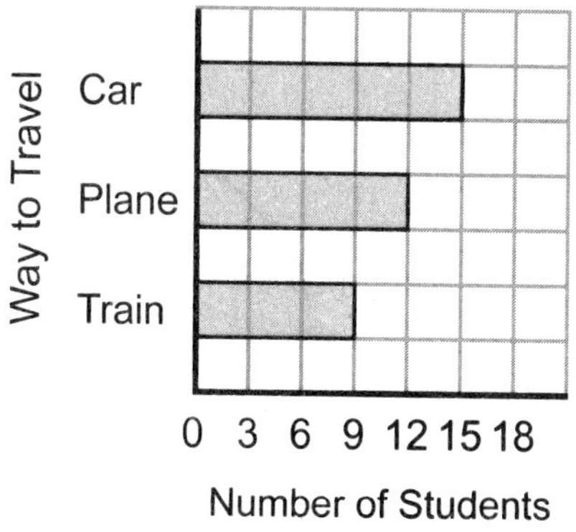

a) What number does the scale count by? ______

b) How many students prefer to travel by train? ______

c) How many more students prefer the car to the plane? ______

d) How many students were surveyed altogether? ______

BONUS ▶ Could a bar on this graph end in the middle of a block? Explain.

____

____

A bar can end between two numbers on a bar graph.

3. Students voted for their favourite summer activity. The bar graph shows the results.

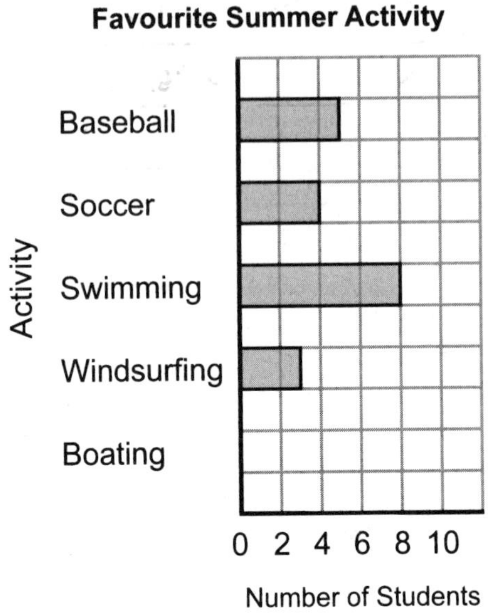

a) Fill in the table.

Favourite Activity	**Number of Students**
Baseball	*5*
Soccer	
Swimming	
Windsurfing	

b) 9 students picked boating. Add this to the table. Add the bar for boating to the bar graph.

c) Fill in the blank.

i) ______ times as many students picked boating as windsurfing.

ii) ______ times as many students picked swimming as soccer.

iii) ______ students picked water activities.

iv) ______ times as many students chose water activities as soccer.

v) ______________________ was the most popular activity.

vi) ______________________ was the least popular activity.

vii) How many students were surveyed? ______________

BONUS ▶

d) Kyle thinks that the bar for swimming is 2 blocks longer than the bar for soccer, so 2 more students voted for swimming. Is he correct? Explain.

____

____

____

e) On Sports Day, the class can choose three of these activities. Which three should they choose? Explain.

____

____

PDM4-5 Creating Bar Graphs

1. Sara is researching different dog breeds.

   a) Fill in the table using Bar Graph 1.

Dog Breed	Mass (kg)
Beagle (B)	
Collie (C)	
Dalmatian (D)	
Husky (H)	
Pug (P)	

Bar Graph 1
Dog Breeds and Masses

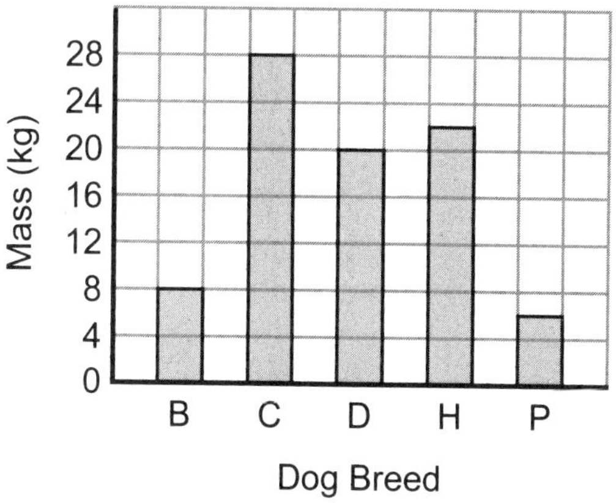

   b) What number does the scale skip count by? ______

   c) Are there bars that end between the numbers? ______

   d) How many blocks long is the tallest bar? ______

   e) Use the table to complete Bar Graph 2 with a scale that skip counts by 2 to show the same information.

Bar Graph 2
Dog Breeds and Masses

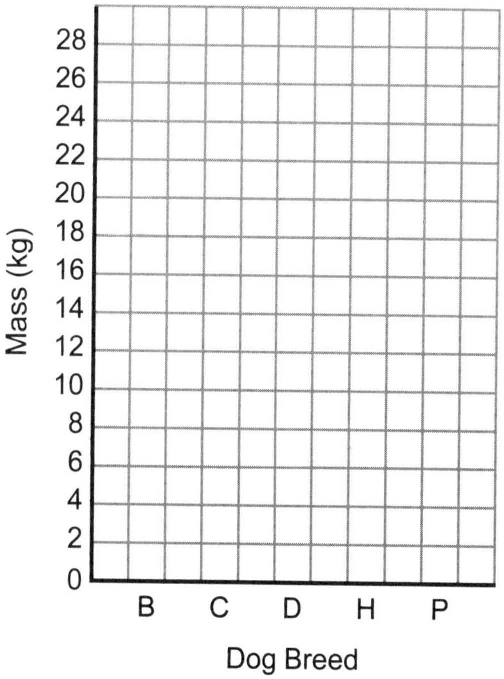

   f) Are there bars that end between the numbers? ______

   g) Which graph takes more space? ______

   h) Use the graphs to find out which dog breed has a mass 8 kg greater than a dalmatian.

   ____

   Which graph makes this easier to answer? ______

   i) Use the graphs to find out which breed weighs 22 kg less than a collie.

   ____

   Which graph makes this easier to answer? ______

   j) How much would 2 beagles, 1 collie, 1 dalmation, 2 huskies, and 3 pugs weigh altogether? __________

2. Tasha surveyed her grade about their favourite pizza. She gave students four choices.

a) Here are the results of Tasha's survey. Tally the data.

Plain cheese: 𝍸 𝍸 𝍸 𝍸 𝍸 𝍸 36

Pepperoni: 𝍸 𝍸 𝍸 𝍸 𝍸 𝍸 𝍸 ____

Hawaiian: 𝍸 𝍸 𝍸 ____

Vegetarian: 𝍸 𝍸 𝍸 𝍸 𝍸 𝍸 𝍸 𝍸 𝍸 ____

b) Fill in the title and axis labels on the bar graph.

c) Choose a number to count by. Fill in the numbers on the axis.

d) Complete the bar graph.

Title: ______________________________

____

Plain Cheese									
Pepperoni									
Hawaiian									
Vegetarian									

0 ___ ___ ___ ___ ___ ___ ___ ___ ___

____

e) Write the pizzas in order from most to least popular.

____________ ____________ ____________ ____________

f) How many students were surveyed altogether? ____________

g) How many times as many people preferred vegetarian to Hawaiian? ____________

h) How many times as many people preferred plain cheese to Hawaiian? ____________

BONUS ▶ Tasha uses the information in Question 2 to buy pizzas for her grade.

a) If 1 pizza can feed 5 people, how many pizzas should she buy? ____________

b) How many of each type of pizza should she buy?

Plain: ________ Pepperoni: ________ Hawaiian: ________ Vegetarian: ________

c) If 1 pizza can feed 8 people, how many of each type should she buy?

Plain: ________ Pepperoni: ________ Hawaiian: ________ Vegetarian: ________

Comparing Graphs

Karen, Sal, and Yu collected some leaves. They each made a graph.

Karen's graph:

Leaves Collected

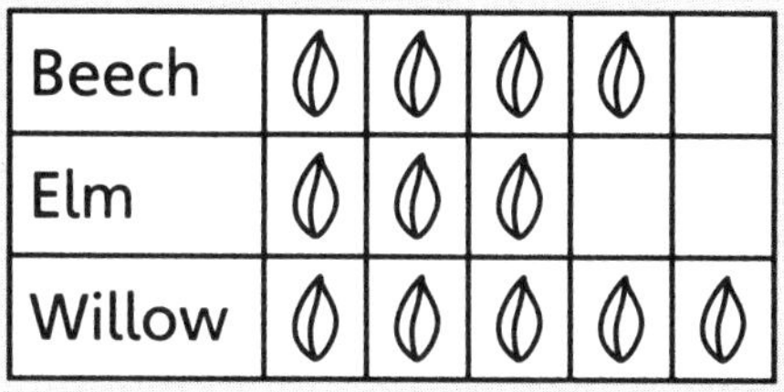

Sal's graph:

Leaves Collected

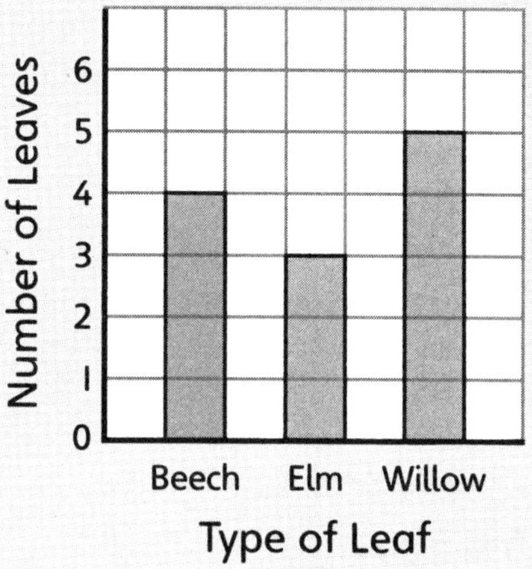

Yu's graph:

Lengths of Leaves

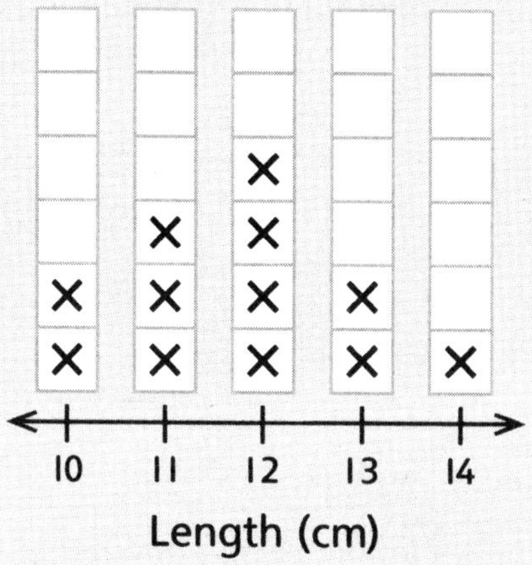

1. a) What type of graph did each student draw?

Karen: ________________ Sal: ________________ Yu: ________________

b) What does each graph have? Write ✓ or ✗.

Feature	**Pictograph**	**Bar Graph**	**Line Plot**
Title			
Labels			
Number line			
Vertical axis			
Scale			
Symbols			

c) How many leaves did Karen, Sal, and Yu collect? __________
How does each graph show this?

Pictograph: ____

Bar graph: ____

Line plot: ____

2. Use the graphs that Karen, Sal, and Yu made to answer the question. Say which graph or graphs you could use to answer the question.

		Answer	Graph(s)
a)	How many more willow leaves than beech leaves did they collect?	*1*	*pictograph, bar graph*
b)	How many fewer elm leaves than beech leaves did they collect?		
c)	How many leaves longer than 12 cm did they collect?		
d)	How many fewer 14 cm long leaves than 10 cm long leaves were there?		
e)	What was the most common type of leaf?		

3. Students voted for their favourite type of book.

a) Make a bar graph showing the same data as the pictograph.

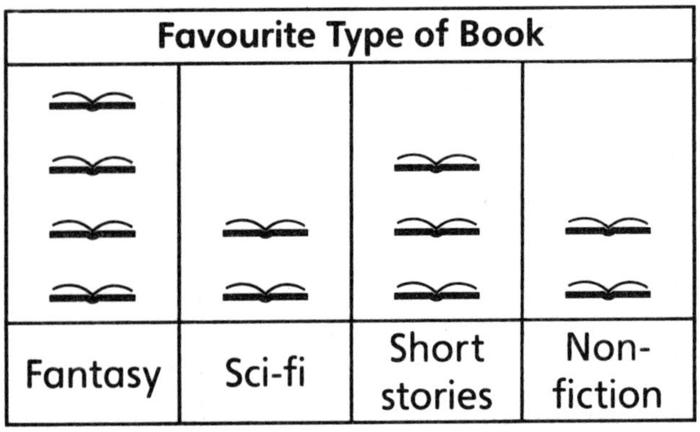

= 1 student

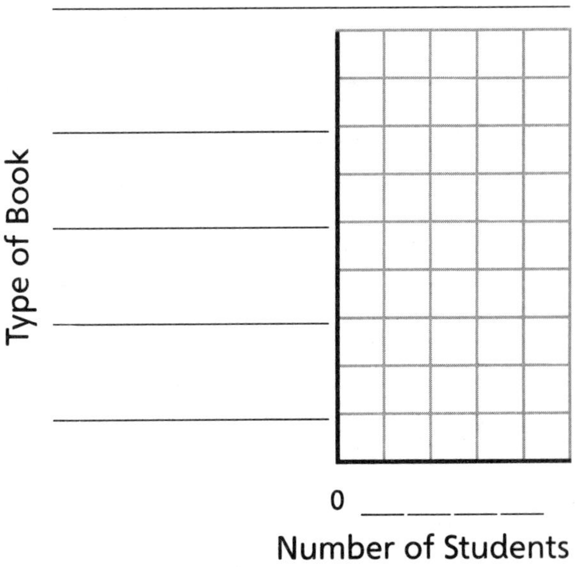

b) How many more students voted for fantasy books than for science fiction?

c) How many fewer students voted for non-fiction books than for short stories?

PDM3-11 Surveys

1. Megan asked her classmates to circle their favourite season. She gave them the choices below.

   Spring Summer Winter

   a) Are there enough choices? ______ Explain. ______________________________

   ____

   b) What choice should she add? ______________

2. Alex asked his classmates to circle the number of siblings (brothers or sisters) they have. He offered the answers below.

   0 1 2 3

   Anne has 4 siblings, and Carl has 6 siblings.

   a) Can Anne and Carl answer the survey? ______

   b) What **one** choice could Alex add so that both Carl and Anne can answer the survey? ______________

3. Ask your classmates how they got to school today.

   a) Tally your results.

   Title: ______________________________________

Way to Get to School	Tally
School bus	
Car	
Walk	
Bike	
Scooter	
Other	

   b) Make a pictograph. ☺ = 2 students

To write a survey question,

- Decide what you want to know.

  Example:
  What is the favourite fruit of my classmates?

- Make sure the question does not have too many possible responses. One of the responses could be "other."

Example:
What is your favourite fruit? — ✗ This question may give you too many answers.

What fruit do you like? — ✗ People could give more than one answer.

☐ apple ☐ grape ☐ orange ☐ other

Which is your favourite fruit? — ✓ This is a better survey question.

☐ apple ☐ grape ☐ orange ☐ other

4. a) Write a survey question to find out what pizza toppings students like best.

____

____

____

b) Write the possible responses to your question.

☐ __________ ☐ __________ ☐ __________

☐ __________ ☐ __________ ☐ other

5. Write a different survey question you could ask your classmates.

____

____

____

6. a) Survey your classmates to find out their favourite school subjects. Use the table to tally and count your results.

School Subject	Tally	Count
English		
French		
Gym		
Math		
Science		
Other		

b) What scale (counting by 1s, 2s, 3s, 5s, or 10s) would be the best for a bar graph of your data? ______ Explain. ______________________________

____

c) Use the scale you picked in part b). Create a bar graph of the data you collected.

Title: ______________________________

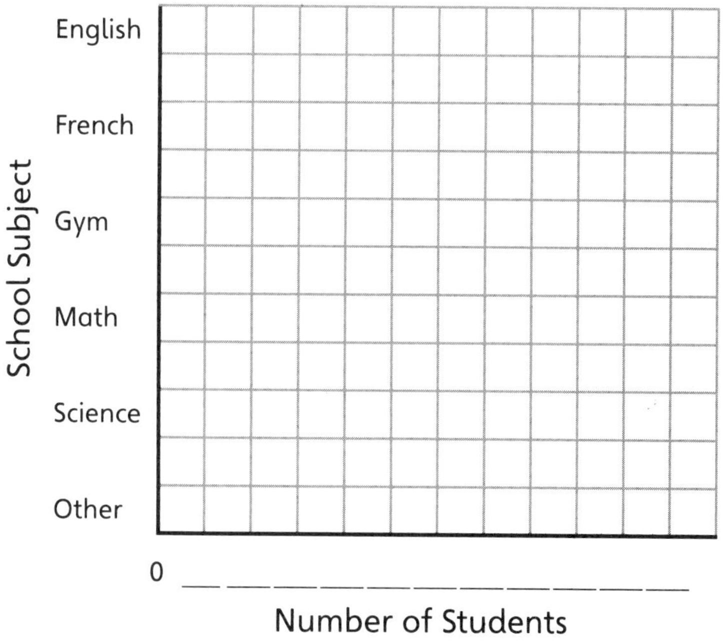

d) List three conclusions you can make from your bar graph.

PDM3-2 Line Plots

1. Measure the heights of the flowers to the nearest centimetre.

_____ cm

_____ cm

_____4_____ cm _____ cm

_____ cm

_____ cm

_____ cm

_____ cm

_____ cm

_____ cm

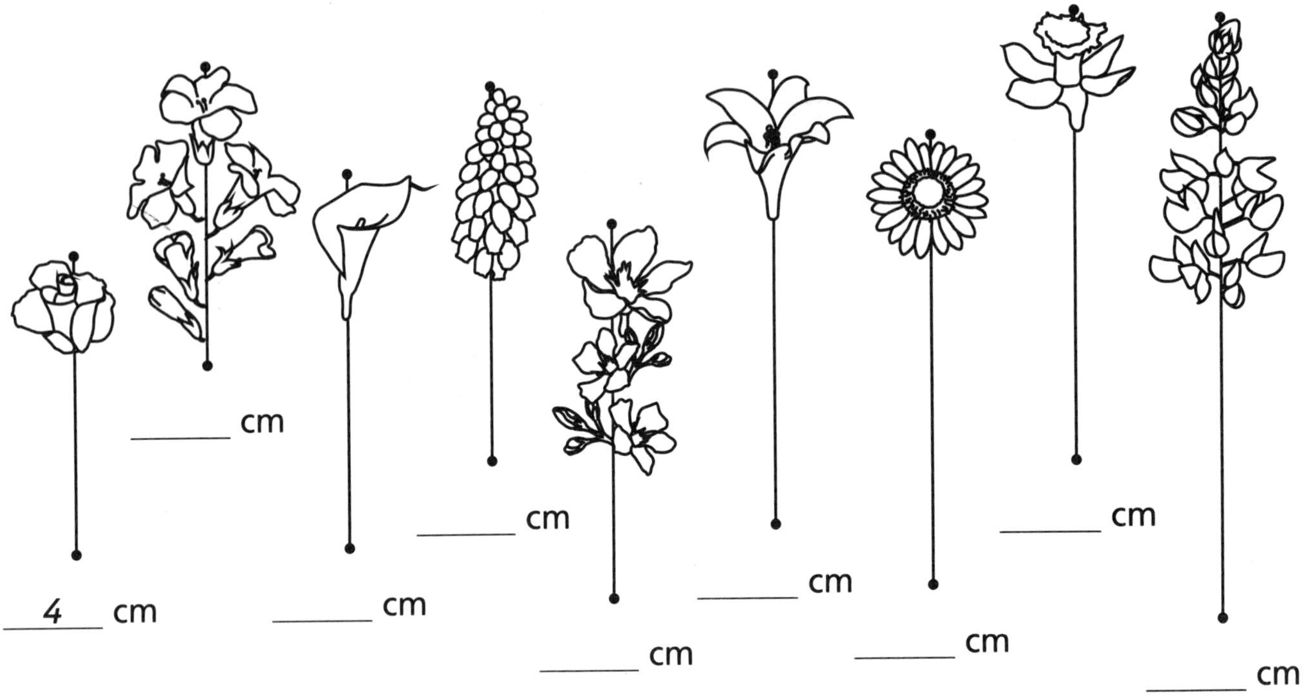

We can show measurements using a **line plot**.

This is a line plot for the data in Question 1.

Each **✗** shows one data value.

Heights of Flowers ← title

Height (cm) ← label

number line

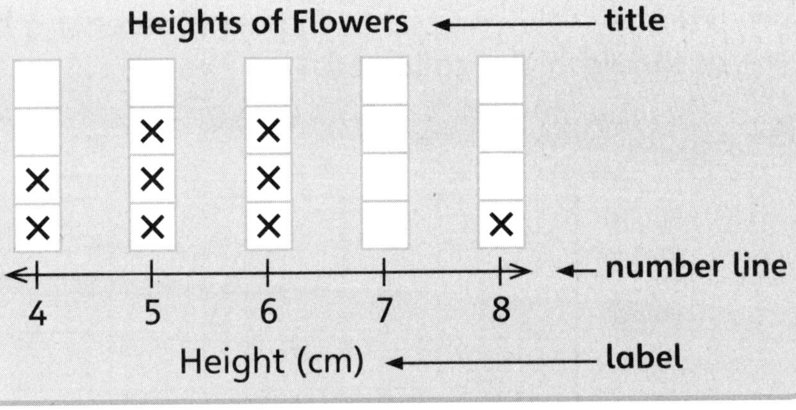

2. a) Use the line plot in the grey box to fill in the table.

 b) How many flowers are 7 cm tall? _____

 How does the line plot show this?

 c) Where is it easier to see the number of flowers of each length, on the line plot or in the table? _____

Height (cm)	Number of Flowers
4	2
5	
6	
7	
8

3. a) Measure the lengths of the pencils to the nearest centimetre.

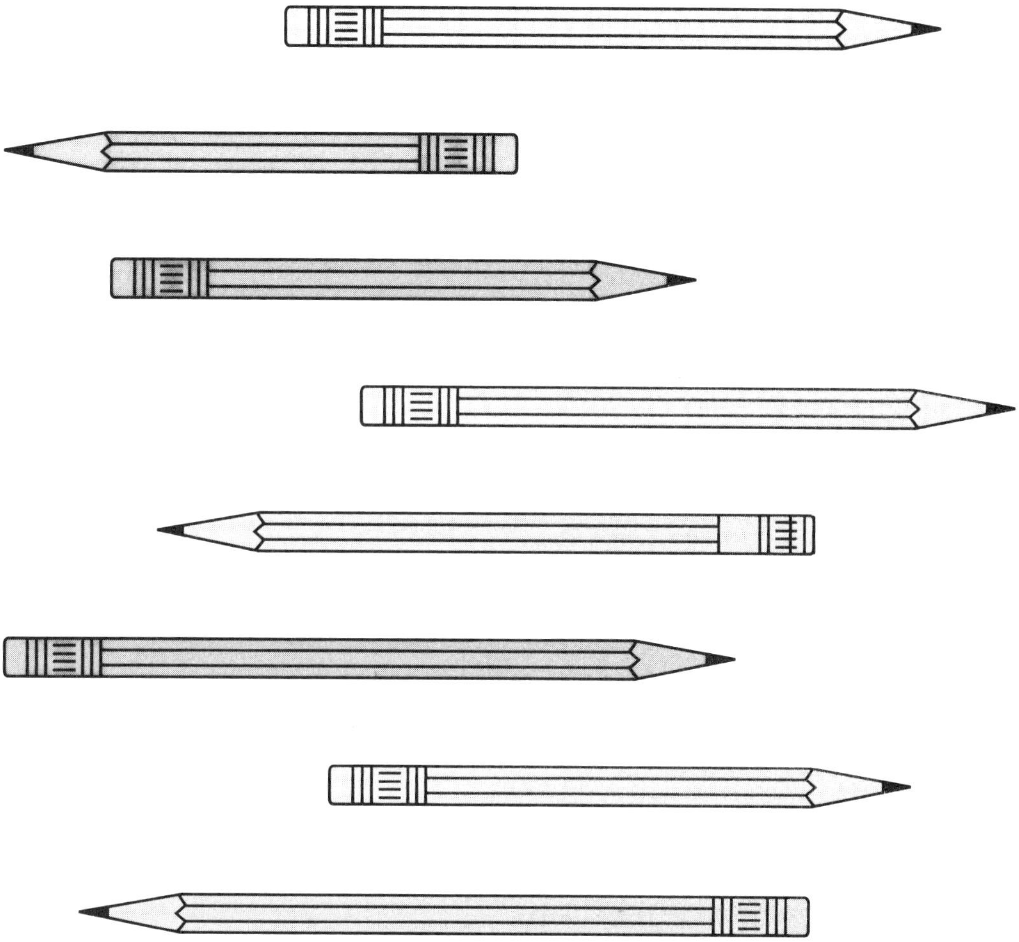

________ cm

________ cm

________ cm

________ cm

________ cm

________ cm

________ cm

________ cm

b) What is the title of the line plot below?

____

What is the label? ____________________

c) What is the length of the shortest pencil? __________

What is the length of the longest pencil? __________

d) Fill in the number line for the line plot. Start with the length of the shortest pencil.

e) Draw an ✕ on the line plot for each pencil's length. Cross out the length in part a) after you draw the ✕ for it.

f) What is the most common pencil length?

____

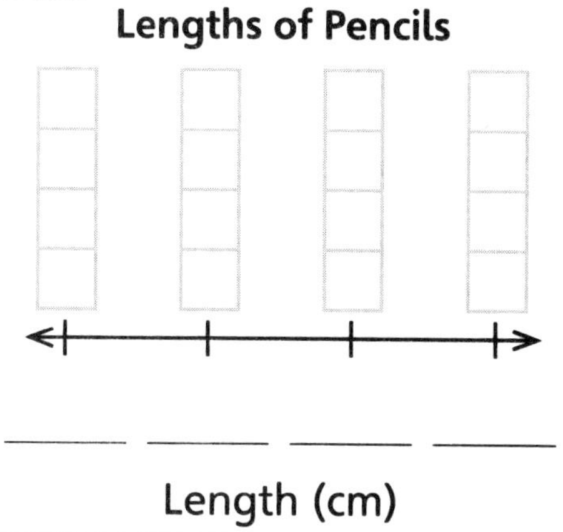

4. The students in Mary's class measure the heights of 10 bamboo shoots to the nearest centimetre. Mary records the heights in a table.

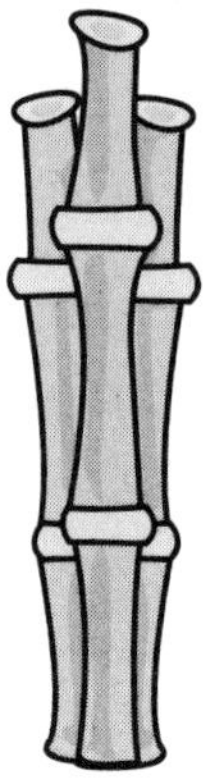

Height (cm)	32	32	33	33	33	35	35	36	37	37

a) The line plot below will show the heights of the bamboo shoots. Write a title and a label for the line plot. Include the unit in the label.

b) Complete the number line for the line plot.

c) Draw an **X** in the line plot for each height in the table. Cross out the height in the table after you draw the **X** for it.

Title ______________________

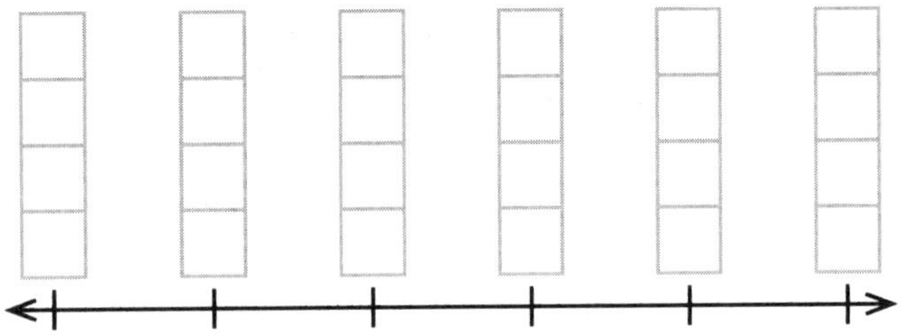

______ ______ ______ ______ ______ ______

Label ______________________

d) Use the line plot to answer the questions.

How many bamboo shoots have a height of 33 cm? ______

How many bamboo shoots are 34 cm tall? ______

How many bamboo shoots have a height of 36 cm? ______

What is the total number of bamboo shoots? ______

How many bamboo shoots are less than 34 cm tall? ______

BONUS ▶ How many bamboo shoots are more than 35 cm tall? ______

e) What is the length of the longest bamboo shoot? ____________

What is the length of the shortest bamboo shoot? ____________

What is the most common length of the bamboo shoots? ____________

f) Are most of the bamboo shoots longer or shorter than 34 cm? Explain.

BONUS ▶ How many bamboo shoots are more than 33 cm tall and less than 36 cm tall?

PDM3-3 Reading Line Plots

1. Students count the pockets on their clothes. The line plot shows how many students have each number of pockets.

Pockets on Our Clothes Today

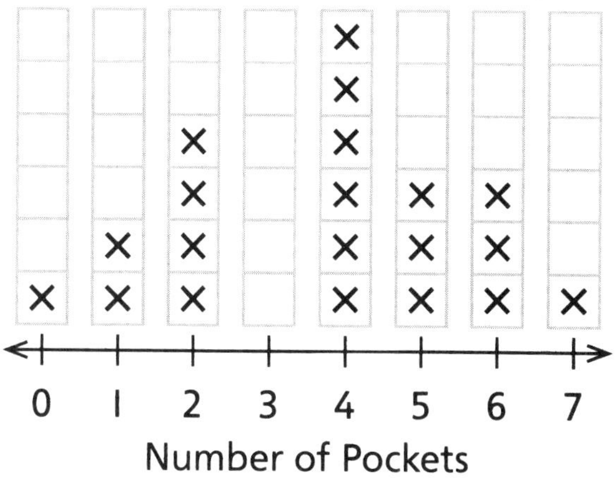

a) How many people have each number of pockets?

1 pocket ______

5 pockets ______

0 pockets ______

3 pockets ______

7 pockets ______

b) What is the largest number of pockets? ______

What is the smallest number of pockets? ______

c) What is the most common number of pockets? ______

d) How many students counted their pockets in total? ______

How do you know? ______________________________

In the line plot in Question 1, the 4 Xs above number 2 on the number line show that 4 students have 2 pockets on their clothes.

2. Students count the buttons on their clothes.

Buttons on Our Clothes Today

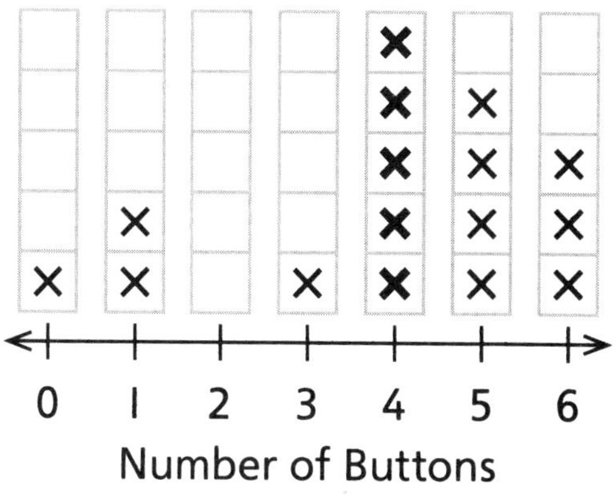

a) One student has 3 buttons. Circle the X that shows this.

b) The thick **X**s show that ______ students have ______ buttons on their clothes.

c) What is the largest number of buttons on students' clothes in the line plot? ______

d) What is the most common number of buttons on the clothes in the line plot? ______

How many students have that many buttons? ______

e) How many students counted their buttons for the line plot? ______

The **mode** is the most common data value.

In the set 2, 3, 4, 4, 5, 5, 5, the mode is 5.

3. Circle the mode in the set of data values.

a) 2, 3, 3, 4, 5

b) 10, 10, 10, 13, 14, 14

c) 1, 3, 5, 5, 7, 7, 7

4. Write the data in order from least to greatest. Circle the mode.

a) 1, 3, 5, 7, 3, 5, 3 ____________________

b) 10, 15, 13, 11, 21, 15 ____________________

c) 321, 321, 87, 903 ____________________

5. Look at the line plots in Questions 1 and 2.

a) What is the mode in Question 1? ________ pockets

b) What is the mode in Question 2? ________ buttons

c) How can you find the mode from a line plot? ______________________________

____

The data set 3, 3, 4, 4, 5, 6, 7 has two modes, the numbers 3 and 4.

The data set 3, 3, 5, 5 has no mode. Each value appears the same number of times.

6. Jake collected 12 birch leaves. The table shows the lengths of the leaves.

Length (cm)	3	5	4	7	3	5	5	3	7	7	4	8

a) Make a line plot showing the lengths of the leaves.

b) What are the modes of the data set?

c) How many more 7 cm leaves than 8 cm leaves are there?

How can you see that from the line plot?

d) Jake places all the leaves of the same length end to end. How long is each chain of leaves? Use multiplication to find the answers.

3 cm leaves   4 cm leaves   5 cm leaves   7 cm leaves

e) Jake places all 12 leaves end to end. What is the total length of all the leaves?

PDM5-7 Primary and Secondary Data

Data you collect yourself is called **primary** (or **first-hand**) data.

Data collected by someone else, such as data from books, the internet, or electronic databases, is called **secondary** (or **second-hand**) data.

1. Would you use primary or secondary data to answer the question?

a) How many pets do people in my class have? ____________________

b) How many pets do people in Canada have? ____________________

c) What is the average number of words you can type in 1 minute? ____________________

d) What is the largest number of words anyone can type in 1 minute? ____________________

e) What is the average age of maple trees in Quebec? ____________________

f) Which languages do people in my class speak at home? ____________________

g) Which languages do people in my province speak at home most often? ____________________

2. Choose one of your answers in Question 1 and explain how you know. ____________________

____

There are three ways to collect primary data.

Survey: People answer your questions or vote.

Measurement: You perform an experiment and use tools to measure and record data.

Observation: You perform an experiment and record what you see.

3. Would you use a survey, an observation, or a measurement to answer the question?

a) Which season are more of my friends born in? ____________________

b) Does it take me longer to run 3 km or to walk 1 km? ____________________

c) How many people in my class have brown eyes? ____________________

d) How many birds visit the school yard during the day? ____________________

e) What is the most popular dessert among people in my neighbourhood? ____________________

f) Which of my friends has the longest hair? ____________________

4. Choose one of your answers in Question 3 and explain how you know.

____

____

5. Would everyone know the answer to the survey question? Write "yes" or "no."

a) What is your favourite colour? ________

b) At what time of day were you born? ________

c) What is your hair colour? ________

d) What is your eyeglass prescription? ________

6. Add a category so that everyone can answer the survey question.

a) What is your favourite ice cream flavour?

☐ strawberry ☐ vanilla ☐ chocolate ☐ ________________

b) In which season were you born?

☐ winter ☐ spring ☐ summer ☐ ________________

c) Which of these colours do you like best?

☐ red ☐ yellow ☐ blue ☐ green ☐ ________________

d) How tall are you, to the nearest centimetre?

☐ under 120 cm ☐ 120 to 129 cm ☐ 130 to 139 cm ☐ 140 to 149 cm ☐ ________________

7. a) Write a survey question to ask students in your class.

____

____

b) Write the possible responses to your question.

☐ ____________________ ☐ ____________________

☐ ____________________ ☐ ____________________

☐ ____________________ ☐ ____________________

8. a) Write a question that you will need secondary data to answer.

____

____

____

b) Why can't you collect the data for your question in part a) yourself?

____

____

____

NS4-45 Naming Fractions

The area is cut into 4 equal parts.

1 part out of 4 is shaded.

$\frac{1}{4}$ of the area is shaded.

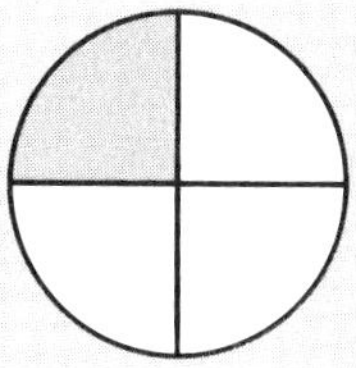

$\frac{1}{4}$ — The **numerator** (1) tells you one part is shaded. The **denominator** (4) tells you how many equal parts are in a whole.

1. Write the fraction shown by the shaded part of the image.

a) 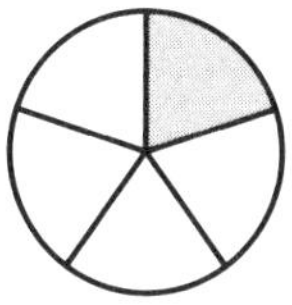

b) 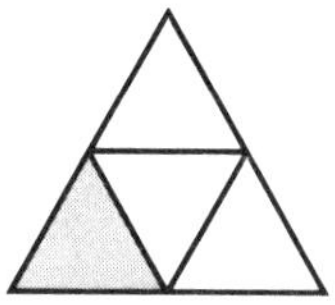

c) 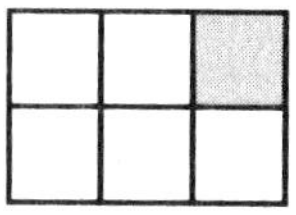

d) 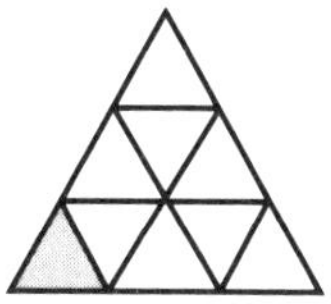

e) 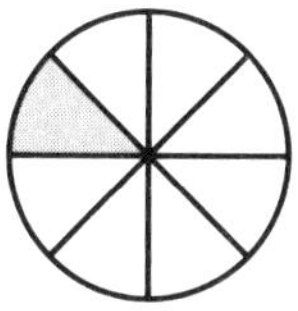

f) 

2. Shade the fraction.

a) $\frac{1}{6}$ 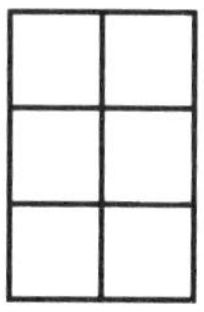

b) $\frac{1}{5}$ 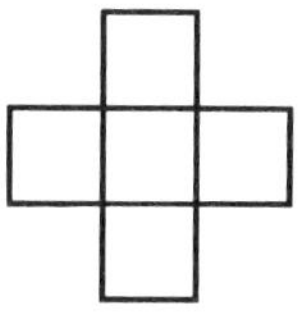

c) $\frac{1}{9}$ 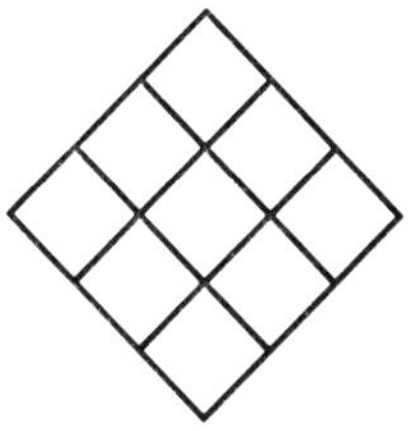

d) $\frac{1}{10}$ 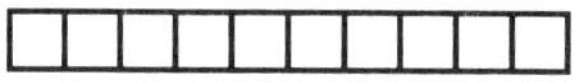

e) $\frac{1}{100}$ 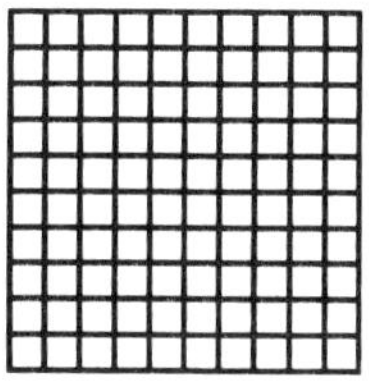

f) $\frac{1}{20}$ 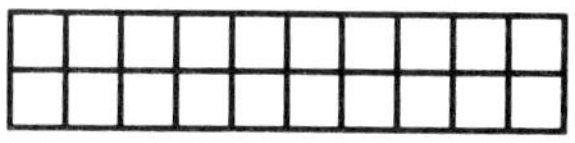

3. Write the words that describe each square in the figure.

one fourth   **one fifth**   **one sixth**   **one seventh**   **one eighth**   **one ninth**

a) 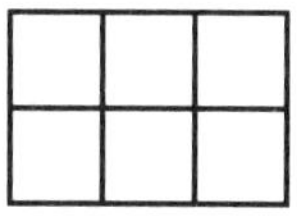

____

b) 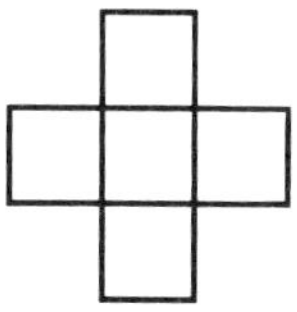

____

c) 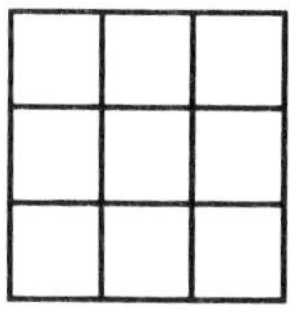

____

4. Write the fraction shown by the shaded part of the figure.

a)

b)

c)

d)

e)

f)

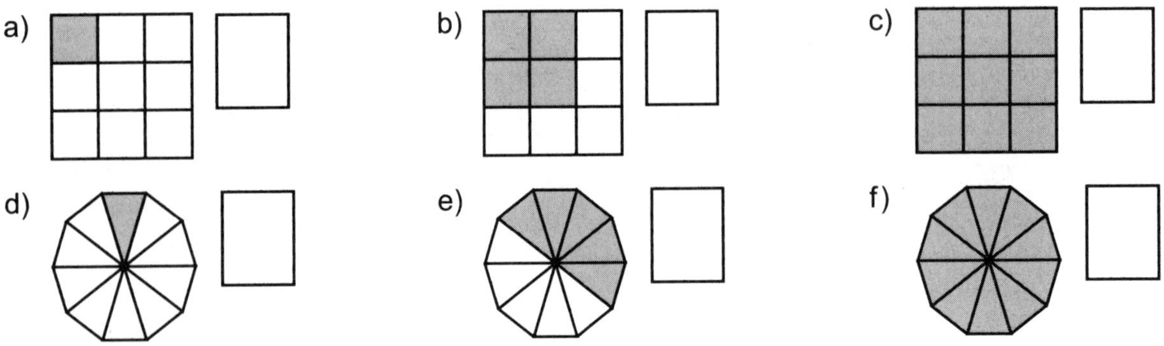

5. Shade the fraction.

a) $\dfrac{1}{7}$

b) $\dfrac{3}{7}$

c) $\dfrac{6}{7}$

d) $\dfrac{1}{8}$

e) $\dfrac{5}{8}$

f) $\dfrac{7}{8}$

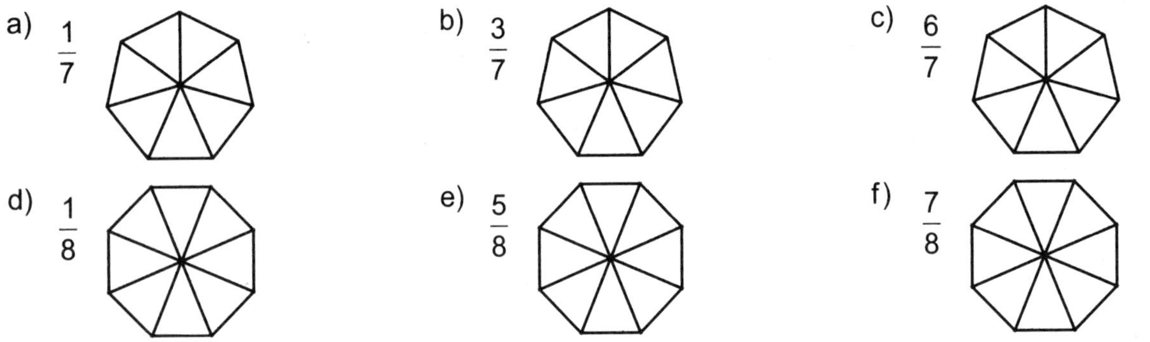

6. Find a fraction in the top row that is equal to a fraction in the bottom row.
Fill in the blank with the letter from the fraction in the top row.

A.

B.

C.

D.

a)

b)

c)

d)

_____ _____ _____ _____

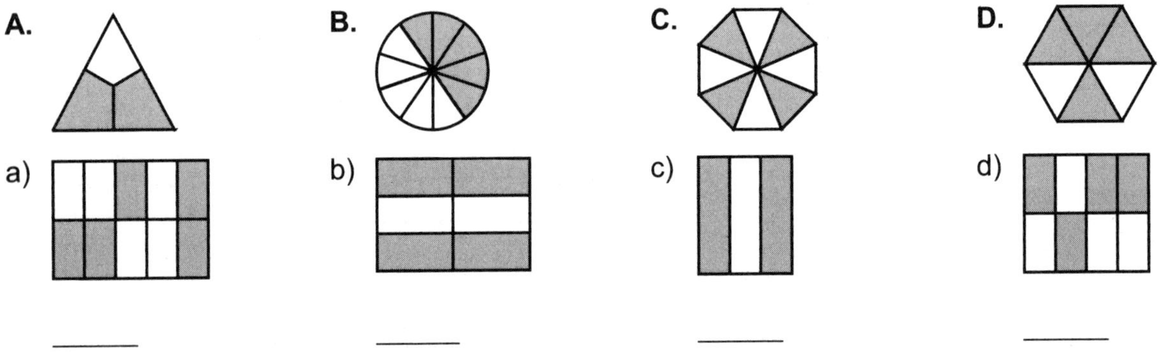

7. Shade the fraction twice. Put a ✔ under the figure with the larger amount of shading.

a) $\dfrac{1}{10}$

b) $\dfrac{4}{10}$

c) $\dfrac{7}{10}$

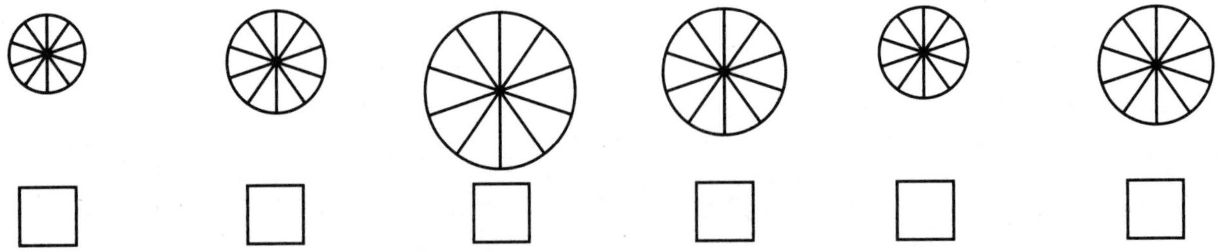

NF4-2 Comparing Fractions (Introduction)

1. Which strip has more shaded? Circle its fraction.

a)
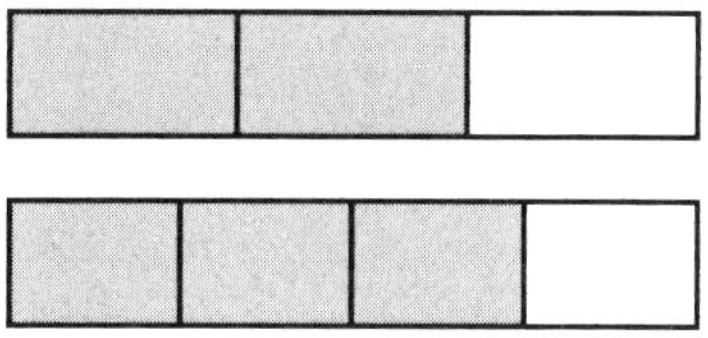
$\frac{2}{3}$ $\frac{3}{4}$ (circled)

b)
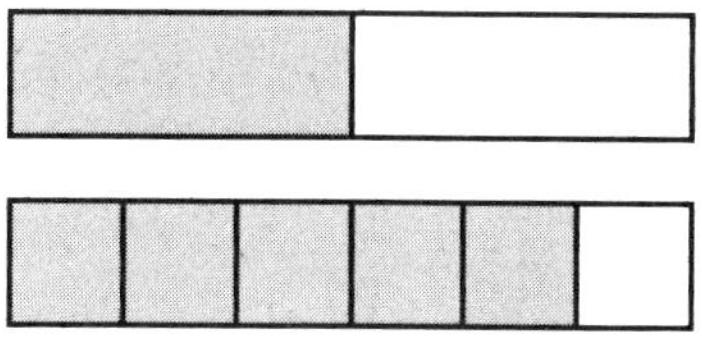
$\frac{1}{2}$ $\frac{5}{6}$

c)
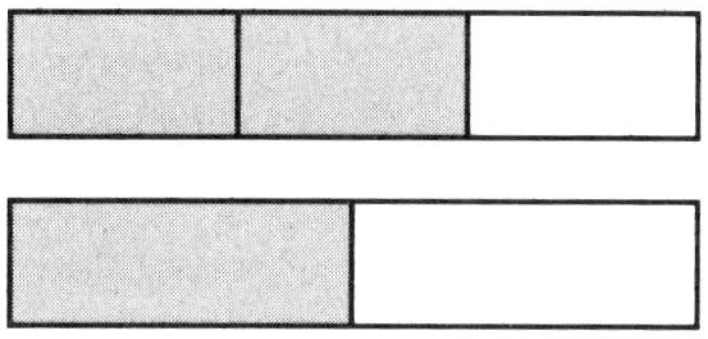
$\frac{2}{3}$ $\frac{1}{2}$

d)
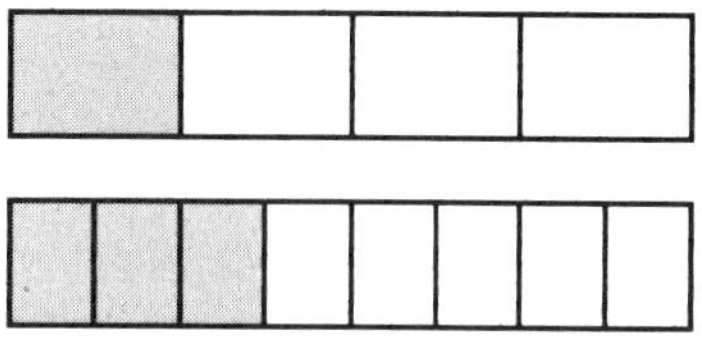
$\frac{1}{4}$ $\frac{3}{8}$

e)
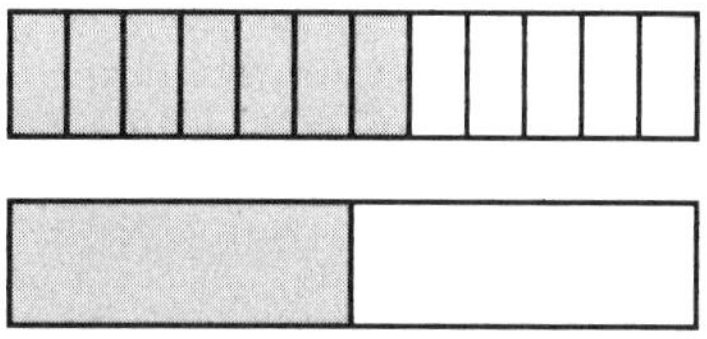
$\frac{7}{12}$ $\frac{1}{2}$

f)
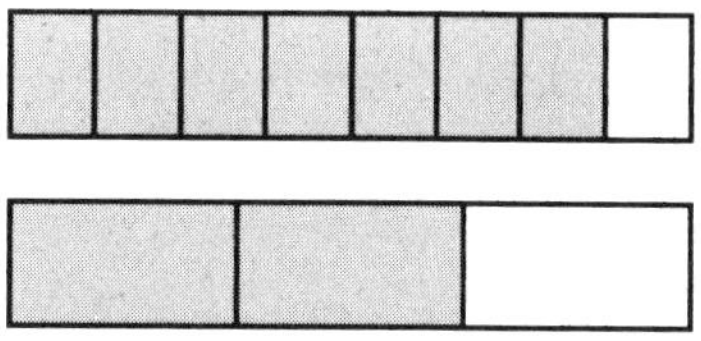
$\frac{7}{8}$ $\frac{2}{3}$

$\frac{1}{2}$ is **greater than** $\frac{1}{3}$ because more is shaded.

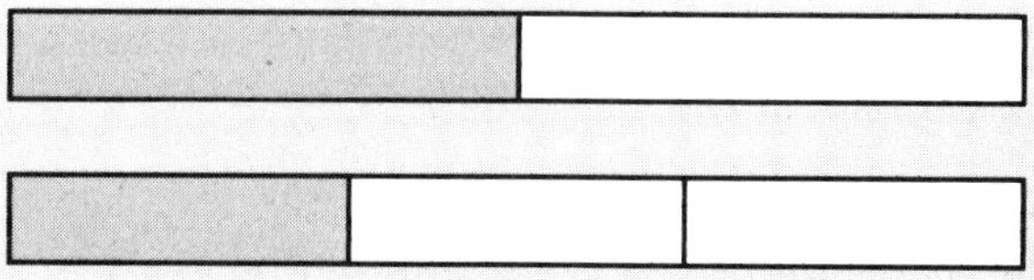
$\frac{1}{2}$ $\frac{1}{3}$

2. Shade the amounts. Circle the greater fraction.

a)
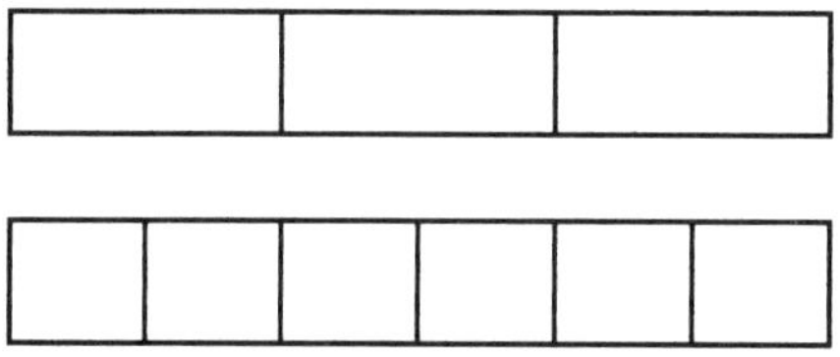
$\frac{2}{3}$ $\frac{5}{6}$

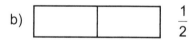

b)
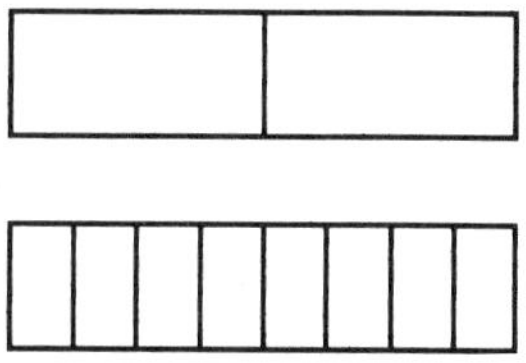
$\frac{1}{2}$ $\frac{3}{8}$

c)
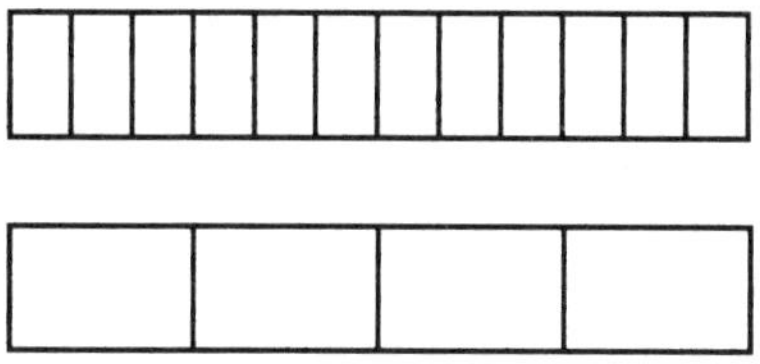
$\frac{10}{12}$ $\frac{3}{4}$

d)
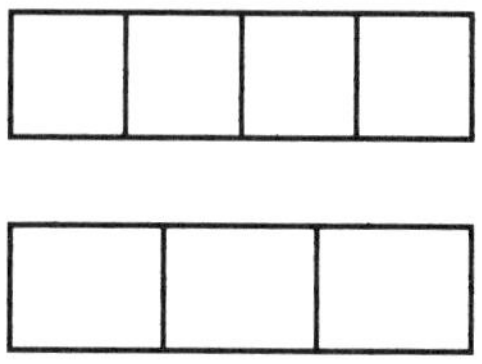
$\frac{1}{4}$ $\frac{1}{3}$

"5 is greater than 3" is written $5 > 3$.

"3 is less than 5" is written $3 < 5$.

3. Write your answers to Question 2 using $<$ or $>$.

a) $\frac{2}{3}$ ☐ $\frac{5}{6}$ b) $\frac{1}{2}$ ☐ $\frac{3}{8}$ c) $\frac{10}{12}$ ☐ $\frac{3}{4}$ d) $\frac{1}{4}$ ☐ $\frac{1}{3}$

NS4-46 Comparing Fractions to Benchmarks

1. Shade half of the figure. Write two fractions to describe the shaded part.

a) 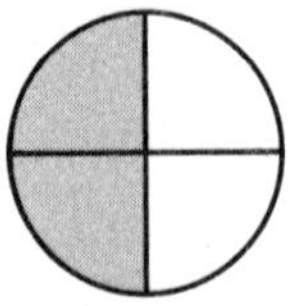 $\frac{1}{2}$ = $\frac{2}{4}$

b) 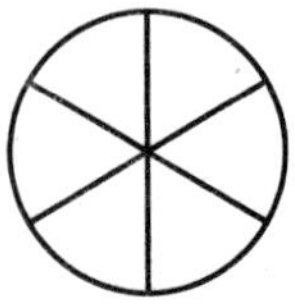 □ = □

c) 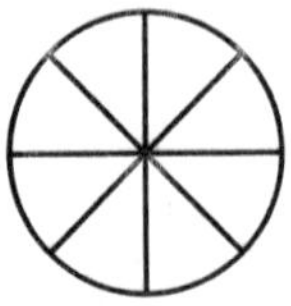 □ = □

d)  □ = □

2. Circle the fractions that are more than half.

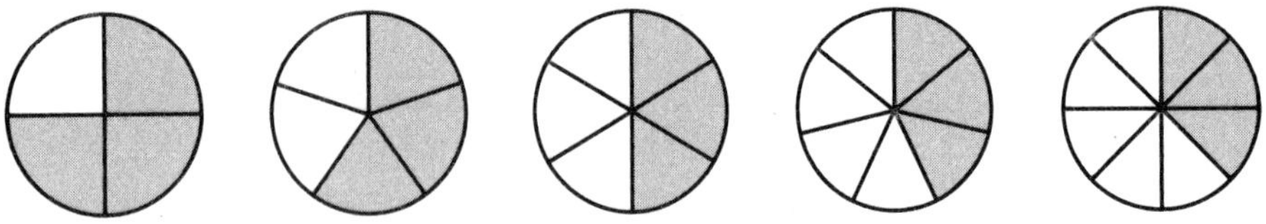

$\frac{3}{4}$ $\frac{3}{5}$ $\frac{3}{6}$ $\frac{3}{7}$ $\frac{3}{8}$

Is $\frac{3}{5}$ more than $\frac{1}{2}$ or less than $\frac{1}{2}$?

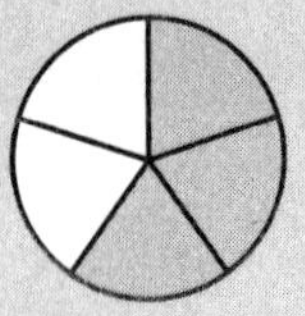

There are 5 parts altogether. 5 − 3 = 2 parts are not shaded.

When more parts are shaded than not shaded, the fraction is greater than $\frac{1}{2}$, so $\frac{3}{5} > \frac{1}{2}$.

3. How many shaded parts does the fraction show? How many parts are not shaded?

a) 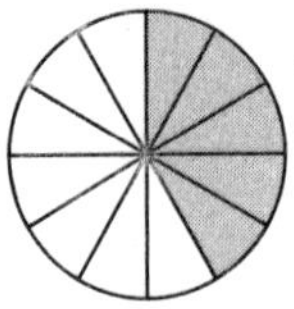 _____ shaded _____ not shaded

b) 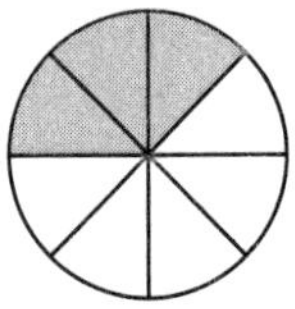 _____ shaded _____ not shaded

c) 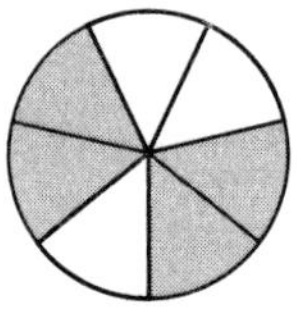 _____ shaded _____ not shaded

4. Write > or <.

a) $\frac{2}{5}$ □ $\frac{1}{2}$ b) $\frac{4}{9}$ □ $\frac{1}{2}$ c) $\frac{6}{11}$ □ $\frac{1}{2}$ d) $\frac{13}{25}$ □ $\frac{1}{2}$ e) $\frac{23}{50}$ □ $\frac{1}{2}$ f) $\frac{5}{11}$ □ $\frac{1}{2}$

5. Karen drank $\frac{3}{8}$ of a bottle of milk. Ella drank $\frac{6}{11}$ of it. Who drank more milk?

Hint: Compare the fractions to $\frac{1}{2}$. ______________

6. Glen ran around $\frac{3}{5}$ of a track. Yu ran around $\frac{1}{3}$ of it. Who ran farther? ______________

Rob really likes pizza! The pizza has 4 slices, and Rob ate 4 slices:

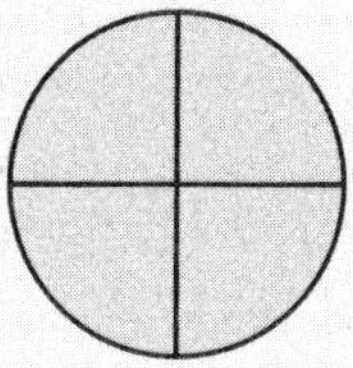

Rob ate $\frac{4}{4}$ of a pizza. Rob ate 1 pizza.

7. Write the shaded fraction.

a) 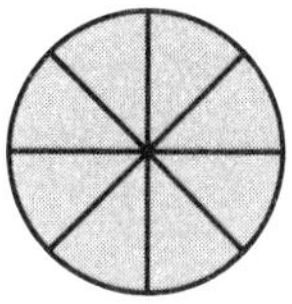 ☐

b) 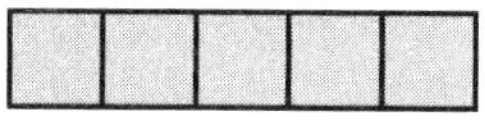 ☐

c) 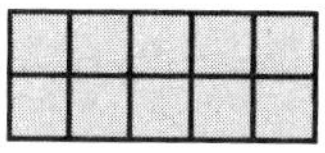 ☐

8. A fraction is equal to 1 if its numerator and denominator are ________________.

Rob does not like this pizza at all! The pizza has 4 slices, and Rob ate 0 slices:

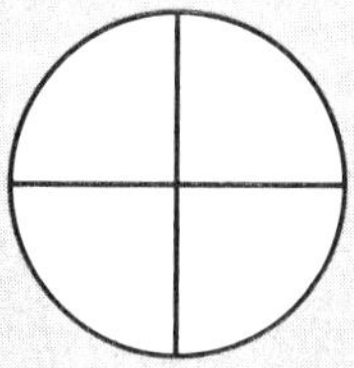

Rob ate $\frac{0}{4}$ of a pizza. Rob ate none of the pizza.

9. Write if the fraction is "equal to" or "greater than" 0.

a) The fraction 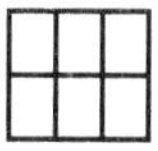 is ________________ 0.

b) The fraction 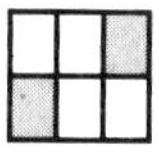 is ________________ 0.

10. A fraction is equal to 0 if its numerator is _____.

11. Shade two different fractions between 0 and $\frac{1}{2}$, and then write the fractions.

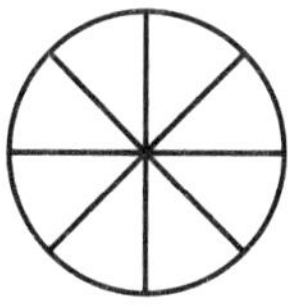

This fraction is ☐.

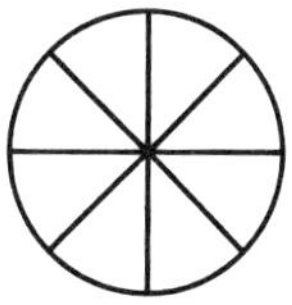

This fraction is ☐.

12. Shade two different fractions between $\frac{1}{2}$ and 1, and then write the fractions.

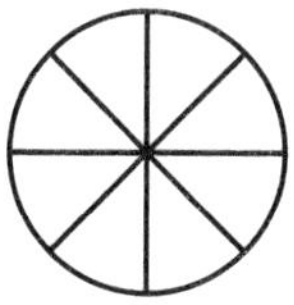

This fraction is ☐.

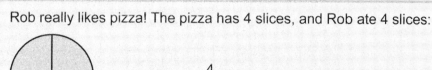

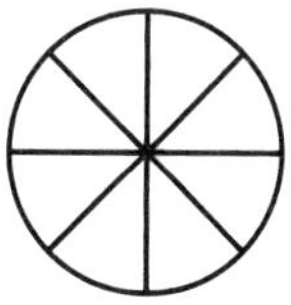

This fraction is ☐.

Equivalent Fractions

1. How many times as many parts are there?

a)  has _______ times as many parts as 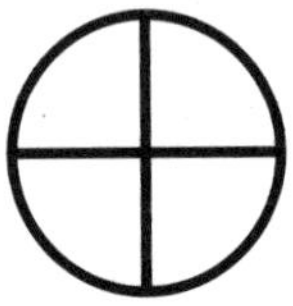.

b) 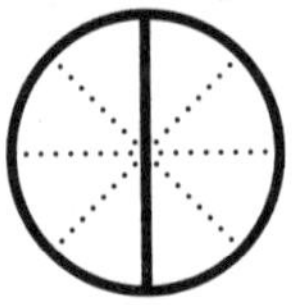 has _______ times as many parts as 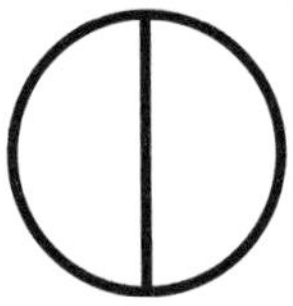.

c) 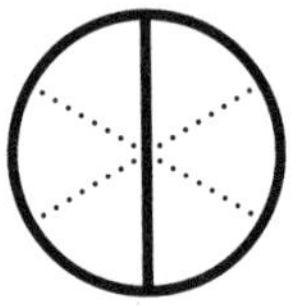 has _______ times as many parts as 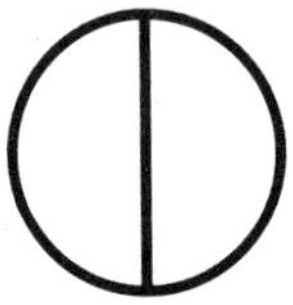.

d)  has _______ times as many parts as .

2. Fill in the blanks.

a) A has _______ times as many parts as B.

A has _______ times as many shaded parts as B.

A
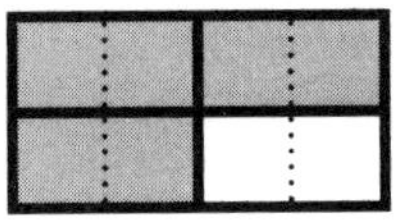
B
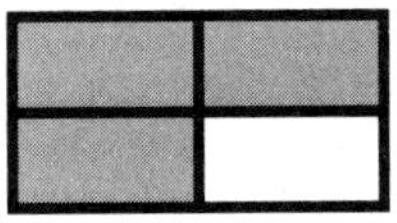

b) A has _______ times as many parts as B.

A has _______ times as many shaded parts as B.

A
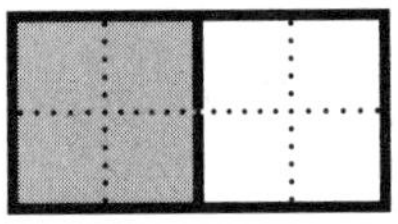
B
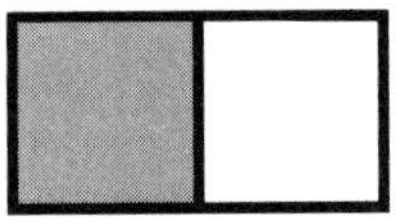

c) A has _______ times as many parts as B.

A has _______ times as many shaded parts as B.

A
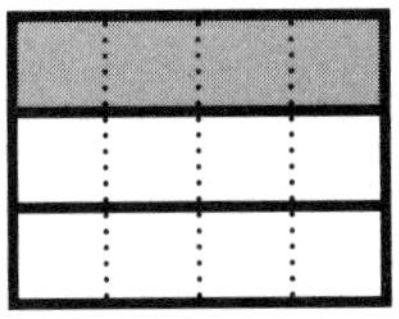
B
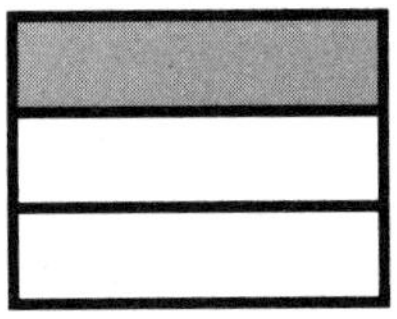

d) A has _______ times as many parts as B.

A has _______ times as many shaded parts as B.

A
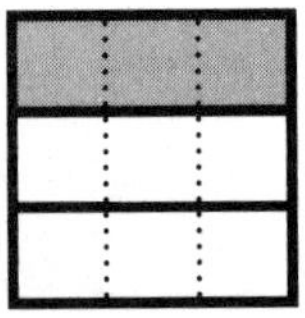
B
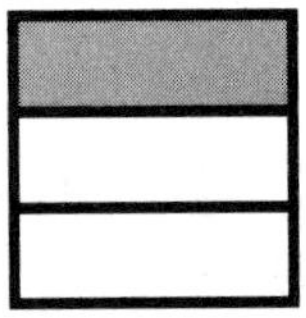

3. The picture shows two equivalent fractions. Fill in the blanks.

a) 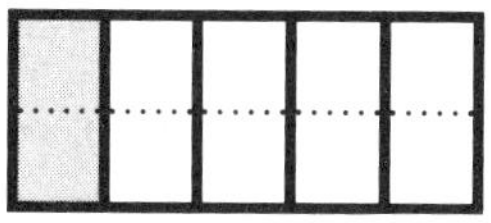 $\frac{1}{5}$ and $\frac{2}{10}$

2 is ______ times as much as 1.

10 is ______ times as much as 5.

b) 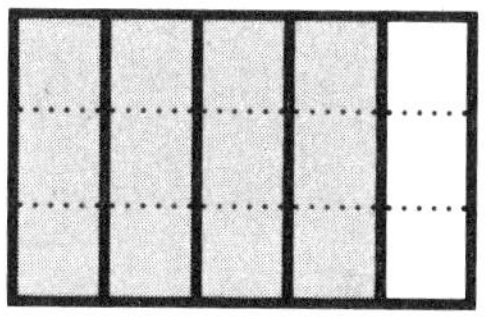 $\frac{4}{5}$ and $\frac{12}{15}$

12 is ______ times as much as 4.

15 is ______ times as much as 5.

c) 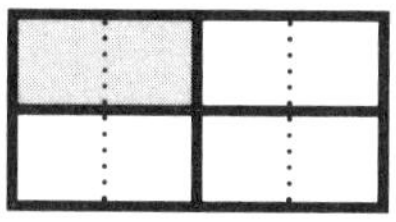 $\frac{1}{4}$ and $\frac{2}{8}$

2 is ______ times as much as 1.

8 is ______ times as much as 4.

d) 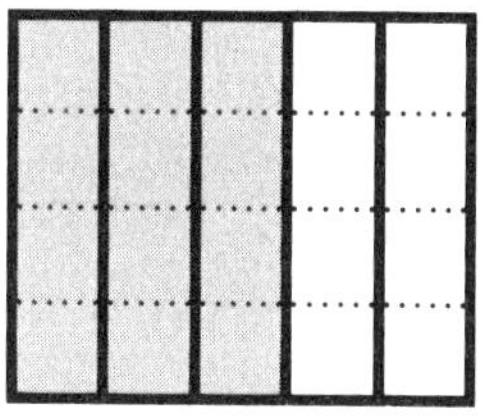 $\frac{3}{5}$ and $\frac{12}{20}$

12 is ______ times as much as 3.

20 is ______ times as much as 5.

4. Write an equivalent fraction for the picture. Then write how many times as much the new numerator and denominator are.

a) 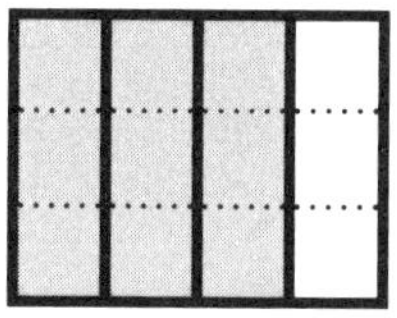 $\frac{3}{4} = \boxed{\frac{9}{12}}$

__*3*__ times as much

b) 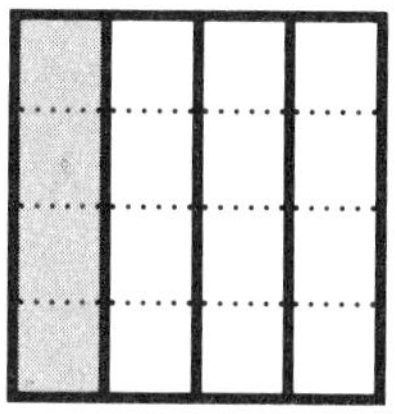 $\frac{1}{4} = \square$

______ times as much

c) 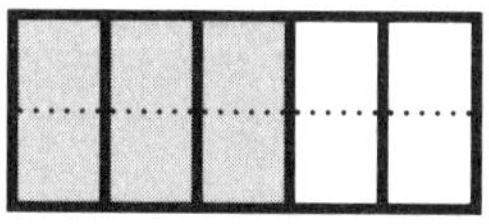 $\frac{3}{5} = \square$

______ times as much

BONUS ▶

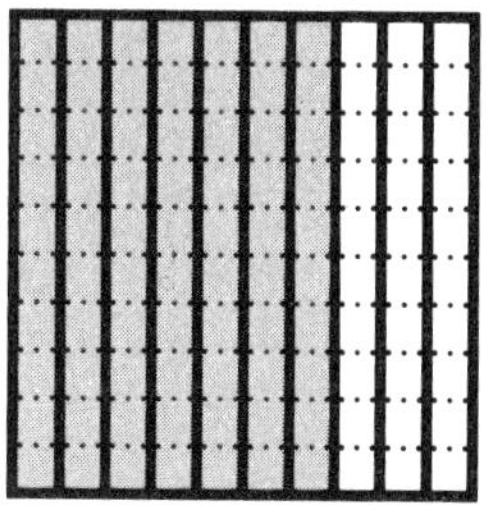 $\frac{7}{10} = \square$

______ times as much

To get an equivalent fraction, multiply the numerator **and** denominator by the same number.

Example: Picture A

$$\frac{3}{4} \xrightarrow{\times 2} \frac{6}{8} \quad \left(\frac{3}{4} = \frac{6}{8}\right)$$

Picture B

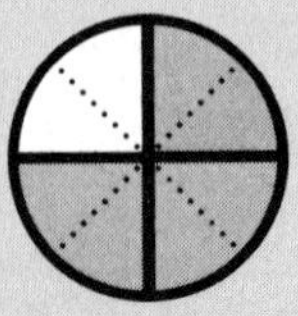

Picture B has twice as many **parts** as Picture A.
Picture B has twice as many **shaded parts** as Picture A.

5. Draw lines to cut the pies into more equal pieces. Then fill in the numerators of the equivalent fractions.

a)

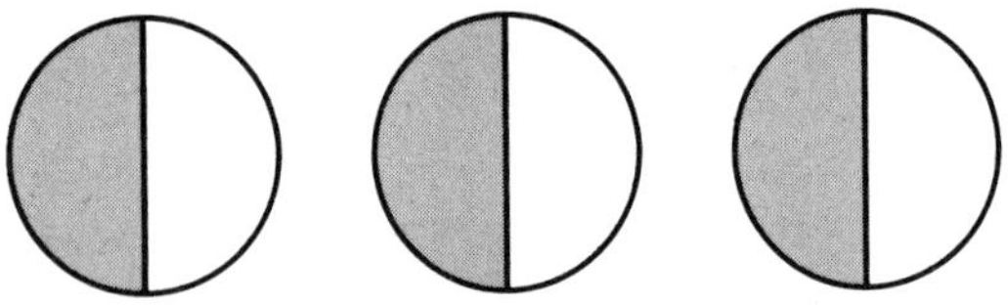

4 pieces 6 pieces 8 pieces

$\frac{1}{2} = \frac{}{4} = \frac{}{6} = \frac{}{8}$

b)

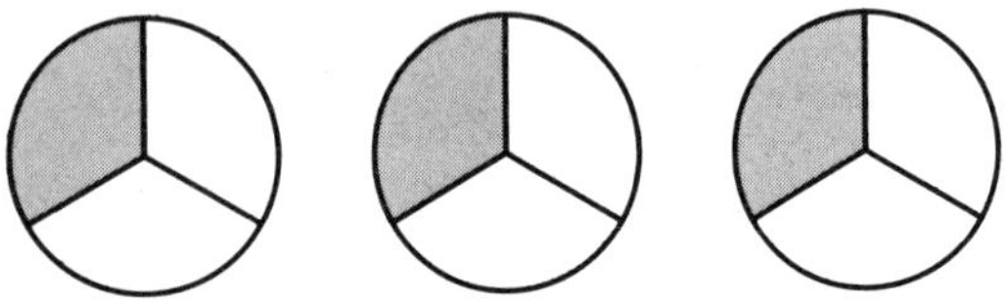

6 pieces 9 pieces 12 pieces

$\frac{1}{3} = \frac{}{6} = \frac{}{9} = \frac{}{12}$

6. Draw lines to cut the pie into more pieces. Then fill in the missing numbers.

a)

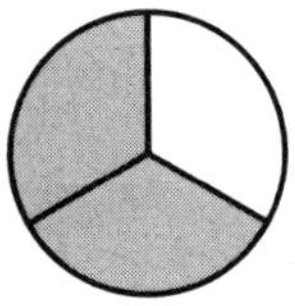

$\frac{2 \xrightarrow{\times 2}}{3 \xrightarrow[\times 2]{}} = \frac{}{6}$

b)

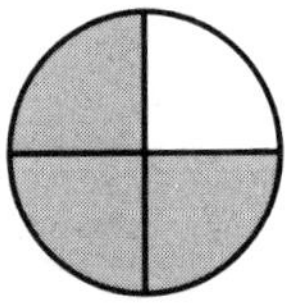

$\frac{3 \xrightarrow{\times}}{4 \xrightarrow[\times]{}} = \frac{}{8}$

c)

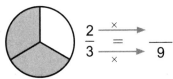

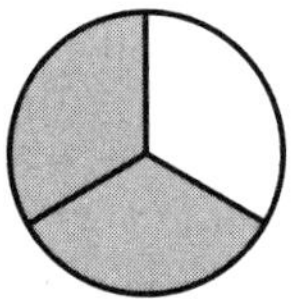

$\frac{2 \xrightarrow{\times}}{3 \xrightarrow[\times]{}} = \frac{}{9}$

This number tells you how many pieces to cut each slice into.

7. Use multiplication to find the equivalent fraction.

a) $\frac{1 \times 2}{3 \times 2} = \frac{}{6}$

b) $\frac{1 \times}{2 \times} = \frac{}{10}$

c) $\frac{2}{5} = \frac{}{10}$

d) $\frac{3}{4} = \frac{}{8}$

e) $\frac{1}{4} = \frac{}{12}$

f) $\frac{4}{5} = \frac{}{15}$

g) $\frac{5}{6} = \frac{}{12}$

h) $\frac{3}{10} = \frac{}{100}$

i) $\frac{5}{9} = \frac{}{72}$

8. Write five fractions equivalent to $\frac{2}{3}$.

$\frac{2}{3} = \square = \square = \square = \square = \square$

NF5-12 Flexibility with Equivalent Fractions and Lowest Terms

You can divide the numerator and denominator by the same number to get an equivalent fraction.

Example: Picture A Picture B

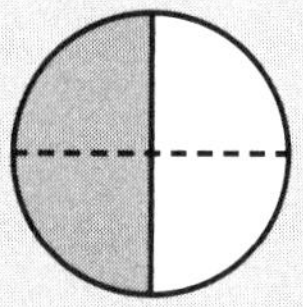

$$\frac{2}{4} \overset{\div 2}{\underset{\div 2}{=}} \frac{1}{2}$$

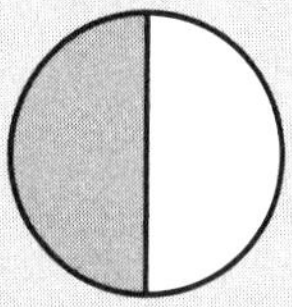

Picture A has twice as many **parts** as Picture B.
Picture A has twice as many **shaded parts** as Picture B.

1. Use division to find the equivalent fractions.

a) $\frac{2}{6} \overset{\div 2}{\underset{\div 2}{=}} \frac{\square}{3}$

b) $\frac{5}{10} \overset{\div 5}{\underset{\div 5}{=}} \frac{\square}{2}$

c) $\frac{2}{10} \overset{\div 2}{\underset{\div 2}{=}} \frac{1}{\square}$

d) $\frac{3}{6} \overset{\div 3}{\underset{\div 3}{=}} \frac{1}{\square}$

e) $\frac{10}{15} \overset{\div 5}{\underset{\div 5}{=}} \frac{\square}{3}$

f) $\frac{8}{28} \overset{\div 4}{\underset{\div 4}{=}} \frac{2}{\square}$

2. Use division to write three fractions equivalent to …

a) $\frac{8}{32} = \square = \square = \square$

b) $\frac{27}{54} = \square = \square = \square$

c) $\frac{12}{36} = \square = \square = \square$

d) $\frac{30}{60} = \square = \square = \square$

NF4-4 Fractions on Number Lines

We can use number lines instead of fraction strips to show fractions.

$\frac{3}{4}$ of the strip is shaded.

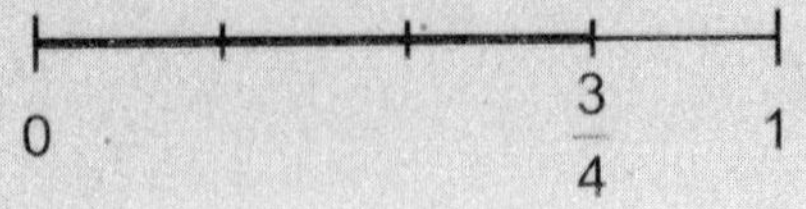

$\frac{3}{4}$ of the number line from 0 to 1 is shaded.

1. Find what fraction of the number line from 0 to 1 is shaded.

a) 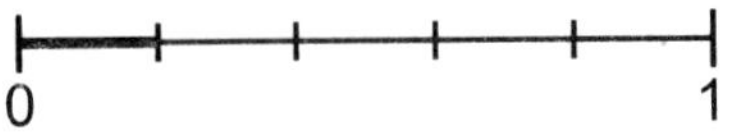

☐ is shaded.

So ☐ is shaded.

b) 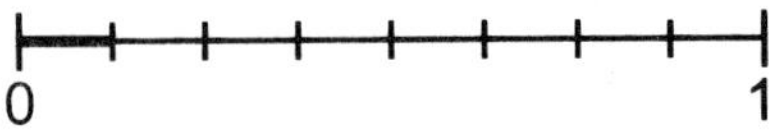

☐ is shaded.

So ☐ is shaded.

To find $\frac{3}{4}$ on a number line, divide the number line from 0 to 1 into **4** equal parts.
Then start at 0 and take **3** parts.

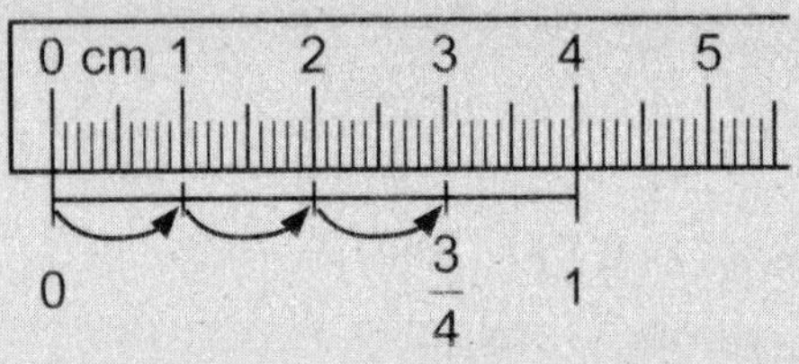

2. Use a ruler to divide the number line from 0 to 1 into equal parts, and then mark the fraction.

a) 3 equal parts and mark $\frac{1}{3}$

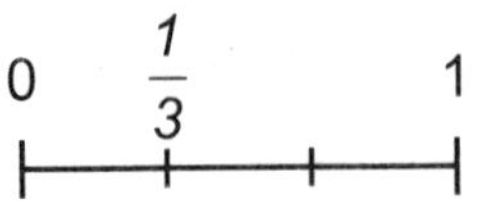

b) 5 equal parts and mark $\frac{2}{5}$

c) 6 equal parts and mark $\frac{3}{6}$

d) 8 equal parts and mark $\frac{6}{8}$

3. Pamela marks $\frac{3}{4}$ on the number line. John marks $\frac{2}{3}$ on the same number line.

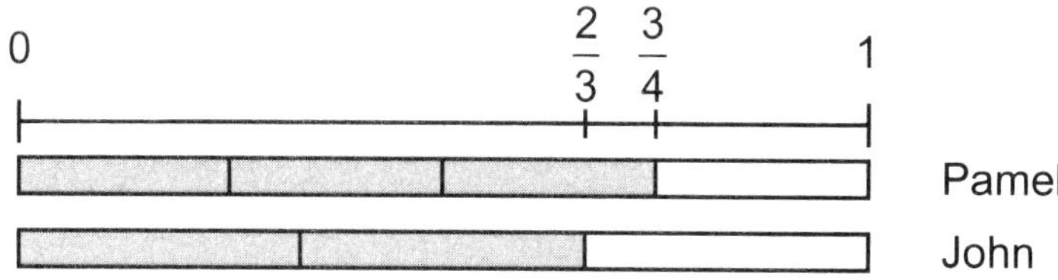

Which fraction is bigger? ☐

> You can use number lines to compare fractions.
>
> $\frac{3}{4}$ is greater than $\frac{2}{4}$ because it is farther to the right: $\frac{3}{4} > \frac{2}{4}$.
>
> 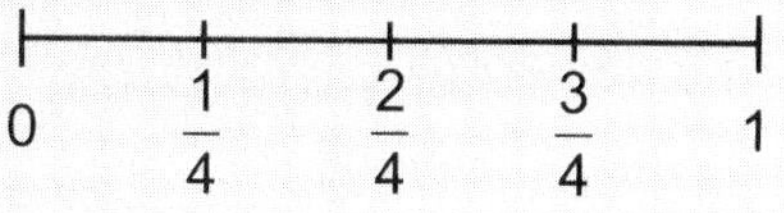
>

4. Anna placed fractions with different denominators on the same number line.

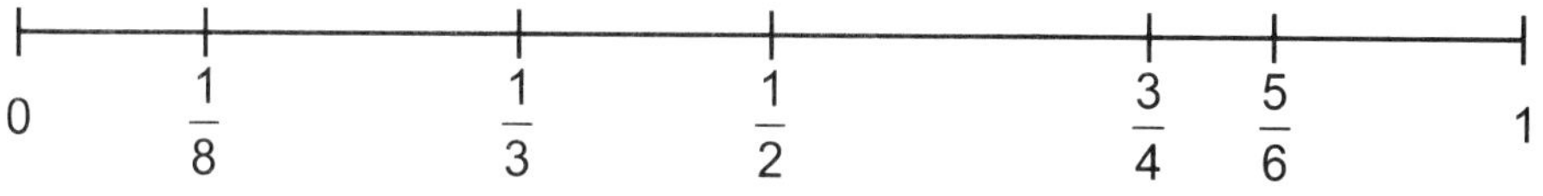

a) Write $<$ (less than) or $>$ (greater than).

i) $\frac{1}{8}$ ☐ $\frac{1}{2}$ ii) $\frac{3}{4}$ ☐ $\frac{1}{3}$ iii) $\frac{5}{6}$ ☐ $\frac{3}{4}$

b) Circle these fractions on the number line above. Then write them from greatest to least.

$\frac{1}{2}$, $\frac{5}{6}$, $\frac{1}{3}$ ☐ $>$ ☐ $>$ ☐

> Two fractions are equivalent if they mark the same place on a number line from 0 to 1.

5. Use the number lines to find equivalent fractions.

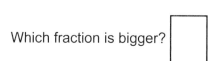

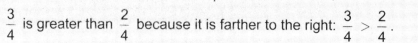

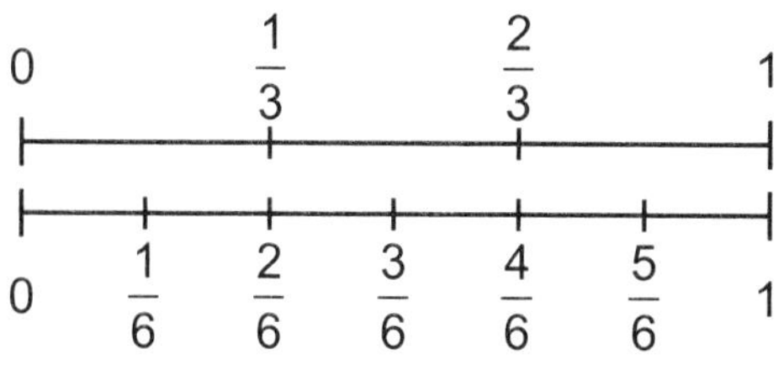

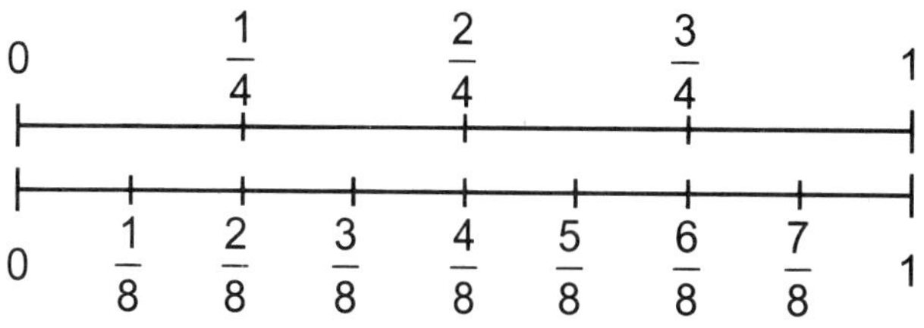

a) $\frac{1}{3} = \frac{\quad}{6}$ b) $\frac{2}{3} = \frac{\quad}{6}$ c) $\frac{1}{4} = \frac{\quad}{8}$ d) $\frac{3}{4} = \frac{\quad}{8}$

NS4-48 Comparing and Ordering Fractions

1. a) Write the numerators of the shaded fractions.

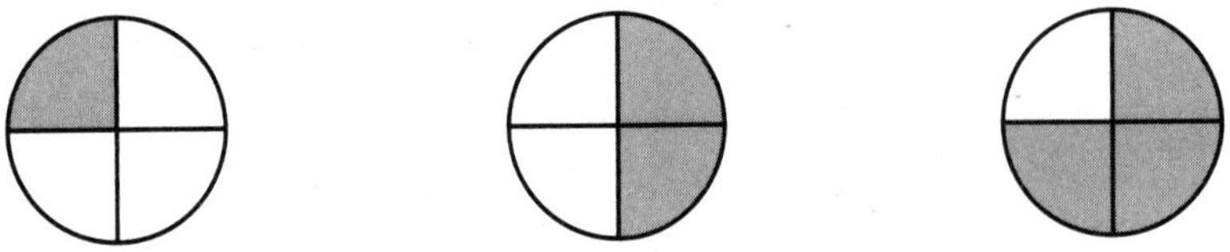

$\frac{\quad}{4}$ $\qquad$ $\frac{\quad}{4}$ $\qquad$ $\frac{\quad}{4}$

b) Look at the pictures and fractions in part a) from left to right. Write "increases," "decreases," or "stays the same."

i) Numerator ____________________.

ii) Denominator ____________________.

iii) Shaded fraction ____________________.

Comparing fractions when ...

the numerator changes **and** **the denominator stays the same**

$\frac{1}{5}$

fewer shaded parts →

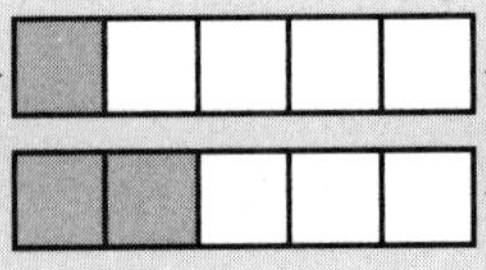

more shaded parts →

← same number and size of parts

$\frac{2}{5}$

So $\frac{2}{5} > \frac{1}{5}$ because more parts are shaded.

---

2. Circle the greater fraction.

a) $\frac{2}{5}$ or $\frac{4}{5}$ $\qquad$ b) $\frac{3}{4}$ or $\frac{1}{4}$ $\qquad$ c) $\frac{4}{10}$ or $\frac{9}{10}$ $\qquad$ d) $\frac{3}{3}$ or $\frac{1}{3}$

3. Write any number in the blank that makes the relationship correct.

a) $\frac{3}{7} > \frac{1}{7}$ $\qquad$ b) $\frac{\quad}{29} < \frac{14}{29}$ $\qquad$ c) $\frac{61}{385} > \frac{\quad}{385}$ $\qquad$ **BONUS ▶** $\frac{\quad}{1000} < \frac{2}{1000}$

4. Two fractions have the same denominator but different numerators. How can you tell which fraction is greater?

____

____

5. Use the number line to order the fractions from least to greatest.
Draw an **X** to mark the position of each fraction.

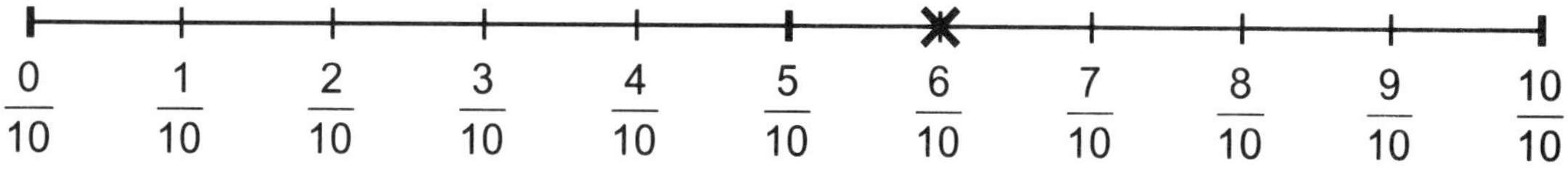

$\frac{6}{10}$ $\frac{1}{10}$ $\frac{8}{10}$ $\frac{4}{10}$ $\frac{2}{10}$ $\frac{9}{10}$ $\frac{5}{10}$

☐ < ☐ < ☐ < ☐ < ☐ < ☐ < ☐

6. Order the fractions from least to greatest by considering the numerators and denominators.

a) $\frac{3}{5}$ $\frac{0}{5}$ $\frac{2}{5}$ $\frac{5}{5}$ $\frac{1}{5}$

☐ < ☐ < ☐ < ☐ < ☐

b) $\frac{6}{10}$ $\frac{1}{10}$ $\frac{4}{10}$ $\frac{2}{10}$ $\frac{9}{10}$

☐ < ☐ < ☐ < ☐ < ☐

7. a) What fraction of a litre is in the container?

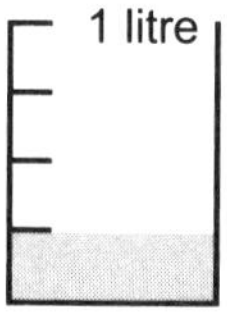

☐

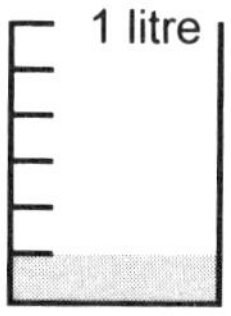

☐

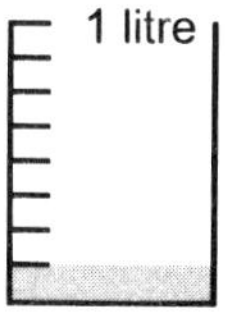

☐

b) Which fraction in part a) is …

i) the smallest? ☐ ii) the biggest? ☐ iii) in the middle? ☐

c) Write “smaller” or “bigger.” As the denominator gets bigger, each part gets _______________.

Comparing fractions when …

the numerator stays the same **and** **the denominator changes**

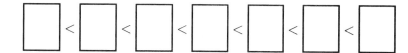

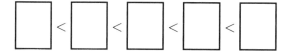

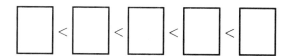

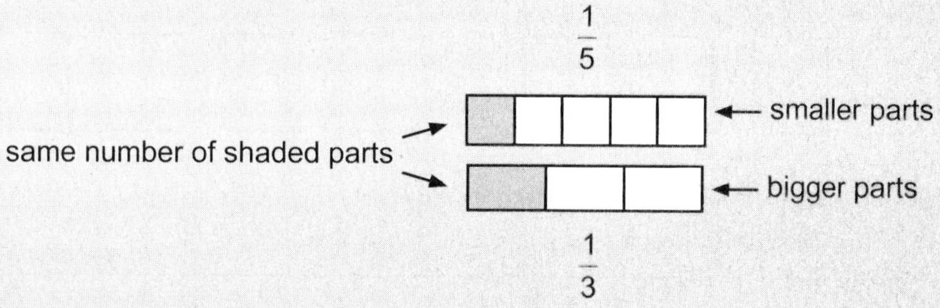

So $\frac{1}{5} < \frac{1}{3}$ because the parts are smaller in the shape with more parts.

8. Circle the greater fraction.

a) $\frac{2}{5}$ or $\frac{2}{3}$ b) $\frac{3}{4}$ or $\frac{3}{5}$ c) $\frac{4}{5}$ or $\frac{4}{10}$ d) $\frac{3}{4}$ or $\frac{3}{3}$

9. Write any number in the blank that makes the relationship correct.

a) $\frac{3}{5} > \frac{\_\_\_}{8}$ b) $\frac{\_\_\_}{15} > \frac{14}{29}$ c) $\frac{9}{16} > \frac{9}{\_\_\_}$ d) $\frac{20}{\_\_\_} < \frac{20}{27}$

10. Two fractions have the same numerator but different denominators.
How can you tell which fraction is greater?

____

____

11. a) Order the fractions from least to greatest by matching each fraction to the strip it represents and then shading it.

i) $\frac{1}{4}$ $\frac{1}{10}$ $\frac{1}{2}$ $\frac{1}{5}$ $\frac{1}{3}$

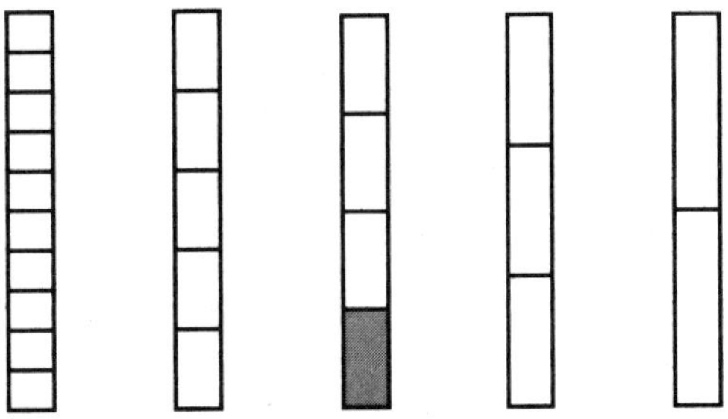

☐ < ☐ < $\frac{1}{4}$ < ☐ < ☐

ii) $\frac{2}{2}$ $\frac{2}{4}$ $\frac{2}{10}$ $\frac{2}{3}$ $\frac{2}{5}$

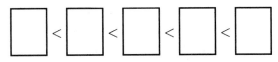

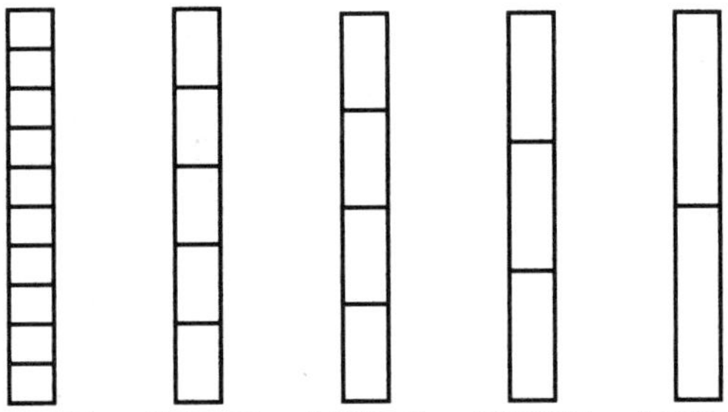

☐ < ☐ < ☐ < ☐ < ☐

b) Order the fractions from least to greatest by considering the numerators and denominators.

i) $\frac{1}{4}$ $\frac{1}{10}$ $\frac{1}{2}$ $\frac{1}{5}$ $\frac{1}{3}$

☐ < ☐ < ☐ < ☐ < ☐

ii) $\frac{2}{2}$ $\frac{2}{4}$ $\frac{2}{10}$ $\frac{2}{3}$ $\frac{2}{5}$

☐ < ☐ < ☐ < ☐ < ☐

c) Are your answers for parts a) and b) the same? Explain.

____

____

12. Randi says that $\frac{1}{2}$ of a pie is less than $\frac{1}{10}$ of a pie. Is she correct? Explain.

____

____

13. Ray, Hanna, and Lynn each brought 1 cake to school for their year-end class party. None of the cakes are the same size. The teacher cut each cake into 8 equal pieces, so everyone in the class can have a piece. Ray says, "That's not fair at all!" and Lynn says, "That's perfectly fair!"

a) Why does Ray think it's unfair?

____

____

b) Why does Lynn think it's fair?

____

____

14. a) Write the fractions in the correct category.

~~$\frac{3}{4}$~~	$\frac{1}{3}$	$\frac{2}{5}$	$\frac{4}{6}$
$\frac{4}{9}$	$\frac{3}{7}$	$\frac{7}{8}$	$\frac{6}{10}$
$\frac{5}{9}$	$\frac{2}{3}$	$\frac{1}{6}$	$\frac{3}{10}$

0 to $\frac{1}{2}$	**$\frac{1}{2}$ to 1**
	$\frac{3}{4}$

b) Use the results from part a) to write "<" or ">" in the box between the pair of fractions.

i) $\frac{6}{10}$ ☐ $\frac{3}{7}$ ii) $\frac{1}{3}$ ☐ $\frac{3}{4}$ iii) $\frac{4}{6}$ ☐ $\frac{4}{9}$ iv) $\frac{2}{5}$ ☐ $\frac{5}{9}$

v) $\frac{2}{3}$ ☐ $\frac{3}{10}$ vi) $\frac{3}{7}$ ☐ $\frac{7}{8}$ vii) $\frac{5}{9}$ ☐ $\frac{1}{6}$ viii) $\frac{4}{9}$ ☐ $\frac{3}{4}$

NS4-51 Fraction Word Problems

1. $\frac{5}{9}$ of the community pool is reserved for swimming lengths. What fraction of the pool

 is not reserved for swimming lengths? ☐

2. A pitcher of fruit drink is made by mixing water and canned orange juice.

 a) If $\frac{1}{4}$ of the fruit drink is canned orange juice, what fraction of the drink is water? ☐

 b) How would the taste of the fruit drink change if $\frac{1}{2}$ of it were canned orange juice instead of $\frac{1}{4}$?

 c) If you added some club soda to a glass of fruit drink, would the fraction of canned juice in the glass of fruit drink get bigger or smaller? Explain.

3. The picture represents a set of stickers.

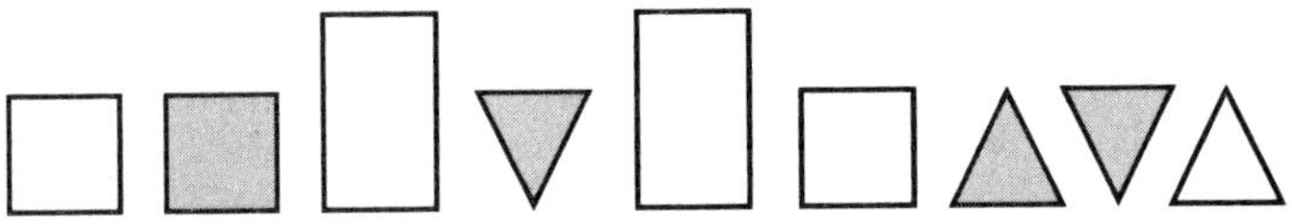

 a) What are two examples of $\frac{4}{9}$ of the stickers? _____

 b) What fraction of the stickers are quadrilaterals (have exactly four sides)? ☐

 c) What fraction of the quadrilaterals do not have four equal sides? ☐

 d) What other group can be represented with the same fraction as in c)?

4. The picture represents the fraction of Earth's surface that is covered by water.

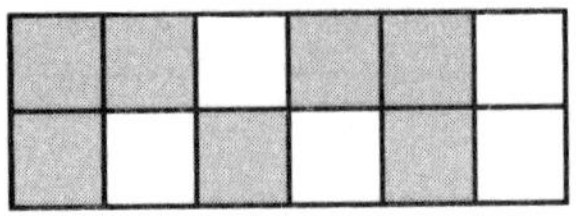

a) What fraction of Earth's surface is covered by water (shaded)? ☐

 b) What fraction of Earth's surface is not covered by water? ☐

 c) Which is there more of, Earth's surface with water or without water? _____

5. Lela and Ray went to the park. The pictures represent the fraction of time each spent on the swings.

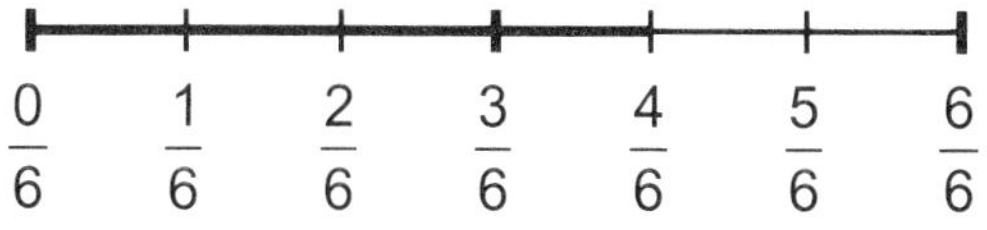

Lela

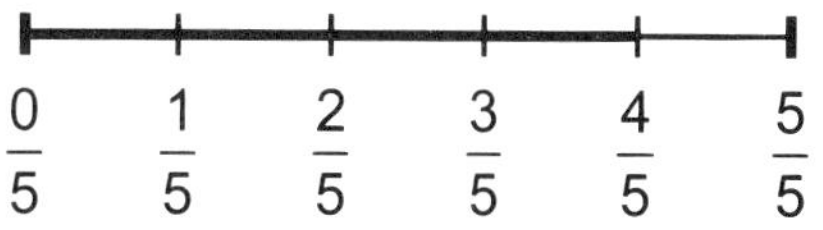

Ray

a) What fraction of the time at the park did Lela spend on the swings? ☐

b) What fraction of the time at the park did Ray spend on the swings? ☐

c) Who spent more time on the swings? ____________

6. A teacher is going to order 10 pizzas for a year-end party. More than half of the pizzas must be vegetarian.

a) Will there be enough vegetarian pizzas if 3 are vegetarian? ______

b) Will there be enough vegetarian pizzas if 6 are vegetarian? ______

c) If 6 pizzas are vegetarian, what fraction of the pizzas are not vegetarian? ☐

d) Give another example of a fraction that would have enough vegetarian pizzas by shading the pizzas below.

7. Soccer Team A won $\frac{3}{9}$ of the games they played this season. Soccer Team B lost $\frac{5}{9}$ of the games they played this season. Soccer Team C won $\frac{3}{5}$ of the games they played this season.

a) What fraction of their games did Team A lose? ☐

b) What fraction of their games did Team B win? ☐

c) What fraction of their games did Team C lose? ☐

d) Which team won a greater fraction of their games, Team A or Team B? ______

e) Which team won a greater fraction of their games, Team A or Team C? ______

Decimal Tenths and Place Value

A **tenth** (or $\frac{1}{10}$) can be represented in different ways.

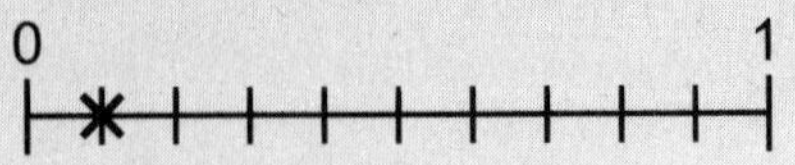

A tenth of the distance between 0 and 1

A tenth of a pie

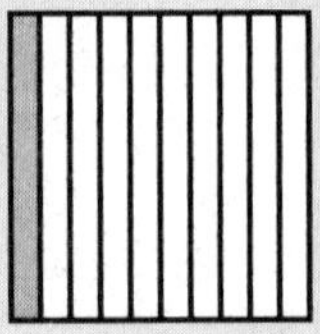

A tenth of a square

Mathematicians invented decimal tenths as a short form for tenths: $\frac{1}{10} = 0.1$, $\frac{2}{10} = 0.2$, and so on.

1. Write a fraction and a decimal for the shaded part in the boxes.

a) 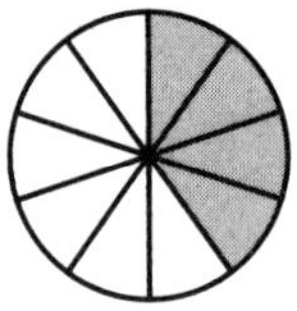 $\frac{4}{10}$ | 0.4

b) 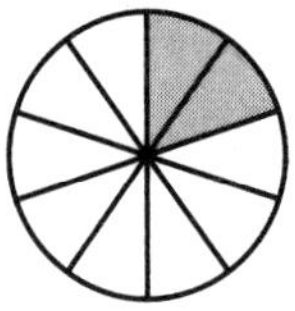 $\frac{2}{10}$ | 0,2

c) 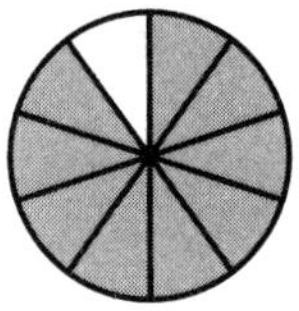 $\frac{9}{12}$ | 9.1

2. Write the decimal.

a) 5 tenths = 0.5 b) 7 tenths = 0.7 c) 6 tenths = 0.6 d) 9 tenths = 0.9

e) 2 tenths = 0.2 f) 8 tenths = 0.8 g) 3 tenths = 0.3

BONUS ▶ 0 tenths = 0.0

3. Shade to show the decimal.

a) 0.3 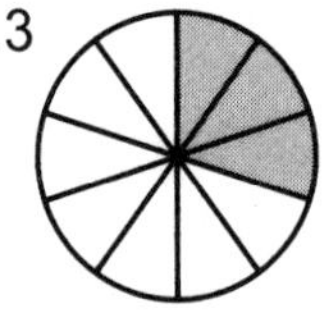

b) 0.8 

c) 0.5 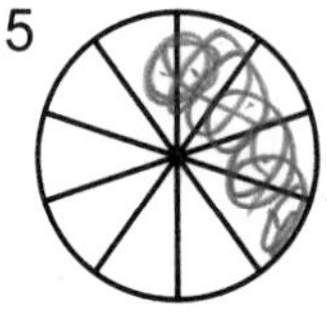

d) 0.6 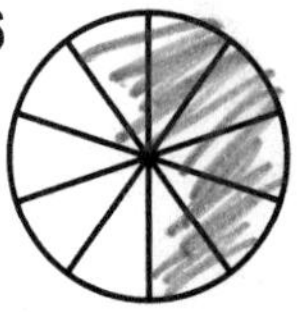

4. Show the decimal on the number line.

a) 0.8 of the distance from 0.0 to 1.0

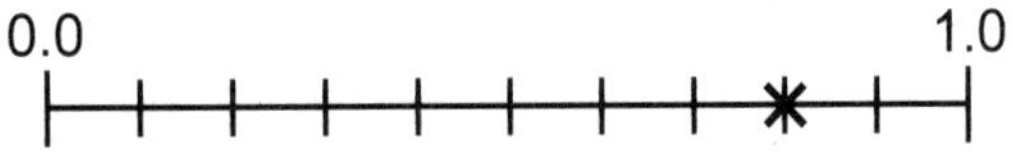

b) 0.3 of the distance from 0.0 to 1.0

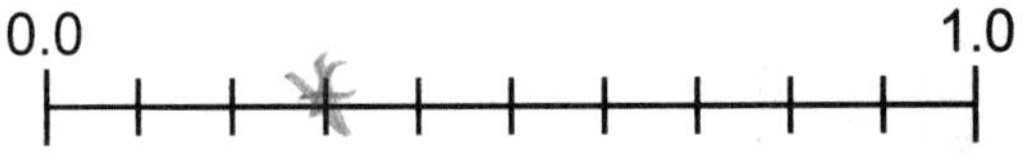

c) 0.5 of the distance from 0.0 to 1.0

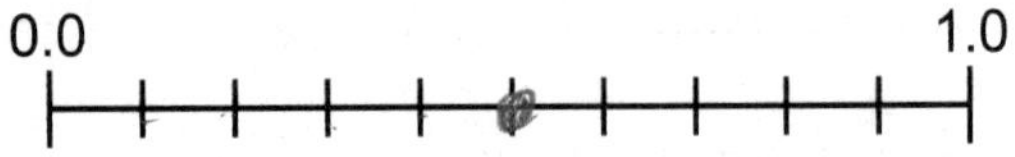

d) 0.9 of the distance from 0.0 to 1.0

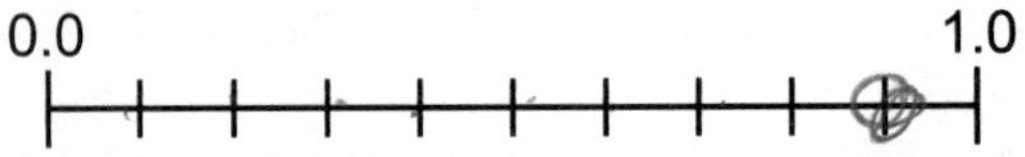

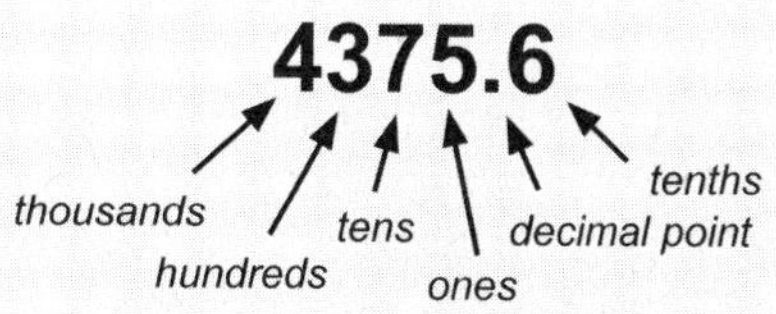

5. Write the place value of the underlined digit.

a) $\underline{2}$.7 *ones* b) 53.$\underline{9}$ ______ c) 107.$\underline{1}$ ______

d) $\underline{2}$36.4 ______ e) $\underline{4}$501.8 ______ f) 73$\underline{3}$4.5 ______

g) 4$\underline{0}$0.3 ______ h) $\underline{9}$21.2 ______ i) 367$\underline{7}$.8 ______

6. Write the place value of the digit 3 in the number.
Hint: First underline the 3 in the number.

a) 2361.9 ______ b) 405.3 ______ c) 713.8 ______

d) 30.2 ______ e) 3919.1 ______ f) 2854.3 ______

g) 392.7 ______ h) 1636.2 ______ i) 3544.5 ______

You can also write numbers using a place value chart. Example:

This is the number 7102.8 in a place value chart:

Thousands	Hundreds	Tens	Ones	Tenths
7	1	0	2 •	8

7. Write the number into the place value chart.

		Thousands	Hundreds	Tens	Ones	Tenths
a)	5227.6	*5*	*2*	*2*	*7* •	*6*
b)	8053.4				•	
c)	489.2				•	
d)	27.8				•	
e)	9104.5				•	
f)	8.7				•	
g)	706.0				•	
h)	6.1				•	

In the number 2836.5:

the **digit** 2 has a value of 2000—the **value** of the digit 2 is 2000;

the digit 8 has a value of 800—the value of the digit 8 is 800;

the digit 3 has a value of 30—the value of the digit 3 is 30;

the digit 6 has a value of 6—the value of the digit 6 is 6; and

the digit 5 has a value of $\frac{5}{10}$—the value of the digit 5 is $\frac{5}{10}$.

8. Write the value of each digit.

a) b) c)

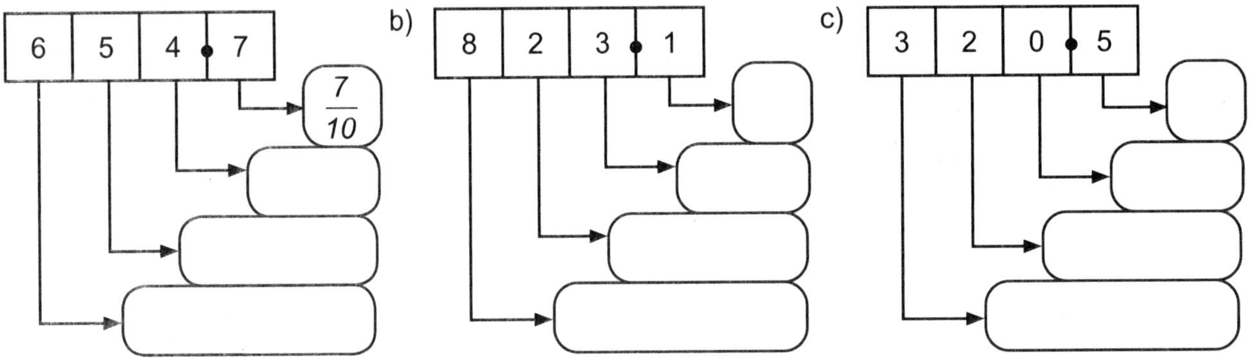

9. What value does the digit 7 have in the number?

a) 732.6 *700*

b) 4107.9

c) 6171.2

d) 7384.5

e) 9062.7

f) 467.8

g) 1894.7

h) 2744.8

i) 7250.5

j) 6000.7

k) 3975.4

l) 743.1

10. Fill in the blank.

a) In the number 1969.5, the digit 6 stands for *60*.

b) In the number 5873.2, the digit 3 stands for ________.

c) In the number 7451.3, the value of the digit 7 is ________.

d) In the number 8003.9, the value of the digit 9 is ________.

e) In the number 4855.7, the value of the digit 8 is ________.

f) In the number 9201.4, the digit ______ is in the ones place.

g) In the number 3495.6, the digit ______ is in the hundreds place.

h) In the number 6467.5, the digit ______ is in the tenths place.

Decimal Fractions and Place Value

Decimals are a way to record place values based on decimal fractions.

decimal point
5 thousands → **5342.67** ← 7 hundredths
3 hundreds, 4 tens, 2 ones, 6 tenths

1. Write the place value of the underlined digit.

a) 2.7 *ones* b) 53.9 ______ c) 107.1 ______

d) 236.4 ______ e) 501.08 ______ f) 734.58 ______

2. Write the place value of the digit 3 in the number. Hint: First underline the 3 in the number.

a) 261.93 ______ b) 405.03 ______ c) 7103.8 ______

d) 3.02 ______ e) 3919.1 ______ f) 2854.30 ______

You can also write numbers using a place value chart. Example:

This is the number 7102.85 in a place value chart:

Thousands	Hundreds	Tens	Ones	Tenths	Hundredths
7	1	0	2 •	8	5

3. Write the number into the place value chart.

		Thousands	Hundreds	Tens	Ones	Tenths	Hundredths
a)	5227.60	*5*	*2*	*2*	*7* •	*6*	*0*
b)	853.4				•		
c)	0.05				•		
d)	27.00				•		
e)	4.58				•		

4. What is the value of the digit 9 in each decimal? Write the answer two ways.

a) 0.49 $\frac{9}{100}$ or 9 *hundredths* b) 3.92 $\frac{9}{\_\_}$ or 9 ______

c) 8.90 $\frac{9}{\_\_}$ or 9 ______ d) 3.09 $\frac{9}{\_\_}$ or 9 ______

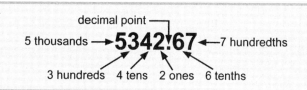

NS4-53 Relating Fractions and Decimals—to Tenths

1. a) Write a fraction in each blank above the number line.

b) Write a decimal in each blank below the number line.

$\frac{0}{10}$ ___ ___ ___ ___ ___ ___ ___ ___ ___ $\frac{10}{10}$

0.0 0.1 ___ ___ ___ ___ ___ ___ ___ ___ 1.0

c) Which decimal is equal to the fraction?

i) $\frac{5}{10}$ = ______ ii) $\frac{10}{10}$ = ______ iii) $\frac{0}{10}$ = ______

2. a) Write a decimal in each blank below the number line.

b) Cross out each incorrect fraction and write the correct fraction above it.

$\frac{0}{10}$ ___ $\frac{2}{10}$ ___ ___ ___ ___ ___ ___ ___ ___

$\frac{0}{10}$ $\frac{7}{10}$ ~~$\frac{3}{10}$~~ $\frac{2}{10}$ $\frac{4}{10}$ $\frac{10}{10}$ $\frac{6}{10}$ $\frac{5}{10}$ $\frac{8}{10}$ $\frac{9}{10}$ $\frac{1}{10}$

0.0 0.1 ___ ___ ___ ___ ___ ___ ___ ___ 1.0

3. a) Write a fraction in each blank above the number line.

b) Cross out each incorrect decimal on the number line and write the correct decimal below it.

$\frac{0}{10}$ $\frac{1}{10}$ ___ ___ ___ ___ ___ ___ ___ ___ ___

0.0 0.3 0.2 0.7 0.4 0.9 0.6 0.1 0.8 0.5 1.0

___ ___ ___ ___ ___ ___ ___ ___ ___ ___ ___

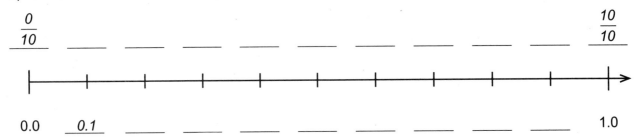

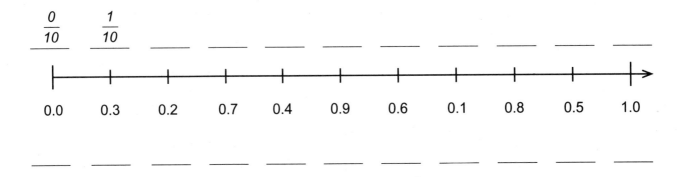

4. a) Fill in the missing numerators and decimals on the number lines.

$\frac{0}{2}$ ____ $\frac{}{2}$ ____ $\frac{}{2}$ ____

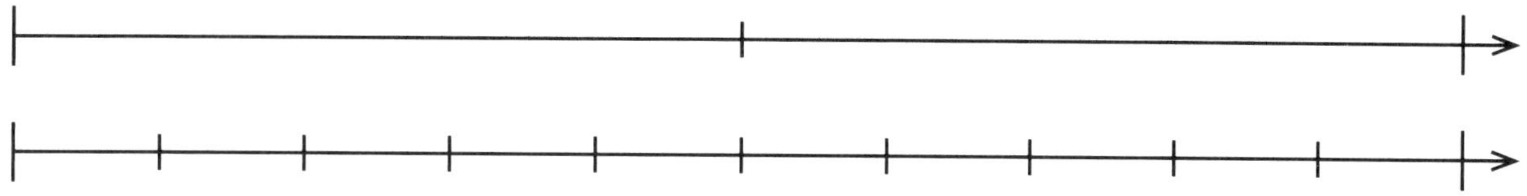

0.0 ____ ____ ____ ____ ____ ____ ____ ____ ____ ____

b) Write the decimal that the fraction is equal to.

i) $\frac{0}{2}=$ 0.0 ii) $\frac{1}{2}=$ ________ iii) $\frac{2}{2}=$ ________

BONUS ▶ Write the decimals that are not equal to any fraction in part b).

0.1 0.2 ________ ________ ________ ________ ________ ________

5. a) Fill in the missing fractions and decimals.

$\frac{0}{5}$ ____ ____ ____ ____ ____

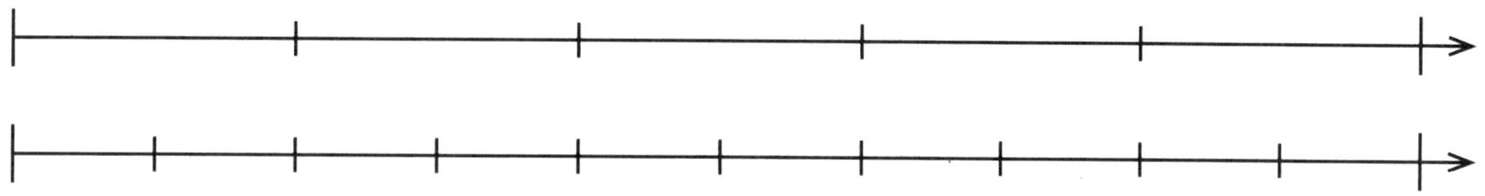

0.0 ____ ____ ____ ____ ____ ____ ____ ____ ____ ____

b) Write the decimal the fraction is equal to in part b).

i) $\frac{4}{5}=$ ________ ii) $\frac{2}{5}=$ ________ iii) $\frac{5}{5}=$ ________

iv) $\frac{1}{5}=$ ________ v) $\frac{0}{5}=$ ________

BONUS ▶ Write the decimals that are not equal to any fraction in part b).

0.1 0.3 ________ ________ ________ ________

NS4-54 Decimals Greater Than 1—to Tenths

1. Write a decimal in each blank below the number line.

a) 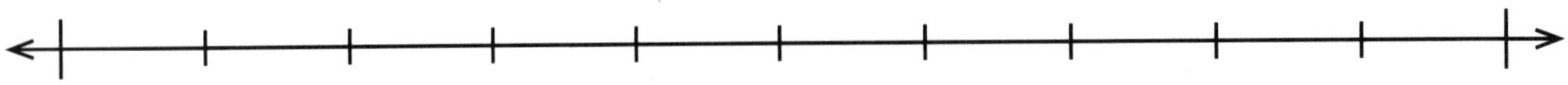

1.0   *1.1*   ____   ____   ____   ____   ____   ____   ____   ____   2.0

b) 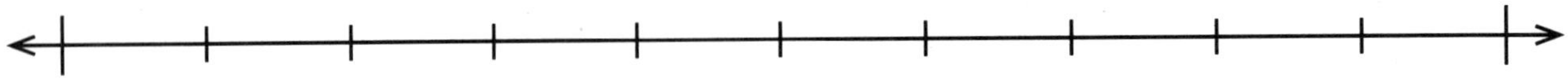

5.7   ____   ____   ____   ____   ____   ____   ____   ____   ____   ____

c) 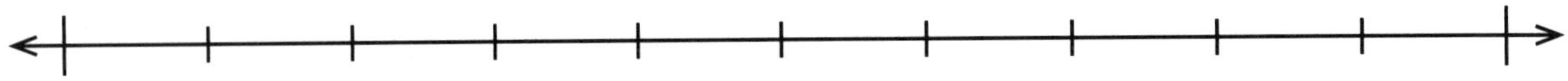

63.4   ____   ____   ____   ____   ____   ____   ____   ____   ____   ____

2. a) How are the scales in Question 1 different from each other?

____

____

b) How are the scales in Question 1 the same as each other?

____

____

You can write a decimal in words. Use "and" for the decimal point.

Examples: 12.3 = twelve **and** three tenths   2.8 = two **and** eight tenths

3. Fill in the missing number word.

a) 3.1 = three and ____*one*____ tenth

b) 18.7 = eighteen and ______________ tenths

c) 6.5 = ______________ and five tenths

d) 20.8 = ______________ and eight tenths

4. Write the equivalent words or decimal.

a) 7.4 = ____

b) 4.9 = ____

c) nineteen and one tenth = __________

d) sixty-two and four tenths = __________

5. Count the shaded tenths. Write the amount two ways.

a) 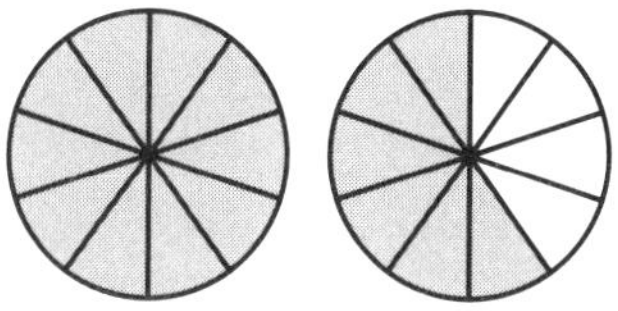

16 tenths = 1.6

b) 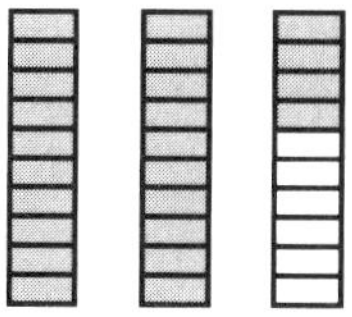

_______ tenths = _______

c) 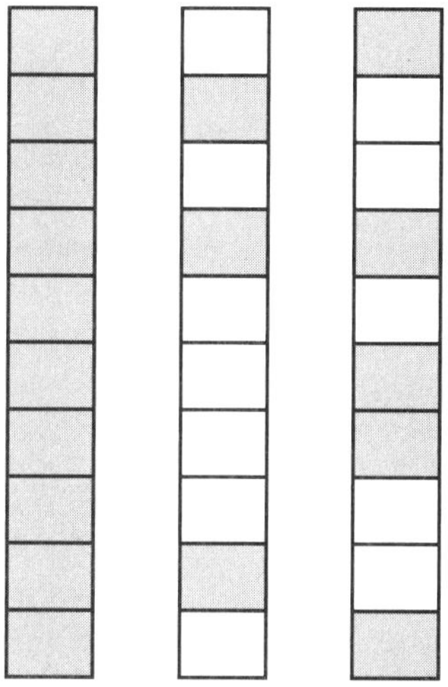

_______ tenths = _______

d) 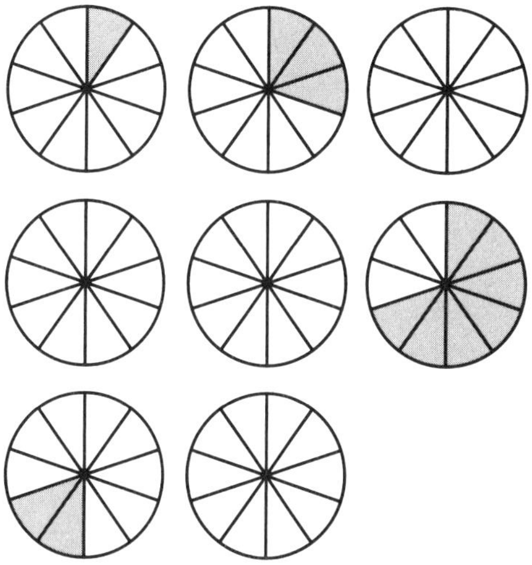

_______ tenths = _______

e) 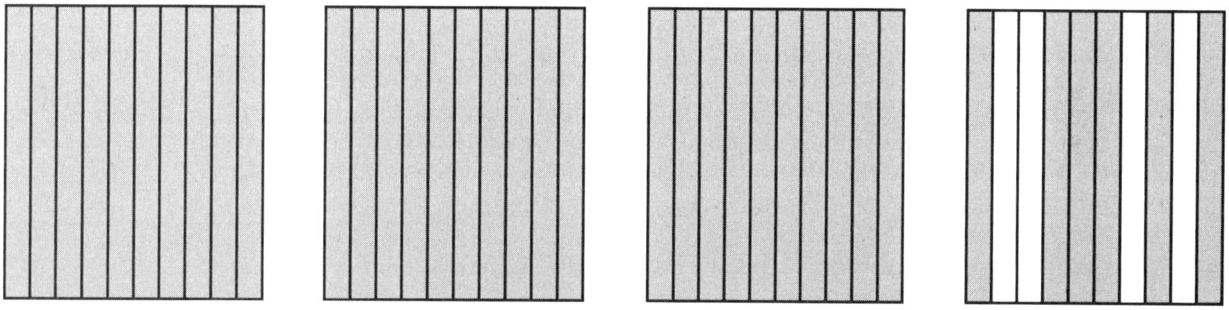

_______ tenths = _______

BONUS ▶

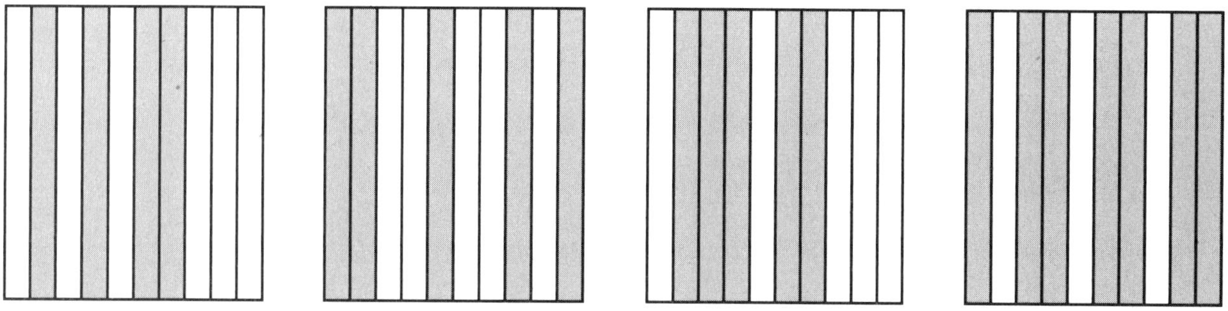

_______ tenths = _______

NF4-27 Decimals Greater Than 1

A mixed number can be written as a decimal.

Examples: $12\frac{3}{10} = 12.3$ $2\frac{85}{100} = 2.85$

The decimal point separates the whole number part (on the left) and the fraction part (on the right).

1. Write the mixed number as a decimal.

a) $3\frac{4}{10} =$ ______ b) $12\frac{5}{10} =$ ______ c) $8\frac{45}{100} =$ ______ d) $46\frac{3}{100} =$ ______

REMINDER ▶

The number of digits to the right of the decimal point = the number of zeros in the denominator

Examples: $3.\mathbf{45} = 3\frac{45}{\mathbf{100}}$ $34.\mathbf{5} = 34\frac{5}{\mathbf{10}}$ $34.\mathbf{05} = 34\frac{5}{\mathbf{100}}$

2. Write the denominator of the fraction part for the equivalent mixed number.

a) 4.9 ______ b) 1.58 ______ c) 15.08 ______ **BONUS ▶** 18.3402 ______

3. Write the decimal as a mixed number.

a) 3.81 = b) 6.9 = c) 7.04 = d) 18.15 =

e) 13.4 = f) 17.06 = g) 193.45 = **BONUS ▶** 7.004 =

You can write a decimal in words. Use "and" for the decimal point.

Examples: $12\frac{3}{10} = 12.3$ = twelve **and** three tenths $2\frac{85}{100} = 2.85$ = two **and** eighty-five hundredths

4. Write "tenths" or "hundredths." Hint: Count the digits to the right of the decimal point.

a) 3.12 = three and twelve ______ b) 18.7 = eighteen and seven ______

c) 6.05 = six and five ______ d) 20.8 = twenty and eight ______

5. Write the equivalent words or decimal.

a) 7.4 = ______

b) 4.09 = ______

c) seventy-four and eleven hundredths = ______ d) twenty and four tenths = ______

REMINDER ▶ You can change an improper fraction to a mixed number by dividing.

Example: $\frac{28}{10}$

$28 \div 10 = 2 \text{ R } 8$, so $\frac{28}{10} = 2\frac{8}{10}$

6. Change the improper fraction to a mixed number.

a) $\frac{74}{10}$ $74 \div 10 =$ _______ R _______

So $\frac{74}{10} =$

b) $\frac{684}{100}$ $684 \div 100 =$ _______ R _______

So $\frac{684}{100} =$

7. Change the improper fraction to a mixed number and then to a decimal.

a) $\frac{35}{10} = 3\frac{5}{10} = 3.5$

b) $\frac{387}{100} = 3\frac{87}{100} = 3.87$

c) $\frac{41}{10} =$

d) $\frac{642}{10} =$

e) $\frac{564}{100} =$

f) $\frac{4\,208}{100} =$

NS4-55 Comparing and Ordering Numbers—to Tenths

 = 1  = 0.1

1. Write the number for each base ten model using numerals (in the box). Then circle the greater number in the pair.

a) 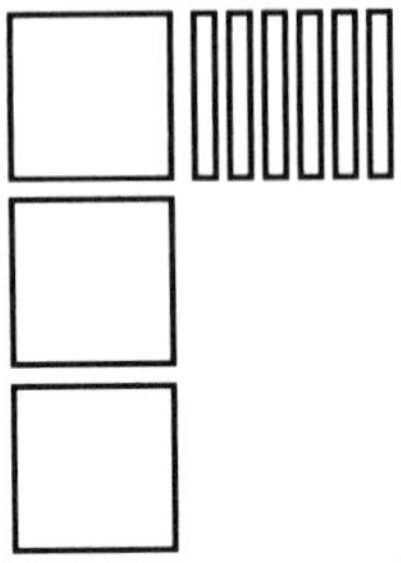 *3.6* 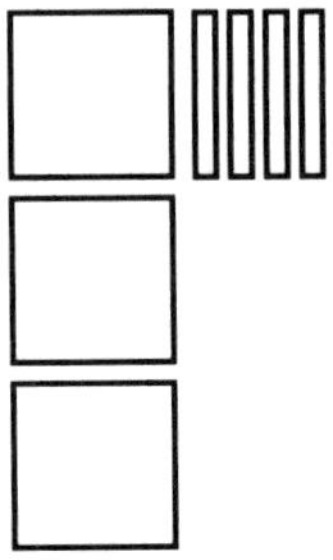 ☐

b) 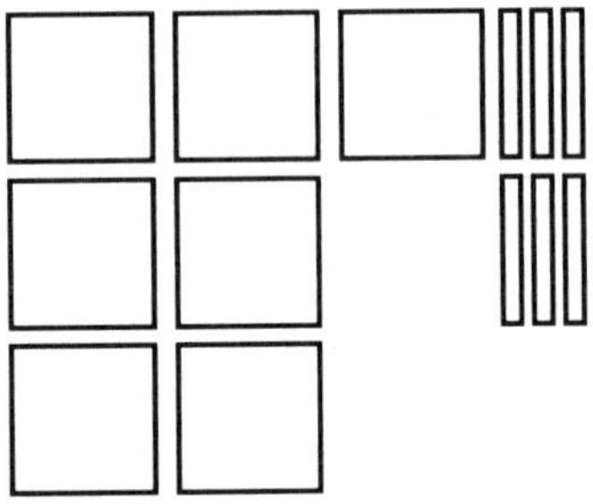 ☐ 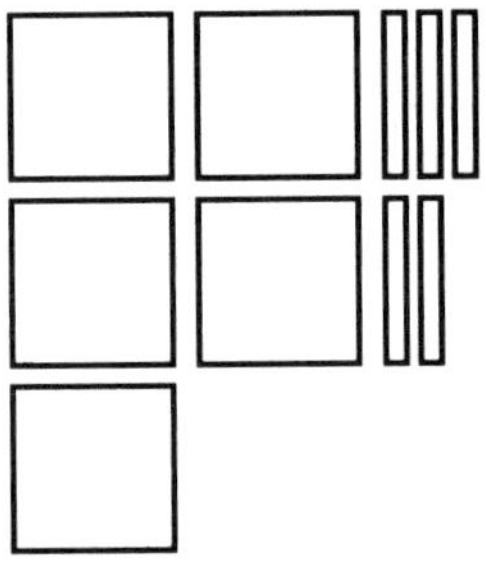 ☐

c) Explain how you knew which number in part a) was greater.

2. Draw base ten models for the pair of numbers. Then circle the greater number.

a) nine and seven tenths 7.9

b) twelve and eight tenths 8.2

3. Write the value of each digit. Then complete the sentence.

a)

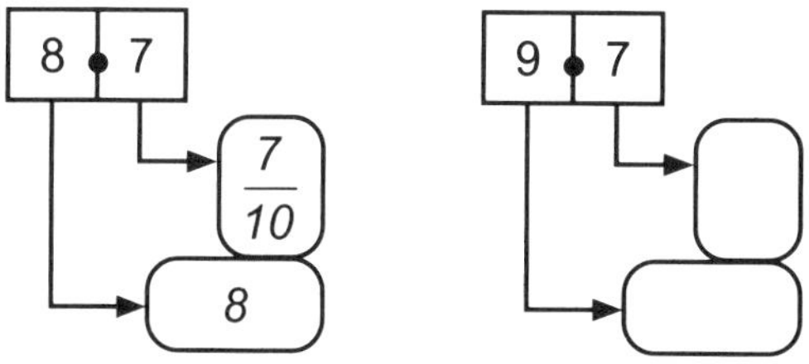

________ is greater than ________.

b)

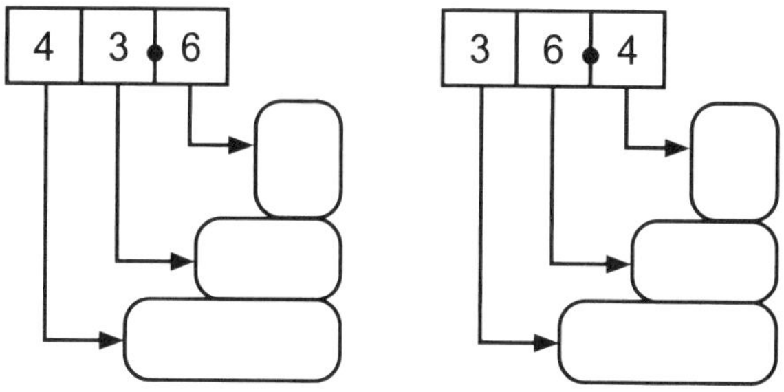

________ is greater than ________.

c)

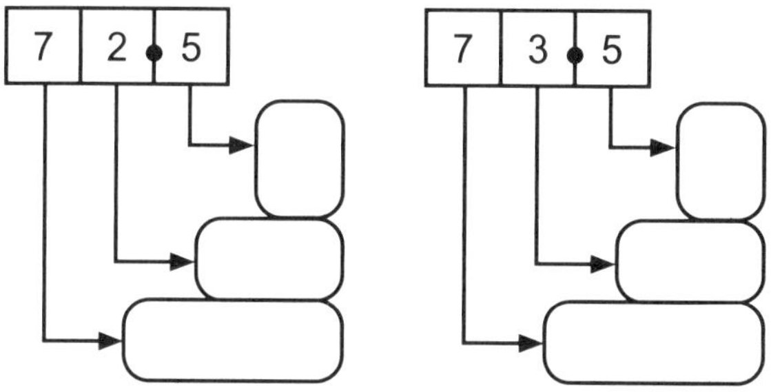

________ is greater than ________.

d)

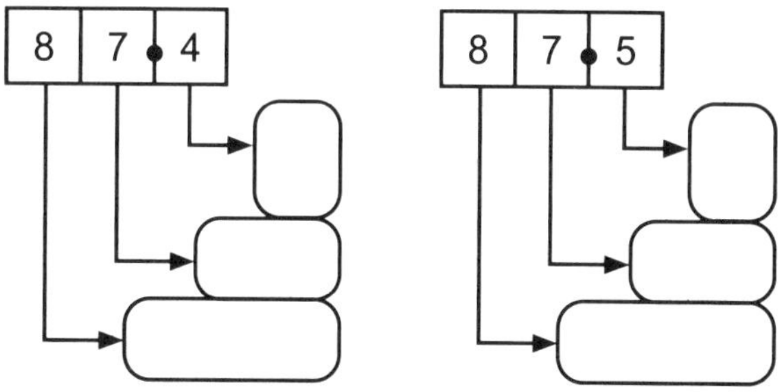

________ is greater than ________.

4. Circle the digits that are different in the pair of numbers. Then write the greater number in the box.

a) 247.5
246.5
247.5

b) 136.0
126.0

c) 4852.5
4858.5

d) 632.5
732.5

5. Read the numbers from left to right. Circle the first pair of digits you find that are different. Then write the greater number in the box.

a) 4323.3
4332.3

b) 5090.7
5900.7

c) 756.2
776.8

BONUS ▶ 12 146.6
12 086.4

6. Circle the greater number.

a) 8147.6 9147.6

b) 352.1 325.9

c) 5098.1 5089.9

7. Write “<” (less than) or “>” (greater than) in the box to make the statement true.

a) 6726.2 ☐ 6726.6

b) 788.8 ☐ 788.7

c) 4303.2 ☐ 3403.9

8. Write the second number below the first number with the decimal points lined up. Then circle the greater number.

a) (1296.8) 689.8 b) 416.2 96.2 c) 5137.2 5371.2 d) 7358.2 735.8

689.8 ________ ________ ________

9. Circle the greatest number.

a) 68.1 86.1 81.6

b) 98.3 109.3 319.4

c) 3670.1 3063.7 736.6

d) 5228.2 2558.2 852.8

10. Arrange the numbers in descending order.

a) 549.1 5490.1 954.1

________, ________, ________

b) 1300.4 10 002.4 989.7

________, ________, ________

c) 826.7 762.8 800.0

________, ________, ________

d) 400.1 1000.4 410.0

________, ________, ________

11. Write a number in each blank so the three numbers are arranged in ascending order.

a) 529.9, ________, 592.2

________, 529.9, 592.2

529.9, 592.2, ________

b) 614.4, 641.1, ________

614.4, ________, 641.1

________, 614.4, 641.1

c) ________, 79.3, 790.3

79.3, 790.3, ________

79.3, ________, 790.3

12. a) Mark the numbers on the number line using an **X**. Then write the numbers in ascending and descending order: 519.7, 519.3, 520.0.

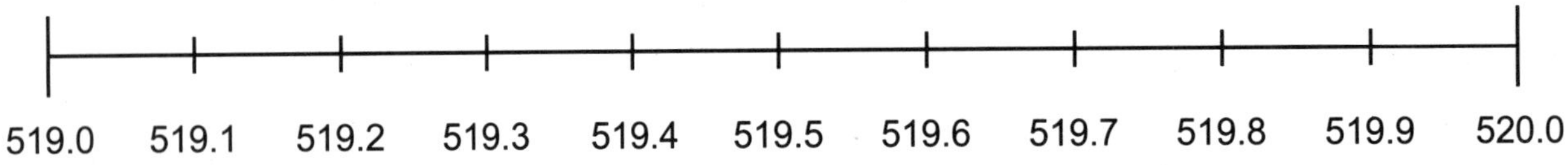

Ascending order: ________, ________, ________

Descending order: ________, ________, ________

b) Explain why it would be difficult to make a number line to mark the numbers 43.9, 9432.2, and 432.9 on.

____

____

____

Adding and Subtracting Decimals—to Tenths

A base ten representation for decimal tenths:

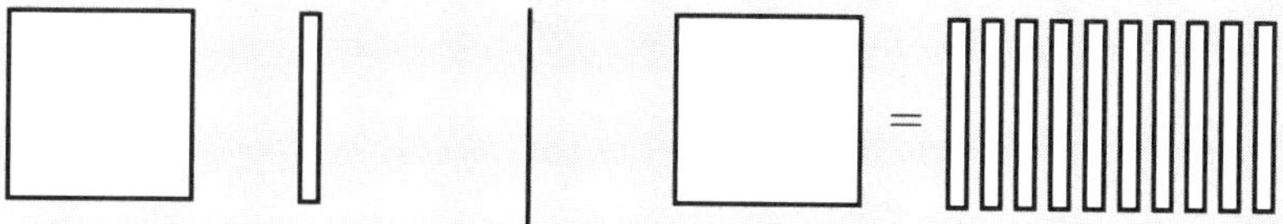

1 one   1 tenth | 1 one = 10 tenths

1. Regroup every 10 tenths as 1 one.

a)

Ones	Tenths	
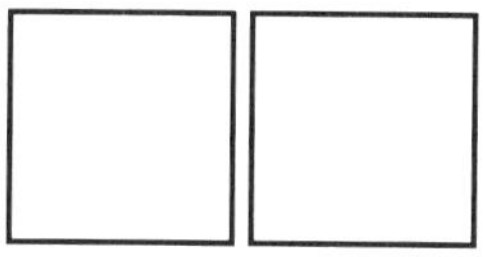	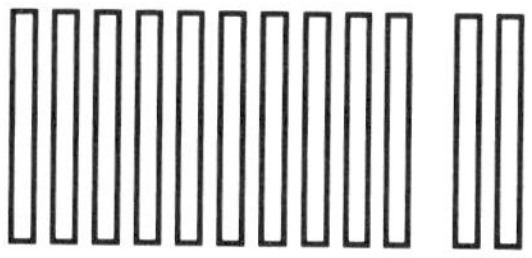	______ ones + ______ tenths
		______ ones + ______ tenths

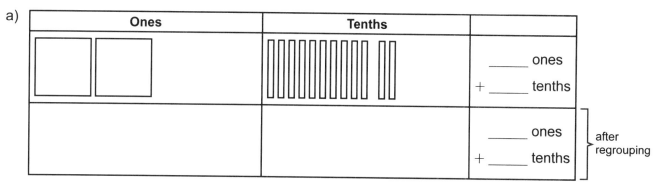

} after regrouping

b) 16 tenths = ______ ones + ______ tenths

c) 23 tenths = ______ ones + ______ tenths

d) 49 tenths = ______ ones + ______ tenths

e) 52 tenths = ______ ones + ______ tenths

2. Regroup so that the tenths place value has a single digit.

a) 3 tenths + 12 tenths = ___*1*___ one + ___*5*___ tenths

b) 7 ones + 14 tenths = ______ ones + ______ tenths

c) 8 tens + 6 ones + 36 tenths = ______ tens + ______ ones + ______ tenths

d) 6 hundreds + 5 tens + 4 ones + 54 tenths = ______ hundreds + ______ tens + ______ ones + ______ tenths

BONUS ▶ 9 thousands + 3 hundreds + 7 tens + 2 ones + 28 tenths = ______ thousands + ______ hundreds + ______ tens + ______ ones + ______ tenths

3. Add by adding each place value.

a) 35.4 + 2.3

	Tens	Ones	Tenths
	3	*5* .	*4*
+		*2* .	*3*
	3	*7* .	*7*

b) 146.1 + 22.8

	Hundreds	Tens	Ones	Tenths
			.	
+			.	
			.	

4. Add by adding each place value. Then regroup.

a) 14.5 + 3.6

	Tens	Ones	Tenths
	1	4 .	5
+		3 .	6
	1	7 .	11
	1	8 .	1

← after regrouping →

b) 25.8 + 12.6

	Tens	Ones	Tenths
		.	
+		.	
		.	
		.	

5. Add the decimals by lining up the decimal points.

a) 6.5 + 3.2

	6 .	5
+	3 .	2
	9 .	7

b) 11.3 + 32.5

c) 65.6 + 2.3

d) 37.2 + 42.6

You can show regrouping on a grid. Example: 4.8 + 3.5

	1	
	4 .	8
+	3 .	5
	8 .	**3**

8 tenths + 5 tenths = 13 tenths were regrouped as **1** one and **3** tenths

6. Add the decimals by lining up the decimal points. You will need to regroup.

a) 6.7 + 1.8

	1	
	6 .	7
+	1 .	8
	8 .	**5**

b) 24.7 + 4.3

c) 57.2 + 31.9

d) 63.4 + 12.6 + 1.5

7. On a grid, line up the decimal points and add the numbers. You may need to regroup more than once.

a) 19.6 + 3.6 b) 37.9 + 30.5 c) 126.8 + 2.9 d) 314.5 + 56.7

8. Clara buys 3.8 kg of red apples and 2.9 kg of green apples. What is the total mass of the apples?

9. Jake weighs 45.9 kg and his dog, Spot, weighs 3.7 kg. What is their total weight in kg?

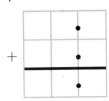

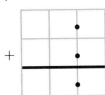

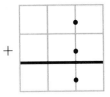

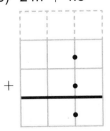

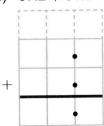

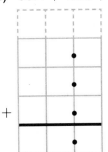

10. Subtract by crossing out ones and tenths blocks.

a) 2.8 – 0.6 = 2.2

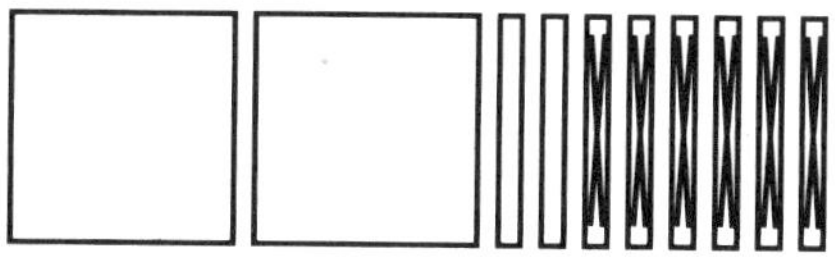

b) 3.5 – 1.4 = ______

c) 5.7 – 3.5 = ______

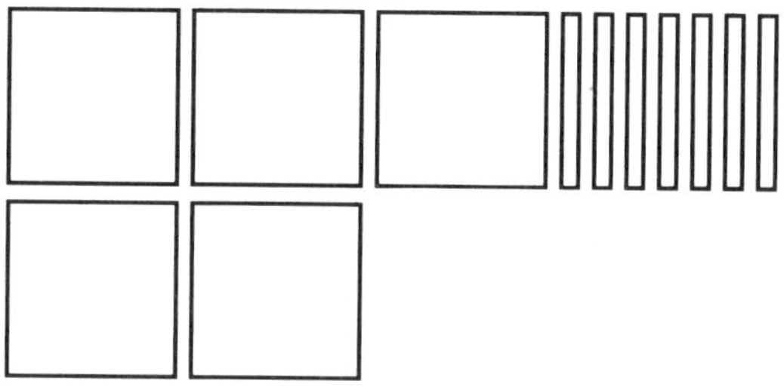

d) 8.9 – 4.3 = ______

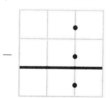

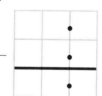

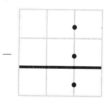

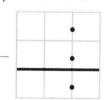

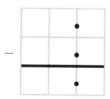

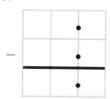

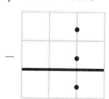

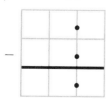

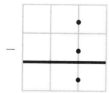

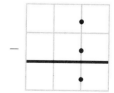

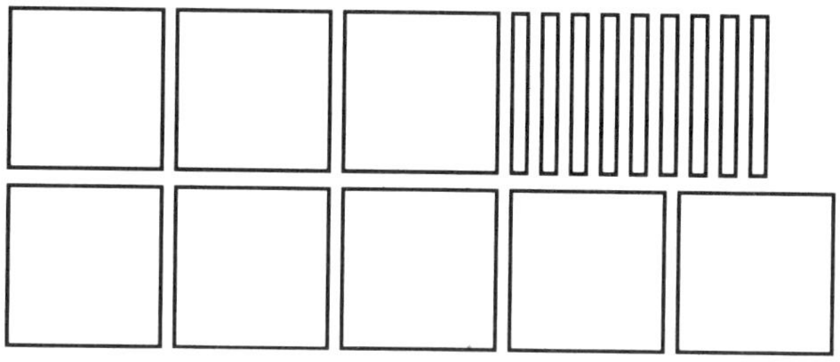

11. Represent some of the subtractions from Question 10 in tables by lining up the decimal points.

a) 2.8 – 0.6 = 2.2

	Ones	Tenths
	2 .	8
–	0 .	6
	2 .	2

b) 5.7 – 3.5 = ______

	Ones	Tenths
	.	
–	.	
	.	

c) 8.9 – 4.3 = ______

	Ones	Tenths
	.	
–	.	
	.	

12. Subtract the decimals by lining up the decimal points.

a) 10.7 – 10.3

	1	0 .	7
–	1	0 .	3
	0	0 .	4

b) 20.5 – 10.2

c) 13.4 – 2.2

d) 16.4 – 0.3

e) 52.5 – 11.5

f) 63.7 – 2.6

g) 78.8 – 7.1

h) 95.1 – 93.0

i) 4.8 – 4.4

j) 21.5 – 1.4

k) 45.5 – 12.4

l) 79.8 – 42.7

When subtracting decimals, you may have to regroup.

Example:

	5 . 7	
−	1 . 8	
	.	

	4 17	
	~~5~~ . ~~7~~	
−	1 . 8	
	.	

	4 17	
	~~5~~ . ~~7~~	
−	1 . 8	
	3 . 9	

Regroup 1 one as 10 tenths.

13. Exchange 1 one for 10 tenths.

a) 4 ones + 0 tenths = *3* ones + *10* tenths

b) 8 ones + 0 tenths = ______ ones + ______ tenths

c) 4 ones + 3 tenths = ______ ones + ______ tenths

d) 6 ones + 8 tenths = ______ ones + ______ tenths

e) 7 ones + 4 tenths = ______ ones + ______ tenths

BONUS ▶ 9823 ones + 19 tenths = ______ ones + ______ tenths

14. Subtract the decimals. Put a decimal point in your answer on the grid.

a) 8.1 − 5.8

	7 *11*	
	~~8~~ . ~~1~~	
−	5 . 8	
	2 . 3	

b) 5.7 − 3.9

	.	
−	.	
	.	

c) 6.1 − 4.2

d) 2.4 − 0.7

e) 4.5 − 2.6

f) 31.1 − 22.2

g) 57.4 − 6.6

BONUS ▶ 105.2 − 1.9

15. To calculate the sum, write the decimals as fractions with a common denominator.

a) $0.27 + 0.6 = \frac{27}{100} + \frac{6}{10} = \frac{27}{100} + \frac{\_\_}{100} = \frac{\_\_}{100} = \_\_.\_\_\ \_\_$

b) $0.57 + 0.76 = \frac{57}{100} + \frac{76}{100} = \frac{\_\_}{100} = \_\_.\_\_\ \_\_$

c) $2.02 + 0.99 = \frac{\_\_}{100} + \frac{\_\_}{100} = \frac{\_\_}{100} = \_\_.\_\_\ \_\_$

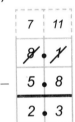

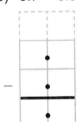

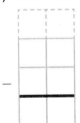

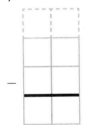

16. Subtract the decimals.

a) 8.7 − 2.6

b) 29.4 − 13.1

c) 75.8 − 43.6

17. Add or subtract mentally.

a) 0.5 + 0.3 = ________

b) 4.9 − 2.8 = ________

c) 7.9 − 4.2 = ________

d) 2.3 + 1.2 = ________

e) 5.7 − 1.6 = ________

f) 6.7 − 2.5 = ________

g) 6.3 + 2.5 = ________

h) 4.3 − 2.1 = ________

i) 9.4 − 7.4 = ________

18. What is the difference in the thickness of the coins?

a) a quarter (1.6 mm) and a dime (1.2 mm)

b) a nickel (1.8 mm) and a quarter (1.6 mm)

19. Sara made fruit drink by mixing 1.2 L of juice with 0.9 L of ginger ale. How many litres of fruit drink did she make?

20. A large leopard, including its head, body, and tail, is 3.3 m long. Its tail is 1.4 m long. What is the length of the leopard's head and body altogether?

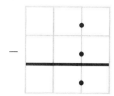

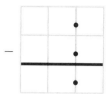

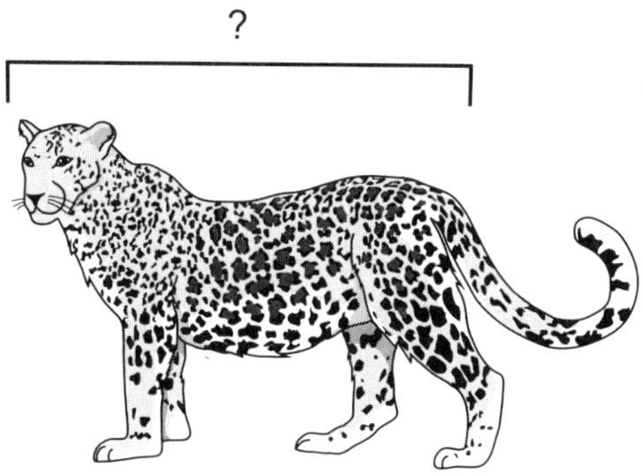

NS4-57 Estimating Sums and Differences—to Tenths

1. Draw an arrow pointing to 0.0 or 1.0 to show whether the circled decimal is closer to 0.0 or 1.0.

a)
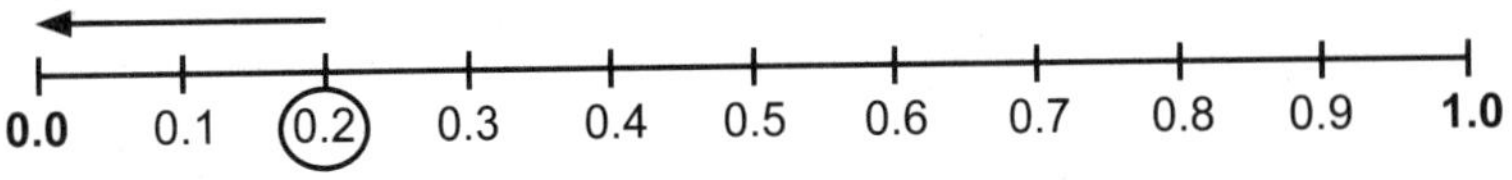

b)
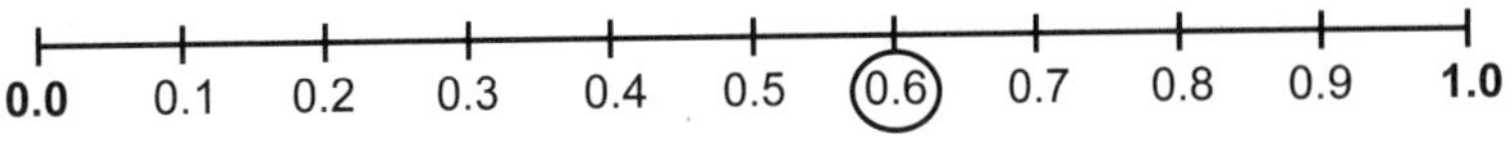

c)
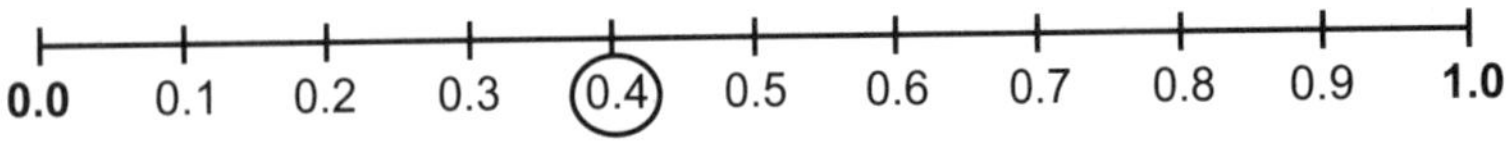

d)
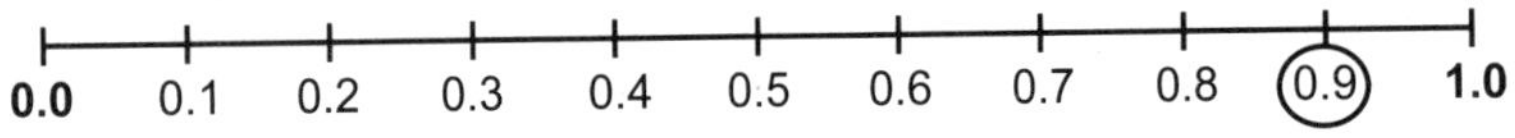

2. a) Which decimal numbers are closer to the number?

i) 0.0 ____________ ii) 1.0 ____________

b) Why is 0.5 a special case? ____________

3. Draw an arrow to show which whole number you would round the circled number to. Then round the number.

a)
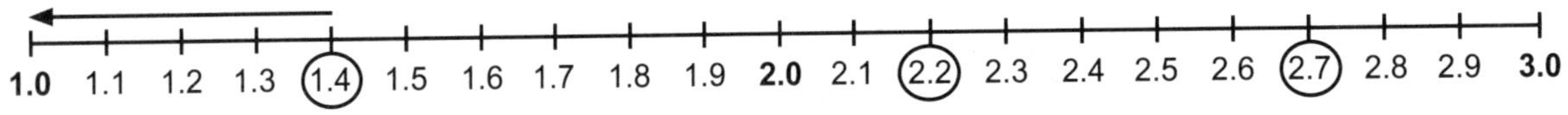

Round to 1.0 ______ ______

b)
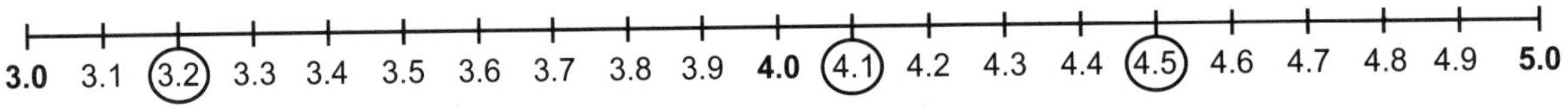

Round to ______ ______ ______

BONUS ▶
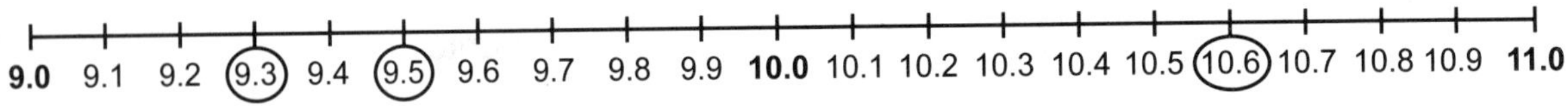

Round to ______ ______ ______

4. Circle the correct answer.

a) 2.9 is closer to: 2.0 or 3.0

b) 1.4 is closer to: 1.0 or 2.0

c) 3.6 is closer to: 3.0 or 4.0

d) 7.2 is closer to: 7.0 or 8.0

e) 25.4 is closer to: 25.0 or 26.0

f) 48.8 is closer to: 48.0 or 49.0

g) 93.6 is closer to: 93.0 or 94.0

h) 59.6 is closer to: 59.0 or 60.0

REMINDER ▶ The sign $\approx$ means **approximately equal to**.

5. Estimate by rounding to the nearest *one*.

a) 6.8 → [7] + 1.2 → + [1] = [8]

b) 12.7 + 5.4 → [ ] + [ ] = [ ]

c) 34.8 + 14.7 → [ ] + [ ] = [ ]

d) 9.5 − 6.3 → [ ] − [ ] = [ ]

e) 46.2 − 15.8 $\approx$ *46 − 16* = *30*

f) 31.9 − 19.5 $\approx$ ______ = ______

g) 165.2 − 54.7 $\approx$ ______ = ______

h) 149.7 − 24.9 $\approx$ ______ = ______

i) 115.4 − 9.7 $\approx$ ______ = ______

j) 78.6 + 10.9 $\approx$ ______ = ______

k) 220.3 − 4.6 $\approx$ ______ = ______

l) 27.5 + 31.7 $\approx$ ______ = ______

6. Estimate by rounding to the nearest *one*.

a) Oscar the puppy is 39.6 cm long. His basket is 60.3 cm long. Approximately how much longer is the basket than Oscar?

______

b) The longest paddle in a shed is 154.6 cm long. The shortest paddle is 49.7 cm long. Approximately how much longer is the long paddle?

______

c) Emma's favourite hike is 16.7 km long. Her second favourite hike is 9.5 km long.

i) Approximately how much longer is her favourite hike?

ii) Approximately how long are the hikes altogether?

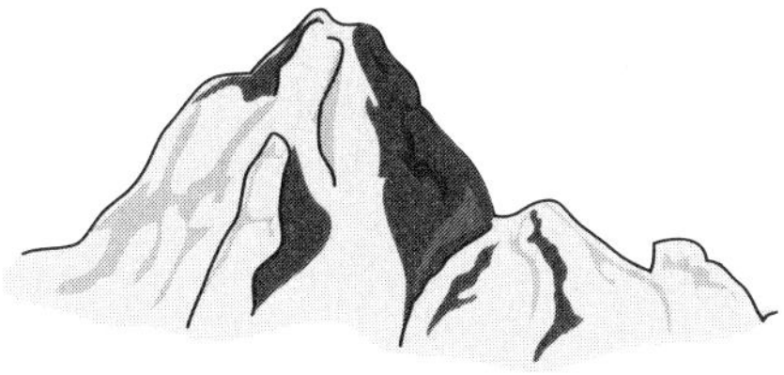

d) The shallow end of a pool is 0.4 m deep, and the deep end is 4.5 m deep.

i) Approximately how much deeper is the deep end than the shallow end?

ii) Does it make sense to use estimation for this problem? Explain.

NS4-60 Combining Tenths and Hundredths

1. Describe the shaded parts in two ways.

a) 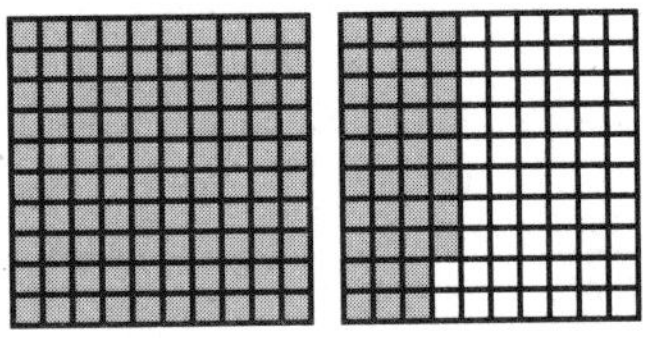

1.38 = *1* one *3* tenths *8* hundredths

b) 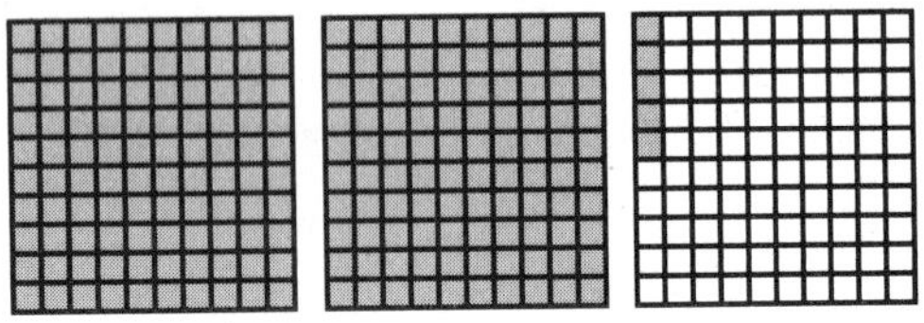

_______ = _______ ones _______ tenths _______ hundredths

c) 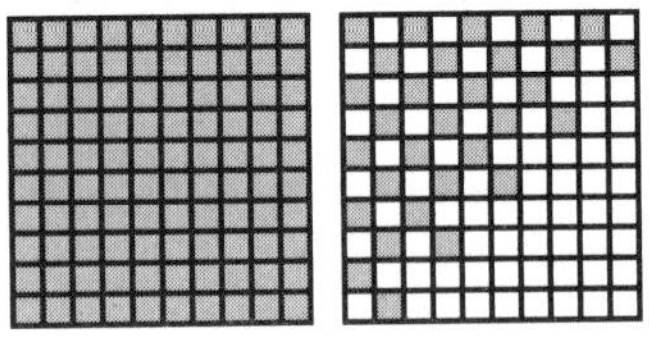

_______ = _______ one _______ tenths _______ hundredths

d) 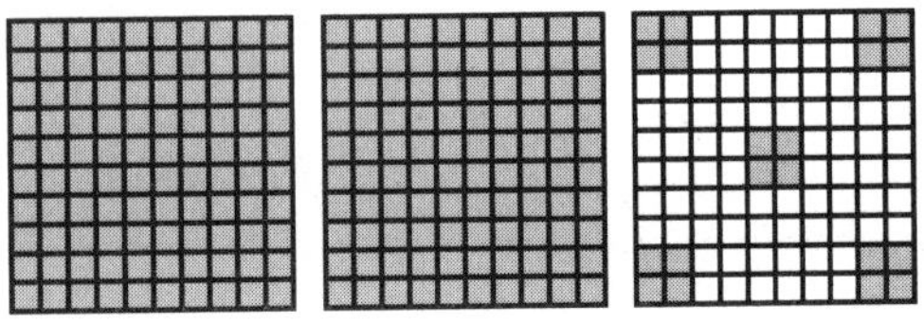

_______ = _______ ones _______ tenths _______ hundredths

2. Fill in the blanks.

a) 71 hundredths = *7* tenths *1* hundredth

$\frac{71}{100}$ = 0. *7* *1*

b) 28 hundredths = ____ tenths ____ hundredths

$\frac{\_\_\_}{100}$ = 0. ____ ____

c) 41 hundredths = ____ tenths ____ hundredth

$\frac{\_\_\_}{100}$ = 0. ____ ____

d) 60 hundredths = ____ tenths ____ hundredths

$\frac{\_\_\_}{100}$ = 0. ____ ____

e) 53 hundredths = ____ tenths ____ hundredths

$\frac{\_\_\_}{100}$ = 0. ____ ____

f) 12 hundredths = ____ tenth ____ hundredths

$\frac{\_\_\_}{100}$ = 0. ____ ____

g) 36 hundredths = ____ tenths ____ hundredths

$\frac{\_\_\_}{100}$ = 0. ____ ____

h) 92 hundredths = ____ tenths ____ hundredths

$\frac{\_\_\_}{100}$ = 0. ____ ____

3. Describe the decimal in two ways.

a) 3.70 = _3_ ones _7_ tenths _0_ hundredths
= _3 and 70 hundredths_

b) 0.04 = _0_ tenths _4_ hundredths
= _4 hundredths_

c) 0.52 = ____ tenths ____ hundredths
= ______________________

d) 6.02 = ____ ones ____ tenths ____ hundredths
= ______________________

e) 0.83 = ____ tenths ____ hundredths
= ______________________

f) 5.55 = ____ ones ____ tenths ____ hundredths
= ______________________

g) 1.06 = ____ one ____ tenths ____ hundredths
= ______________________

h) 8.90 = ____ ones ____ tenths ____ hundredths
= ______________________

4. Write the number in expanded form.

a) 2.95 = ______ + ______ + ______

b) 5408.41 = ______ + ______ + ______ + ______ + ______ + ______

c) 237.06 = ______ + ______ + ______ + ______ + ______

d) 67.23 = ______ + ______ + ______ + ______

Cameron describes the distance covered on a number line in two ways.

43 hundredths = 4 tenths 3 hundredths

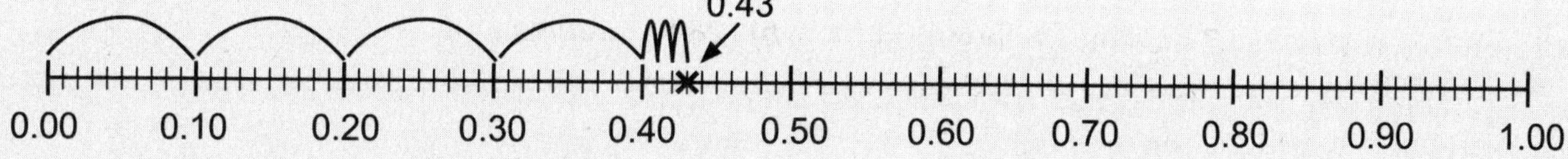

5. Write the distance covered in two ways.

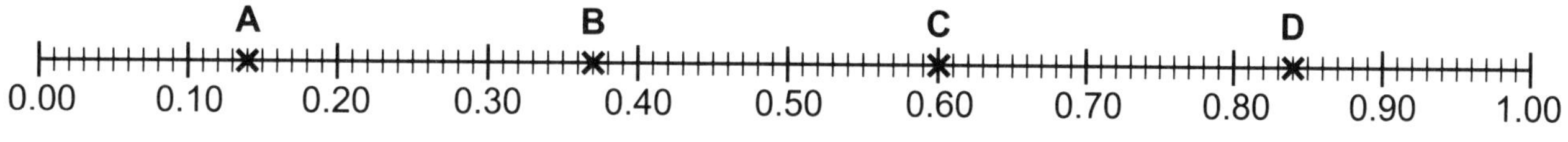

A. ____ tenth ____ hundredths
= ____ hundredths

B. ____ tenths ____ hundredths
= ____ hundredths

C. ____ tenths ____ hundredths
= ____ hundredths

D. ____ tenths ____ hundredths
= ____ hundredths

REMINDER ▶ A metre is 100 centimetres.

6. What part of a metre is the length shown? Write your answer as a decimal and a fraction.

a)

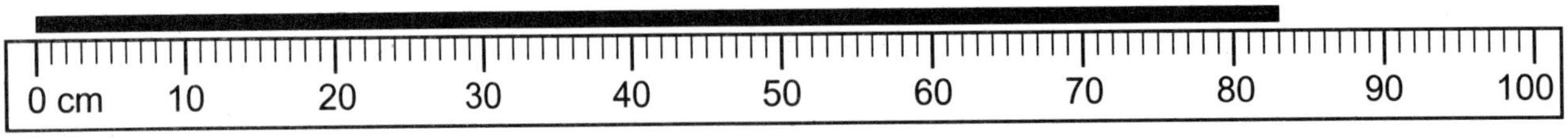

83 cm = *0.83* m = $\frac{83}{100}$ m

b)

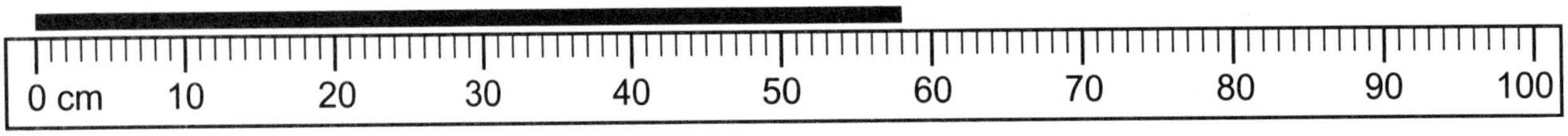

58 cm = ________ m = ☐ m

c)

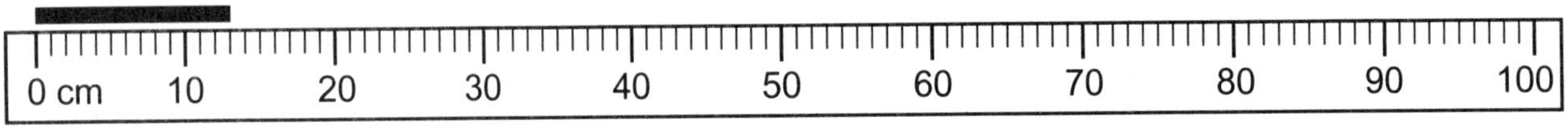

13 cm = ________ m = ☐ m

d)

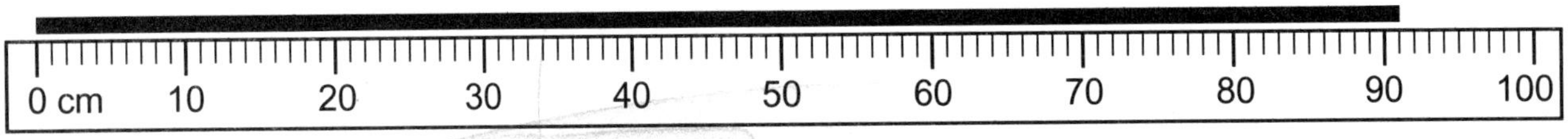

91 cm = ________ m = ☐ m

e)

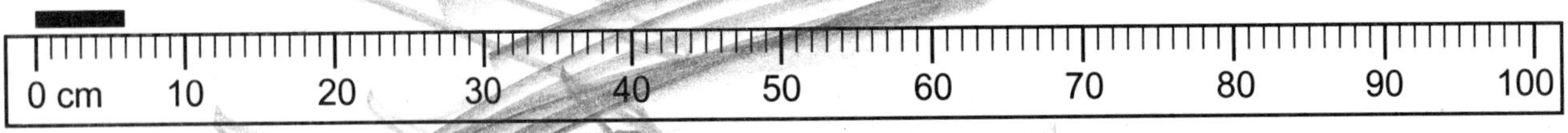

6 cm = ________ m = ☐ m

f)

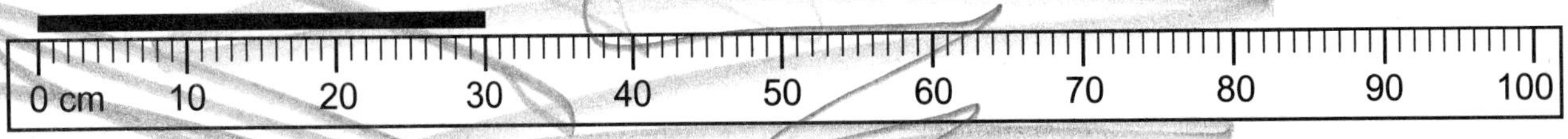

30 cm = ________ m = ☐ m

Adding and Subtracting to Hundredths

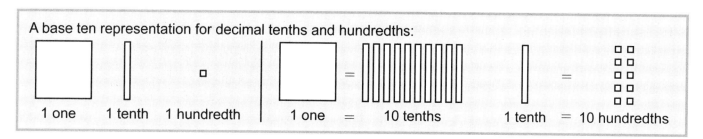

A base ten representation for decimal tenths and hundredths:

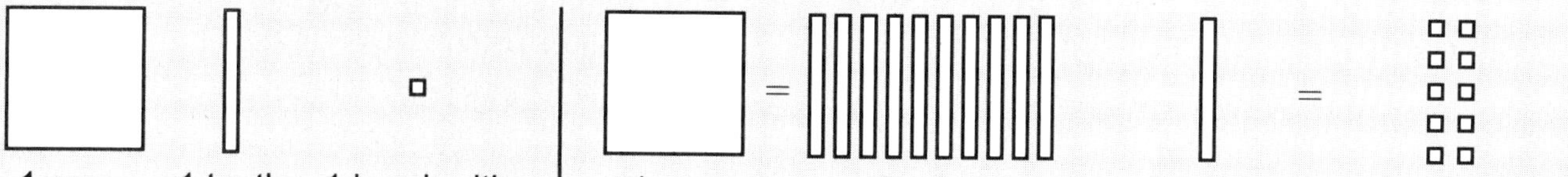

1 one   1 tenth   1 hundredth | 1 one = 10 tenths   1 tenth = 10 hundredths

1. Regroup so that each place value has a single digit.

a) 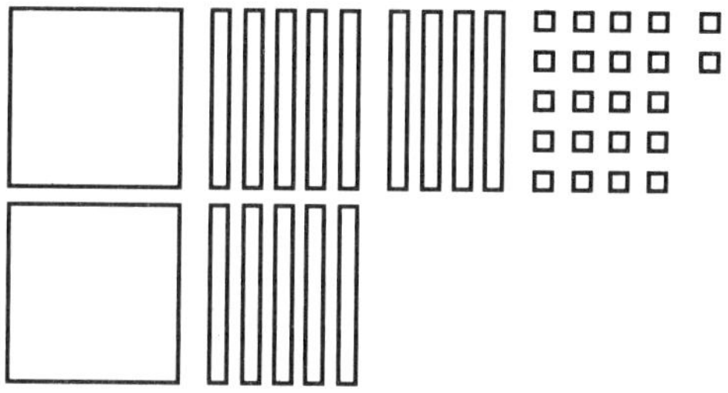

2 ones + 14 tenths + 22 hundredths

= *3 ones + 6 tenths + 2 hundredths*

b) 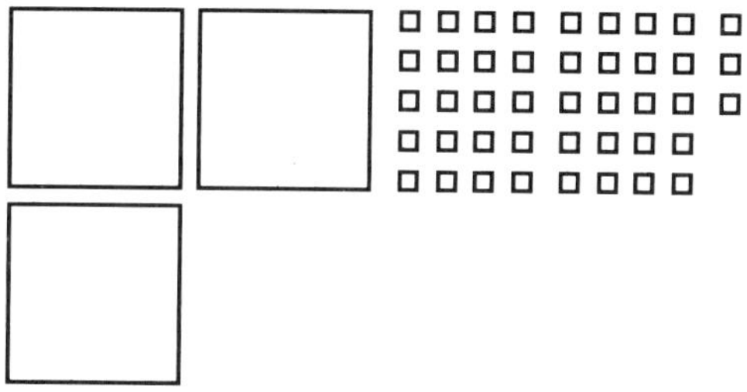

3 ones + 43 hundredths

= ________________

c) 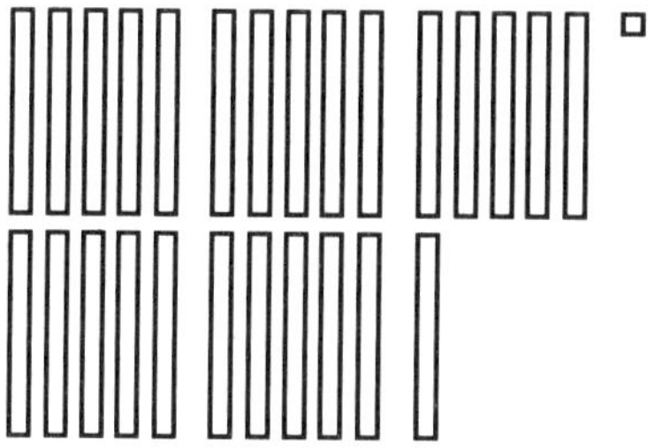

26 tenths + 1 hundredth

= ________________

d) 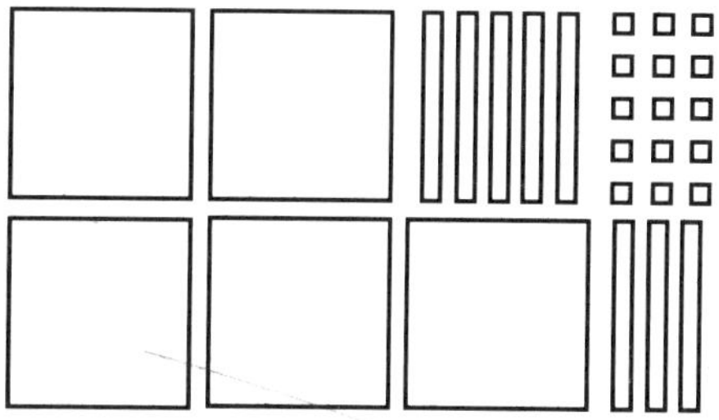

5 ones + 8 tenths + 15 hundredths

= ________________

2. Regroup so that each place value has a single digit.

a) 5 ones + 12 tenths + 17 hundredths = ___*6*___ ones + ___*3*___ tenths + ___*7*___ hundredths

b) 16 tenths + 22 hundredths = ________ one + ________ tenths + ________ hundredths

c) 7 ones + 13 tenths + 20 hundredths = ________ ones + ________ tenths + ________ hundredths

d) 1 one + 76 tenths + 16 hundredths = ________ ones + ________ tenths + ________ hundredths

BONUS ▶ 9 ones + 13 tenths + 52 hundredths = ________ ten + ________ ones + ________ tenths + ________ hundredths

3. Add by lining up the decimal points. You may need to regroup more than once.

a) 7.15 + 2.46

		1	
	7 .	1	5
+	2 .	4	6
	9 .	6	1

b) 34.64 + 21.27

c) 68.89 + 22.31

4. On a grid, line up the decimal points and then add.

a) 34.9 + 5.77 b) 62.95 + 27.1 c) 53.8 + 8.03 d) 1.46 + 17.8

e) 0.41 + 3.8 f) 4.25 + 1.9 g) 7.8 + 12.64 h) 2.54 + 53.7

5. Exchange 1 tenth for 10 hundredths.

a) 6 tenths + 0 hundredths = ___5___ tenths + ___10___ hundredths

b) 9 tenths + 4 hundredths = ______ tenths + ______ hundredths

c) 1 tenth + 6 hundredths = ______ tenths + ______ hundredths

d) 8 tenths + 8 hundredths = ______ tenths + ______ hundredths

6. Subtract by lining up the decimal points. You may need to regroup more than once.

a) 1.75 − 0.68

		6	15
	1 .	~~7~~	~~5~~
−	0 .	6	8
	1 .	0	7

b) 4.12 − 0.09

c) 7.23 − 6.14

d) 9.14 − 1.06

e) 43.52 − 25.9

f) 35.3 − 18.49

g) 63.07 − 2.7

h) 78.4 − 54.72

7. a) Iva draws three lines. The first line is 14.4 cm long, the second line is 25.62 cm long, and the third line is 6.08 cm long. What is the total length of the lines?

b) Iva erases 2.4 cm from the line that is 6.08 cm long. What is the total length of the lines now?

c) Did you need to know which line she erased from to answer the question in part b)? Explain.

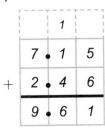

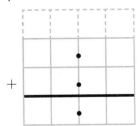

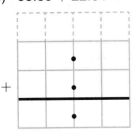

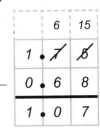

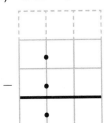

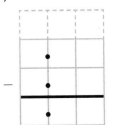

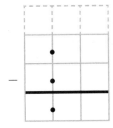

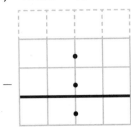

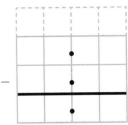

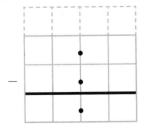

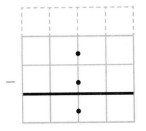

NS4-62 Dollar and Cent Notation

The tables show how to represent money in cent notation and in dollar notation.

	Cent Notation	Dollar (Decimal) Notation
Sixty-five cents	65¢	$0.65 (*dimes* 6, *cents* 5)

	Cent Notation	Dollar (Decimal) Notation
Seven cents	7¢	$0.07 (*dimes* 0, *cents* 7)

The dot between the 0 and the number of dimes is called a **decimal point**.

1. Write the total amount of money in cent notation and in dollar (decimal) notation.

a)

Dimes	Cents
3	4

= *34* ¢ = $ *0.34*

b)

Dimes	Cents
0	5

= ______¢ = $________

c)

Dimes	Cents
4	3

= ______¢ = $________

d)

Dimes	Cents
8	7

= ______¢ = $________

e)

Dimes	Cents
5	4

= ______¢ = $________

f)

Dimes	Cents
0	9

= ______¢ = $________

g)

Dimes	Cents
0	2

= ______¢ = $________

h)

Dimes	Cents
7	5

= ______¢ = $________

i)

Dimes	Cents
0	1

= ______¢ = $________

100¢ = $1.00 (*dollars*: 1; *dimes*: 0; *cents*: 0)

345¢ = $3.45 (*dollars*: 3; *dimes*: 4; *cents*: 5)

1843¢ = $18.43 (*dollars*: 18; *dimes*: 4; *cents*: 3)

2. Complete the table.

	Amount in ¢	Dollars	Dimes	Cents	Amount in $
a)	143¢	*1*	*4*	*3*	*$1.43*
b)	47¢				
c)	325¢				
d)	3¢				
e)	2816¢				

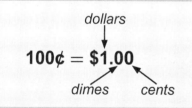

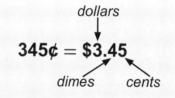

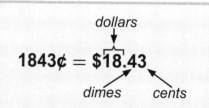

3. Write the amount in cent notation.

a) $3.00 = ______ b) $0.60 = ______ c) $0.09 = ______ d) $1.00 = ______

e) $7.00 = ______ f) $12.00 = ______ g) $15.00 = ______ h) $1.99 = ______

i) $1.51 = ______ j) $0.98 = ______ k) $0.03 = ______ l) $0.08 = ______

4. Write the amount in dollar notation.

a) 254¢ = *$2.54* b) 103¢ = ______ c) 216¢ = ______ d) 375¢ = ______

e) 300¢ = ______ f) 4¢ = ______ g) 7¢ = ______ h) 90¢ = ______

i) 600¢ = ______ j) 99¢ = ______ k) 1200¢ = ______ l) 1604¢ = ______

5. Complete the table as shown in part a).

	Dollars	Cents	Total
a)	 = *$3*	 = *35¢*	*$3.35*
b)	 = ______	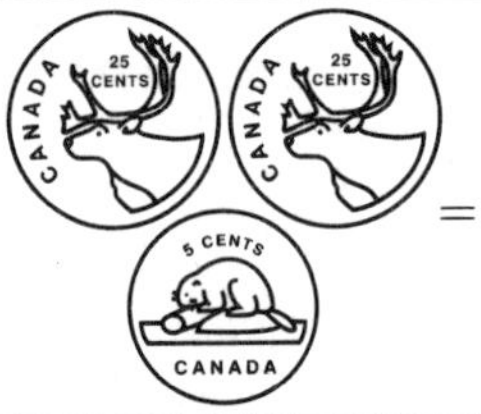 = ______	______
c)	 = ______	 = ______	______
d)	 = ______	 = ______	______

6. Lela paid for a pencil with 3 coins. The pencil cost $0.75. Which coins did she use?

7. Ansel bought a pack of markers for $3.50. He paid for it with 5 coins. Draw the money he used.

8. Show two ways to make $5.25 with 6 coins.

Money Math

1. You have $10. Find the difference owed when you need to pay the given amount.

	Amount to Pay	Paid	Calculation	Difference Owed
a)	$2	$10	*$10 – $2*	*$8*
b)	$4	$10		
c)	$7	$10		
d)	$3	$10		
e)	$6	$10		

2. You have $1. Find the difference owed when you need to pay the given amount.

	Amount to Pay	Paid	Calculation	Difference Owed
a)	70¢	$1	*100¢ – 70¢*	*30¢*
b)	40¢	$1		
c)	60¢	$1		
d)	90¢	$1		
e)	50¢	$1		
f)	10¢	$1		

3. Find the difference to the next highest dollar.

a) $12.30 → [*70¢*] → *$13.00*

b) $15.20 → [ ] → *$16.00*

c) $14.40 → [ ] → ______

d) $11.70 → [ ] → ______

e) $21.60 → [ ] → ______

f) $35.10 → [ ] → ______

g) $59.40 → [ ] → ______

BONUS ▶ $87.80 → [ ] → ______

You need to pay $16.40. You pay with a 20-dollar bill ($20.00). What is the difference owed?

Step 1: Find the next highest whole dollar after $16. $17

Step 2: Write the amount of money given. $20

Step 3: Find the differences in the steps. 60¢, $3

Step 4: Add the differences. $3.60

($16.40) —60¢→ [$17] —$3→ ($20)

Difference owed = $3.60

4. You need to pay the given amount. You have a 20-dollar bill. Find the difference owed.

a) ($13.60) —[ ]→ [*$14*] —[ ]→ (*$20*) Difference owed = ______

b) ($12.80) —[ ]→ [ ] —[ ]→ (*$20*) Difference owed = ______

c) ($17.10) —[ ]→ [ ] —[ ]→ ( ) Difference owed = ______

BONUS ▶ You need to pay the given amount. You have a 50-dollar bill. Find the difference owed.

d) ($48.20) —[ ]→ [ ] —[ ]→ ( ) Difference owed = ______

e) ($43.10) —[ ]→ [ ] —[ ]→ ( ) Difference owed = ______

f) ($4.70) —[ ]→ [ ] —[ ]→ ( ) Difference owed = ______

g) ($19.90) —[ ]→ [ ] —[ ]→ ( ) Difference owed = ______

h) ($20.20) —[ ]→ [ ] —[ ]→ ( ) Difference owed = ______

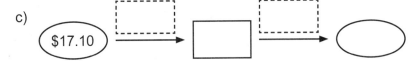

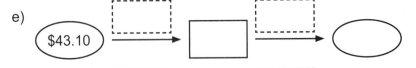

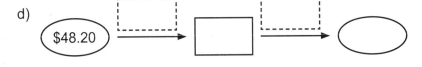

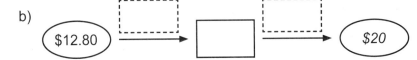

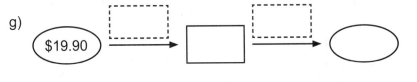

5. You need to pay the given amount. You have a 20-dollar bill. Find the difference owed.

a) ($13.25) —5¢→ [$13.30] —70¢→ [$14] —$6→ ($20)   Difference owed = $6.75

b) ($17.65) —→ [ ] —→ [ ] —→ ($20)   Difference owed = ______

c) ($12.15) —→ [ ] —→ [ ] —→ ( )   Difference owed = ______

6. Round the given amount to the nearest nickel by rounding the number of cents to the nearest multiple of 5.

	Money	**$**	**¢**	**Cents Rounded to the Nearest Nickel**	**Money Rounded to the Nearest Nickel**
a)	$18.43	$18	43¢	45¢	$18.45
b)	$22.21				
c)	$49.78				
d)	$13.07				
e)	$59.97				

7. You need to pay the amount shown. You have a 50-dollar bill. Round the amount to the nearest nickel. Then find the difference owed.

a) $44.73   ($44.75) —5¢→ [$44.80] —→ [$45] —→ ($50)   Difference owed = ______

b) $46.13   ( ) —→ [ ] —→ [ ] —→ ( )   Difference owed = ______

c) $47.12   ( ) —→ [ ] —→ ( )   Difference owed = ______

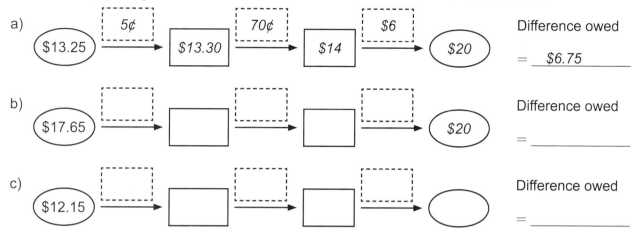

NS5-57 Adding and Subtracting Money

1. Add.

a) $5.45 + $3.23

	$	5	. 4	5
+	$	3	. 2	3
	$		.	

b) $26.15 + $32.23

	$		.	
+	$		.	
	$		.	

c) $19.57 + $50.32

	$		.	
+	$		.	
	$		.	

2. Add. You will have to regroup.

a)

	$	1	6	. 6	0
+	$	2	3	. 7	5
	$			.	

b)

	$	2	7	. 4	5
+	$	4	5	. 1	2
	$			.	

c)

	$	8	7	. 4	1
+	$		6	. 3	9
	$			.	

d)

	$	3	4	. 6	0
+	$	2	6	. 0	0
	$			.	

e)

	$	3	2	. 4	7
+	$	4	4	. 2	5
	$			.	

f)

	$	1	6	. 0	8
+	$	4	8	. 0	5
	$			.	

3. Subtract. You will have to regroup.

a)

	$	2	4	. 5	0
−	$	2	1	. 7	5
	$			.	

b)

	$	3	6	. 4	5
−	$	1	3	. 8	0
	$			.	

c)

	$	4	7	. 2	3
−	$		6	. 7	2
	$			.	

d)

	$	5	3	. 0	4
−	$	1	6	. 0	3
	$			.	

e)

	$	7	0	. 6	2
−	$	2	5	. 5	1
	$			.	

f)

	$	8	4	. 1	7
−	$	3	9	. 0	9
	$			.	

4. Jasmin bought a pair of mittens for $7.25 and a T-shirt for $13.53. How much did Jasmin spend in total?

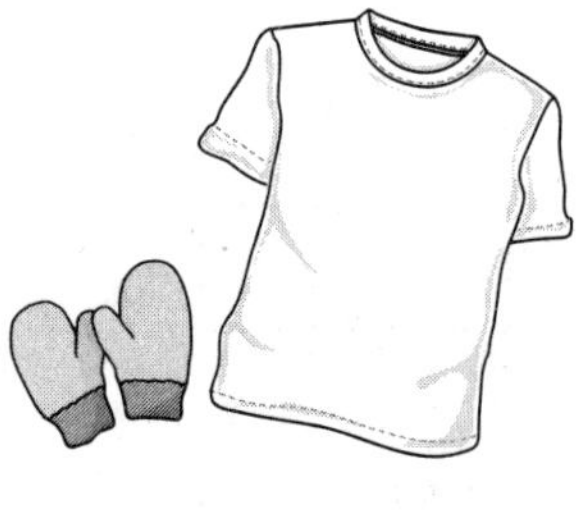

5. A library spent $270.25 on novels and $389.82 on movies and music. How much did the library spend in total?

6. Eric bought two baseball hats that cost $21.30 each. Add to find out how much he paid in total.

7. Raj has $25. If he buys a board game for $9.50 and a book for $10.35, will he have enough money left to buy a second book for $5.10?

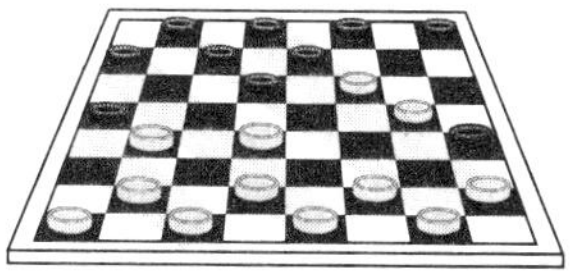

8. The regular price for a pair of glasses is $69.99. Today only, they are on sale for $10.50 off per pair. If Lynn buys her glasses today, how much will she pay?

BONUS ▶ If Lynn buys one pair of glasses today and one pair next week, how much will she pay in total?

9. Answer the question by looking at the items and their prices below.

a) If you bought a pair of shoes, a camera, and a water bottle, how much would you pay?

b) Which costs more: shoes and a soccer ball or pants?

c) Could you buy a water bottle, a hockey shirt, and shoes with $60? Explain how you found the answer.

d) What is the total cost of the three most expensive items?

BONUS ▶ How much would it cost to buy two pairs of pants? Explain how you could use a mental math strategy to simplify the calculation.

10. Try to find the answer mentally.

a) How much do 4 loaves of bread cost at $2.10 each?

b) Apples cost 50¢ each. How many could you buy with $3.00?

c) Permanent markers cost $3.10 each. How many could you buy if you had $12.00?

11. Sam spent $3.27 on apples, 563¢ on peaches, and four dollars and ninety-six cents on grapes. Write each amount in dollar notation. Use graph paper to find the total amount Sam spent.

NS5-60 Multiplying Decimals by Powers of 10

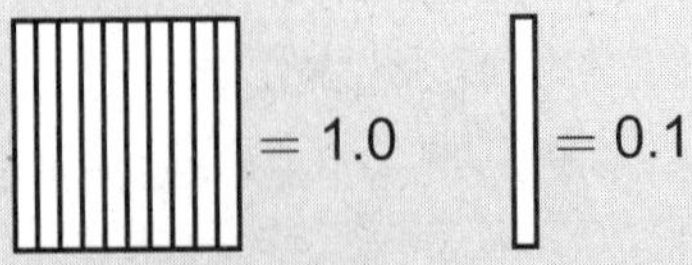

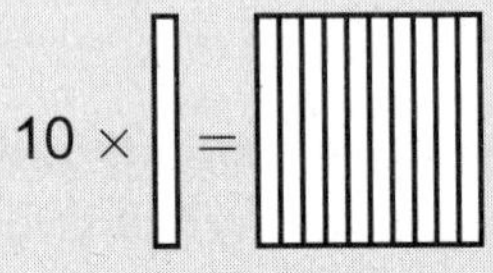

If a hundreds block represents 1 whole, then a tens block represents 1 tenth (or 0.1), and

10 tenths make 1 whole: $10 \times 0.1 = 1.0$

1. Multiply the number of tens blocks by 10. Then show how many hundreds blocks there are to complete the multiplication statement.

a)

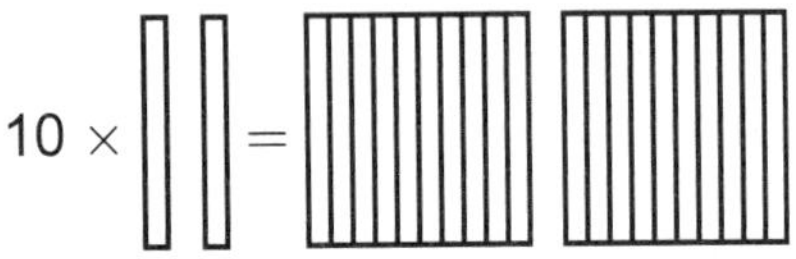

$10 \times 0.2 =$ __2__

b)

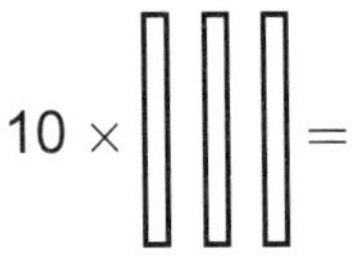

$10 \times 0.3 =$ ______

c)

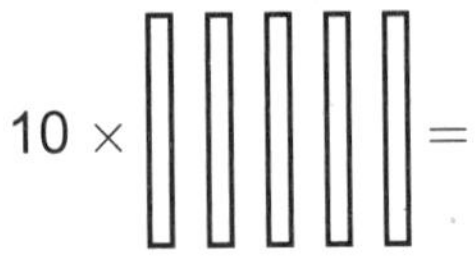

$10 \times 0.5 =$ ______

2. Multiply by 10 by shifting the decimal point one place to the right.

a) $10 \times 0.5 =$ __5__
b) $10 \times 2.6 =$ ________
c) $10 \times 1.4 =$ ________
d) $10 \times 2.4 =$ ________
e) $3.5 \times 10 =$ ________
f) $14.5 \times 10 =$ ________
g) $10 \times 2.06 =$ __20.6__
h) $10 \times 12.75 =$ ________
i) $10 \times 97.6 =$ ________

To convert from metres to centimetres, you multiply by 100. There are 100 cm in 1 m.

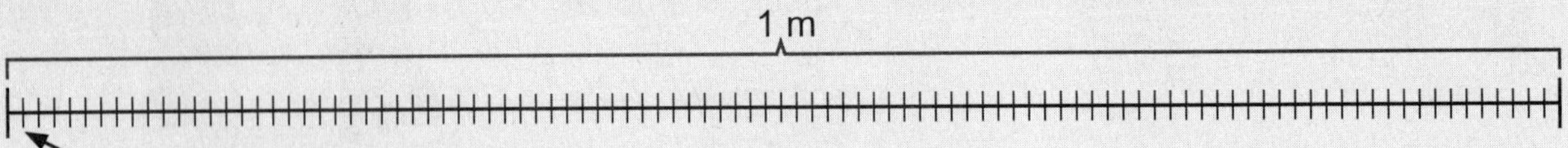

$1 \text{ cm} = \frac{1}{100} \text{ m} = 0.01 \text{ m}$ $\quad$ $1 \text{ cm} \times 100 = 1 \text{ m}$

3. Convert the measurement in metres to centimetres.

a) 0.4 m = ______ cm
b) 0.8 m = ______ cm
c) 3.4 m = ______ cm

4. 10×5 can be written as a sum: $5 + 5 + 5 + 5 + 5 + 5 + 5 + 5 + 5 + 5$.
Write 10×0.5 as a sum and skip count by 0.5 to find the answer.

5. A dime is a tenth of a dollar (10¢ = \$0.10). Draw a picture or use play money to show that $10 \times \$0.10 = \$1.00$.

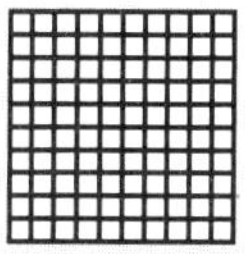 = 1.0

If a hundreds block represents 1 whole, then

□ = 0.01

a ones block represents 1 hundredth (or 0.01), and

100 × □ = 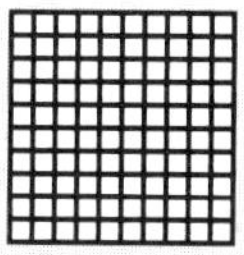

100 hundredths make 1 whole: 100 × 0.01 = 1.00.

6. Write a multiplication statement for the picture.

a) 100 × □□□ = 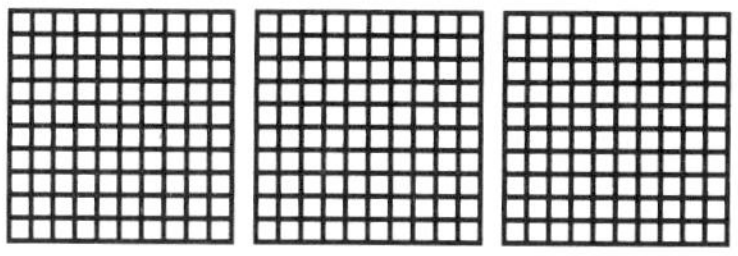

100 × 0.03 = ________

b) 100 × □□ = 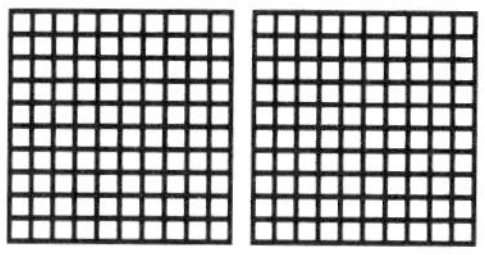

________ = ________

The picture shows why the decimal point shifts two places to the right when multiplying by 100:

100 × 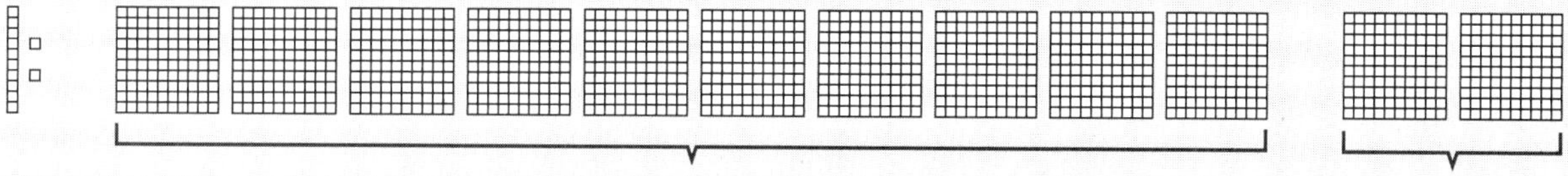

100 × 0.12 = 12

100 × 0.1 = 10

100 × 0.02 = 2

7. Multiply by 100. Do your rough work in the grid.

a) 100 × 0.8 = *80*

b) 100 × 3.5 = ______

c) 7.2 × 100 = ______

d) 6.0 × 100 = ______

e) 100 × 0.34 = ______

f) 100 × 0.07 = ______

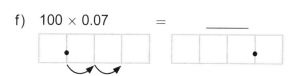

We can use zero as a placeholder when multiplying decimals. Example: 2.35 × 1000:

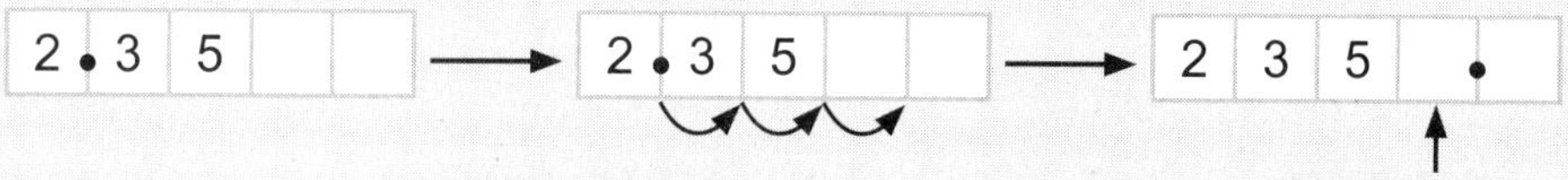

= 2350

Write 0 as a placeholder.

BONUS ▶ Multiply by 1000 by shifting the decimal point three places to the right.

a) 1000 × 0.93 = ________

b) 6.32 × 1000 = ________

c) 1000 × 0.72 = ________

8. a) Fill in the table.

Metres	1	2		4		6
Centimetres	*100*		300		500	

b) To convert a measurement from metres to centimetres, you multiply by ______.

c) Write "more" or "fewer" in the blank: To change a measurement from a larger unit to a smaller unit, you need __________ of the smaller unit.

d) Write "m" or "cm" in the blanks: In the measurement 6.04 m, the 6 stands for ______ and the 4 stands for ______.

e) Write "as large as" or "as small as" in the blanks: Metres are 100 times ____________________ centimetres, and centimetres are 100 times ____________________ metres.

REMINDER ▶ To multiply a decimal by 100, shift the decimal point two places to the right.

9. Convert the measurement from metres to centimetres by multiplying by 100.

a) 5.0 m × 100 = *500* cm

b) 0.2 m × 100 = ________ cm

c) 0.83 m × 100 = ________ cm

d) 4.9 m × 100 = ________ cm

REMINDER ▶ There are 1000 m in 1 km. To convert from kilometres to metres, multiply by 1000.

10. Convert the measurement from kilometres to metres by multiplying by 1000.

a) 8.0 km × 1000 = *8000* m

b) 2.4 km × 1000 = ________ m

c) 0.16 km × 1000 = ________ m

d) 0.04 km × 1000 = ________ m

11. Convert the measurement.

a) 0.9 km × *1000* = ________ m

b) 3.7 m × ________ = ________ cm

c) 1.04 m × ________ = ________ cm

d) 9.02 km × ________ = ________ m

12. Kim thinks that 0.15 km plus 48 m equals 48.15 m.

a) Is her answer correct? ______

b) If her answer is not correct, explain her mistake and add the lengths correctly.

Multiplying and Dividing Decimals by Powers of 10

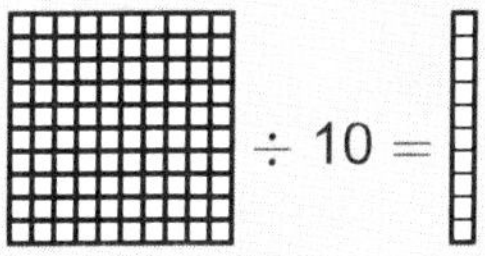

Divide 1 whole into 10 equal parts; each part is 1 tenth.
1.0 ÷ 10 = 0.1

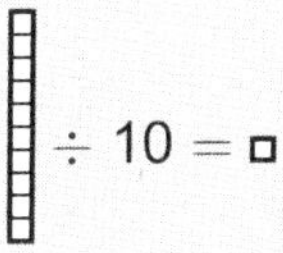

Divide 1 tenth into 10 equal parts; each part is 1 hundredth.
0.1 ÷ 10 = 0.01

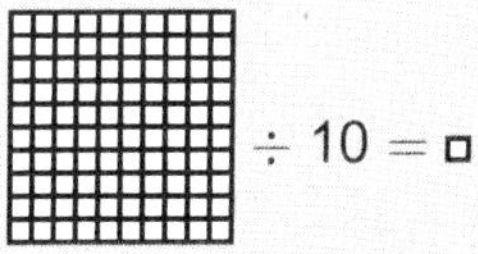

Divide 1 whole into 100 equal parts; each part is 1 hundredth.
1.0 ÷ 100 = 0.01

1. Complete the picture and write a division equation.

a) 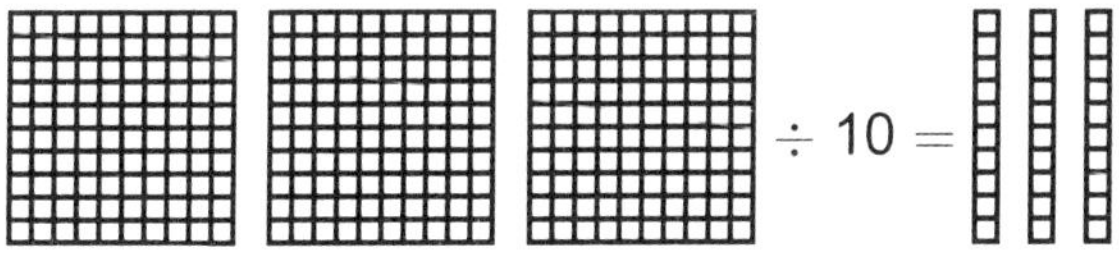

3.0 ÷ 10 = *0.3*

b) 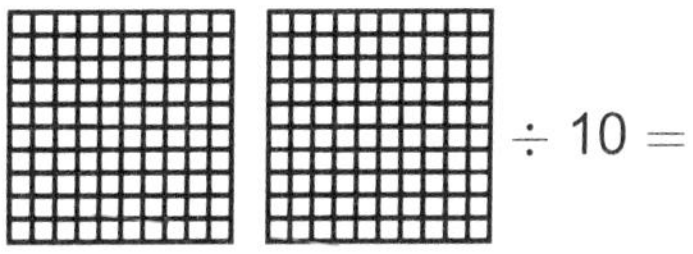

__________ = ______

c) 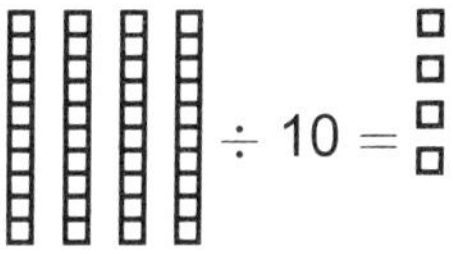

0.4 ÷ 10 = ______

d) 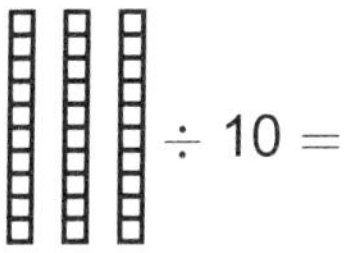

__________ = ______

e) 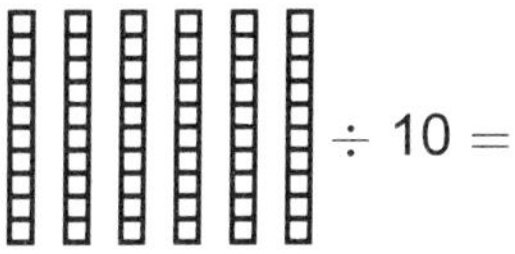

__________ = ______

f) 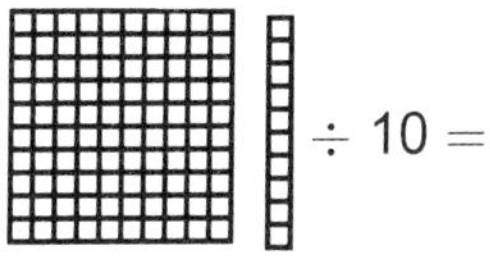

1.1 ÷ 10 = ______

g) 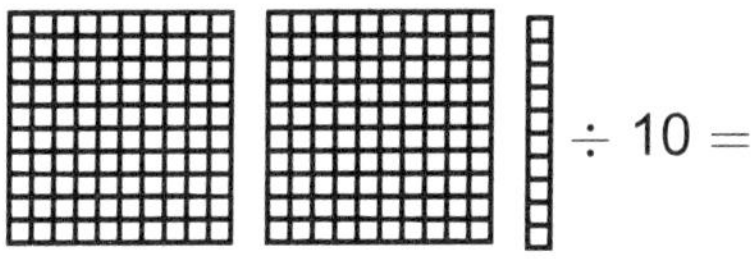

__________ = ______

h) 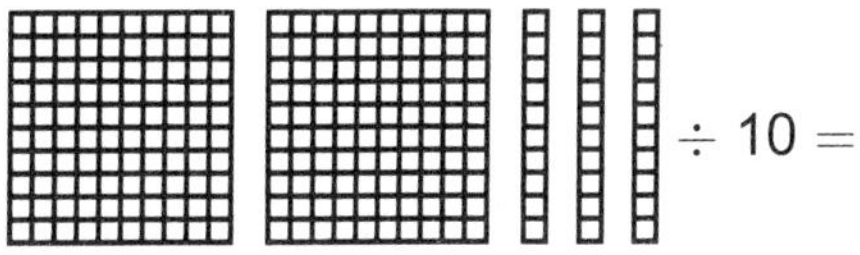

__________ = ______

REMINDER ▶ Division can be used to "undo" a multiplication. $4 \xrightarrow{\times 2} 8$ and $8 \xrightarrow{\div 2} 4$

2. How do you undo multiplying by 100 or 1000?

a) To multiply by 100, I move the decimal point ______ places to the ________________,

so to divide by 100, I move the decimal point ______ places to the ________________.

b) To multiply by 1000, I move the decimal point ______ places to the ________________,

so to divide by 1000, I move the decimal point ______ places to the ________________.

3. Shift the decimal point one or two places to the left. Draw an arrow to show a shift.

a) 0.4 ÷ 10 = *.04 or 0.04*

		0.	4

	.	0	4

b) 0.7 ÷ 10 = ______

		0.	7

	.		

c) 0.6 ÷ 10 = ______

		0.	6

	.		

d) 3.1 ÷ 10 = *0.31*

		3.	1

	.	3	1

e) 15.0 ÷ 10 = ______

	1	5.	0

	.		

f) 81.4 ÷ 10 = ______

		.	

	.		

g) 25.4 ÷ 10 = ______

		.	

	.		

h) 23.0 ÷ 10 = ______

		.	

	.		

i) 0.5 ÷ 100 = *0.005*

		0.	5

0.	0	0	5

j) 7.0 ÷ 100 = ______

		7.	0

.			

k) 9.1 ÷ 100 = ______

		.	

.			

l) 91.0 ÷ 100 = ______

		.	

.			

4. a) To multiply by 10, I move the decimal point *1* place to the *right*.

b) To multiply by 1000, I move the decimal point ______ places to the __________.

c) To multiply by 10 000, I move the decimal point ______ places to the __________.

d) To divide by 100, I move the decimal point ______ places to the __________.

e) To divide by 10, I move the decimal point ______ place to the __________.

f) To multiply by 100, I move the decimal point ______ places to the __________.

g) To ______________ by 10, I move the decimal point ______ place to the left.

h) To ______________ by 100, I move the decimal point ______ places to the right.

i) To ______________ by 10, I move the decimal point ______ place to the right.

j) To ______________ by 100, I move the decimal point ______ places to the left.

k) To ______________ by 1000, I move the decimal point ______ places to the right.

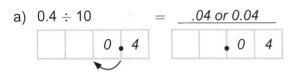

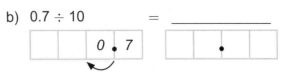

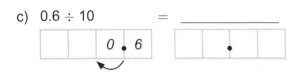

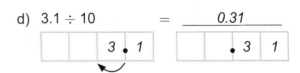

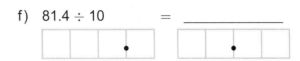

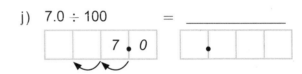

NS5-5 Multi-Digit Addition

1. Add the numbers by drawing base ten materials and adding the digits. Use the base ten materials to show how to combine the numbers and how to regroup.

a) 14 + 37

	With Base Ten Materials		With Numerals	
	Tens	Ones	Tens	Ones
14			*1*	*4*
37			*3*	*7*
sum		*regroup 10 ones as a ten*	*4*	*11*
	after regrouping		*5*	*1*

b) 35 + 27

	With Base Ten Materials		With Numerals	
	Tens	Ones	Tens	Ones

2. Add the ones digits. Show how you would regroup 10 ones as 1 ten.

a) [*1*] ← *tens go here*
$1\ 4 + 1\ 9$ = [*3*] ← *ones go here*

b) $3\ 6 + 4\ 9$

c) $6\ 4 + 2\ 8$

d) $3\ 5 + 4\ 5$

e) $2\ 6 + 1\ 9$

3. Add the numbers by regrouping.

a) *1*
$3\ 6 + 4\ 9$ = *8 5*

b) $1\ 9 + 3\ 2$

c) $6\ 4 + 2\ 9$

d) $7\ 7 + 1\ 8$

e) $3\ 6 + 3\ 6$

f) $8\ 5 + 6$

g) $2\ 9 + 3\ 2$

h) $4\ 3 + 1\ 8$

i) $2\ 1 + 5\ 9$

j) $7\ 8 + 2\ 8$

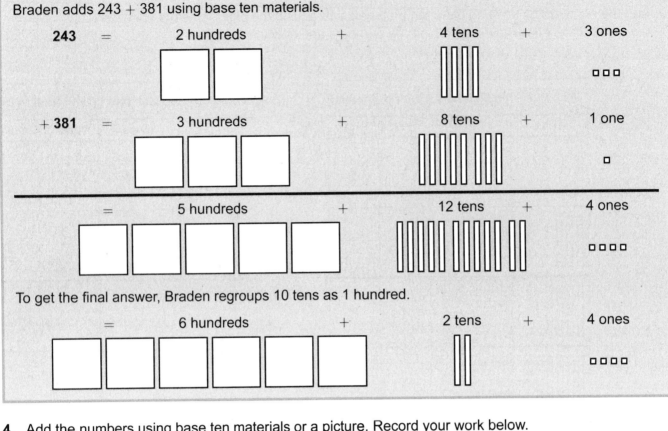

Braden adds 243 + 381 using base ten materials.

243 = 2 hundreds + 4 tens + 3 ones

+ 381 = 3 hundreds + 8 tens + 1 one

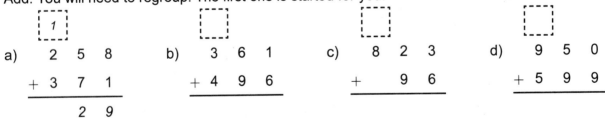

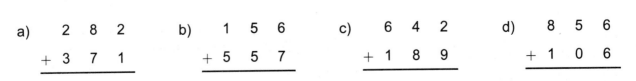

= 5 hundreds + 12 tens + 4 ones

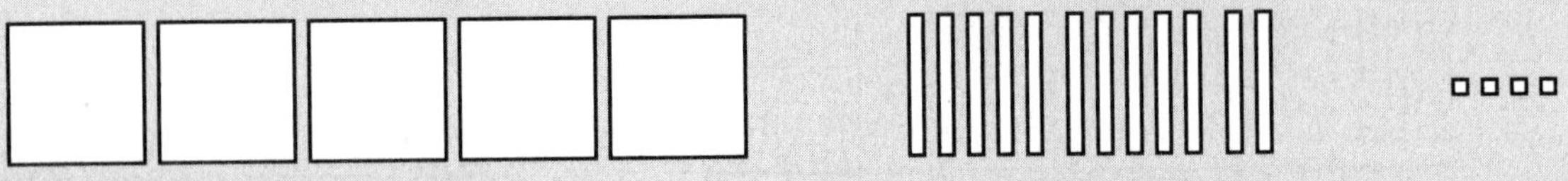

To get the final answer, Braden regroups 10 tens as 1 hundred.

= 6 hundreds + 2 tens + 4 ones

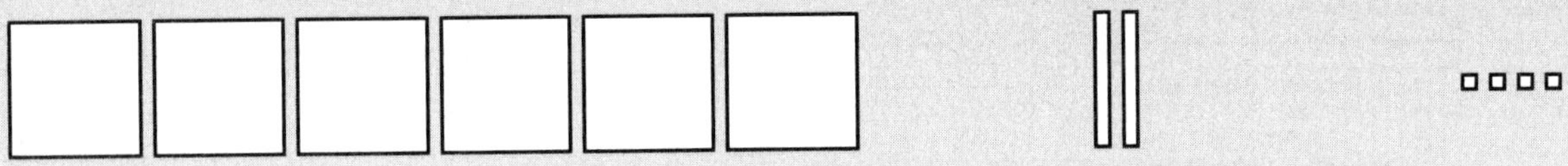

4. Add the numbers using base ten materials or a picture. Record your work below.

572   ______ hundreds + ______ tens + ______ ones

+ 251   + ______ hundreds + ______ tens + ______ one

= ______ hundreds + ______ tens + ______ ones

after regrouping = ______ hundreds + ______ tens + ______ ones

5. Add. You will need to regroup. The first one is started for you.

a)
```
   1
  2 5 8
+ 3 7 1
-------
    2 9
```

b)
```
  3 6 1
+ 4 9 6
-------
```

c)
```
  8 2 3
+   9 6
-------
```

d)
```
  9 5 0
+ 5 9 9
-------
```

6. Add, regrouping where necessary.

a)
```
  2 8 2
+ 3 7 1
-------
```

b)
```
  1 5 6
+ 5 5 7
-------
```

c)
```
  6 4 2
+ 1 8 9
-------
```

d)
```
  8 5 6
+ 1 0 6
-------
```

7. Add by lining the numbers up correctly in the grid. The first one is started for you.

a) 643 + 182

	6	4	3
+	1	8	2

b) 547 + 236

c) 405 + 368

d) 256 + 92

8. Add the numbers, either by using base ten materials or by drawing a picture in your notebook. Use ⬚ to show a thousand. Record your work here.

6826	=	______ thousands + ______ hundreds + ______ tens + ______ ones
+ 2543	=	______ thousands + ______ hundreds + ______ tens + ______ ones
	=	______ thousands + ______ hundreds + ______ tens + ______ ones
after regrouping	=	______ thousands + ______ hundreds + ______ tens + ______ ones

9. Add. You will need to regroup the hundreds as thousands.

a)
```
   2 3 7 6
 + 3 8 2 3
 ---------
     1 9 9
```
b)
```
   5 8 2 6
 + 2 7 5 2
```
c)
```
   7 5 6 9
 + 1 8 3 0
```
d)
```
   7 6 5 6
 + 1 5 2 3
```

10. Add. You will need to regroup the tens as hundreds.

a)
```
   5 2 6 6
 + 1 4 6 2
```
b)
```
   5 6 8 2
 + 3 1 6 5
```
c)
```
   3 4 7 5
 + 2 4 5 4
```
d)
```
   9 2 6 8
 +   3 9 1
```

11. Add, regrouping when necessary.

a)
```
   3 5 6 2
 + 3 6 2 4
```
b)
```
   2 2 6 1
 + 6 9 2 5
```
c)
```
   7 5 6 7
 + 1 3 8 2
```
d)
```
   9 2 0 5
 +   7 5 8
```
e)
```
   5 4 5 5
 + 1 2 7 3
```
f)
```
   6 5 4 7 3
 + 2 7 2 5 4
```
g)
```
   4 5 6 8 3
 + 2 9 2 3 4
```
h)
```
   5 4 3 7 3 6
 + 3 4 4 6 5 2
```

12. a) Grace drove 1280 km on Saturday and 970 km on Sunday. How many kilometres did she drive altogether?

b) Two cars have prices of $31 400 and $42 700. What is the total price of both cars?

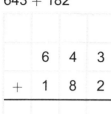

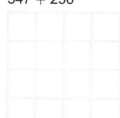

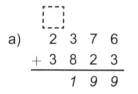

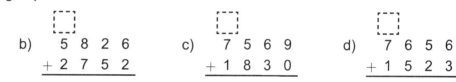

NS5-6 Multi-Digit Subtraction

Ken subtracts 34 − 16 using base ten blocks.

Step 1:
Ken represents 34 with base ten materials.

Tens	Ones
3	4

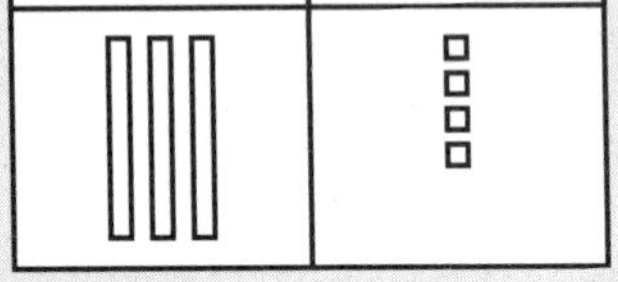

Here is how Ken uses numerals to show his work:

	3	4
−	1	6

Step 2:
6 (the ones digit of 16) is greater than 4 (the ones digit of 34), so Ken exchanges a tens block for 10 ones.

Tens	Ones
2	14

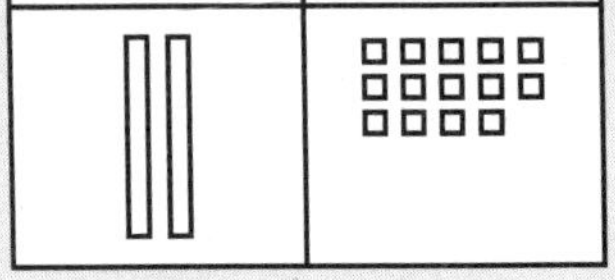

Here is how Ken shows the regrouping:

	2	14
	~~3~~	~~4~~
−	1	6

Step 3:
Ken subtracts 16 (he takes away 1 tens block and 6 ones).

Tens	Ones
1	8

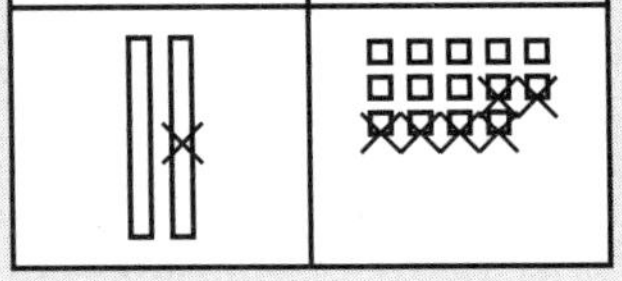

And now Ken can subtract 16:

	2	14
	~~3~~	~~4~~
−	1	6
	1	8

1. Ken doesn't have enough ones to subtract. Help him by regrouping a tens block as 10 ones. Show how he would rewrite his subtraction statement.

a) 66 − 37

Tens	Ones
6	6

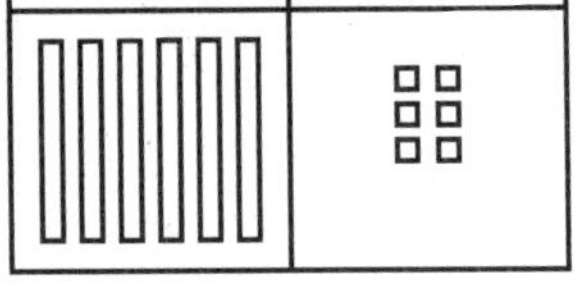

Tens	Ones
5	16

	6	6
−	3	7

→

	5	16
	~~6~~	~~6~~
−	3	7

b) 75 − 46

Tens	Ones
7	5

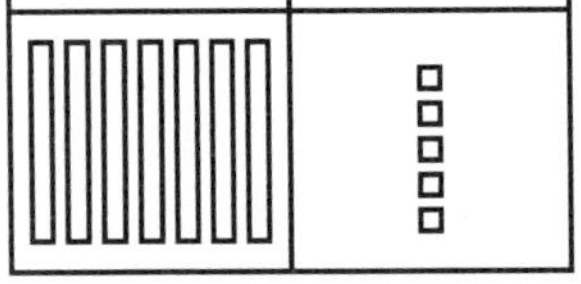

Tens	Ones

	7	5
−	4	6

→

	7	5
−	4	6

2. Subtract by regrouping.

a)

	6	13
	~~7~~	~~3~~
−	4	5
	2	8

b)

	6	2
−	3	4

c)

	8	1
−	2	3

d)

	7	4
−	3	5

e)

	9	6
−	5	8

3. Subtract by regrouping 1 hundred as 10 tens.

a)

	7	5	4
−	3	6	2

b)

	7	3	9
−	1	7	4

c)

	5	2	2
−	2	5	1

d)

	7	4	8
−	5	8	8

4. Subtract by regrouping 1 ten as 10 ones. The first one has been started for you.

a)

		4	*13*
	6	~~5~~	~~3~~
−	5	2	6

b)

	5	7	2
−	4	3	9

c)

	9	6	4
−	6	3	8

d)

	8	9	0
−	4	1	6

Sometimes you need to regroup twice. Example:

Step 1:

```
   1 15
 7 2̸ 5̸
− 4 6 7
```

Step 2:

```
   1 15
 7 2̸ 5̸
− 4 6 7
      8
```

Step 3:

```
    11
 6 1̸ 15
 7̸ 2̸ 5̸
− 4 6 7
      8
```

Step 4:

```
    11
 6 1̸ 15
 7̸ 2̸ 5̸
− 4 6 7
    5 8
```

Step 5:

```
    11
 6 1̸ 15
 7̸ 2̸ 5̸
− 4 6 7
  2 5 8
```

5. Subtract, regrouping twice.

a)

	5	2	7
−	2	7	9

b)

	2	3	1
−		7	4

c)

	5	2	5
−	4	3	8

d)

	4	7	1	5
−	3	7	4	2

6. The Volga River is about 3692 km long, and the Yangtze River is 6301 km long. How much longer is the Yangtze River than the Volga River?

7. An ocean clam called a quahog can live up to 400 years. A bowhead whale can live up to 211 years. How much longer than a bowhead whale can a quahog live?

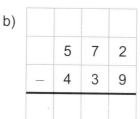

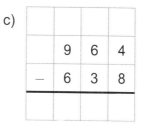

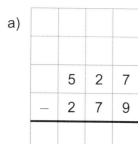

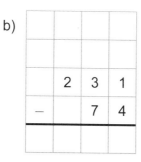

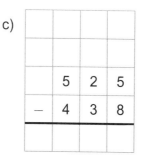

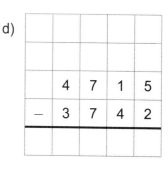

Sometimes you need to regroup *three* times (regroup 1 ten as 10 ones, 1 hundred as 10 tens, and 1 thousand as 10 hundreds). Example:

Step 1:

```
     2 16
  8 4 3̸ 6̸
− 2 5 6 8
```

Step 2:

```
     2 16
  8 4 3̸ 6̸
− 2 5 6 8
        8
```

Step 3:

```
      12
    3 2̸ 16
  8 4̸ 3̸ 6̸
− 2 5 6 8
      6 8
```

Step 4:

```
  7 13 12
    3̸ 2̸ 16
  8̸ 4̸ 3̸ 6̸
− 2 5 6 8
    8 6 8
```

Step 5:

```
  7 13 12
    3̸ 2̸ 16
  8̸ 4̸ 3̸ 6̸
− 2 5 6 8
  5 8 6 8
```

8. Subtract, regrouping three times.

a)

	9	5	4	2
–	1	7	6	3

b)

	3	2	7	5
–	2	3	8	6

c)

	5	1	2	3
–	3	5	4	4

d)

	8	4	7	8
–	5	6	8	9

9. Subtract, regrouping two, three, or four times. Example:

Step 1:

```
  0 10
  1̸ 0̸ 0 0
−   3 7 1
```

Step 2:

```
      9
  0 10̸ 10
  1̸ 0̸ 0̸ 0
−   3 7 1
```

Step 3:

```
      9  9
  0 10̸ 10̸ 10
  1̸ 0̸ 0̸ 0̸
−   3 7 1
```

Step 4:

```
      9  9
  0 10̸ 10̸ 10
  1̸ 0̸ 0̸ 0̸
−   3 7 1
    6 2 9
```

a)

	1	0	0	0
–		4	6	8

b)

	1	0	0
–		3	2

c)

	1	0	0	0	0
–		5	3	7	9

10. Seventy-five students signed up for a trip. Thirty-six of the students are wearing hats. How many are not wearing hats?

11. The shoreline of Lake Michigan is 2633 km long. The shoreline of Lake Erie is 1402 km. How much longer is the shoreline of Lake Michigan than the shoreline of Lake Erie?

12. The National Arts Centre in Ottawa, ON, can sell up to 2323 tickets for an upcoming concert. The Centre sold 1152 tickets on the first day of sales, 549 on the second day, and 426 on the third day. How many tickets for the concert were left?

NS5-7 Addition and Subtraction Word Problems

1. The bars in each picture represent a quantity of red and green apples. Fill in the blanks.

a) 7 red apples
3 green apples

7 red

3 green

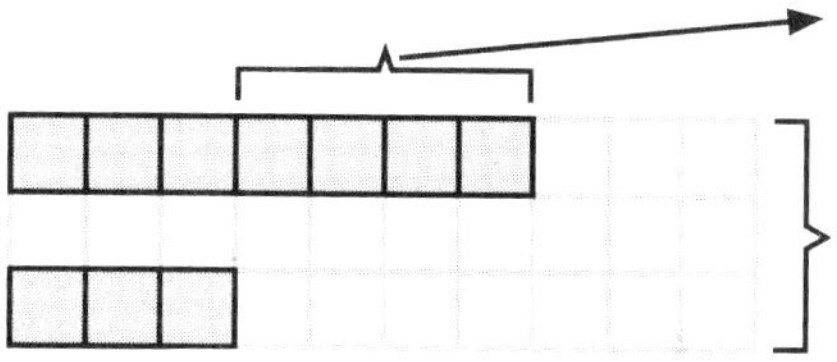

difference: *4 apples*

total: *10 apples*

b) 6 red apples
3 more green apples than red apples

______

______

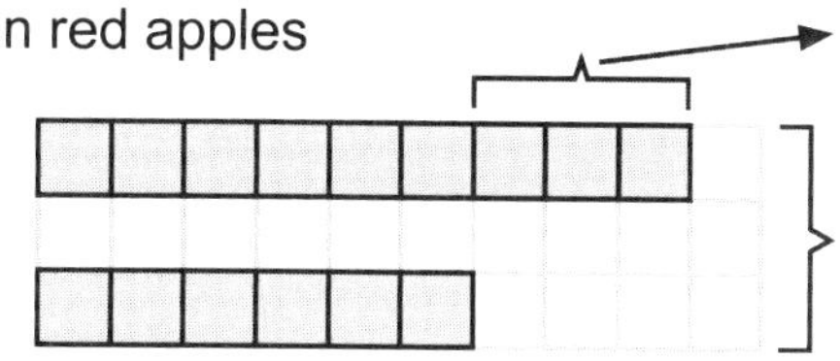

difference: ______

total: ______

c) 6 red apples
2 more green apples than red apples

______

______

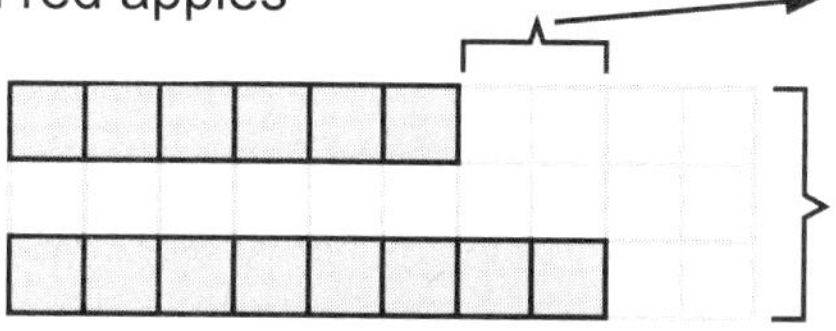

difference: ______

total: ______

d) 9 apples in total
4 green apples

______

______

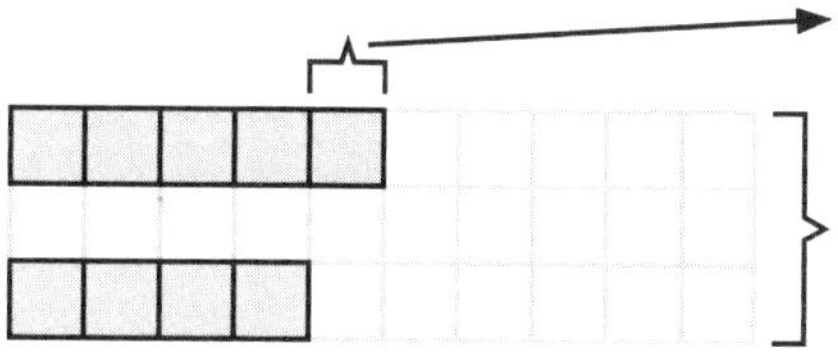

difference: ______

total: ______

2. Write the missing numbers and answer the question.

	Red Apples	Green Apples	Total Number of Apples	How Many More of One Colour of Apple?
a)	3	5	8	*2 more green apples than red apples*
b)	4		9	
c)		1	8	
d)	8			3 more red apples than green apples

3. Draw a picture (as in Question 1) and make a table (as in Question 2) for the quantities.

a) 5 red apples
4 more green apples
than red apples

b) 13 apples in total
6 green apples

BONUS ▶ 9 apples in total
1 more red apple
than green apples

4. The addition **3 + 4 = 7** has three other equations in its **fact family**: **4 + 3 = 7**, **7 − 4 = 3**, and **7 − 3 = 4**. Write the fact family for the equation.

a) 2 + 4 = 6 ______________________________

b) 7 + 3 = 10 ______________________________

c) 12 + 5 = 17 ______________________________

5. Complete the table.

	Green Grapes	Purple Grapes	Total Number of Grapes	Fact Family	How Many More of One Type of Grape?
a)	8	2	10	*8 + 2 = 10 2 + 8 = 10 10 − 8 = 2 10 − 2 = 8*	6 more green grapes than purple
b)	5		9		
c)	3	6			
d)		4			3 more purple grapes than green
e)	11		15		

6. Write the correct sign (+ or −) in the box.

a) number of red apples ☐ number of green apples = total number of apples

b) number of red apples ☐ number of green apples = How many more red than green?

c) number of green grapes ☐ number of purple grapes = How many more green than purple?

d) number of purple grapes ☐ number of green grapes = total number of grapes

7. Draw a picture on grid paper (as in Question 1 on the previous page) for the question.

a) Lynn has 12 red stickers and 5 blue stickers. How many stickers does she have?

b) Cam has 6 pets. Two are cats. The rest are dogs. How many dogs does he have?

c) Rani walked 8 km. Luc walked 5 km. How much farther did Rani walk than Luc?

8. Alexa has $57 and Jin has $12. How much money do they have altogether?

9. Cathy cycled 2375 km one year and 5753 km the next year. How many kilometres did she cycle altogether?

10. The maximum depth of the Pacific Ocean is 10 994 m. The maximum depth of the Atlantic Ocean is 8486 m. How much deeper is the Pacific Ocean than the Atlantic Ocean?

11. Mount Kilimanjaro in Tanzania is 5895 m tall, and Mount Fuji in Japan is 3776 m tall. How much taller is Mount Kilimanjaro than Mount Fuji?

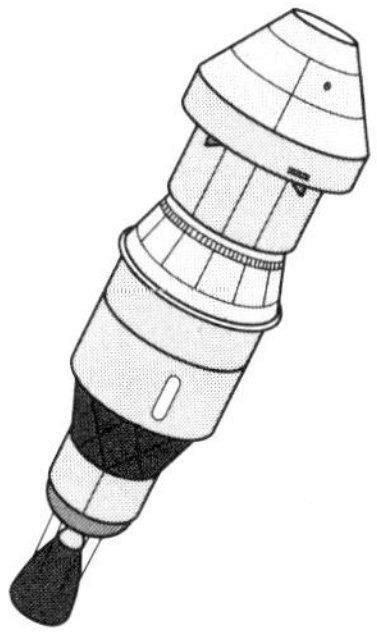

12. In space, the Apollo 10 command module travelled 39 937 km per hour. How far did it travel in two hours?

13. Two nearby towns have populations of 28 475 and 35 832 people. What is the total population of both towns?

14. The United States declared independence from the Kingdom of Great Britain in 1776. How many years ago did the US declare independence?

15. In the number 432 ...

- the hundreds digit is 1 more than the tens digit.
- the tens digit is 1 more than the ones digit.

a) Make up your own number with this property. ____ ____ ____

b) Now write the number backwards. ____ ____ ____

c) Write your two numbers in the grid and subtract (put the greater number on top).

−			

d) Try this again with several other numbers. You will always get 198!

BONUS ▶ Try to explain why this works.

16. Sam had 87 stickers. He put 25 in a book and gave 14 to his friend Nina. How many stickers were leftover?

17. John has 26 marbles. Dory has 15 fewer marbles than John. Carl has 10 more marbles than John. How many marbles do Dory and Carl have altogether?

18. Mike had $73 by the end of September and he saved $18 each month. Mary had $64 by the end of September and she saved $21 each month. Who has more money by the end of December?

NS4-58 Tenths and Hundredths (Fractions)

One dime is $\frac{1}{10}$ of a dollar. One cent is $\frac{1}{100}$ of a dollar.

1. Write the fraction of a dollar the amount represents.

a) 4 cents ____ b) 3 dimes ____ c) 6 dimes ____ d) 34 cents ____

2. Write how many cents the dimes are worth. Then write a fraction equation.

a) 3 dimes = *30* cents

$\frac{3}{10} = \frac{30}{100}$

b) 7 dimes = ______ cents

c) 8 dimes = ______ cents

d) 5 dimes = ______ cents

3. Complete the table.

	Fraction of a Dollar (Tenths)	Number of Dimes	Number of Cents	Fraction of a Dollar (Hundredths)
a)	$\frac{4}{10}$	*4*	*40*	$\frac{40}{100}$
b)		6		
c)			90	
d)	$\frac{3}{10}$			

4. Yu says 37 pennies are worth more than 5 dimes because 37 coins are more than 5 coins. Is she right? Explain.

5. Shade the same amount in the second square. Then count by 10s to write the number of hundredths.

a) 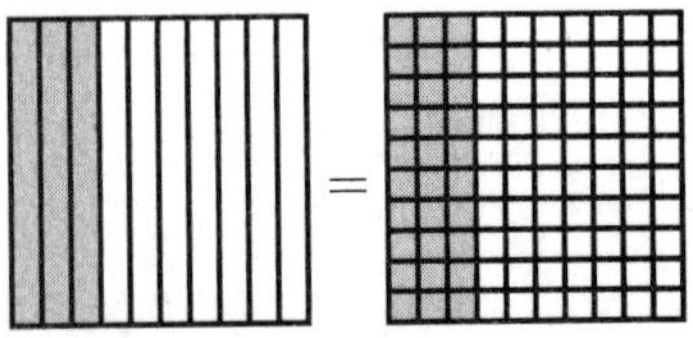

$\frac{3}{10} = \frac{\_\_\_}{100}$

b) 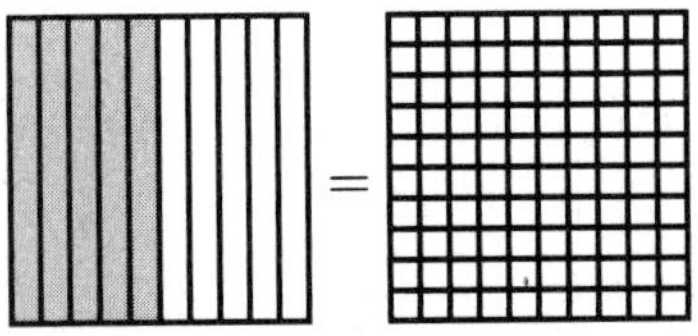

$\frac{5}{10} = \frac{\_\_\_}{100}$

6. Count the columns to write the tenths. Count by 10s to write the hundredths.

a)

Picture	Tenths	Hundredths
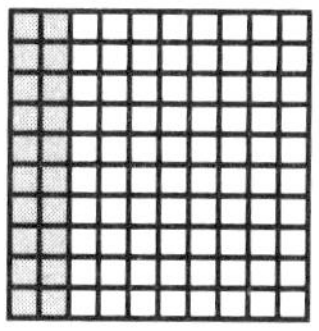	$\frac{2}{10}$	$\frac{20}{100}$

b)

Picture	Tenths	Hundredths

7. Count the number of hundredths. Write your answer two ways.
Hint: Count by tens and then by ones.

a) 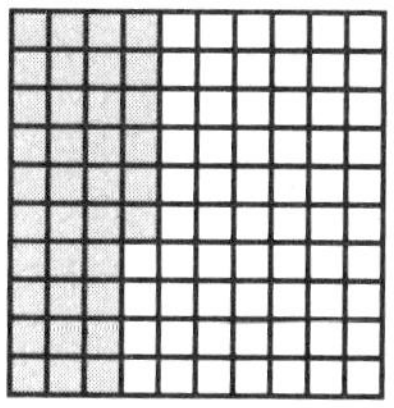 ______ hundredths

= $\frac{\square}{\square}$

b) 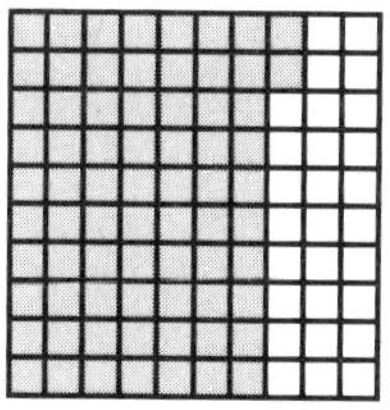 ______ hundredths

= $\frac{\square}{\square}$

8. Shade the fraction.

a) $\frac{47}{100}$

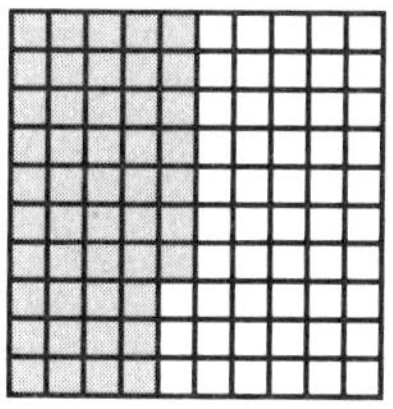

b) $\frac{3}{10}$

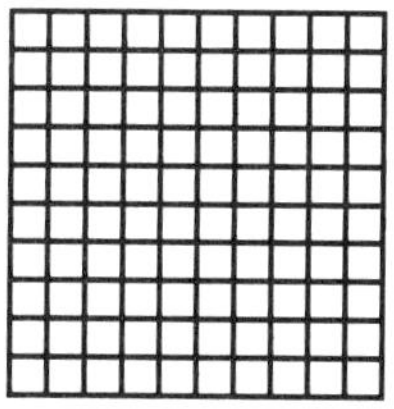

c) 5 hundredths

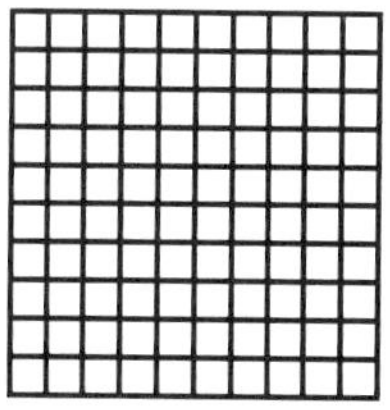

d) 4 tenths

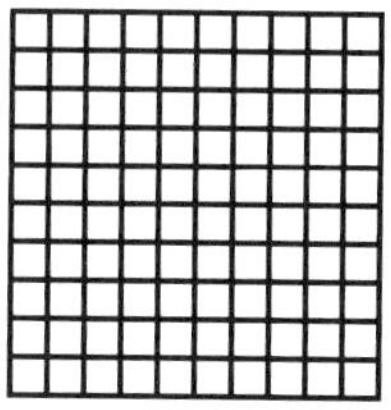

9. Shade the fraction. Then circle the greater fraction in the pair.

a) $\frac{38}{100}$ $\frac{6}{10}$

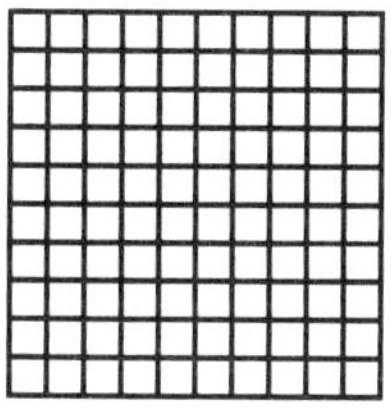 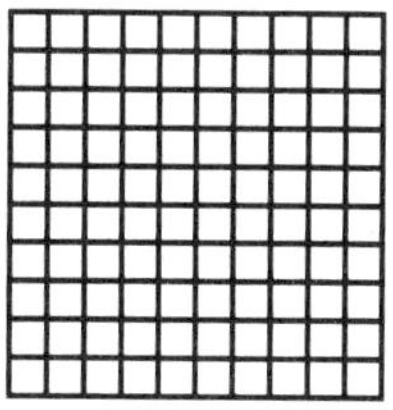

b) $\frac{4}{100}$ $\frac{7}{10}$

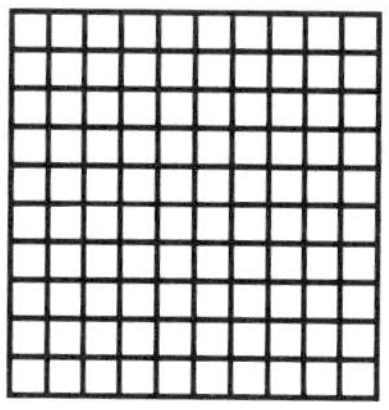 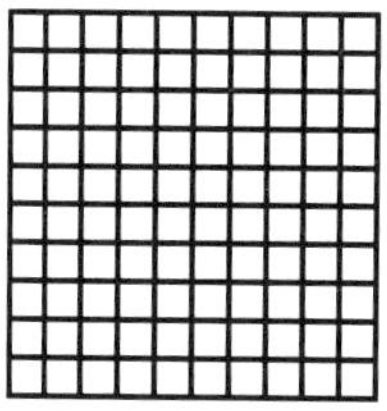

10. Marko says that $\frac{17}{100}$ is greater than $\frac{8}{10}$ because 17 is greater than 8.

Is Marko correct? Explain.

____

____

NS4-59 Decimal Hundredths

A **hundredth** (or $\frac{1}{100}$) can be represented in different ways.

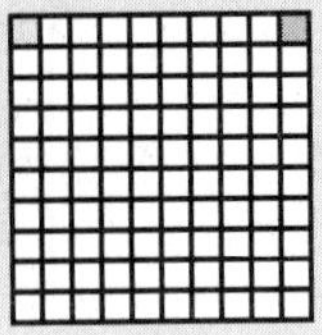

← *A hundredth of the distance from 0 to 1*

Examples: $\frac{1}{100} = 0.01$, $\frac{8}{100} = 0.08$, $\frac{37}{100} = 0.37$

1. Write a fraction for the shaded part of the hundreds block. Then write the fraction as a decimal.
Hint: Count by 10s for each column or row that is shaded.

a) 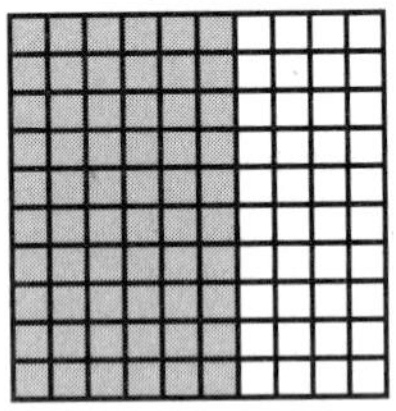 $\frac{60}{100} = 0.60$

b) 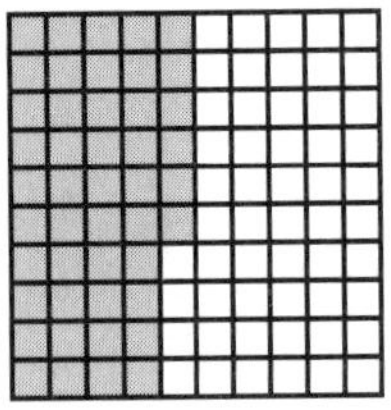

c) 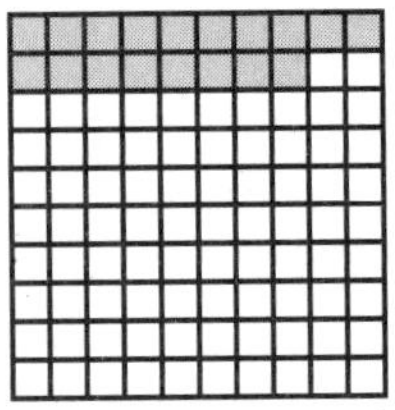

d) 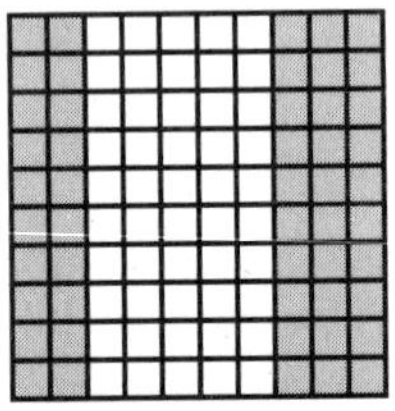

e) 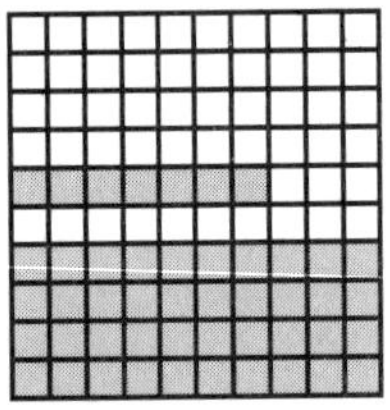

BONUS ▶ 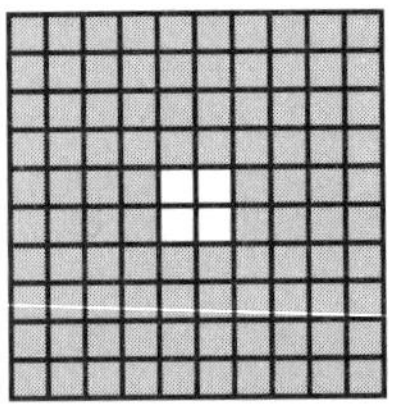

2. Write the decimal hundredths.

a) 18 hundredths = ________
b) 9 hundredths = ________
c) 90 hundredths = ________
d) 10 hundredths = ________
e) 52 hundredths = ________
f) 99 hundredths = ________

3. Shade the same amount in the second square. Then count by 10s to find the number of hundredths. Write your answer as a fraction and a decimal.

a) 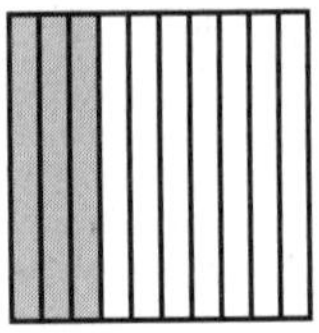 = 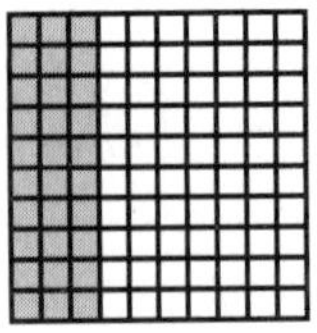

$\frac{3}{10} = \frac{30}{100}$

0.3 = *0.30*

b) 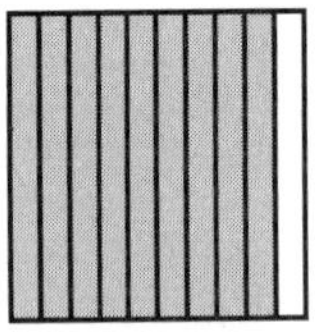 = 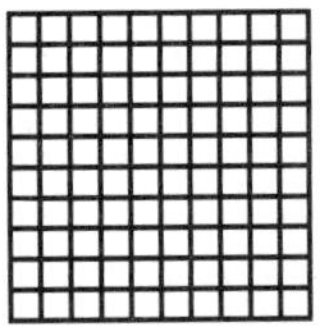

$\frac{9}{10} = \frac{\quad}{100}$

0.9 = ________

c) 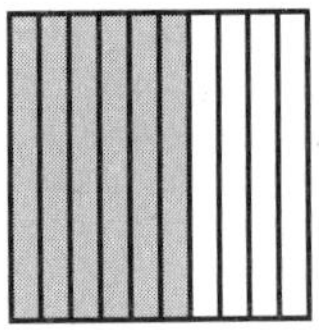 = 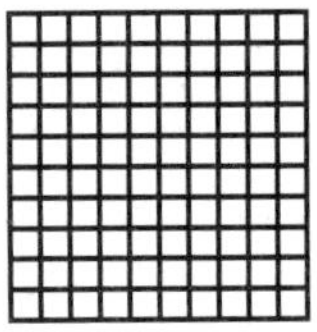

$\frac{6}{10} = \frac{\quad}{100}$

0.6 = ________

4. a) Complete the table.

	Fraction Tenths	Fraction Hundredths	Picture	Decimal Tenths	Decimal Hundredths
i)	$\frac{2}{10}$	$\frac{20}{100}$	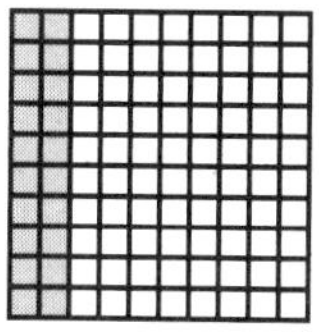	0.2	0.20
ii)			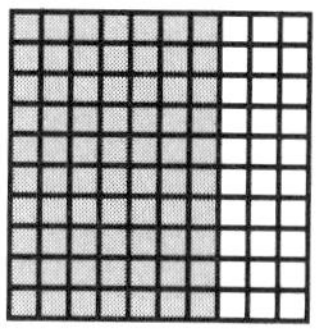		
iii)			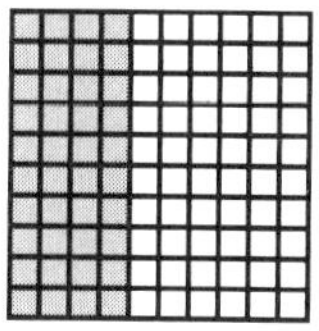		

b) i) Circle the decimal that is greatest and underline the decimal that is least: 0.40 0.20 0.70

ii) Use your answer to part b) i) to write the decimals from least to greatest:

________ < ________ < ________

c) Use your answer to part a) to write the decimals from least to greatest: 0.40 0.20 0.70

________ < ________ < ________

d) Are the answers in part b) ii) and part c) the same? ________

5. Complete the table.

	Fraction Tenths	Fraction Hundredths	Decimal Tenths	Decimal Hundredths
a)	$\frac{4}{10}$	$\frac{40}{100}$	0.4	0.40
b)	$\frac{3}{10}$			
c)			0.8	
d)				0.10

NS6-64 Percentages

A **percentage** is a ratio that compares a number to 100.

The term "percent" means "per 100" or "for every 100" or "out of 100." For example, 84% on a test means 84 out of 100.

You can think of a percentage as a short form for a fraction with denominator 100. Example: $45\% = \frac{45}{100}$

1. Write the percentage as a fraction.

a) 7% b) 92% c) 5% d) 15%

e) 50% f) 100% g) 2% h) 17%

2. Write the fraction as a percentage.

a) $\frac{2}{100}$ b) $\frac{31}{100}$ c) $\frac{52}{100}$ d) $\frac{100}{100}$

e) $\frac{17}{100}$ f) $\frac{88}{100}$ g) $\frac{7}{100}$ h) $\frac{1}{100}$

3. Write the decimal as a fraction and then a percentage.

a) $0.72 = \frac{72}{100} = 72\%$ b) $0.27 =$ c) $0.04 =$

4. Write the fraction as a percentage by first changing it to a fraction with denominator 100.

a) $\frac{3 \times 20}{5 \times 20} = \frac{60}{100} = 60\%$ b) $\frac{2}{5}$

c) $\frac{4}{5}$ d) $\frac{1}{4}$

e) $\frac{3}{4}$ f) $\frac{1}{2}$

g) $\frac{3}{10}$ h) $\frac{7}{10}$

i) $\frac{17}{25}$ j) $\frac{17}{20}$

k) $\frac{3}{25}$ l) $\frac{19}{20}$

m) $\frac{23}{50}$ n) $\frac{47}{50}$

5. Write the decimal as a percentage.

a) $0.2 = \frac{2 \times 10}{10 \times 10} = \frac{20}{100} = 20\%$

b) 0.5

c) 0.7

d) 0.9

6. What percentage of the figure is shaded?

a) 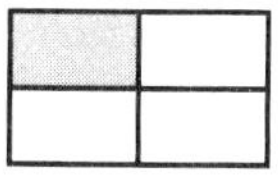

b) 

c) 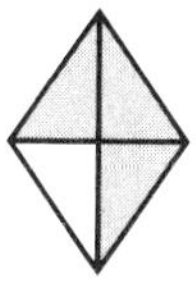

d) 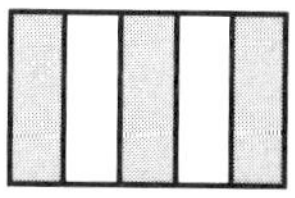

7. Change the fraction to a percentage by first writing it with the smallest numbers.

a) $\frac{9 \div 3}{15 \div 3} = \frac{3}{5} = \frac{3 \times 20}{5 \times 20} = \frac{60}{100} = 60\%$

b) $\frac{12}{15}$

c) $\frac{3}{6}$

d) $\frac{7}{35}$

e) $\frac{21}{28}$

f) $\frac{1}{2}$

g) $\frac{12}{30}$

h) $\frac{10}{40}$

i) $\frac{20}{40}$

j) $\frac{16}{40}$

k) $\frac{60}{150}$

l) $\frac{45}{75}$

m) $\frac{80}{200}$

n) $\frac{72}{80}$

NS6-66 Comparing Decimals, Fractions, and Percentages

1. Is the fraction closest to 10%, 25%, 50%, or 75%?

a) $\frac{3}{5}$ ______ b) $\frac{4}{5}$ ______ c) $\frac{2}{5}$ ______ d) $\frac{2}{10}$ ______

e) $\frac{1}{10}$ ______ f) $\frac{4}{10}$ ______ g) $\frac{9}{10}$ ______ h) $\frac{4}{25}$ ______

i) $\frac{11}{20}$ ______ j) $\frac{16}{20}$ ______ k) $\frac{37}{40}$ ______ l) $\frac{1}{12}$ ______

2. Change the numbers in the pair to fractions with the same denominator. Then write $<$, $>$, or $=$ in the box.

a) $\frac{1}{2}$ 47% b) $\frac{1}{2}$ 53% c) $\frac{1}{4}$ 23% d) $\frac{3}{4}$ 70%

$\frac{50 \times 1}{50 \times 2}$ $\frac{47}{100}$

$\frac{50}{100}$ $\boxed{>}$ $\frac{47}{100}$ ☐ ☐ ☐

e) $\frac{2}{5}$ 32% f) 0.27 62% g) 0.02 11% h) $\frac{1}{10}$ 10%

☐ ☐ ☐ ☐

i) $\frac{19}{25}$ 93% j) $\frac{23}{50}$ 46% k) 0.9 10% l) $\frac{11}{20}$ 19%

☐ ☐ ☐ ☐

3. Write the numbers in order from least to greatest by first changing each number to a fraction.

a) $\frac{3}{5}$, 42%, 0.73 b) $\frac{1}{2}$, 0.67, 80%

c) $\frac{1}{4}$, 0.09, 15% d) $\frac{2}{3}$, 57%, 0.62

PA4-12 Introduction to Algebra—Addition and Subtraction

1. Some apples are inside a box and some are outside. Draw the missing apples in the box.

a)

total number of apples

b)

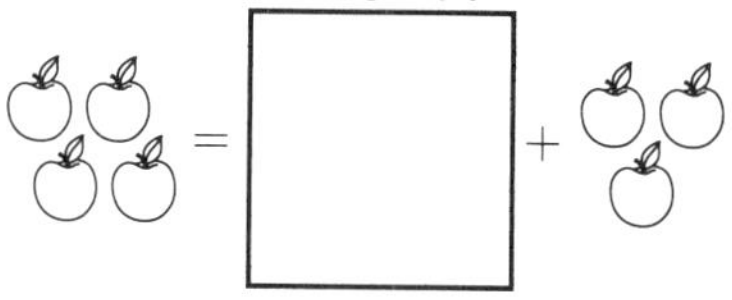

c)

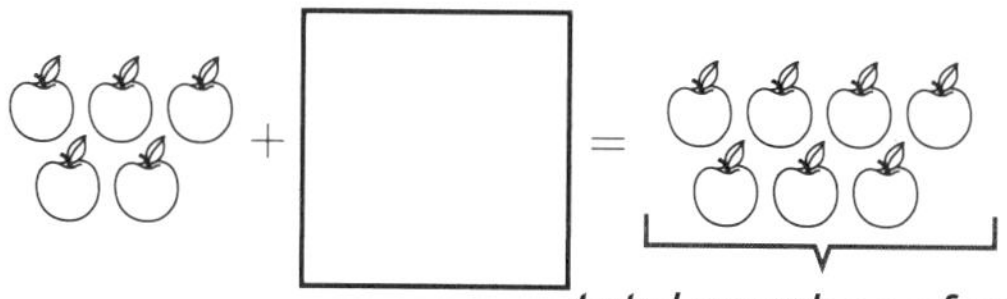

total number of apples

d)

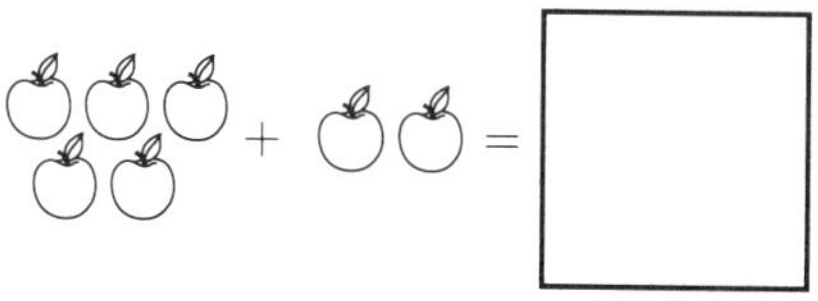

2. Draw the missing apples in the box. Then write the missing number in the smaller box.

a)

6 = 4 + [2]

b)

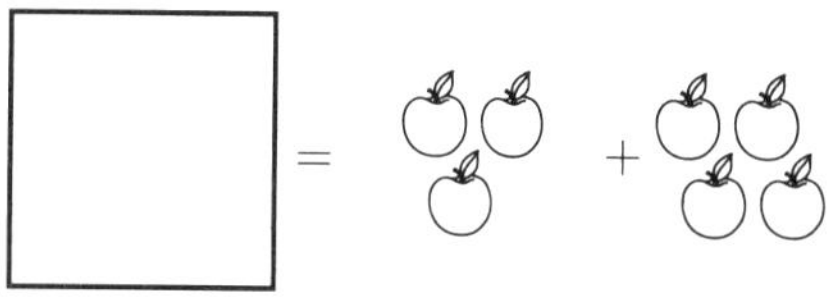

[ ] = 3 + 4

c)

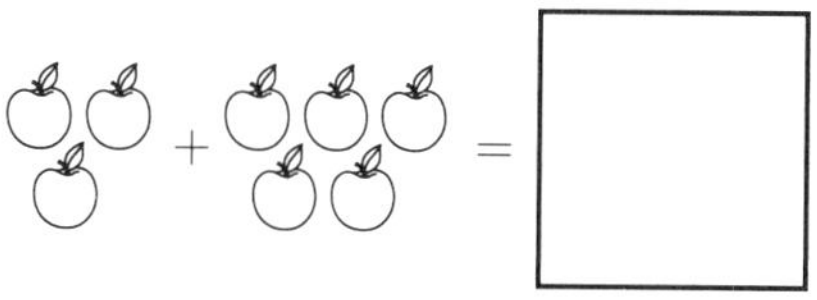

3 + 5 = [ ]

d)

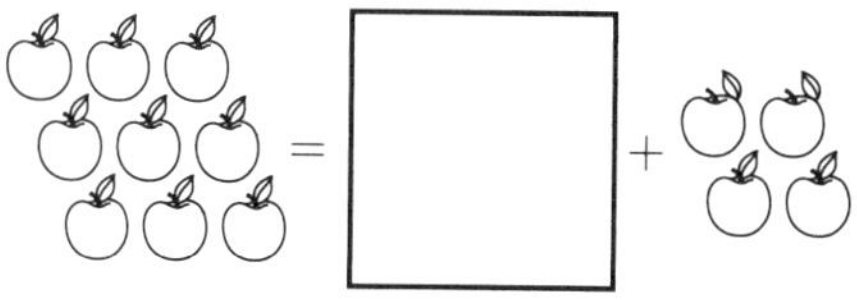

9 = [ ] + 4

Finding the missing number in an equation is called **solving** the equation.

3. Draw a picture for the equation. Use your picture to solve the equation.

a) 5 + [ ] = 9

b) [ ] + 4 = 10

4. Solve the equation by guessing and checking.

a) [ ] + 4 = 21

b) 3 + [ ] = 30

c) 47 = 12 + [ ]

d) 73 = [ ] + 8

5. Some apples are inside a box and some are outside. Draw the missing apples in the box.

a) 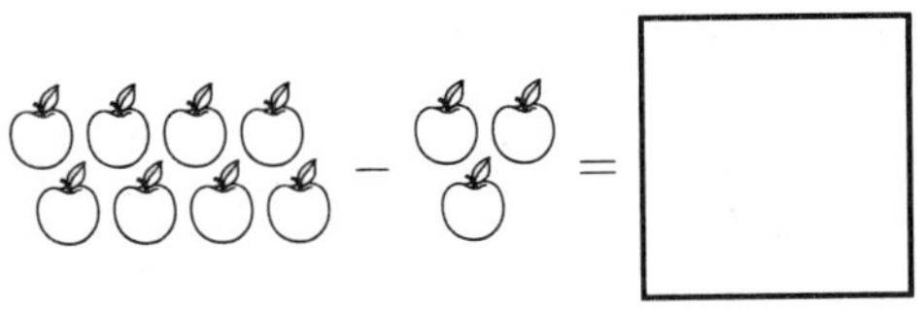

b) 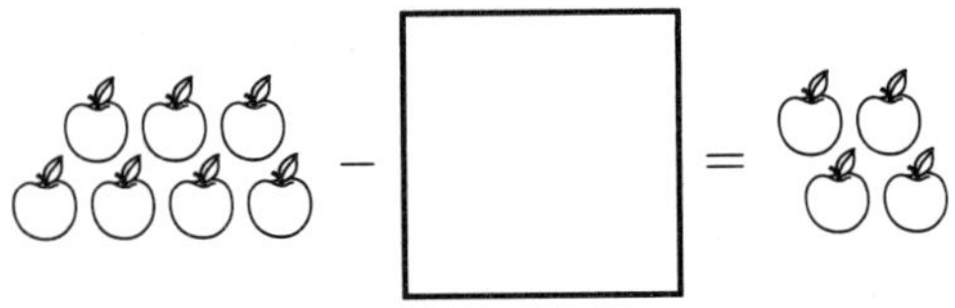

c) 

d) 

6. Draw the missing apples in the box. Then write the missing number in the smaller box.

a) 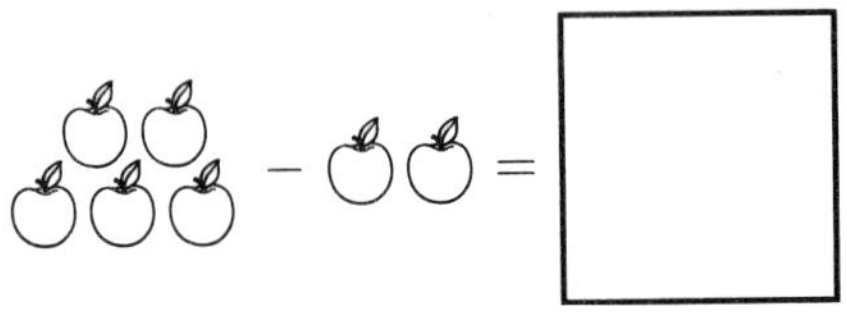

$5 - 2 = \square$

b) 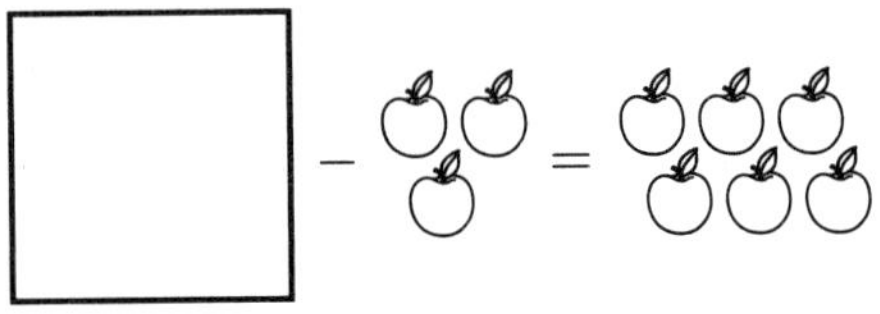

$\square - 3 = 6$

c) 

$6 = 8 - \square$

d) 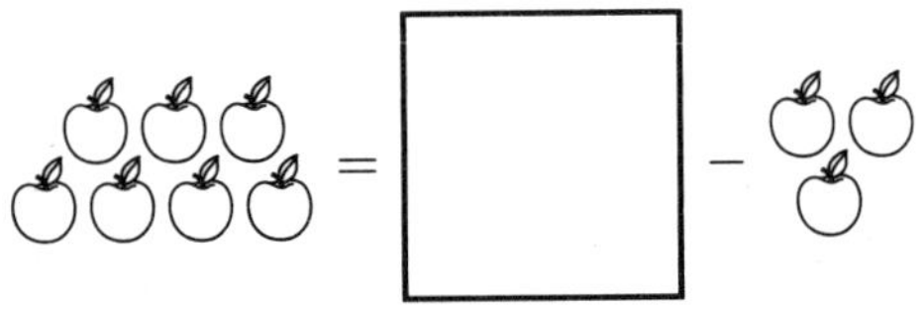

$7 = \square - 3$

7. Draw a picture for the equation. Use your picture to solve the equation.

a) $10 - \square = 7$

b) $5 = \square - 3$

8. Solve the equation by guessing and checking.

a) $\square - 21 = 7$

b) $40 - \square = 15$

c) $89 = \square - 1$

BONUS ▶ $\square = 94 - 63$

Introduction to Algebra—Multiplication and Division

1. Draw the same number of apples in each box. Write the equation for the picture.

a) 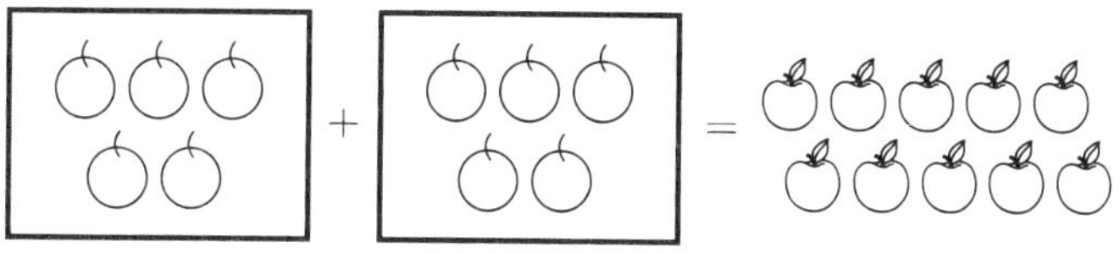

☐ + ☐ = *10*

b) 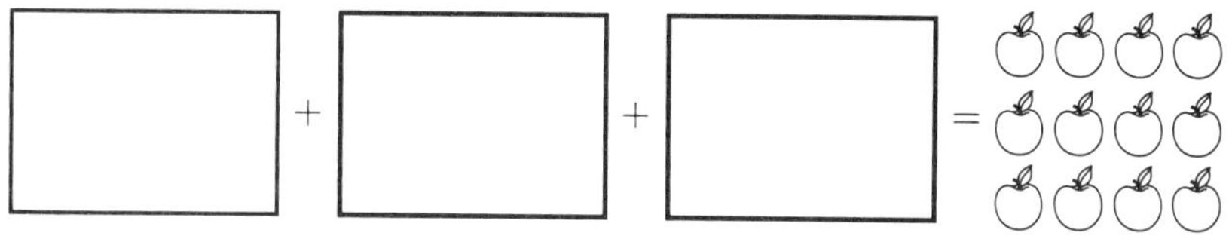

2. Draw a picture for the equation. Use your picture to solve the equation.

a) 3 × 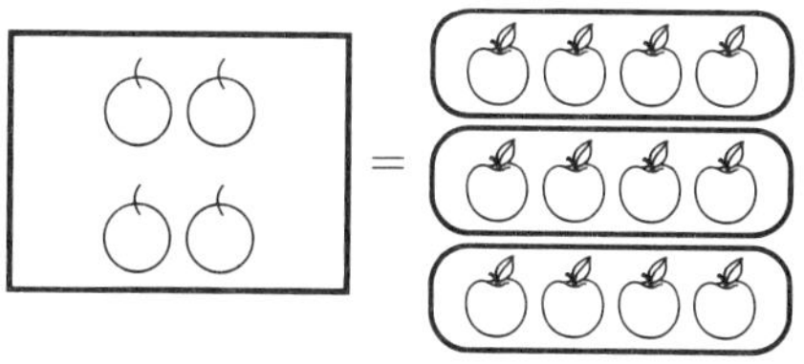

3 × *4* = 12

b) 2 × 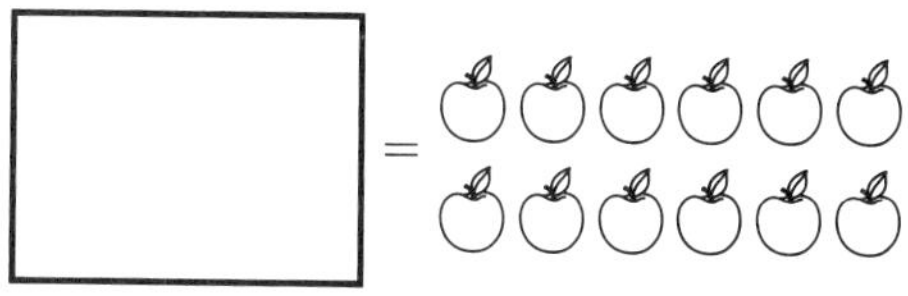

2 × ☐ = 12

c) 3 × 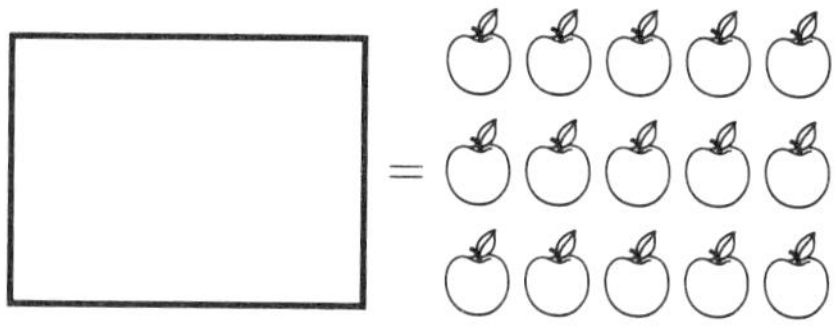

3 × ☐ = 15

d) 6 × 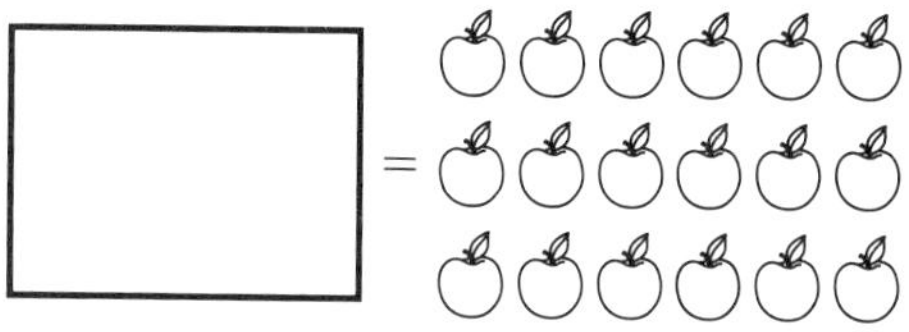

6 × ☐ = 18

e) 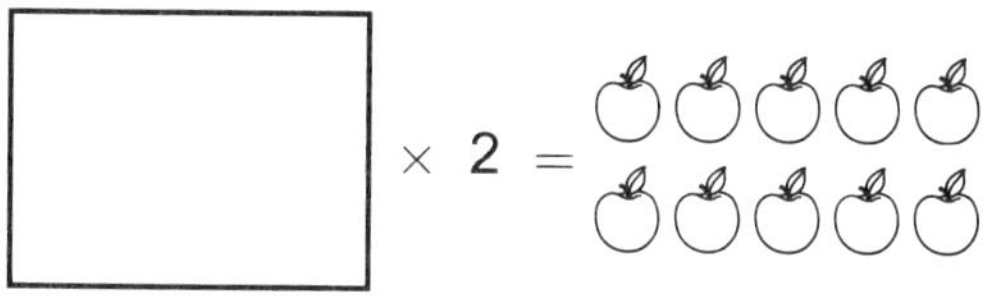

☐ × 2 = 10

f) 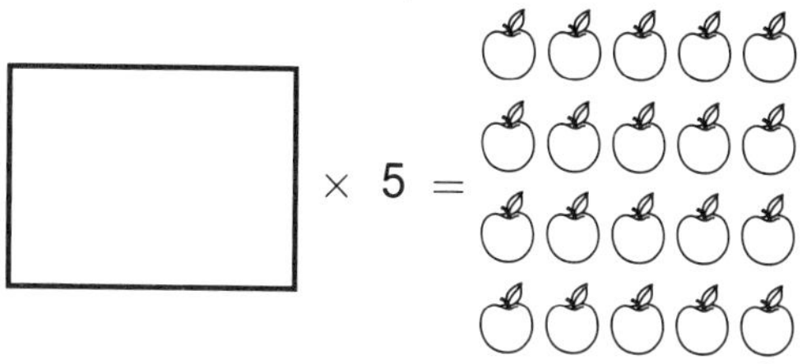

☐ × 5 = 20

3. How many apples should be in the box? Write the number.

a) 2 × [3] = 

b) 2 × [ ] = 

c) 3 ×  = [ ]

d) [ ] × 4 = 

e) [ ] × 3 = 

f) 3 ×  = [ ]

g) [ ] × 2 = 

h) 7 ×  = [ ]

BONUS ▶ There are 10 apples in the bag. What number goes in the box?

3 ×  = [ ]

4. Solve the equation by guessing and checking.

a) 5 × [ ] = 30 b) 18 ÷ 2 = [ ] c) 30 ÷ [ ] = 5 d) [ ] × 7 = 77

e) 24 ÷ [ ] = 6 f) [ ] ÷ 5 = 10 g) 5 × 40 = [ ] h) [ ] ÷ 4 = 7

5. Rewrite the multiplication as division, then solve the equation.

a) [ ] × 2 = 26 b) 96 = 3 × [ ] c) [ ] × 4 = 80

d) 100 = [ ] × 20 e) [ ] × 4 = 88 f) 150 = 50 × [ ]

1. Circle the equations where the unknown is by itself.

$$x = 7 + 2 \qquad w + 5 = 10 \qquad 5 - 3 = a \qquad 6 - b = 4 \qquad k = 12 \div 3$$

Total	
Part 1	Part 2

There are 3 equations for a total and two parts:

Total = Part 1 + Part 2
Part 1 = Total − Part 2
Part 2 = Total − Part 1

2. Write three equations for the table. Circle the equation where the unknown is by itself.

a)

k	
8	5

$$\underset{\text{Total}}{k} = \underset{\text{Part 1}}{8} + \underset{\text{Part 2}}{5}$$

$$\underset{\text{Part 1}}{8} = \underset{\text{Total}}{k} - \underset{\text{Part 2}}{5}$$

$$\underset{\text{Part 2}}{5} = \underset{\text{Total}}{k} - \underset{\text{Part 1}}{8}$$

b)

24	
21	k

$$\underset{\text{Total}}{\rule{1cm}{0.4pt}} = \underset{\text{Part 1}}{\rule{1cm}{0.4pt}} + \underset{\text{Part 2}}{\rule{1cm}{0.4pt}}$$

$$\underset{\text{Part 1}}{\rule{1cm}{0.4pt}} = \underset{\text{Total}}{\rule{1cm}{0.4pt}} - \underset{\text{Part 2}}{\rule{1cm}{0.4pt}}$$

$$\underset{\text{Part 2}}{\rule{1cm}{0.4pt}} = \underset{\text{Total}}{\rule{1cm}{0.4pt}} - \underset{\text{Part 1}}{\rule{1cm}{0.4pt}}$$

c)

17	
k	3

$$\underset{\text{Total}}{\rule{1cm}{0.4pt}} = \rule{1cm}{0.4pt} + \rule{1cm}{0.4pt}$$

$$\underset{\text{Part 1}}{\rule{1cm}{0.4pt}} = \rule{1cm}{0.4pt} - \rule{1cm}{0.4pt}$$

$$\underset{\text{Part 2}}{\rule{1cm}{0.4pt}} = \rule{1cm}{0.4pt} - \rule{1cm}{0.4pt}$$

d)

k	
215	65

$$\underset{\text{Total}}{\rule{1cm}{0.4pt}} = \rule{1cm}{0.4pt} + \rule{1cm}{0.4pt}$$

$$\underset{\text{Part 1}}{\rule{1cm}{0.4pt}} = \rule{1cm}{0.4pt} - \rule{1cm}{0.4pt}$$

$$\underset{\text{Part 2}}{\rule{1cm}{0.4pt}} = \rule{1cm}{0.4pt} - \rule{1cm}{0.4pt}$$

e)

97	
k	18

$$\underset{\text{Total}}{\rule{1cm}{0.4pt}} = \rule{1cm}{0.4pt} + \rule{1cm}{0.4pt}$$

$$\underset{\text{Part 1}}{\rule{1cm}{0.4pt}} = \rule{1cm}{0.4pt} - \rule{1cm}{0.4pt}$$

$$\underset{\text{Part 2}}{\rule{1cm}{0.4pt}} = \rule{1cm}{0.4pt} - \rule{1cm}{0.4pt}$$

f)

312	
78	k

$$\underset{\text{Total}}{\rule{1cm}{0.4pt}} = \rule{1cm}{0.4pt} + \rule{1cm}{0.4pt}$$

$$\underset{\text{Part 1}}{\rule{1cm}{0.4pt}} = \rule{1cm}{0.4pt} - \rule{1cm}{0.4pt}$$

$$\underset{\text{Part 2}}{\rule{1cm}{0.4pt}} = \rule{1cm}{0.4pt} - \rule{1cm}{0.4pt}$$

3. Write an equation where *m* is by itself.

a)

17	
12	*m*

$m = 17 - 12$

b)

8	
m	5

____

c)

m	
11	2

____

d)

9	
m	3

____

4. Fill in the table. Write *m* for the number you are not given.

		Green Grapes	Purple Grapes	Total Number of Grapes	Equation
a)	6 green grapes 14 grapes in total	6	*m*	14	$m = 14 - 6$
b)	5 green grapes 3 purple grapes				
c)	11 grapes in total 9 green grapes				
d)	7 purple grapes 16 grapes altogether				
e)	34 purple grapes 21 green grapes				
f)	71 grapes altogether 45 purple grapes				

BONUS ▶

131 purple grapes 26 green grapes				

5. Circle the total in the story. Then write an equation and solve it.

a) 6 green grapes
9 grapes altogether
x purple grapes

$x = 9 - 6$
$x = 3$

b) 3 green grapes
4 purple grapes
x grapes altogether

c) 11 grapes altogether
7 purple grapes
x green grapes

d) There are 6 cats.
There are 12 dogs.
There are *x* pets altogether.

e) There are 9 marbles.
x of them are red.
5 of them are not red.

f) Rick has 8 cousins.
x of them are boys.
3 of them are girls.

Differences and Equations

Larger Part	
Smaller Part	Difference

There are three equations for a difference and two parts:

Difference = Larger Part − Smaller Part

Larger Part = Smaller Part + Difference

Smaller Part = Larger Part − Difference

1. Write three equations for the table. Circle the equation where the unknown is by itself.

a)

10	
4	b

______ = ______ − ______
Difference Larger Part Smaller Part

______ = ______ + ______
Larger Part Smaller Part Difference

______ = ______ − ______
Smaller Part Larger Part Difference

b)

b	
4	10

______ = ______ − ______
Difference

______ = ______ + ______
Larger Part

______ = ______ − ______
Smaller Part

c)

34	
b	9

______ = ______ − ______
Difference

______ = ______ + ______
Larger Part

______ = ______ − ______
Smaller Part

2. Fill in the table. Write x for the number you are not given. Circle the part that is larger. Write an equation where the unknown is by itself.

		Parts		Difference	Equation
		Cats	**Dogs**		
a)	7 cats; 12 more dogs than cats	*7*	(*x*)	*12*	$x = 12 + 7$
b)	5 cats; 3 dogs				
c)	11 more dogs than cats; 8 cats				
d)	9 dogs; 3 fewer cats than dogs				
e)	17 dogs; 13 fewer dogs than cats				

BONUS ▶

100 cats; 20 fewer dogs than cats				

3. Circle the part that is larger. Underline the difference.

a) There are 9 hats.
There are x scarves.
There are 4 more hats than scarves.

b) There are x hats.
There are 7 scarves.
There are 5 fewer hats than scarves.

c) There are 5 hats.
There are 6 scarves.
There are x fewer hats than scarves.

4. Fill in the table. Write x for the number you are not given. Circle the part that is larger.

	Problem	What Is Compared?	How Many?	Difference	Equation and Solution
a)	Jun has 48 American stamps in his collection. He has 12 more American stamps than Canadian stamps. How many Canadian stamps does he have?	*American stamps*	*48*	*12*	$x = 48 - 12$
		Canadian stamps	x		$x = 36$
b)	Lela has 12 red marbles. She has 8 green marbles. How many more red marbles than green marbles does she have?				
c)	There are 13 dogs in a shelter. There are 7 more cats than dogs in the shelter. How many cats are there?				
d)	A bulldog weighs 7 kg less than a boxer. The boxer weighs 35 kg. How much does the bulldog weigh?				

5. Write an equation where the unknown is by itself. Then solve the equation.

a) Dory hikes 8 km on Saturday. She hikes 3 km more on Sunday than on Saturday. How many kilometres did she hike on Sunday?

b) 17 cars are parked in the school parking lot. There are 8 fewer vans than cars in the same lot. How many vans are there?

c) A dalmatian weighs 29 kg. A dingo weighs 8 kg less. How much does the dingo weigh?

d) Aputik biked 42 km on Saturday. On Sunday, she biked 12 km more than on Saturday. How far did she bike on Sunday?

e) Carl counted 38 robins in his backyard on Monday and 29 robins on Tuesday. How many more robins flew through Carl's backyard on Monday?

f) Sally counted 72 shooting stars on one night. The next night she saw 24 fewer stars than on the first night. How many shooting stars did she see on the second night?

PA4-16 Addition and Subtraction Word Problems

1. Fill in the table. Write *x* for the number you need to find. Cross out the information you do not use.

	Problem	Parts	How Many?	Difference / Total	Equation and Solution
a)	Neka has 4 kg of apples and 5 kg of pears. How many kilograms of fruit does he have?	*apples*	*4 kg*	~~Difference: ____~~	$x = 4 + 5$ $x = 9$
		pears	*5 kg*	Total: x	
b)	Karen biked 47 km on Monday. She biked 54 km on Tuesday. How far did Karen bike in two days?	*distance on Monday*		Difference: ____	
				Total: ____	
c)	Alice raised $32 for charity. Ben raised $9 less than Alice. How much money did Ben raise?			Difference: ____	
				Total: ____	
d)	Alexa bought 3000 millilitres of apple juice. She bought 2000 more millilitres of apple juice than plum juice. How much plum juice did she buy?			Difference: ____	
				Total: ____	
e)	The cafeteria sold 350 cartons of milk. 198 of them were cartons of white milk. The rest were chocolate milk. How many cartons of chocolate milk did the cafeteria sell?			Difference: ____	
				Total: ____	
f)	The height of Mount Kilimanjaro is 5895 m. That is 2953 m less than the height of Mount Everest. How tall is Mount Everest?			Difference: ____	
				Total: ____	

2. The world's tallest tree is about 116 m tall. The Horseshoe Falls at Niagara Falls is about 51 m tall. How much taller is the tallest tree than the Horseshoe Falls?

3. Solve the problem. Use your answer from part i) as data for part ii).

a) i) Tom bought 9 hockey cards and 6 baseball cards. How many cards did he buy altogether?

ii) Tom gave away 5 cards. How many does he have left?

b) There are 24 players on a hockey team, and 15 of them are new to the team.

i) How many players are not new to the team?

ii) How many more new players than not new players are on the team?

4. Solve the two-step problem.

a) Sara bought 8 red jelly beans and 5 white jelly beans. She ate 4 of them. How many jelly beans does she have left?

b) Marko downloaded 7 songs. He downloaded 3 more songs than movies. How many songs and movies did he download altogether?

c) Ray had $32. He bought the book, magazine, and scissors below. How much money does he have left?

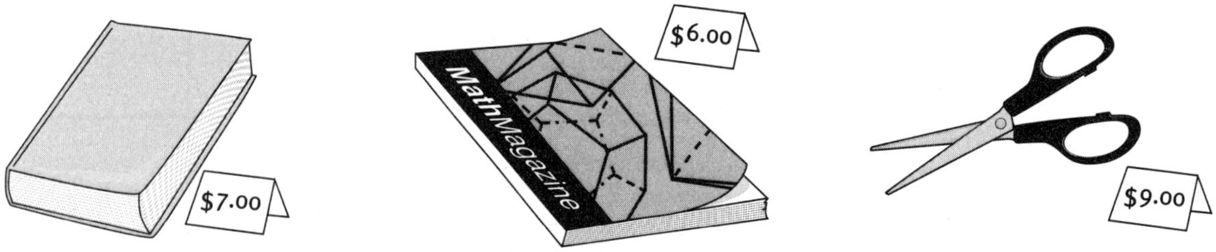

5. Ivan invited 10 friends from school and 8 friends from camp to his birthday party.

a) How many more friends from school than friends from camp were supposed to be at the party?

b) Two friends from school and three friends from camp could not come to the party. How many friends were at the party?

c) Were there more friends from school or more friends from camp at the party? How many more?

6. The table shows the number of cars arriving at the train station parking lot. No cars leave the lot in the morning.

a) How many cars are parked in the lot at 7:00 a.m.?

b) How many cars are parked in the lot at 8:00 a.m.?

c) There are 1008 spaces in total in the lot. How many are still available at 8:00 a.m.?

Before 6:00 a.m.	378
From 6:00 a.m. to 7:00 a.m.	459
From 7:00 a.m. to 8:00 a.m.	125

PA4-17 Models and Times as Many

1. Draw a model for the story.

a) Don has 5 stamps. Jasmin has 3 times as many as Don does.

Don's stamps:	5		
Jasmin's stamps:	5	5	5

b) There are 3 red grapes. There are 5 times as many green grapes as red grapes.

____

____

c) There are 16 green pears. There are 4 times as many red pears as green pears.

____

____

d) Anne has 4 markers. Fred has 5 times as many markers as Anne.

____

____

2. Solve the problem by drawing a model.

a) Ansel has 6 stamps. Jen has 3 times as many stamps as Ansel. How many stamps do they have altogether?

Ansel's stamps:	6			*6 stamps*
Jen's stamps:	6	6	6	*18 stamps*

6 + 18 = 24, so Jen and Ansel have 24 stamps altogether.

b) Lewis studies spiders and scorpions. He has 6 spiders and twice as many scorpions. How many spiders and scorpions does he have altogether?

____

____

____

c) There are 4 hamsters in a store. There are six times as many mice in the store. How many mice and hamsters are there altogether?

3. Draw a model for the story.

a) Mandy has four times as many stickers as Ethan.

Mandy's stickers:

Ethan's stickers:

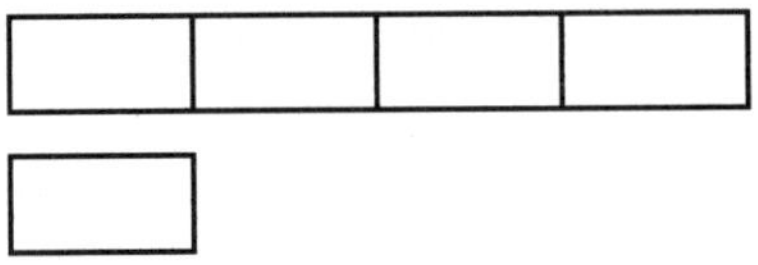

b) Mary is three times as old as Armand.

____

____

c) There are five times as many green grapes as red grapes.

____

____

d) A book is two times thicker than a notebook.

____

____

e) There are three times as many lizards as snakes in the zoo.

____

____

4. Draw a model for the story. Then write the given number beside the correct bar.

a) There are 20 carrots. There are 4 times as many carrots as potatoes.

carrots: 20

potatoes:

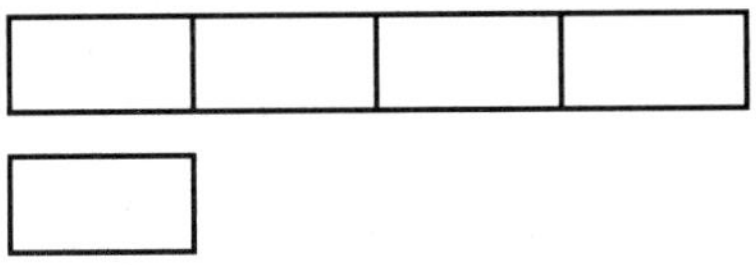

b) There are 30 cars in a parking lot. There are 6 times as many cars as vans in the lot.

____

____

c) Nora chopped up 70 carrots and twice as many little tomatoes for a salad.

____

____

5. Draw the model.

a) Jayden needs three times as many blueberries as raspberries to make jam. He needs 6 cups more blueberries than raspberries. He needs 12 cups of berries altogether.

blueberries: ____________________

raspberries: ____________________

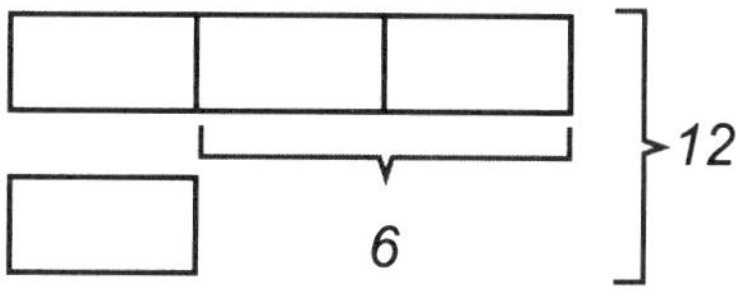

b) Billy's building is 5 times as tall as Grace's. Billy's building is 20 floors taller than Grace's.

____

____

c) There are 3 times as many green apples as red apples. There are 20 apples altogether.

____

____

d) There are twice as many apricots as peaches. There are 32 more apricots than peaches.

____

____

6. All the blocks are the same size. What is the size of each block?

a)
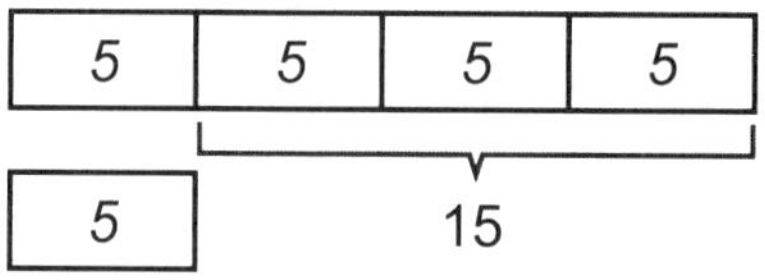

b)
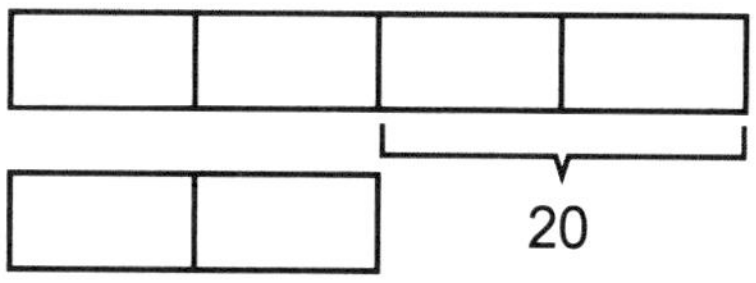

c)
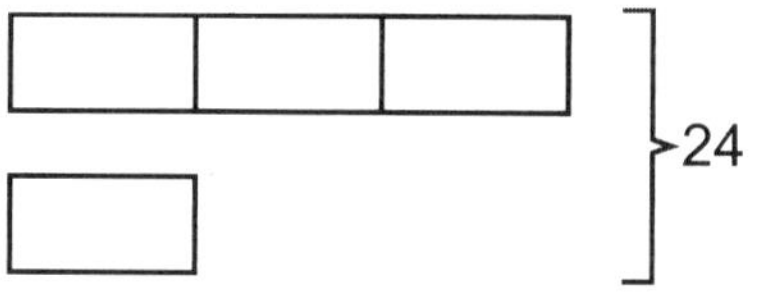

d)
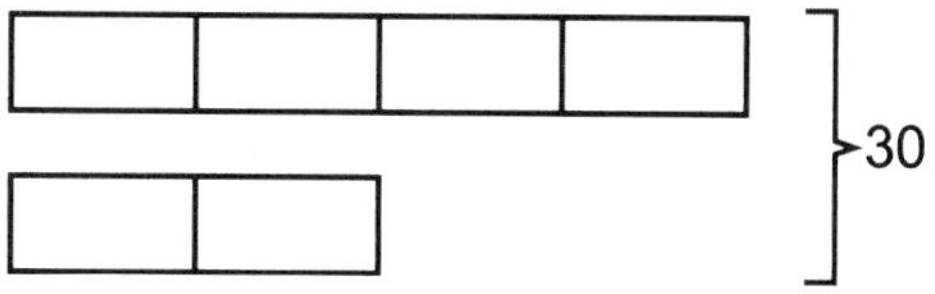

e)
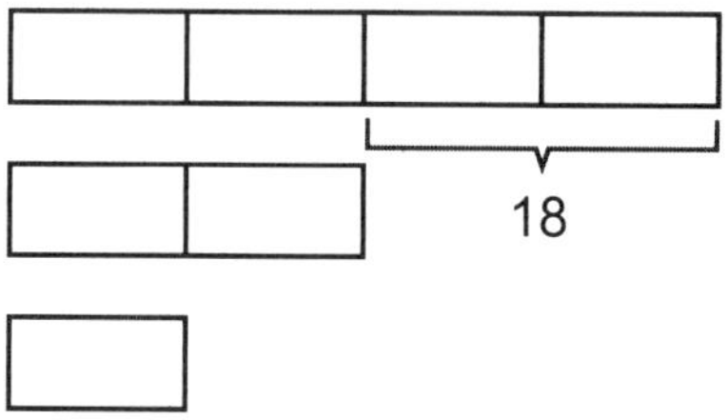

f)
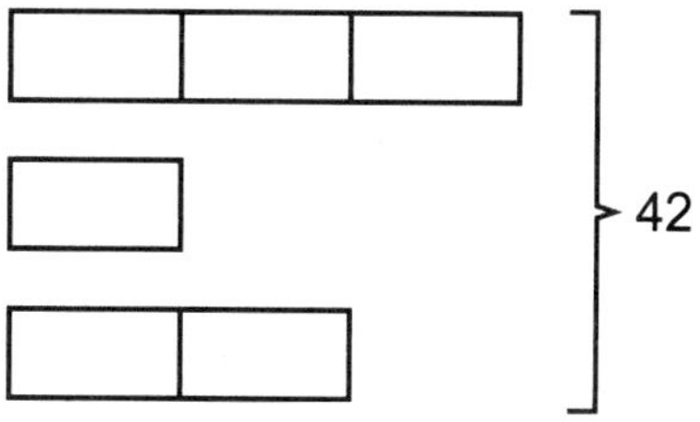

7. Draw the model. Find the size of one block in the model. Then solve the problem.

a) Zack has four times as many stickers as Alex. Zack has 15 more stickers than Alex. How many stickers does each person have?

Zack's stickers:

Alex's stickers:

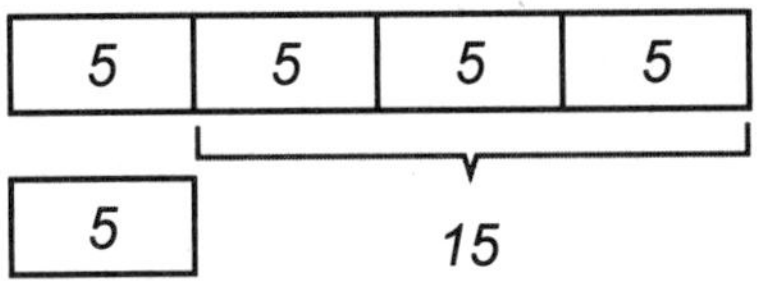

Zack has __20__ stickers and Alex has __5__ stickers.

b) Hanna is three times as old as Marcel. Hanna is 8 years older than Marcel. How old are Hanna and Marcel?

____

____

Hanna is ______ years old and Marcel is ______ years old.

c) There are five times as many green apples as red apples. There are 24 apples altogether. How many apples of each colour are there?

____

____

There are ______ green apples and ______ red apples.

d) A granola recipe calls for seven times as much oatmeal as nuts. Avril wants to make 400 grams of granola. How many grams of nuts and oatmeal does she need?

____

____

Avril needs ______ grams of oatmeal and ______ grams of nuts.

e) A rottweiler weighs five times as much as a Scottish terrier. The Scottish terrier weighs 36 kg less than the rottweiler. How much does each dog weigh?

____

____

The Scottish terrier weighs ______ kg and the rottweiler weighs ______ kg.

f) A pair of pants costs twice as much as a shirt. Fred paid $42 for a pair of pants and a shirt. How much did each item cost?

BONUS ▶ How much would Fred pay for two pairs of pants and three shirts?

PA4-18 Problems and Equations—Multiplication and Division

When the larger part is 3 times the size of the smaller part, we say the **scale factor** is 3.

Smaller Part ☐

Larger Part ☐☐☐

You can find one part from another part using the scale factor.

Larger Part = Smaller Part × Scale Factor

Smaller Part = Larger Part ÷ Scale Factor

1. Circle the larger part and underline the smaller part in the problem. Then fill in the blanks for the equation where the unknown is by itself and cross out the other equation.

a) There are 21 cats and *w* dogs. There are three times as many dogs as cats.

w = *21* × *3* or ~~____ = ____ ÷ ____~~

Larger Part = Smaller Part × Scale Factor or ~~Smaller Part = Larger Part ÷ Scale Factor~~

b) There are 6 plums and *w* pears. There are 2 times as many plums as pears.

____ = ____ × ____ or ____ = ____ ÷ ____

Larger Part = Smaller Part × Scale Factor or Smaller Part = Larger Part ÷ Scale Factor

c) There are 8 cats and *w* dogs. There are 4 times as many dogs as cats.

____ = ____ × ____ or ____ = ____ ÷ ____

Larger Part = Smaller Part × Scale Factor or Smaller Part = Larger Part ÷ Scale Factor

d) There are 12 adults in a chess club. There are twice as many teenagers as adults in the chess club.

____ = ____ × ____ or ____ = ____ ÷ ____

Larger Part = Smaller Part × Scale Factor or Smaller Part = Larger Part ÷ Scale Factor

2. Fill in the table. Write *w* for the number you are not given.
Hint: Circle the larger part and underline the smaller part.

	Problem	Part	How Many?	Equation
a)	There are 20 green apples in a box. There are 4 times as many green apples as red apples.	*green apples*	*20*	*20 ÷ 4 = w*
		red apples	*w*	
b)	There are 16 pears. There are twice as many pears as bananas.			
c)	There are 6 cats in a shelter. There are three times as many dogs as cats in the shelter.			
d)	Sun planted 40 bean seeds. That is 5 times as many as the corn seeds she planted. How many corn seeds did she plant?			

3. Complete the table.

	Total Number of Things	Number of Sets	Number in Each Set	Multiplication or Division Equation
a)	w	6	3	$6 \times 3 = w$
b)	20	4	w	$20 \div 4 = w$
c)	18	w	6	
d)	24	2	w	
e)	w	4	7	
f)	35	w	5	

4. Fill in the table. Write w to show what you don't know. Then write a multiplication or division equation in the last column and solve the problem.

		Total Number of Things	Number of Sets	Number in Each Set	Multiplication or Division Equation
a)	36 people 3 vans	36	3	w	$36 \div 3 = w$ 12 people in each van
b)	10 marbles in each jar 6 jars				______ ____ marbles
c)	35 flowers 5 pots				______ ____ flowers in each pot
d)	6 chairs at each table 7 tables				______ ____ chairs

5. a) A soccer league has 8 teams with 11 players each. How many players are in the league?

b) A birch tree is 15 m tall. A maple tree is twice as tall the birch. How tall is the maple tree?

c) Zara is 35 years old. Zara is 5 times as old as Ken. How old is Ken?

d) A box of pencils costs $2. How much do 25 boxes of pencils cost?

e) Ella paid $15 for three scarves. If all the scarves cost the same amount, how much did each one cost?

BONUS ▶ A male mountain gorilla weighs 200 kg, four times as much as a male chimpanzee. How much does the chimpanzee weigh?

PA6-3 Extending Patterns

1. The pattern below was made by adding 3 to each term to get the next term.

4, 7, 10, 13, 16, …

a) Write the next three terms of the pattern. ______, ______, ______

b) What is the 8th term of the pattern? ______

2. Add, subtract, multiply, or divide to extend the sequence.

a) add 4 — 41, 45, ______, ______, ______

b) subtract 3 — 25, 22, ______, ______, ______

c) add 11 — 20, 31, ______, ______, ______

d) multiply by 2 — 13, 26, ______, ______, ______

e) divide by 3 — 81, 27, ______, ______, ______

3. Extend the sequence to find the 7th term.

a) add 1 — 4, 5, 6, 7, ______________________________

b) subtract 2 — 100, 98, 96, ______________________________

c) add 10 — 30, 40, 50, 60, 70, ______________________________

d) multiply by 2 — 2, 4, 8, 16, ______________________________

e) divide by 10 — 70 000 000, 7 000 000, 700 000, 70 000, ______________________________

4. Extend the sequence. Which term is equal to 64?

a) multiply by 2 — 1, 2, 4, 8, ____________________ 64 is the ________ term.

b) add 10 — 4, 14, 24, 34, ____________________ 64 is the ________ term.

c) add 8 — 8, 16, 24, 32, ____________________ 64 is the ________ term.

BONUS ▶ Extend the pattern.

a) Some terms are added and some are subtracted.

3 (+3) 6 (−1) 5 (+3) 8 (−1) 7 (+3) 10 (−1) 9 ( ) ______ ( ) ______ ( ) ______ ( ) ______

3, 6, 5, 8, 7, 10, 9, ______, ______, ______, ______

b) Some terms are multiplied and some are subtracted.

5 ( ) 10 ( ) 6 ( ) 12 ( ) 8 ( ) 16 ( ) 12 ( ) ______ ( ) ______ ( ) ______ ( ) ______

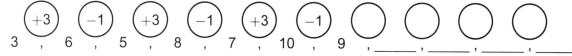

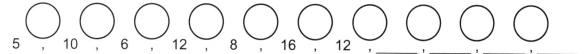

5. The pattern 3, 7, 15, … was made by doubling each term and adding 1 to get the next term.

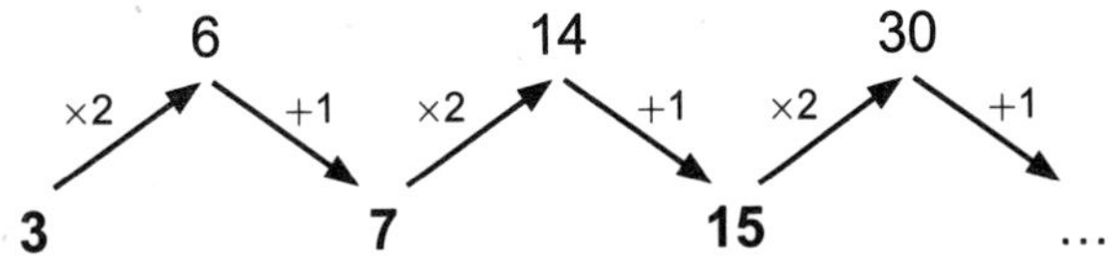

a) Write the next three terms of the pattern. ______, ______, ______

b) What is the 7th term of the pattern? ______

6. Repeat the two operations to extend the sequence that starts with 4.

a) multiply by 2 and add 3

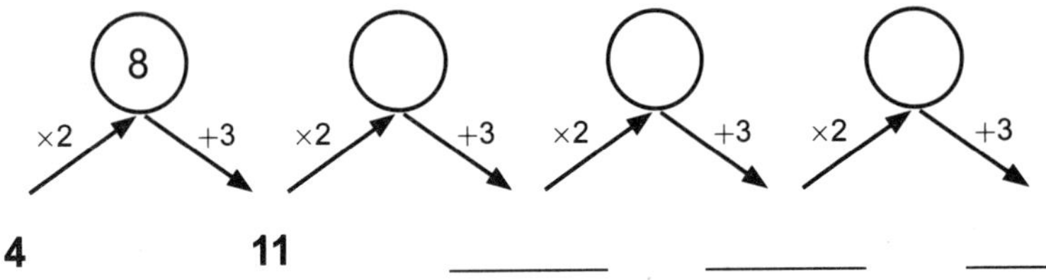

b) multiply by 3 and subtract 1

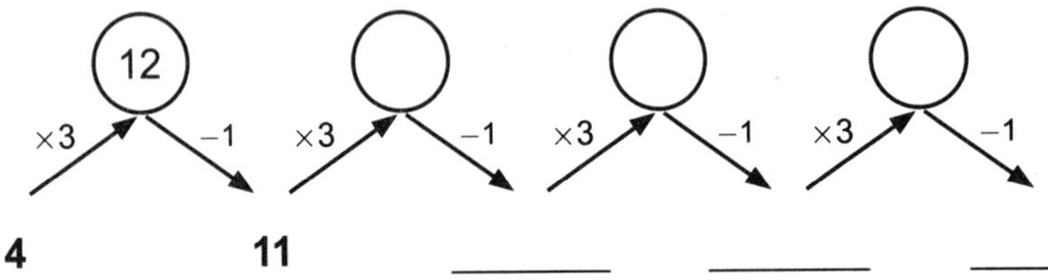

7. Extend the pattern until you reach the 5th term.

a) add 6 3, 9, ______________________________

b) multiply by 3 3, 9, ______________________________

c) multiply by 2 and add 3 3, 9, ______________________________

8. a) Extend the pattern until you reach 79.

i) multiply by 2 and add 1 4, 9, ______________________________

ii) add 10 29, 39, ______________________________

iii) multiply by 3 and add 4 1, 7, ______________________________

b) Which pattern reaches 79 first? ______

BONUS ▶ Extend a sequence that starts "3, 5" two different ways. Describe how you get each next term.

3, 5, ________________________ ______________________________

3, 5, ________________________ ______________________________

OA5-6 Order of Operations and Brackets

Add and subtract in the order you read: from left to right.

1. Add or subtract from left to right.

a) $5 + 4 - 3$
$= 9 - 3$
$= 6$

b) $6 - 4 + 1$

c) $4 + 5 + 3$

d) $9 - 3 - 2$

Multiply and divide in the order you read: from left to right.

2. Multiply or divide from left to right.

a) $3 \times 4 \div 2$
$= 12 \div 2$
$= 6$

b) $6 \div 3 \times 2$

c) $7 \times 3 \times 2$

d) $12 \div 3 \div 2$

When doing operations…

Step 1: Do all multiplications and divisions from left to right.

Step 2: Do all additions and subtractions from left to right.

3. Circle the operation you would do first.

a) $5 + (2 \times 3)$ (circled)
b) $9 - 2 + 5$
c) $10 + 5 \div 5$
d) $11 - 8 \div 2$
e) $12 \div 3 \times 2$
f) $10 - 3 \times 3$
g) $8 + 2 - 5$
h) $5 \times 5 - 6$
i) $18 \div 6 + 3$
j) $15 \div 5 - 2$
k) $2 \times 3 + 4$
l) $4 \times 6 \div 2$

4. Circle and do the first operation. Then rewrite the rest of the expression.

a) $(5 + 8) - 4$ (circled)
$=$ $13 - 4$

b) $5 + (6 \div 3)$ (circled)
$=$ $5 + 2$

c) $12 \div 4 + 2$
$=$ ____________

d) $18 \div 6 \times 3$
$=$ ____________

e) $10 - 5 - 3$
$=$ ____________

f) $2 \times 6 \div 3$
$=$ ____________

g) $16 \div 4 - 3$
$=$ ____________

h) $11 - 5 + 5$
$=$ ____________

i) $2 \times 30 \div 20$
$=$ ____________

j) $7 \times 4 - 3$
$=$ ____________

k) $36 \div 4 + 3$
$=$ ____________

l) $20 - 5 \times 3$
$=$ ____________

Brackets change the order of operations. Do the operations in brackets before all others.

Example: $7 - 3 + 2 = 4 + 2$ but $7 - (3 + 2) = 7 - 5$

$= 6$ $= 2$

5. Do the operation in brackets first. Then write the answer.

a) $(7 + 3) \times 2$

$= 10 \times 2$

$= 20$

b) $7 + (3 \times 2)$

c) $(7 + 3) \div 2$

d) $(7 - 3) \div 2$

e) $7 - (3 \times 2)$

f) $(7 - 3) \times 2$

g) $2 + (3 - 1)$

h) $8 - (6 \div 3)$

i) $4 \times (2 \times 3)$

j) $(4 \times 2) \times 3$

k) $(12 \div 6) \div 2$

l) $12 \div (6 \div 2)$

6. a) Add the same numbers in two ways. Do the addition in brackets first.

i) $(2 + 3) + 8$ $2 + (3 + 8)$

= ____ + 8 = 2 + ____

= ____ = ____

ii) $(5 + 2) + 4$ $5 + (2 + 4)$

= ____ + ____ = ____ + ____

= ____ = ____

b) Does the answer change depending on which addition you do first? ________

7. a) Subtract the same numbers in two ways. Do the subtraction in brackets first.

i) $(9 - 5) - 2$ $9 - (5 - 2)$

= ____ − ____ = ____ − ____

= ____ = ____

ii) $11 - (6 - 5)$ $(11 - 6) - 5$

= ____ − ____ = ____ − ____

= ____ = ____

b) Does the answer change depending on which subtraction you do first? ________

PA5-8 Numerical Expressions

A **numerical expression** is a combination of numbers, operation signs, and sometimes brackets that represents a quantity.

Example: These numerical expressions all represent 10.

$5 + 2 + 3$ $\quad$ $14 - 4$ $\quad$ $70 \div 7$ $\quad$ $(3 + 2) \times 2$

1. Calculate the numerical expression.

a) $2 + 5 + 1$ ______ $\quad$ b) 2×5 ______ $\quad$ c) $3 \times 2 \times 4$ ______

d) $(8 \times 3) \div 2$ ______ $\quad$ e) $(1 + 3) \times 4$ ______ $\quad$ f) $3 + (6 \div 2)$ ______

g) $(6 \times 3) \div 2$ ______ $\quad$ h) $(10 - 4) \div 2$ ______ $\quad$ i) $10 - (4 \div 2)$ ______

2. Write the number 3 in the box and then calculate the expression.

a) $\boxed{3} + 4 \longrightarrow$ _7_ $\quad$ b) $\boxed{3} + 2 \longrightarrow$ ____ $\quad$ c) $9 - \boxed{} \longrightarrow$ ____

d) $\boxed{} - 2 \longrightarrow$ ____ $\quad$ e) $\boxed{} \times 5 \longrightarrow$ ____ $\quad$ f) $18 \div \boxed{} \longrightarrow$ ____

An **equation** is a statement that has two equal expressions separated by an equal sign.

Examples: $14 - 4 = 70 \div 7$ $\quad$ $12 = 3 \times 4$

3. a) Circle two expressions in Question 1 that represent the same number.

b) Write an equation using the two expressions.

____________________ = ____________________

4. Verify that the equation is true.

a) $(4 + 3) \times 2 = (5 \times 3) - 1$

$(4 + 3) \times 2$ and $(5 \times 3) - 1$

$= 7 \times 2$ $\quad$ $= 15 - 1$

$= 14$ $\quad$ $= 14$

b) $2 \times 4 \times 5 = 4 \times 10$

$2 \times 4 \times 5$ and 4×10

c) $3 + 11 = (3 + 1) + (11 - 1)$

$3 + 11$ and $(3 + 1) + (11 - 1)$

d) $3 + 11 = (3 + 2) + (11 - 2)$

$3 + 11$ and $(3 + 2) + (11 - 2)$

PA5-9 Unknown Quantities and Equations

1. Some apples are inside a bag and some are outside the bag. The total number of apples is shown. Draw the missing apples in the bag.

a) 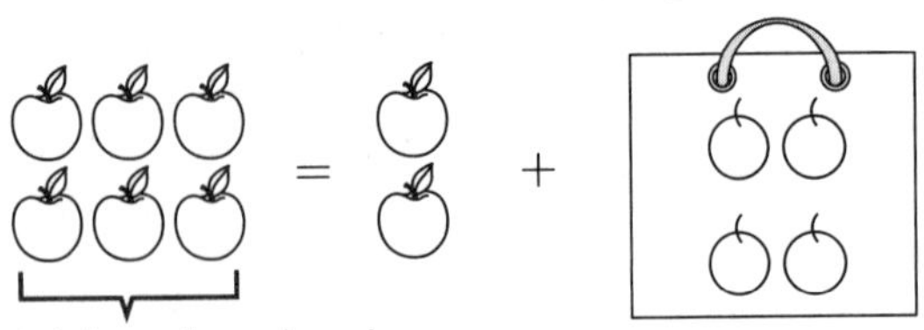
total number of apples

b) 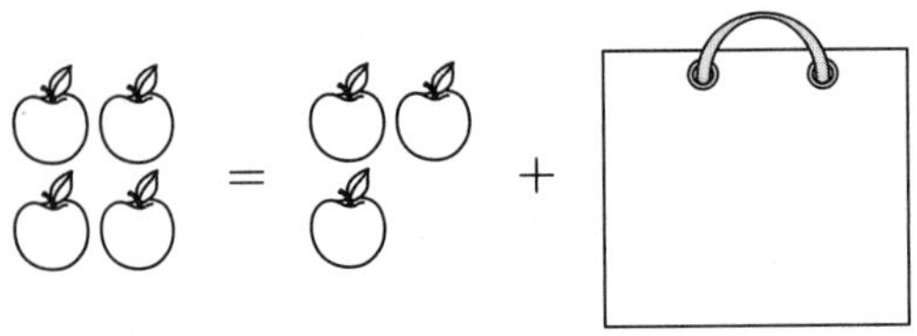

c) 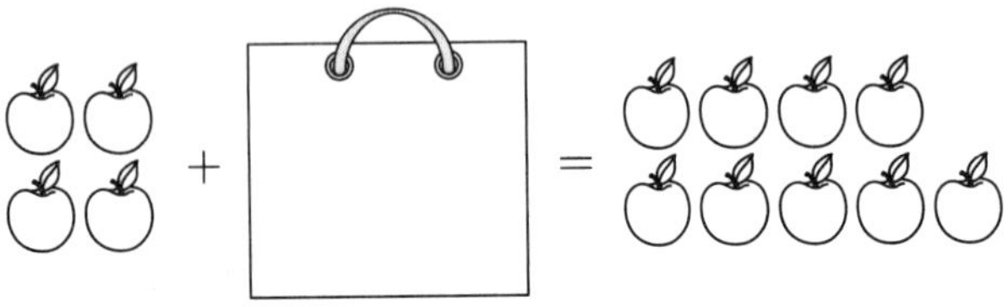

d) 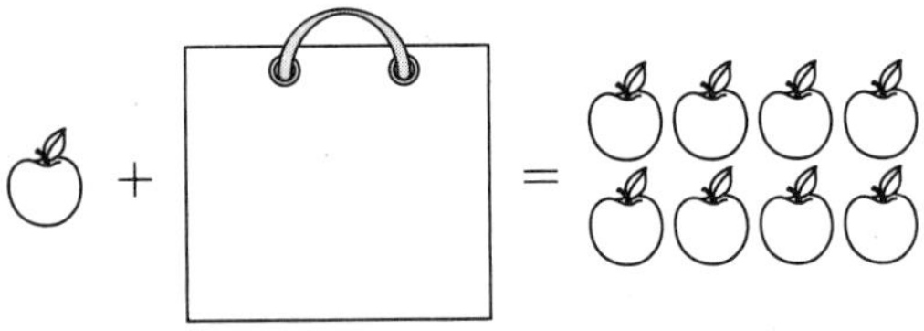

2. Draw the missing apples in the bag. Then write an equation (with numbers) to represent the picture.

a) 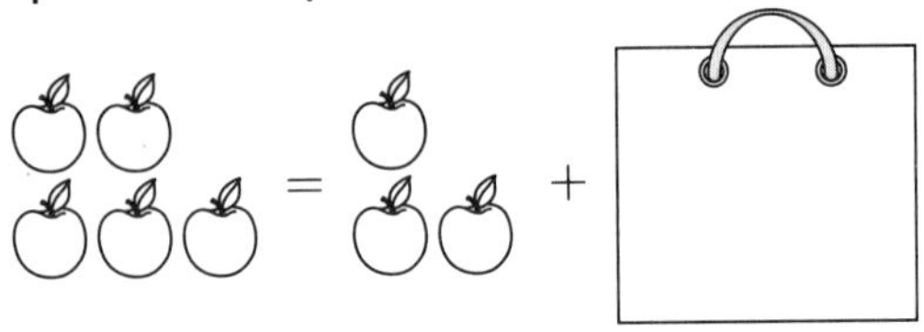

5 = 3 + □

b) 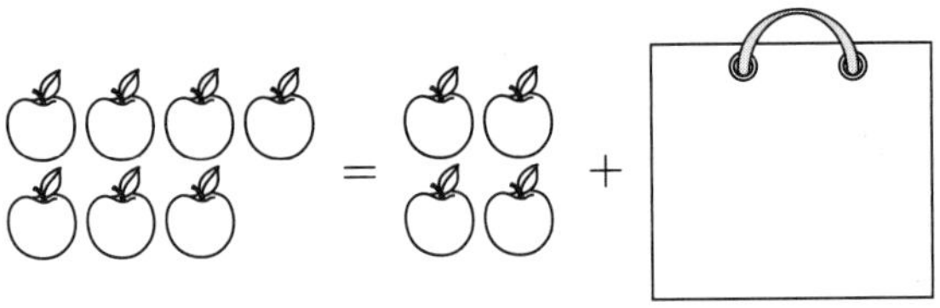

____ = ____ + □

c) 

____ + □ = ____

d) 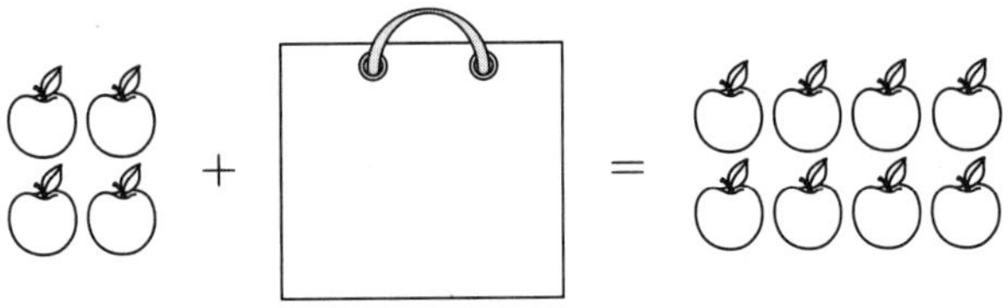

____ + □ = ____

3. Write an equation for each problem. Use a box for the unknown quantity.

a) There are 7 apples altogether. There are 4 outside a basket. How many are inside?

7 = 4 + □

b) There are 9 apples altogether. There are 7 outside a basket. How many are inside?

____ = ____ + □

c) There are 11 plums altogether. There are 5 inside a bag. How many are outside?

d) 17 students are at the library. There are 9 in the computer room. How many are outside the computer room?

4. Jun took some apples from a bag. Show how many apples were in the bag originally.

a) 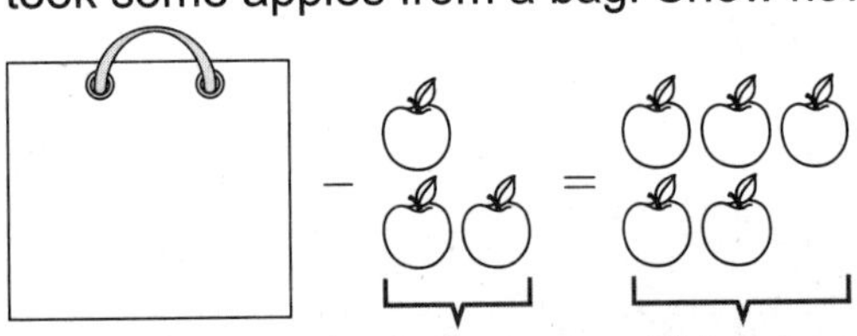
Jun took away this many.
This is how many were left.

b) 

5. Show how many apples were in the bag originally. Then write an equation to represent the picture.

a)

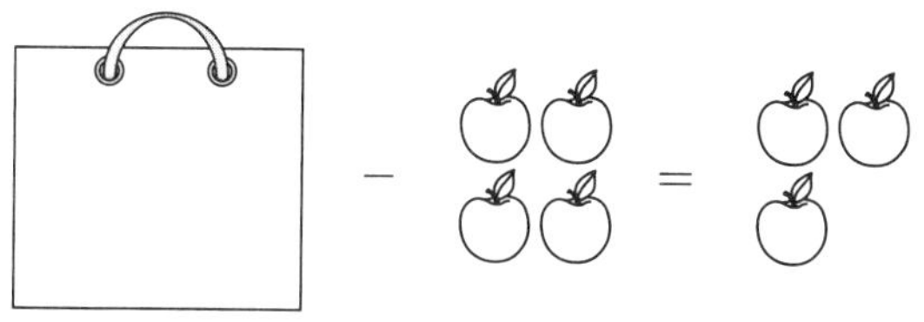

☐ − 4 = 3

b)

☐ − 2 = 5

6. Find the number that makes the equation true and write it in the box.

a) [6] + 3 = 9

b) ☐ + 4 = 9

c) ☐ + 5 = 9

d) 8 − ☐ = 5

e) 13 − ☐ = 11

f) 19 − ☐ = 8

g) 3 + 6 = 5 + ☐

h) 10 − 3 = ☐ + 4

i) 1 + 5 = 7 − ☐

7. Draw the same number of apples in each box. Write the equation for the picture.

a)

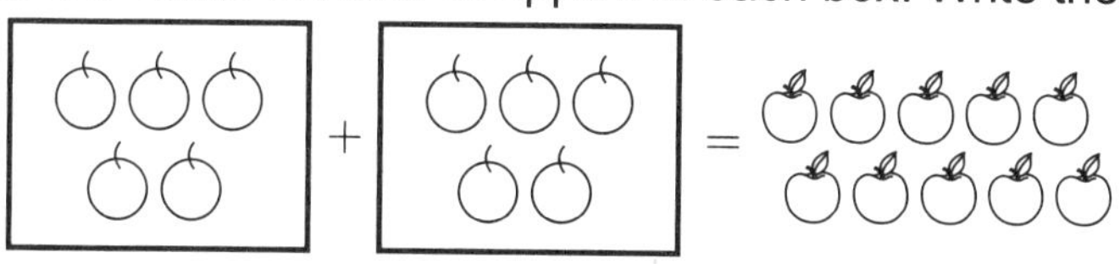

☐ + ☐ = 10

b)

☐ + ☐ + ☐ =

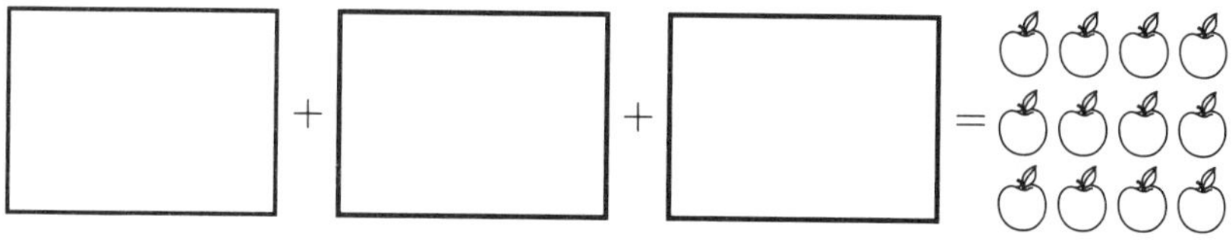

8. Draw a picture for the equation. Use your picture to solve the equation.

a)

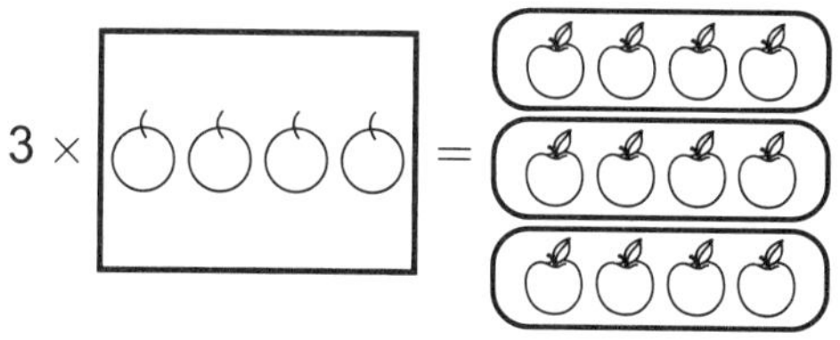

3 × ☐ =

3 × [4] = 12

b)

2 × ☐ =

2 × ☐ = 10

c)

3 × ☐ =

3 × ☐ = 18

d)

☐ × 6 =

☐ × 6 = 24

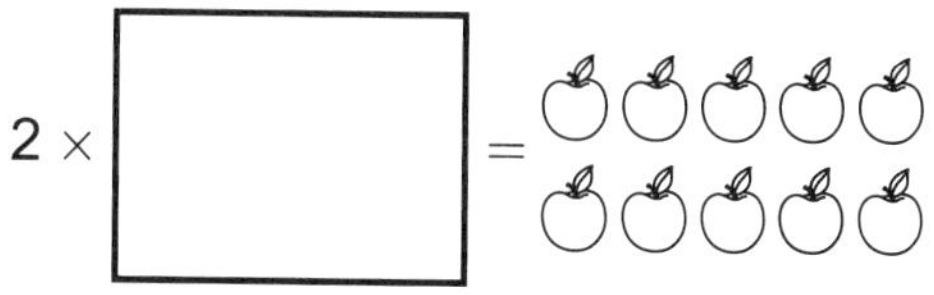

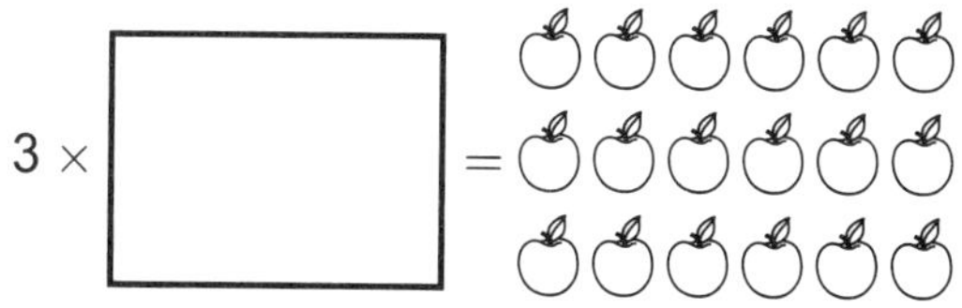

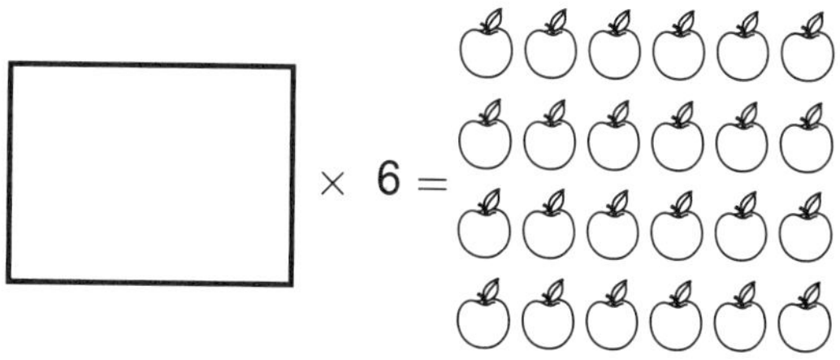

9. How many apples should be in the box? Write the number.

a) $2 \times$ [3] = 

b) $2 \times$ □ = 

c) □ $\times 3 =$ 

d) □ $\times 4 =$ 

e) $3 \times$  = □

f) $3 \times$  = □

g) $8 \times$  = □

h) $7 \times$  = □

BONUS ▶ There are 13 apples in the bag. What number goes in the box?

$4 \times$ () = □

Use circles instead of apples to make your drawing simpler.

10. Draw a picture of each equation. Then solve the equation using your picture.

a) $3 \times 4 =$ □

b) $3 \times$ □ $= 18$

11. Solve the equation by guessing and checking.

a) $6 \times$ □ $= 30$

b) □ $\times 2 = 18$

c) $2 \times$ □ $= 24$

d) □ $\times 7 = 42$

e) $24 \div$ □ $= 6$

f) □ $\div 5 = 6$

g) $5 \times 4 =$ □ $\times 10$

h) $12 \times 3 = 9 \times$ □

12. Solve the equation by writing the unknown by itself.

a) $3 \times$ □ $= 18$

b) □ $\times 7 = 28$

c) □ $\div 4 = 5$

d) $12 \div$ □ $= 6$

e) □ $\times 8 = 32$

f) □ $\div 5 = 7$

g) $24 \div$ □ $= 4$

h) $30 \div$ □ $= 2$

PA5-10 Translating Words into Expressions

1. Match the description with the correct numerical expression.

a)		b)	
2 more than 6	4×6	2 divided into 11	3×11
6 divided by 3	$6 - 2$	11 reduced by 4	$11 \div 2$
2 less than 6	$6 + 2$	11 times 3	$11 + 3$
the product of 6 and 4	$6 - 3$	twice as many as 11	$11 - 4$
6 decreased by 3	$6 \div 3$	11 increased by 3	2×11

2. Write an expression for each description.

a) 4 more than 3 *$3 + 4$*

b) 15 decreased by 8 ____________

c) 24 divided by 8 ____________

d) 2 less than 9 *$9 - 2$*

e) 67 increased by 29 ____________

f) 35 added to 4 ____________

g) twice as many as 5 ____________

h) 15 divided by 5 ____________

i) the product of 7 and 4 ____________

j) 5 times 8 ____________

3. Turn the written instructions into mathematical expressions.

a) Add 8 and 3. *$8 + 3$*

b) Divide 6 by 2. ____________

c) Add 34 and 9. ____________

d) Subtract 5 from 7. ____________

e) Multiply 42 and 2. ____________

f) Decrease 3 by 2. ____________

g) Add 8 and 4. Then divide by 3. ____________________________

h) Divide 8 by 4. Then add 5. ____________________________

i) Divide 4 by 2. Then add 10. Then subtract 4. ____________________________

j) Multiply 6 and 5. Then subtract 20. Then divide by 2. ____________________________

4. Write the mathematical expressions in words.

a) $(6 + 2) \times 3$ *Add 6 and 2. Then multiply by 3.*

b) $(6 + 1) \times 2$ ____________________________

c) $(12 - 5) \times 2$ ____________________________

d) $(3 - 2) \times 4$ ____________________________

BONUS ▶

$4 \times (3 - 1 + 5)$ ____________________________

5. How far will a motorcycle travel at the speed and in the time given? Write the numerical expression.

a) Speed: 60 km per hour
Time: 2 hours

Distance: 60×2 km

b) Speed: 80 km per hour
Time: 4 hours

Distance: ____________ km

c) Speed: 70 km per hour
Time: 5 hours

Distance: ____________ km

6. a) Look at the sign below, then write a numerical expression for the cost of renting a bike for …

i) 1 hour: 5×1 ii) 2 hours: ____________ iii) 4 hours: ____________

b) Complete the description of the expression.

i) 5×3 is the cost of renting a bike for 3 hours.

ii) 5×2 is the cost of renting a bike for ____ hours.

iii) 5×5 is the cost of renting a bike for ____ hours.

7. a) A different rental company charges $3 for each hour. Write the numerical expression for the cost of renting a bike for …

i) 1 hour: 3×1 ii) 2 hours: ____________ iii) 4 hours: ____________

b) Complete the description of the expression.

i) 3×3 is the cost of renting a bike for 3 hours.

ii) 3×2 is the cost of renting a bike for ____ hours.

iii) 3×5 is the cost of renting a bike for ____ hours.

8. A field trip for a Grade 5 class costs $11 per student plus $2 for a snack.

a) Write an expression to represent the cost for 1 student and 1 snack. ____________

b) Write an expression to represent the cost for 3 students and 3 snacks. ____________

BONUS ▸ Write a word problem that could be represented by $19 \times (11 + 2)$.

9. A day pass can be used by 2 adults and 2 children for unlimited one-day bus travel on weekends. Write an expression to represent the number of day passes that are needed for 10 adults and 10 children. Hint: The number of adults and the number of children are the same.

BONUS ▸ 20 students from each class go to the museum. There are 5 classes, along with 13 teachers and 16 parents.

a) Write an expression to represent the number of people who go to the museum.

b) How many buses will be needed if 30 people ride in each bus?

Shapes and Area

Two pattern block squares cover this rectangle.
The squares are the same size.
There are no gaps or overlaps.
The **area** of the rectangle is 2 squares.

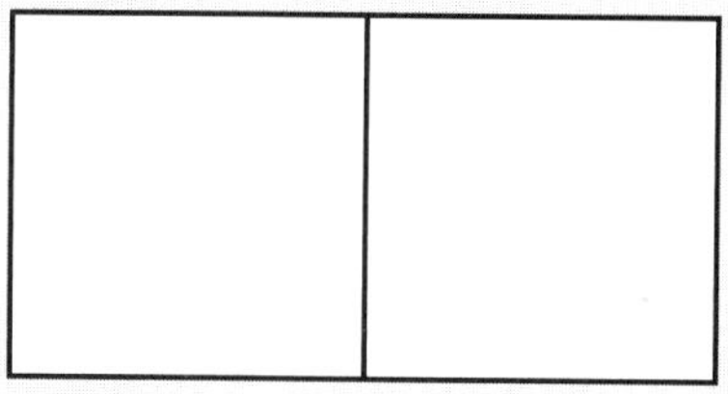

I. Bill measured the area of a book with squares. Write ✓ for what he did correctly. Write ✗ for what he did wrong.

a)

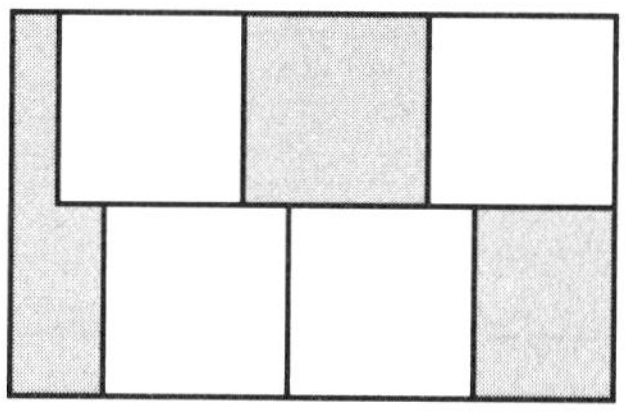

- [✓] The squares are the same size.
- [✗] The book is covered (no gaps).
- [✓] The squares do not overlap.
- [✗] The area is 4 squares.

b)

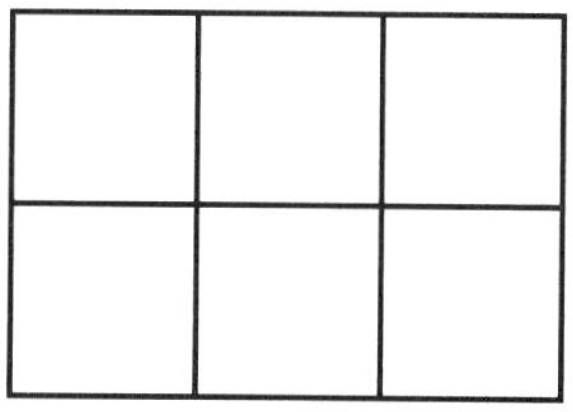

- [ ] The squares are the same size.
- [ ] The book is covered (no gaps).
- [ ] The squares do not overlap.
- [ ] The area is 6 squares.

c)

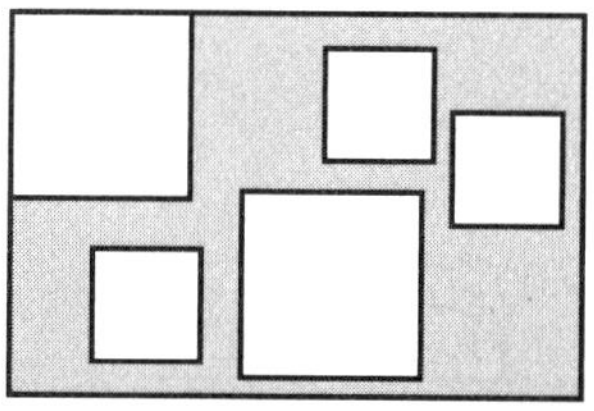

- [ ] The squares are the same size.
- [ ] The book is covered (no gaps).
- [ ] The squares do not overlap.
- [ ] The area is 5 squares.

d)

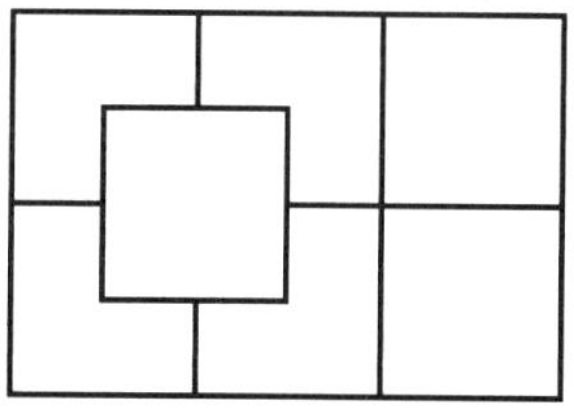

- [ ] The squares are the same size.
- [ ] The book is covered (no gaps).
- [ ] The squares do not overlap.
- [ ] The area is 7 squares.

A **square centimetre** is a square with sides 1 cm long.

We write **cm²** for short.

You can measure area in square centimetres.

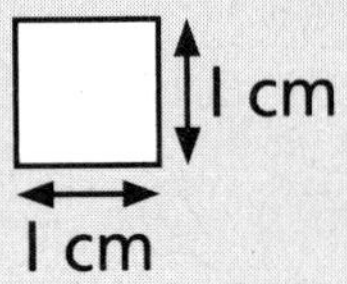

2. Find the area in square centimetres.

a) 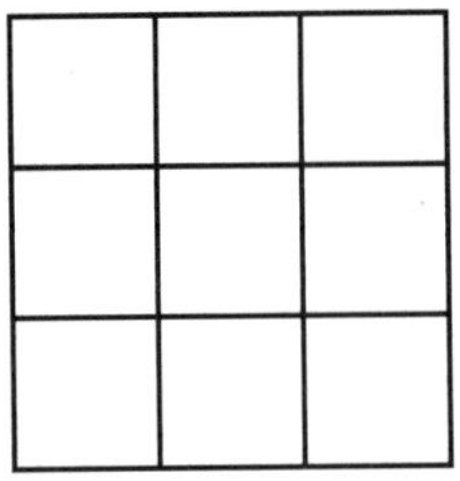

Area = ________ cm^2

b) 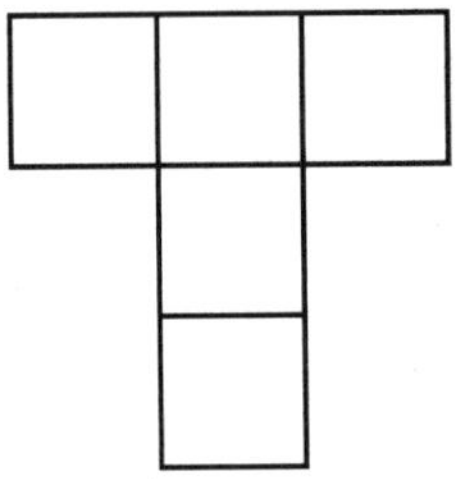

Area = ________ cm^2

c) 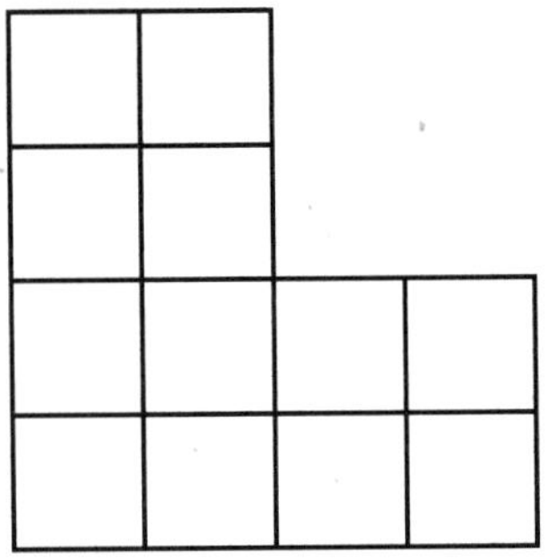

Area = ________ cm^2

d) 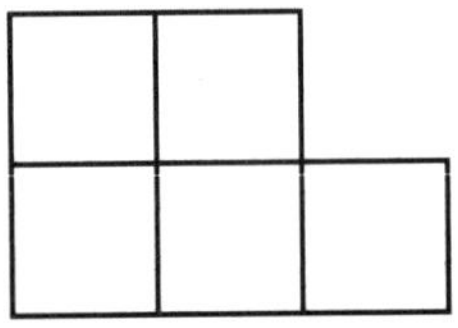

Area = ________ cm^2

e) 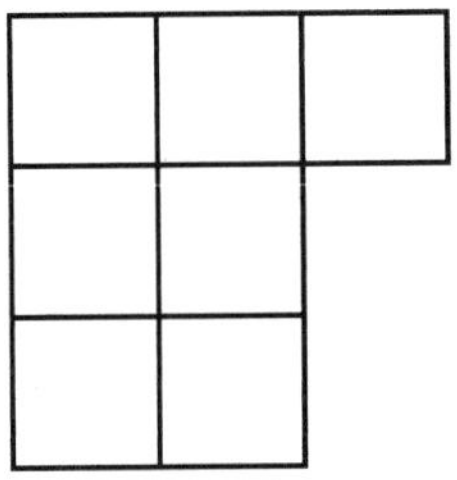

Area = ________ cm^2

f) 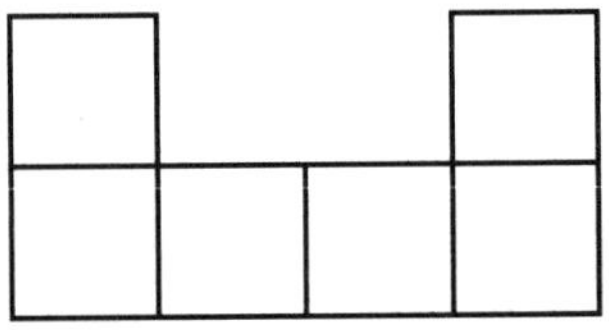

Area = ________ cm^2

3. Use a ruler to join the marks and divide the rectangle into square centimetres. Then find the area in cm^2.

a) 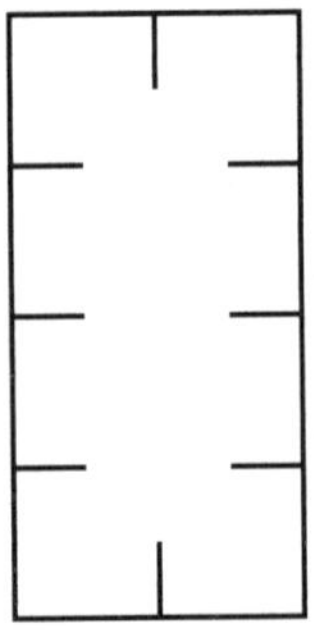

Area = ________ cm^2

b) 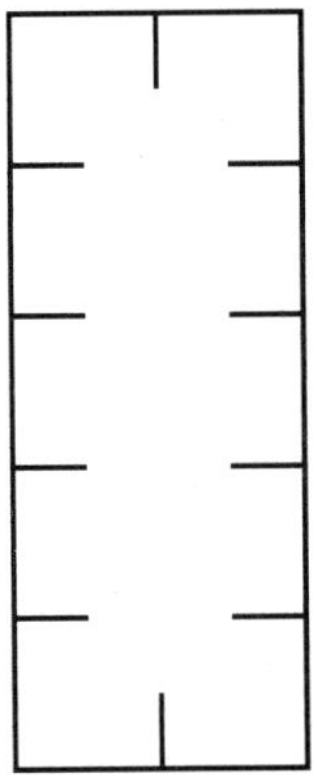

Area = ________ cm^2

c) 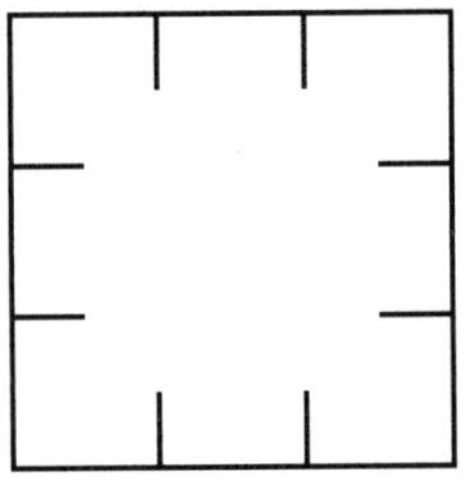

Area = ________ cm^2

4. The small squares on the grid are each 1 cm^2. Find the areas in square units.

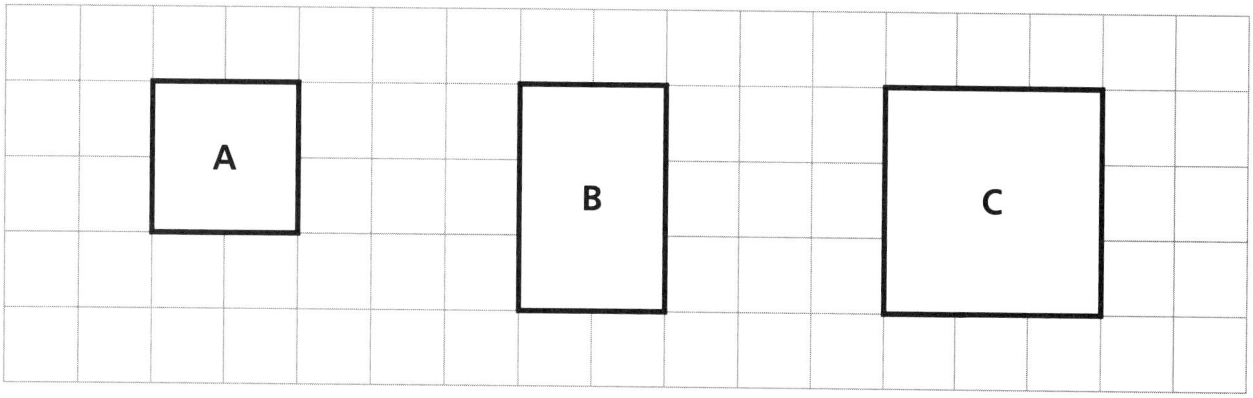

Area of A = ______ cm^2 Area of B = ______ cm^2 Area of C = ______ cm^2

5. Draw 3 shapes on the grid lines. Find the area of each shape.

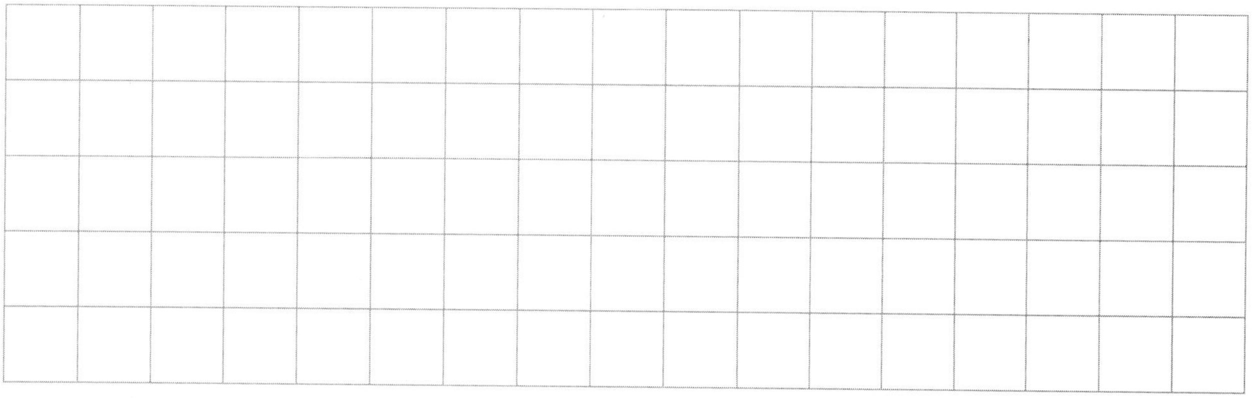

6. a) Draw 3 different shapes on the grid lines, each with an area of 6 cm^2.

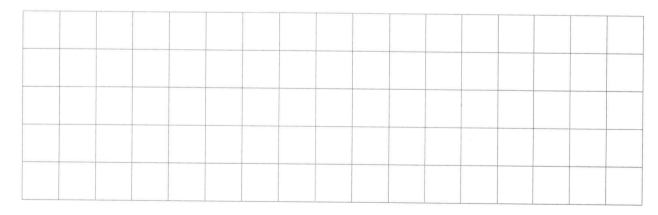

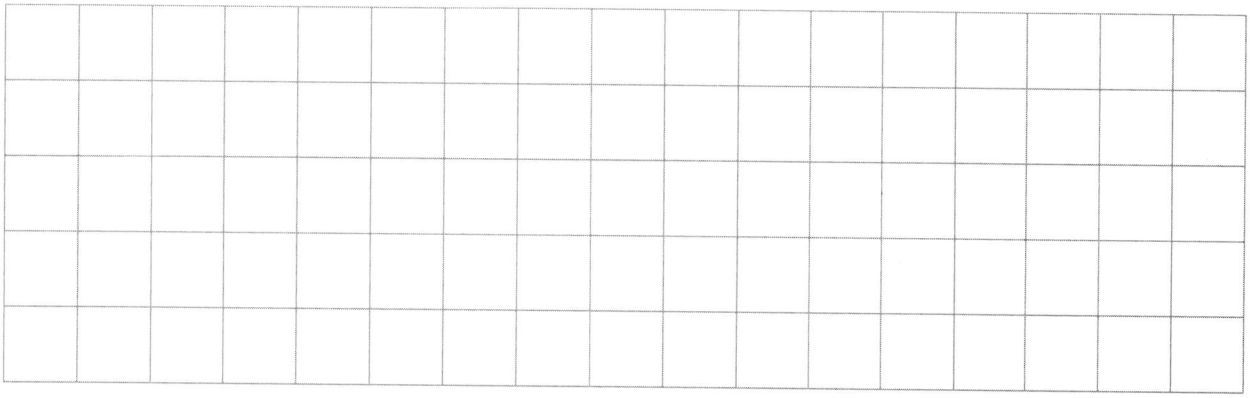

b) Do 2 polygons need to be the same size and shape to have the same area? Explain.

ME4-13 Area in Square Centimetres

The **area** of a flat shape is the amount of space it takes up.

A **square centimetre** (cm^2) is a unit for measuring area.

A square with sides 1 cm has an area of 1 cm^2.

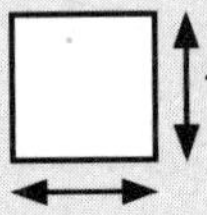

1 cm = **1 cm^2**

1 cm

1. Find the area of the figure in square centimetres.

a) 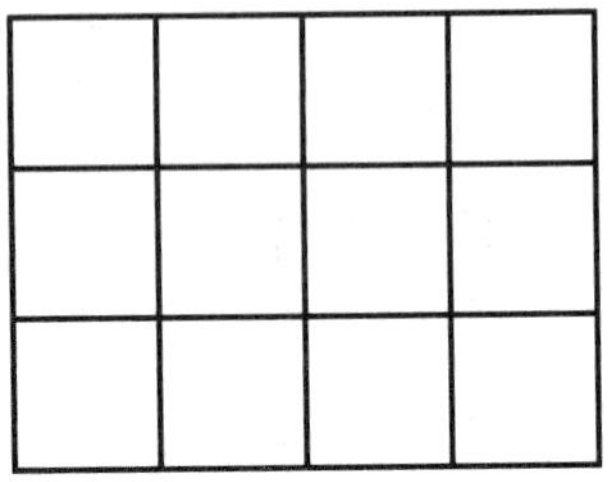

Area = ________ cm^2

b) 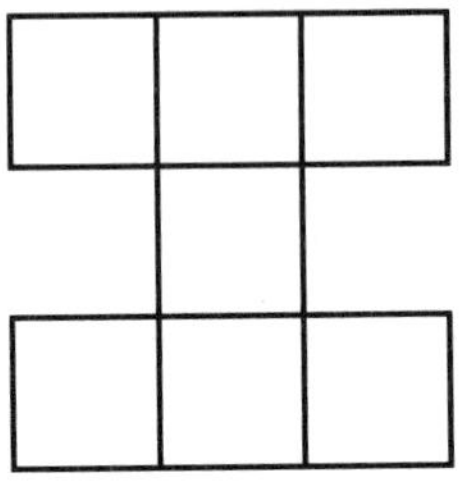

Area = ________ cm^2

c) 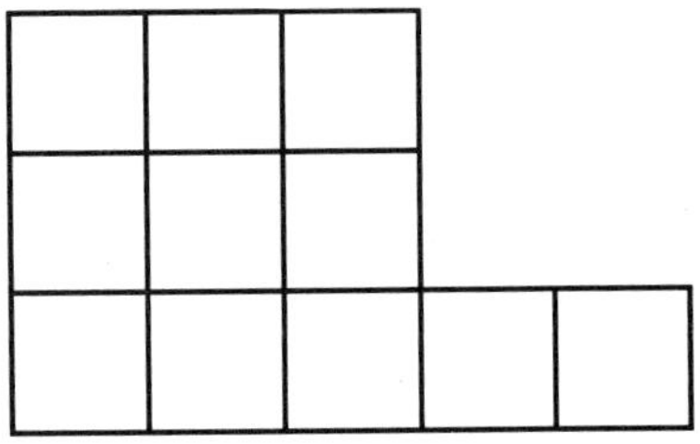

Area = ________ cm^2

2. Using a ruler, draw lines to join the marks and divide the rectangle into square centimetres.

a) 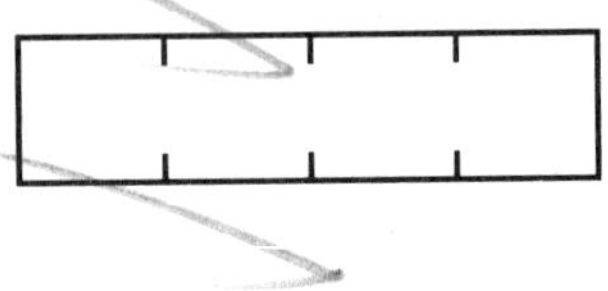

Area = ________ cm^2

b) 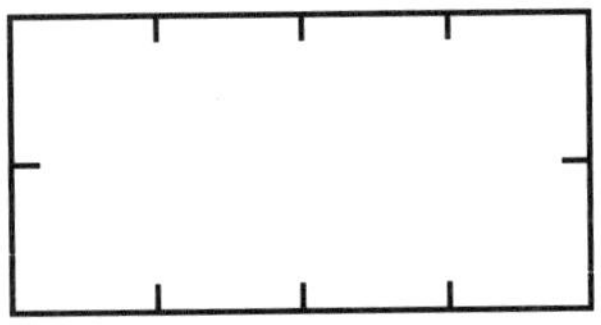

Area = ________ cm^2

c) 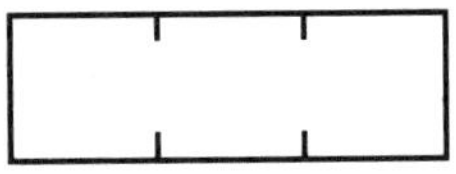

Area = ________ cm^2

3. Find the area of the rectangles in square centimetres.

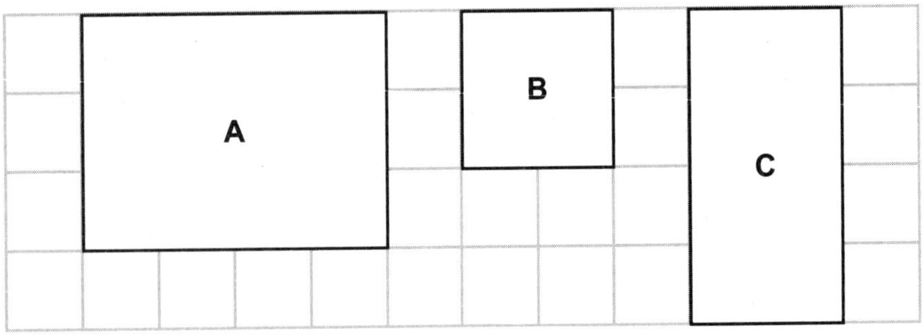

Area of A = ________ cm^2 Area of B = ________ cm^2 Area of C = ________ cm^2

4. Use 1 cm grid paper.

a) Draw two different rectangles with an area of 8 cm^2.

b) Draw two figures that are not rectangles with an area of 8 cm^2.

c) Draw several shapes and find their area.

d) Draw three different rectangles with an area of 12 cm^2.

ME4-14 Area in Square Metres

A **square metre** (m^2) is a unit for measuring area.

A square with sides 1 m has an area of 1 m^2.

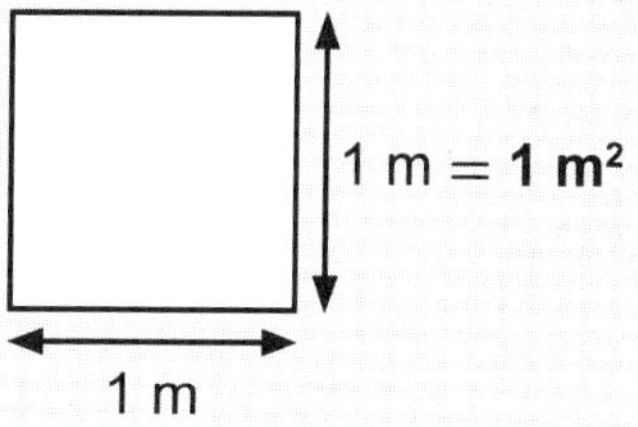

Four unfolded pages from a newspaper are about 1 m^2.

1. Shelly measured the areas of objects at school, but she forgot to write down the units. Fill in the blank with "m^2" or "cm^2."

a) The wall measures 8 ______.

b) The book cover measures 375 ______.

c) The sticky note measures 15 ______.

d) The parking lot measures 475 ______.

2. Choose a unit of measure for the area. Estimate and then measure the area of the object.

	Object	Unit	Estimate	Actual Area
a)	blackboard			
b)	JUMP Math AP Book			
c)	hallway			
d)	desk			
e)	light switch			

3. Ethan says that since there are 100 cm in 1 m, there must be 100 cm^2 in 1 m^2. Is he correct? Explain.

____

____

____

BONUS ▶ Why might someone measure a large area in cm^2?

____

____

____

ME4-15 Area of Rectangles

1. Write a multiplication statement for the array.

a) 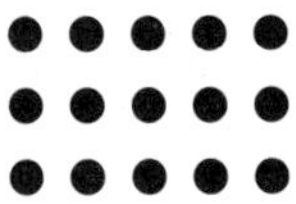 ______

b) 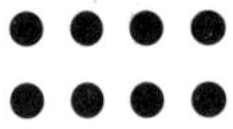 ______

c) 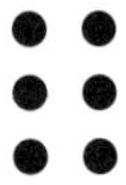 ______

d) 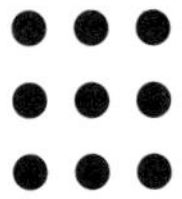 ______

2. Draw a dot in each box. Then write a multiplication statement that tells you the number of boxes in the rectangle.

a) 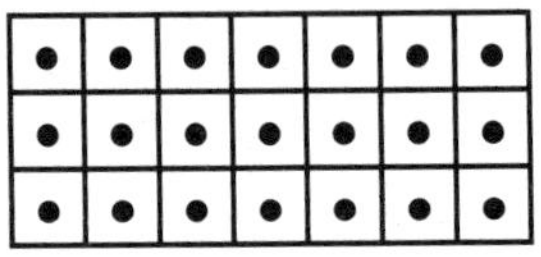 $3 \times 7 = 21$

b) 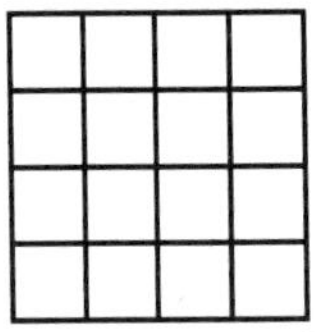 ______

c) 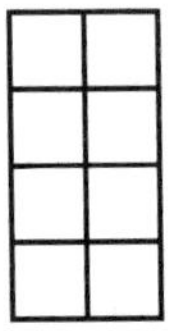 ______

d) 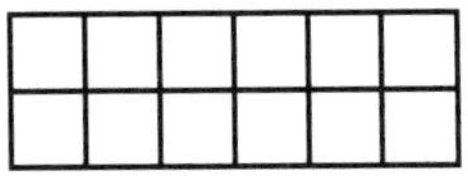 ______

3. Write the number of boxes along the length and the width of the rectangle.
Then write a multiplication equation for the area of the rectangle (in square units).

a) 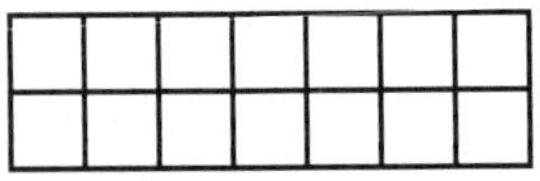 Width = ____

Length = ____

______

b) 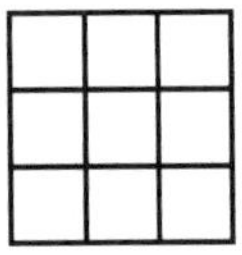 Width = ____

Length = ____

______

c) 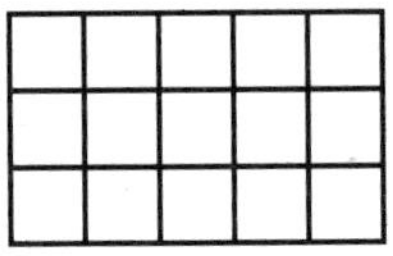 Width = ____

Length = ____

______

4. Using a ruler, draw lines to join the marks and divide the rectangle into square centimetres.
Write a multiplication equation for the area of the rectangle in square centimetres.

a) 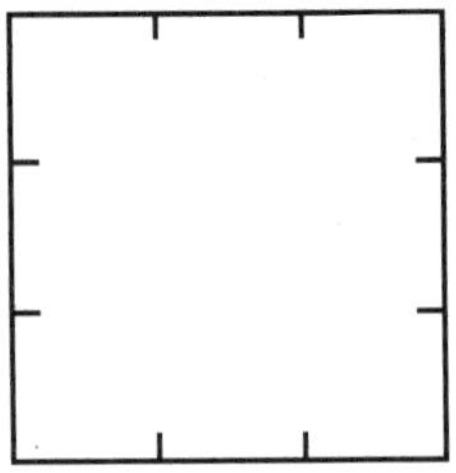

Area = ______

b) 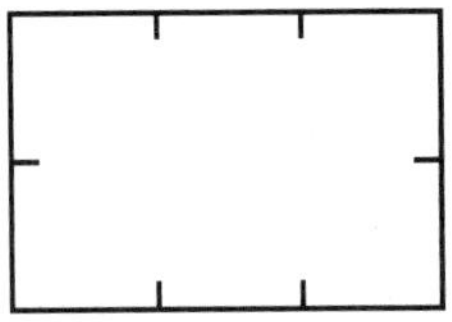

Area = ______

c) 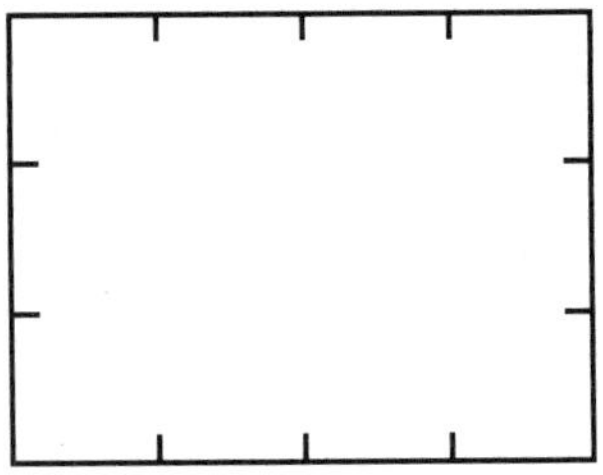

Area = ______

5. How can you find the area of a rectangle from its length and width?

______

______

6. Measure the length and width of the rectangle. Find the area. Include the units!

a) b) c)

__________ __________ __________

7. Area is also measured in other square units. Predict the name of the unit.

a) b) c)

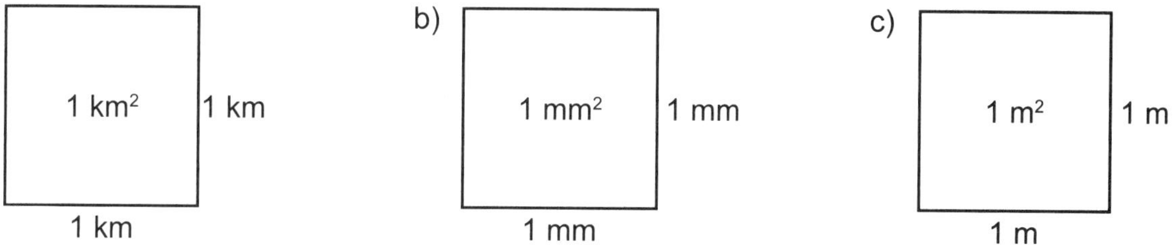

a) *square kilometre* b) __________ c) __________

8. a) Calculate the area of each rectangle (include the units).

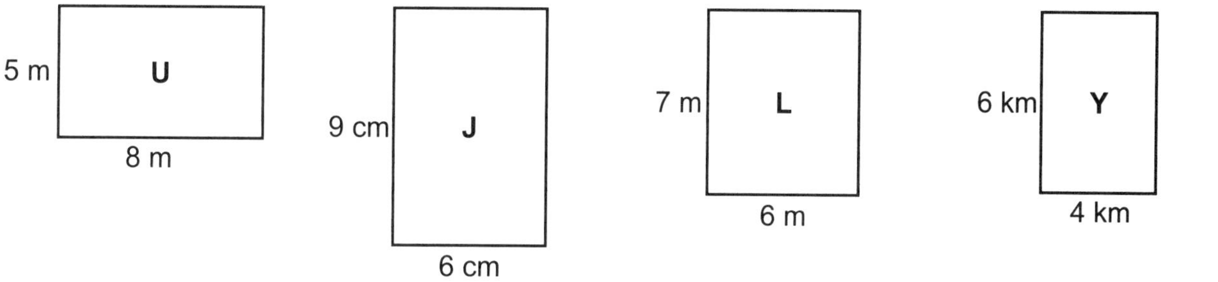

Area = ________ Area = ________ Area = ________ Area = ________

b) List the rectangles from least area to greatest area: ____, ____, ____, ____

What does it spell? __________

9. Find the area of the rectangle using the length and the width. Include the units!

a) Length = 7 m Width = 5 m

Area = *35 m²*

b) Length = 9 m Width = 2 m

Area = ________

c) Length = 8 cm Width = 6 cm

Area = ________

d) Length = 7 cm

Width = 11 cm

Area = ________

e) Length = 9 m

Width = 12 m

Area = ________

f) Length = 12 cm

Width = 3 cm

Area = ________

ME4-16 More Area

1. a) Calculate the area of each figure. Each square represents 1 square centimetre.

i)

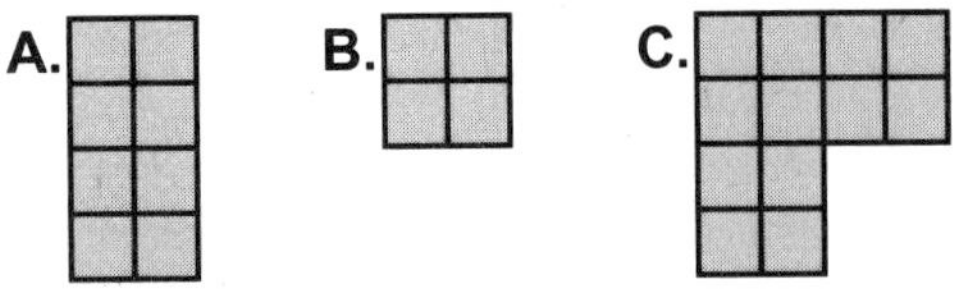

Area of A = ________

Area of B = ________

Area of C = ________

ii)

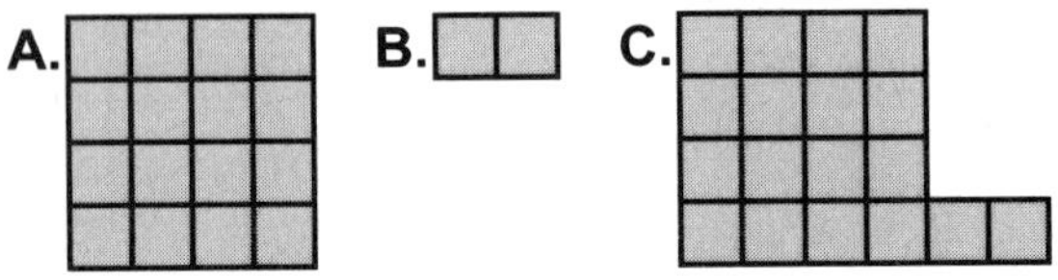

Area of A = ________

Area of B = ________

Area of C = ________

iii)

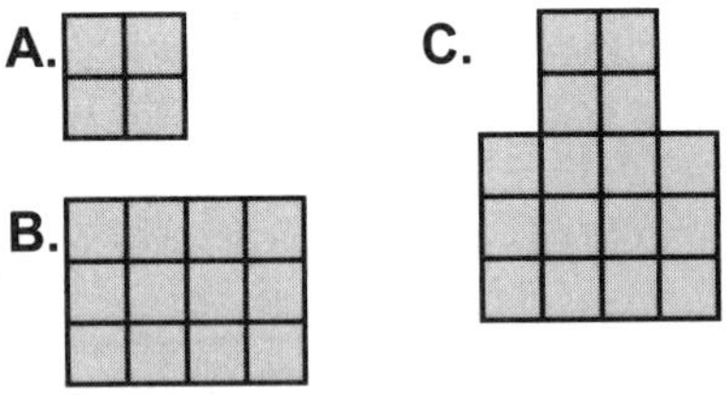

Area of A = ________

Area of B = ________

Area of C = ________

iv)

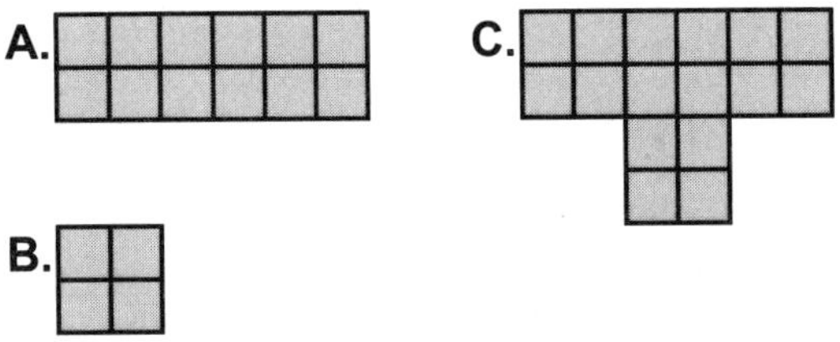

Area of A = ________

Area of B = ________

Area of C = ________

b) Draw a line to show how shape C can be divided into rectangles A and B in part a).

c) How can you get the area of shape C from the areas of rectangles A and B? Write an equation.

Area of C = ____

2. Draw a line to divide the figure into two rectangles. Use the areas of the rectangles to find the total area of the figure.

a)

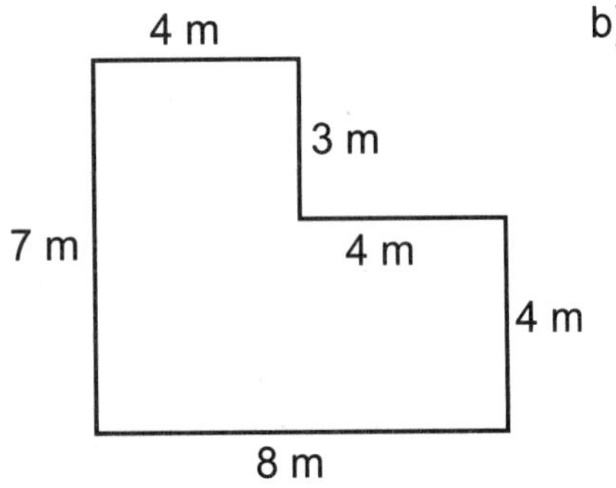

Area of rectangle 1 = ______

Area of rectangle 2 = ______

Total area = ________

b)

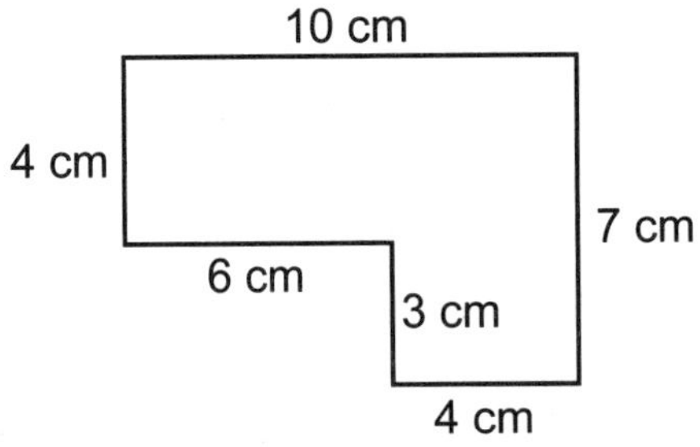

Area of rectangle 1 = ______

Area of rectangle 2 = ______

Total area = ________

c)

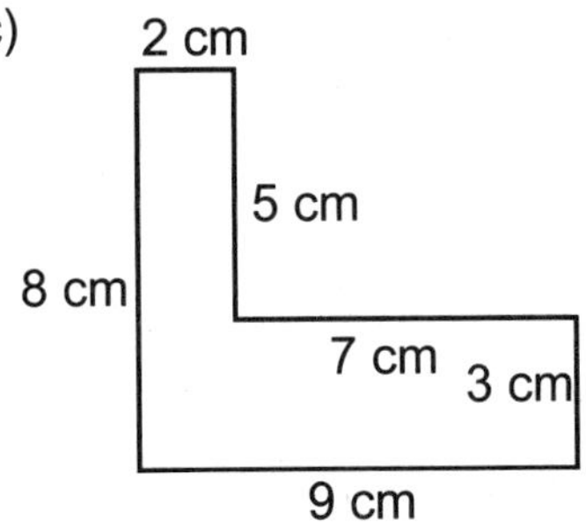

Area of rectangle 1 = ______

Area of rectangle 2 = ______

Total area = ________

3. a) A building is 8 storeys high. The wing is 5 storeys high. How many storeys high is the tower?

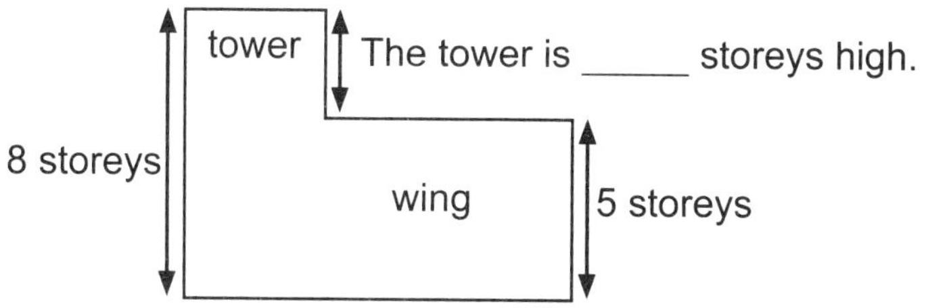

b) The tower of a building is 10 m wide. The base is 50 m wide. How wide is the wing?

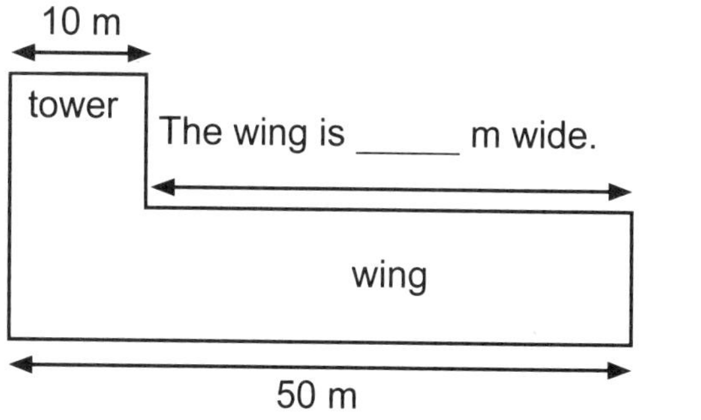

4. Find the missing side lengths. Divide the figure into two rectangles and find their areas. Then find the total area of the figure.

a)

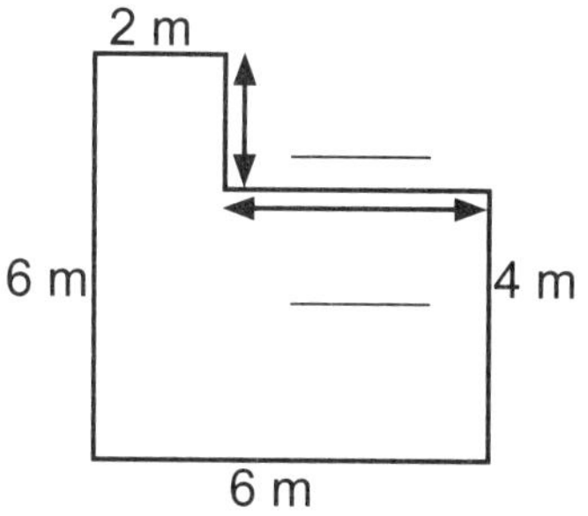

Area of rectangle 1 = ________

Area of rectangle 2 = ________

Total area = ________

b)

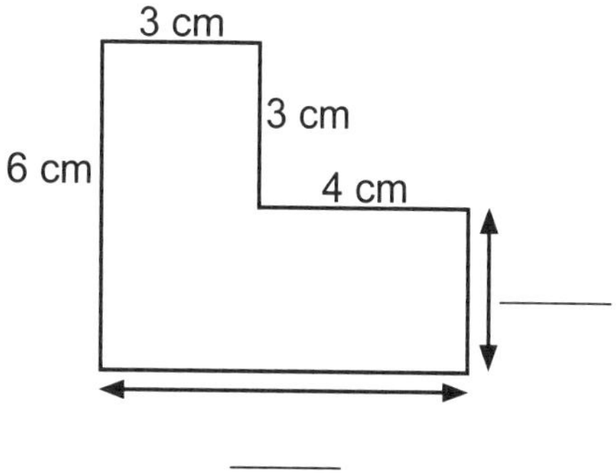

Area of rectangle 1 = ________

Area of rectangle 2 = ________

Total area = ________

5. Find the length of the rectangle.

a) Width = 2 cm Perimeter = 12 cm

Length = ________

b) Width = 4 cm Perimeter = 14 cm

Length = ________

6. Find the area of the rectangle using the clues.
Hint: First find the length of the rectangle.

a) Width = 2 cm Perimeter = 10 cm

Area = ________

b) Width = 4 cm Perimeter = 18 cm

Area = ________

7. On grid paper, draw a **square** with the given perimeter. Then find the area of the square.

a) Perimeter = 12 cm Area = ________

b) Perimeter = 20 cm Area = ________

ME5-15 Area and Perimeter of Rectangles

1. Write a multiplication statement for the array.

a) 

______

b) 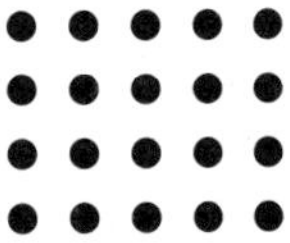

______

c) 

______

d) 

______

2. Draw a dot in each box. Then write a multiplication statement that tells you the number of boxes in the rectangle.

a) 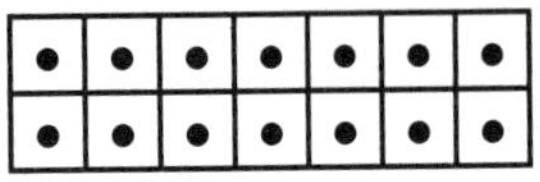

2 × 7 = 14

b) 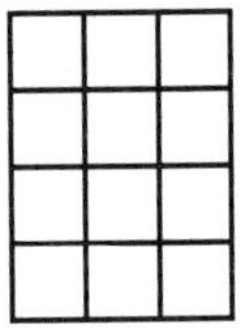

______

c) 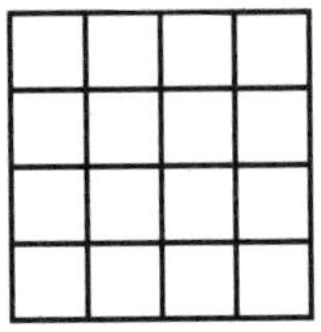

______

d) 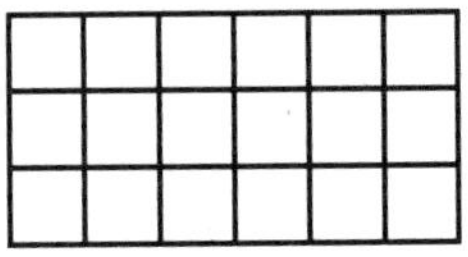

______

3. Write the number of boxes along the length and the width of the rectangle. Then write a multiplication equation for the area of the rectangle (in square units).

a) 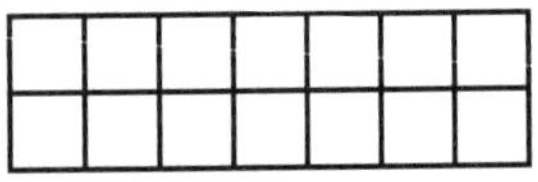

Width = ______

Length = ______

______

b) 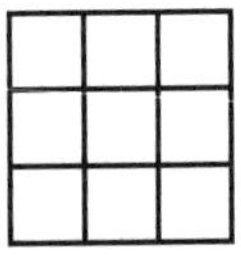

Width = ______

Length = ______

______

c) 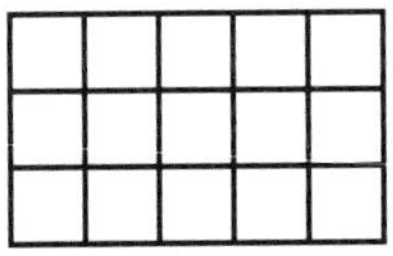

Width = ______

Length = ______

______

4. Using a ruler, draw lines to join the marks and divide the rectangle into square centimetres. Write a multiplication equation for the area of the rectangle in square centimetres.

a) 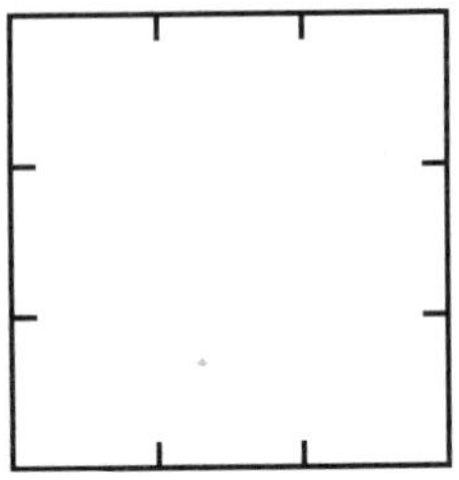

Area = ______

b) 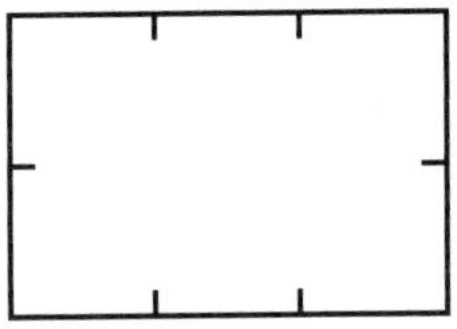

Area = ______

c) 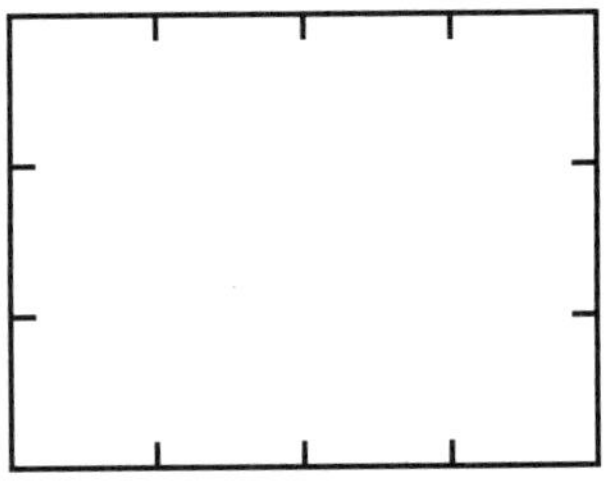

Area = ______

5. How can you find the area of a rectangle from its length and width?

______

______

6. Measure the length and width of the rectangle. Find the area. Include the units!

a) 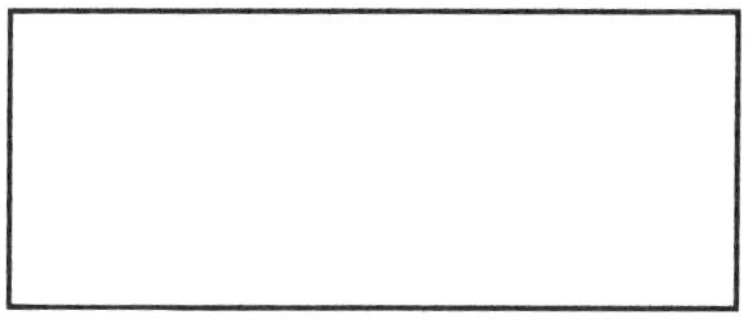

____

b) 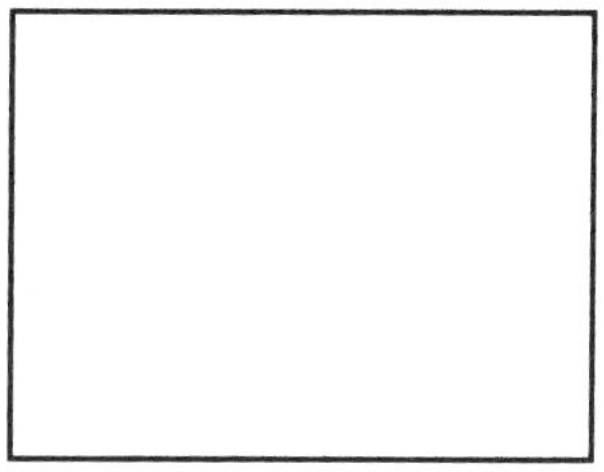

____

c) 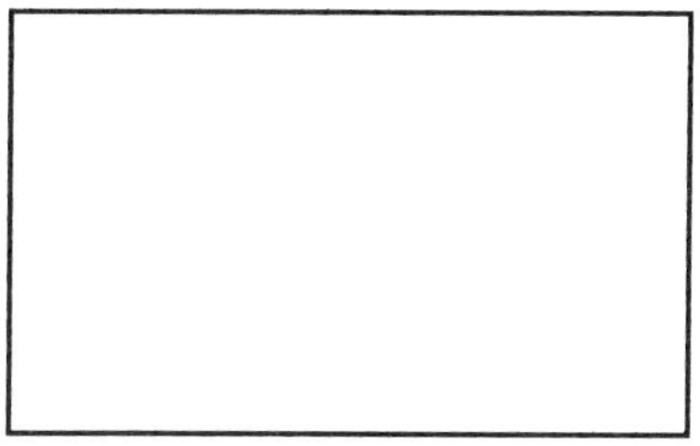

____

7. Area is also measured in other square units. Predict the name of the unit.

a) 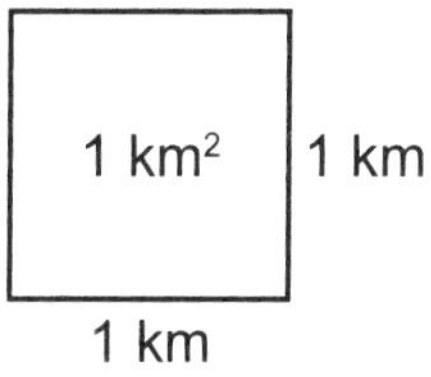

square kilometre

b) 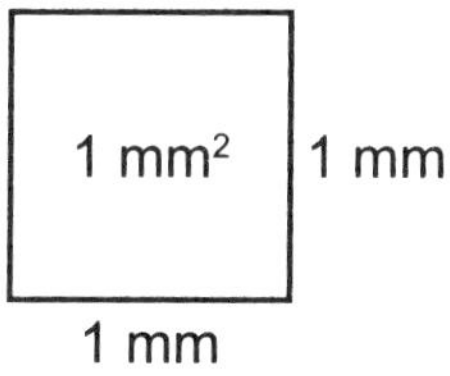

____

c) 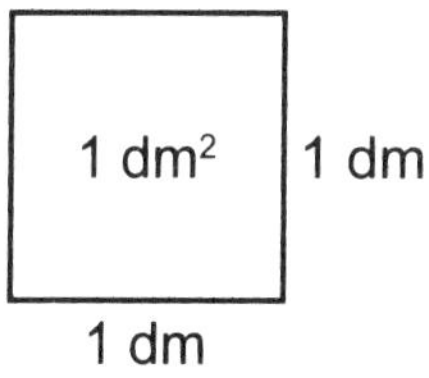

____

8. a) Calculate the area of each rectangle (include the units).

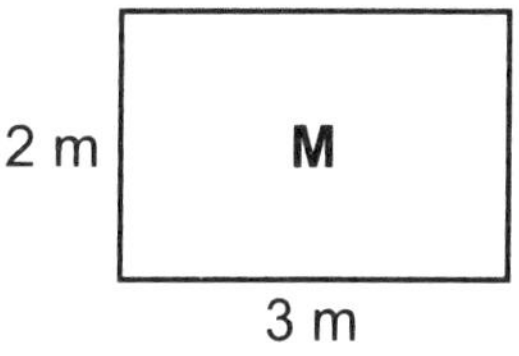

Area = __________

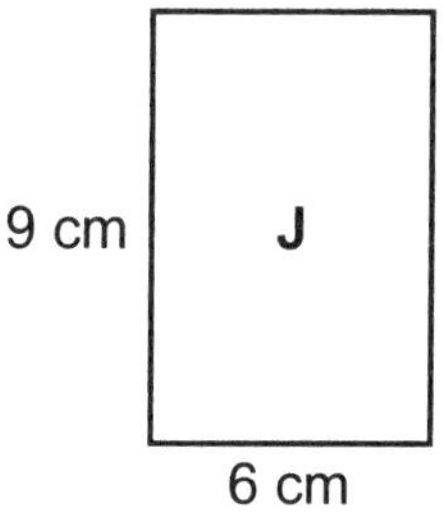

Area = __________

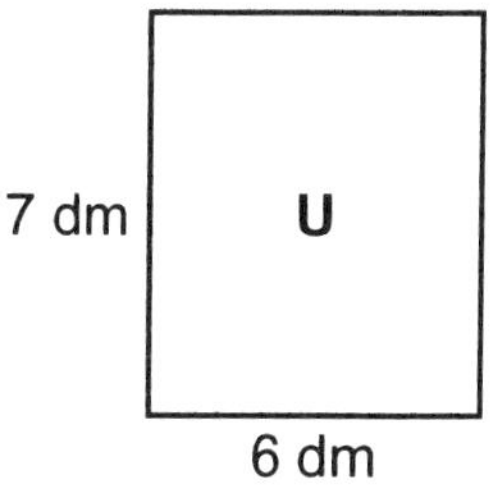

Area = __________

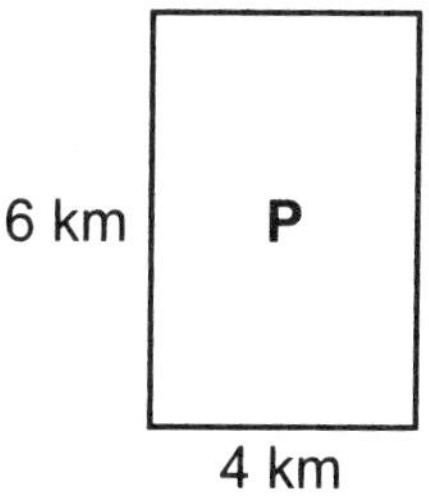

Area = __________

b) List the rectangles from least area to greatest area: ______, ______, ______, ______

What does it spell? ____________________

9. Find the area of the rectangle using the length and the width. Include the units!

a) Length = 7 m
Width = 5 m

Area = *7 m × 5 m*

= *35 m^2*

b) Length = 9 m
Width = 2 m

Area = ________________

= __________

c) Length = 8 cm
Width = 6 cm

Area = ________________

= __________

d) Length = 7 dm
Width = 11 dm

Area = ________________

= __________

e) Length = 9 mm
Width = 12 mm

Area = ________________

= __________

f) Length = 12 km
Width = 3 km

Area = ________________

= __________

10. a) The edge of each grid square represents 1 cm. For each shape, calculate the perimeter and area and write your answers in the chart below.

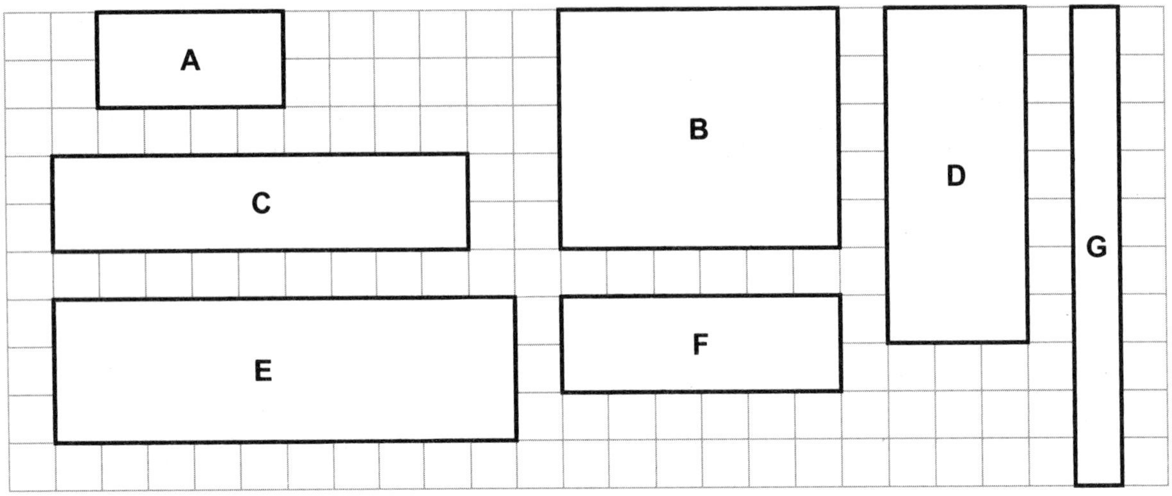

Shape	Perimeter	Area
A	$2 + 4 + 2 + 4 = 12$ cm	$2 \times 4 = 8$ cm^2
B		
C		
D		
E		
F		
G		

b) Shape C has a greater perimeter than shape D. Does it also have a greater area? ________

c) Name two other shapes where one has a greater perimeter and the other a greater area: ________

d) Write the shapes in order from greatest to least perimeter: ____________________

e) Write the shapes in order from greatest to least area: ____________________

f) Are the orders in parts d) and e) the same? ________

g) What is similar about **perimeter** and **area**? What is different?

11. Ethan's lawn is 6 m wide and 9 m long.

a) Find the area of Ethan's lawn.

b) Pieces of sod are sold in 1 m by 2 m rectangular shapes. How many pieces of sod does Ethan need in order to cover the entire lawn?

c) Each 1 m by 2 m piece of sod costs $25. How much will it cost Ethan to cover the entire lawn with sod?

ME4-17 Problems with Area and Perimeter

Area of rectangle = length × width

1. Find the area of the rectangle.

a) Width = 3 m Length = 6 m

Area = ______ × ______

= ______

b) Width = 2 m Length = 9 m

Area = ______ × ______

= ______

c) Width = 6 cm Length = 8 cm

Area = ______ × ______

= ______

2. Write an equation for the area of the rectangle. Then find the unknown length.

a) Length = ℓ m

Width = 5 m

Area = 15 m^2

$\ell \times 5 = 15$

$\ell = 15 \div 5$

$= 3$

b) Length = ℓ m

Width = 2 m

Area = 12 m^2

____

____

____

c) Length = ℓ cm

Width = 6 cm

Area = 24 cm^2

____

____

____

3. Write an equation for the area of the rectangle. Then find the unknown width.

a) Length = 5 m

Width = w m

Area = 20 m^2

$5 \times w = 20$

$w = 20 \div 5$

$= 4$

b) Length = 7 m

Width = w m

Area = 21 m^2

____

____

____

c) Length = 10 cm

Width = w cm

Area = 40 cm^2

____

____

____

4. a) A rectangle has an area of 24 m^2 and a width of 3 m. What is its length?

b) A rectangle has an area of 10 cm^2 and a length of 5 cm. What is its width?

c) A square has an area of 9 cm^2. What is its width?

5. A rectangle with length 3 cm and width 4 cm has area 12 cm^2.

$$3 \times 4 = 12$$

↑ length ↑ width ↑ area

a) Find a different pair of numbers that multiply to equal 12.

b) Draw a rectangle with length and width equal to your numbers.

6. a) Measure the length and the width of each rectangle in centimetres. Find the perimeter and area of each rectangle. Write the answers in the table.

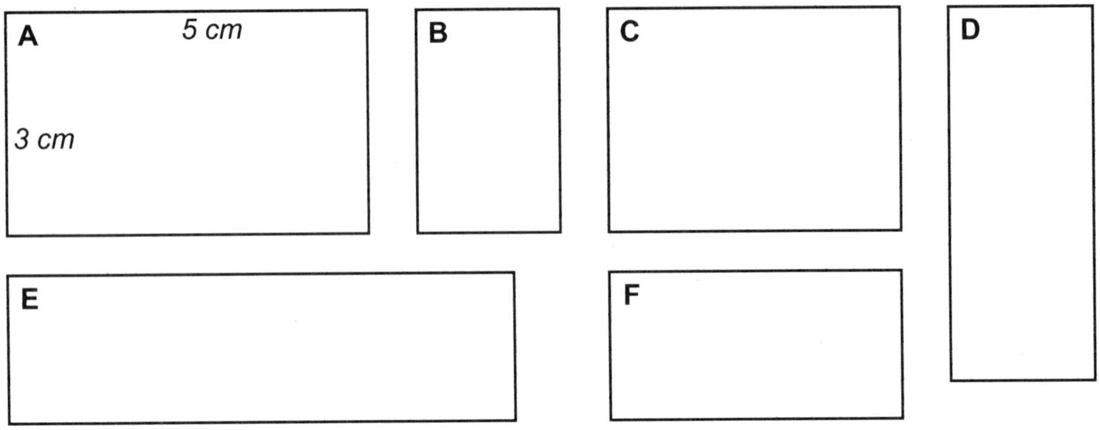

Shape	Perimeter	Area
A	3 cm + 5 cm + 3 cm + 5 cm = 16 cm	5 cm × 3 cm = 15 cm^2
B		
C		
D		
E		
F		

b) Shape E has a greater perimeter than shape A. Does it also have a greater area? ______

c) Name two rectangles that have the same perimeter and different areas. ______ and ______

d) Write the shapes in order from greatest perimeter to least perimeter. ______________________

e) Write the shapes in order from greatest area to least area. ______________________

f) Are the orders in parts d) and e) the same? __________

g) Describe the difference between perimeter and area.

7. Will you use area or perimeter to find ...

a) the amount of paper needed to cover a bulletin board? ______________________

b) the distance around a field? ______________________

c) the amount of carpet needed for a room? ______________________

d) the amount of ribbon needed to make a border for a picture? ______________________

ME4-18 Problems and Puzzles

1. On grid paper, draw a rectangle with …

a) an area of 10 square units and a perimeter of 14 units.

b) an area of 12 square units and a perimeter of 14 units.

2. a) Find the area of the shaded word.

b) There are 33 squares in the grid.
How can you use your answer to part a) to find the number of unshaded squares?

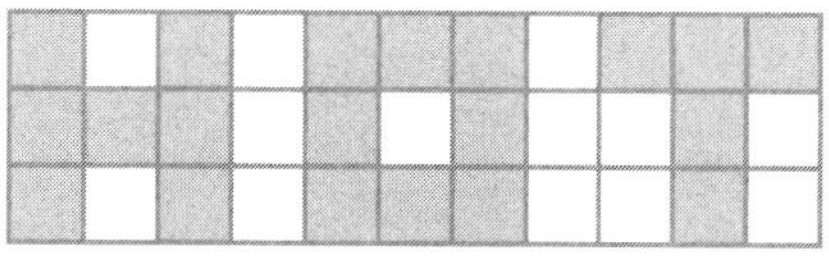

3. Raj wants to build a rectangular flowerbed of width 2 m and perimeter 12 m.

a) Sketch the flowerbed on the grid.

b) What is the length of the flowerbed?

c) Raj wants to build a fence around the flowerbed.
Fencing costs \$3 per metre. How much will the fencing cost?

d) Raj will plant 6 sunflower seeds on each square metre of land. Each sunflower seed costs 2¢. How much will the flowers cost altogether?

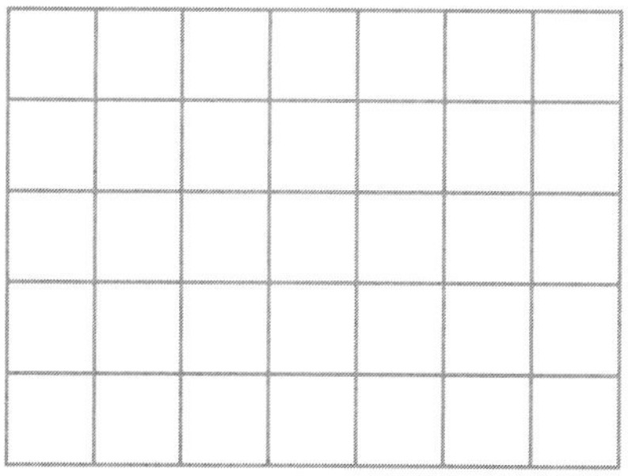

Note: The side of each square in the grid represents 1 metre.

4. a) Draw two rectangles to show that figures with the same area can have different perimeters.

b) Draw two rectangles to show that figures with the same perimeter can have different areas.

5. The area of your thumbnail is about 1 square centimetre (1 cm^2).
Estimate the area of this rectangle using your thumbnail.
Then measure the sides of the rectangle and find its actual area.

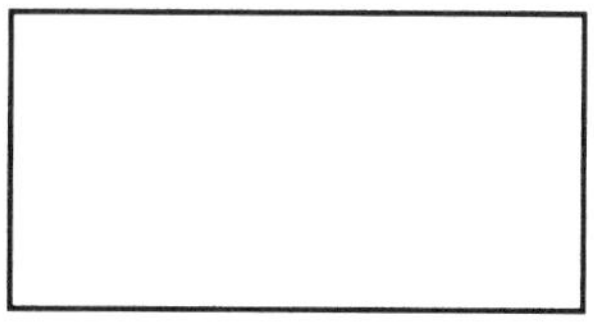

6. On grid paper, draw a figure made of four squares.
Each square must share at least one edge with another square.

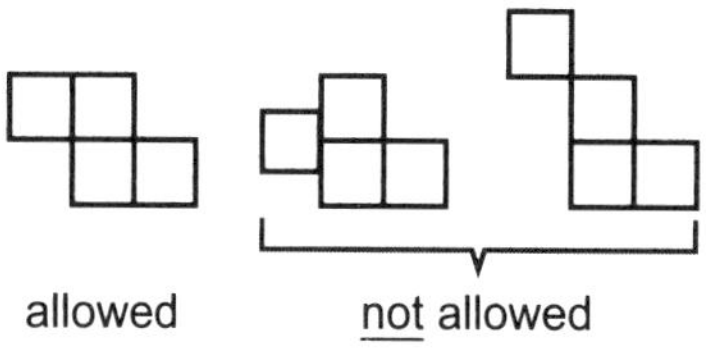

a) How many different figures can you create?

b) What is the area of the figures?

c) Which figure has the smallest perimeter?

d) Ella thinks that two figures with the same perimeter and the same area have to be exactly the same shape and size. Is she correct? Explain.

ME4-19 Scale Drawings

1. Measure to find the actual dimensions of the room according to the scale. Then find the perimeter and area.

a) Scale: 1 cm : 2 m

______ m

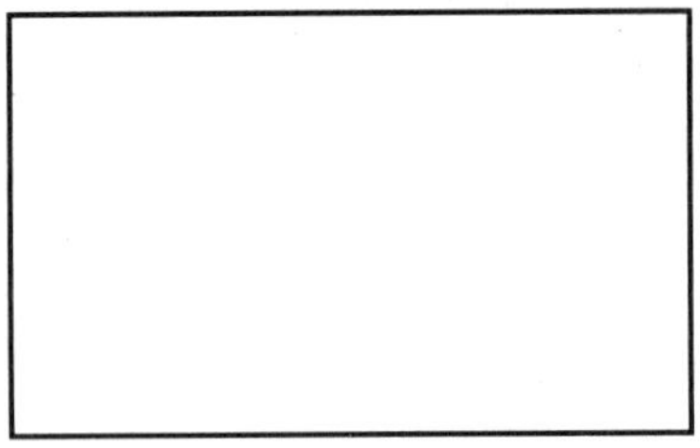

______ m

Perimeter = __________

Area = __________

b) Scale: 1 cm : 3 m

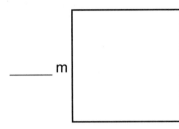

______ m

______ m

Perimeter = __________

Area = __________

2. a) The map shows the eastern-, western-, northern-, and southern-most capitals of Canada and Ottawa. Measure to find how far you would travel if you took the trip shown on the map. Scale: 1 cm : 300 km

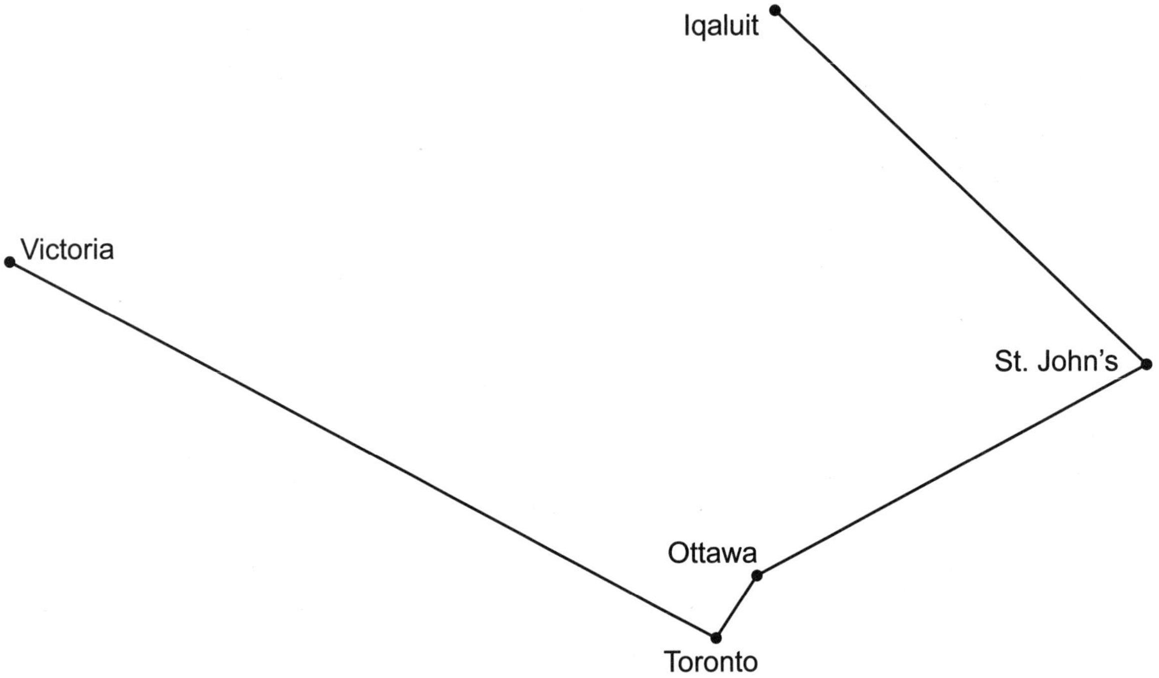

Total distance: ______________________

b) About how far is Victoria from Iqaluit?

3. This is a scale drawing of a park.

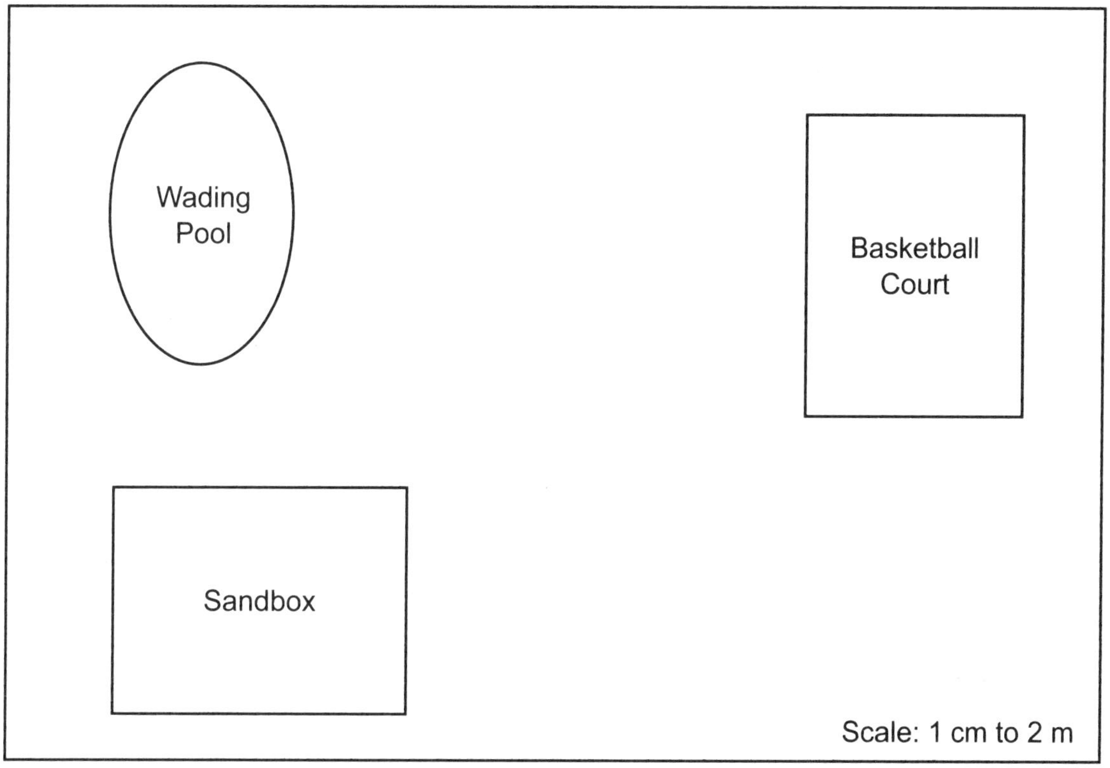

a) What is the length and the width of the park in metres?

b) What is the perimeter and the area of the park in metres?

c) About how far is the basketball court from the wading pool?

d) What is the area of the basketball court in metres?

e) A swing set requires a 6 m by 4 m rectangular area. Add a scale drawing of the swing set to the park.

ME4-20 Grids and Maps

Use the grid to answer Questions 1–3.

	A	B	C	D	E
1	h	e	b	d	r
2	o	t	u	a	y
3	w	n	i	m	s

1. Find the hidden message by writing the letter that appears at the grid location.

____ ____ ____ ____ ____ ____ ____ ____   ____ ____ ____ ____

B2 E1 B1 D2 E3 C2 E1 B1   A1 C2 B3 B2

2. Create a code for the word by writing the location of the letters in the grid.

a) STAR: *E3* *B2* *D2* *E1*

b) HAT: ____ ____ ____

c) OTTAWA: ____ ____ ____ ____ ____ ____

d) WINDSOR: ____ ____ ____ ____ ____ ____ ____

e) WHITEHORSE: ____ ____ ____ ____ ____ ____ ____ ____ ____ ____

3. Choose a word that you can write using the letters in the grid and write a code for it.

4. Draw the symbol in the grid. Write its location.

☆ at *C3*   ♡ at ____   ☾ at ____

☺ at ____   ◇ at ____   △ at ____

	A	B	C
1			
2			
3			☆

BONUS ▶ In a tic-tac-toe game, X took squares B2, C1, and A3. O took squares A1, A2, and B1. Who won the game?

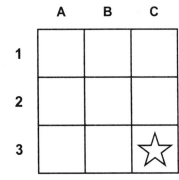

Use the map to answer Questions 5–7.

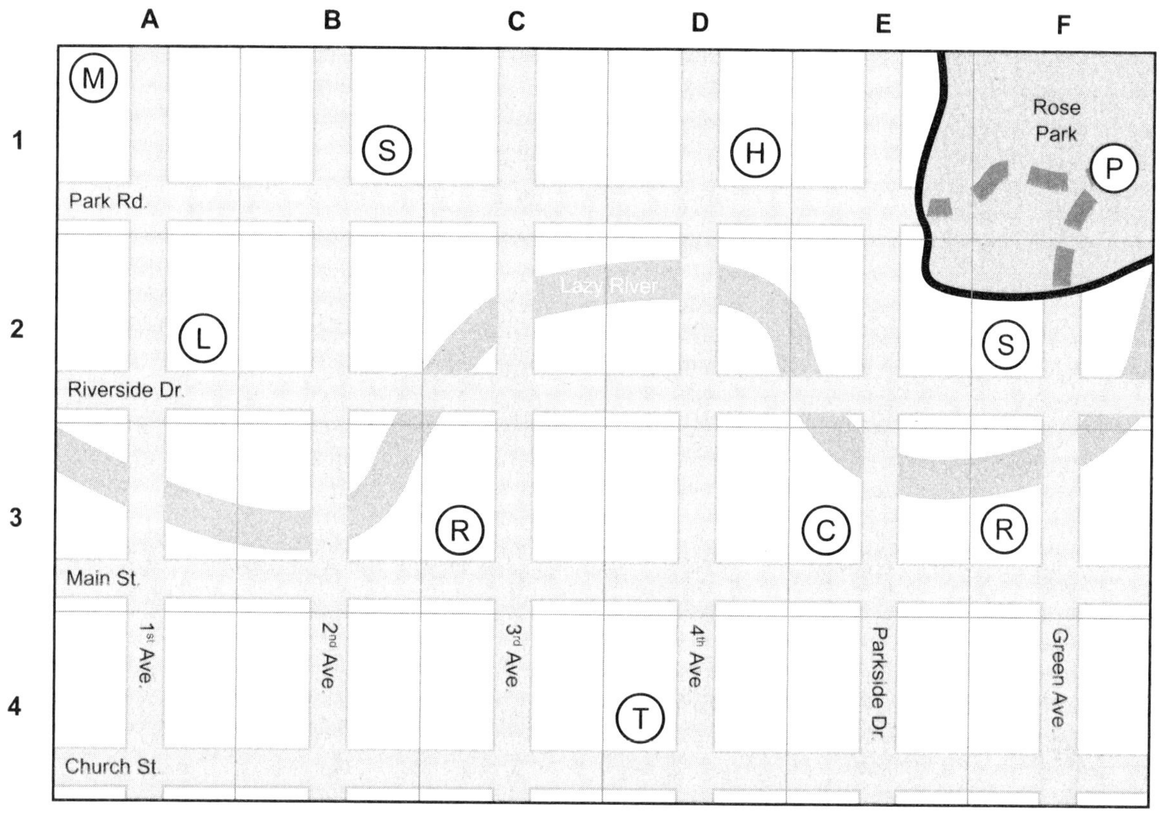

Scale: 1 cm to 100 m

Ⓢ school | Ⓛ library | Ⓡ restaurant | Ⓣ theatre

Ⓗ hospital | Ⓒ city hall | Ⓟ picnic area | Ⓜ mall

5. Find the landmark on the map and write its location.

a) library: ______ b) city hall: ______

c) theatre: ______ d) mall: ______

6. Where is the street on the map? Fill in the blanks.

a) Main St. runs from *A3* to *F3* b) 4th Ave. runs from ______ to ______

c) Green Ave. runs from ______ to ______ d) Park Rd. runs from ______ to ______

7. About how far apart are the two restaurants?

BONUS ▶ Rani walks from the restaurant in C3 to the park entrance in E1. Draw her route on the map. About how far does she walk?

G5-10 Rectangles and Rhombuses

A **rectangle** is a quadrilateral with 4 right angles.

1. Use a corner of a sheet of paper to check for right angles. Mark the right angles. Circle the rectangles.

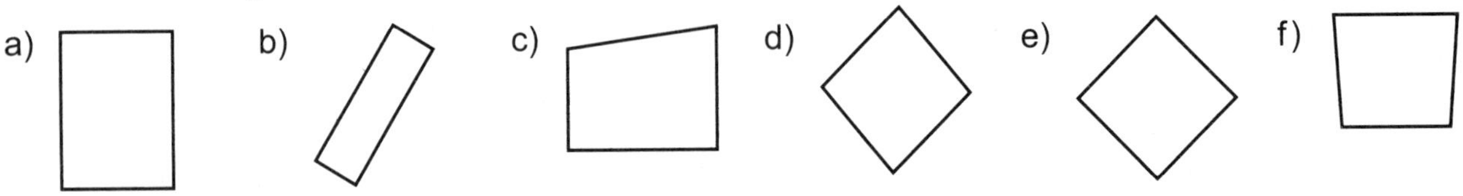

If two lines both meet a third line at a right angle, the two lines are parallel.

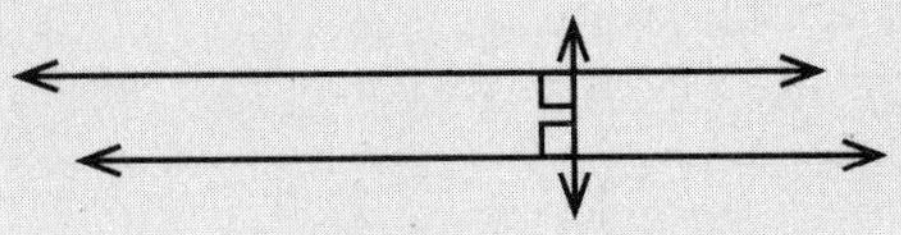

2. a) Are all rectangles also parallelograms? ______ b) Can a rectangle be a trapezoid? ______

3. Explain your answers to Question 2.

____

____

____

4. How were the quadrilaterals sorted? Describe each group.

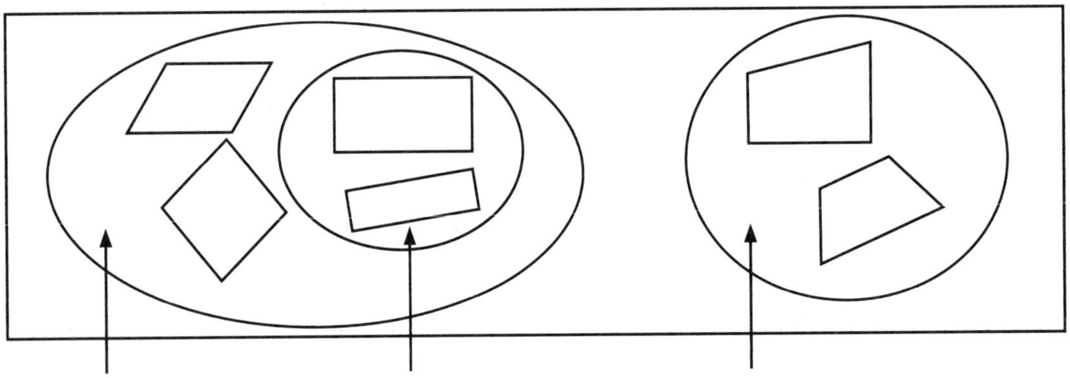

______________ ______________ ______________

5. a) Which Venn diagram will always have an empty region? Cross out that diagram.

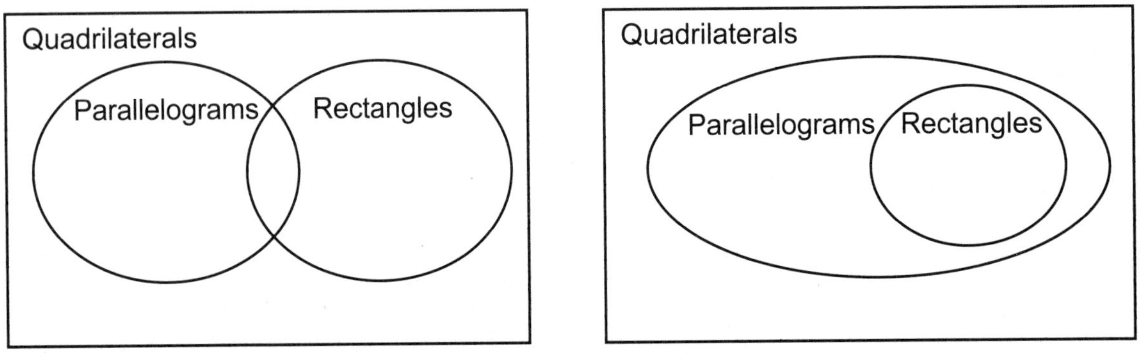

b) Sketch a quadrilateral in every region of the diagram that is not crossed out.

Equilateral polygons have all sides equal. A **rhombus** is an equilateral parallelogram.

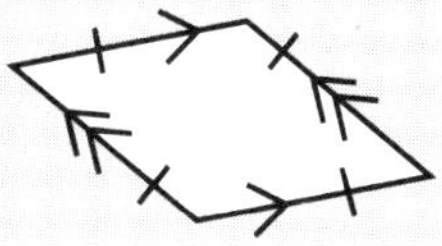

6. a) Measure the sides of the parallelogram to the closest millimetre. Then decide if it is a rhombus.

i)

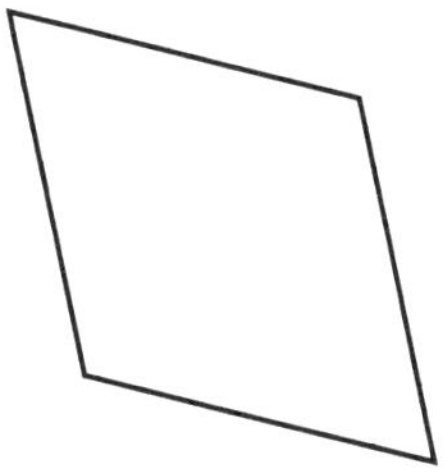

ii)

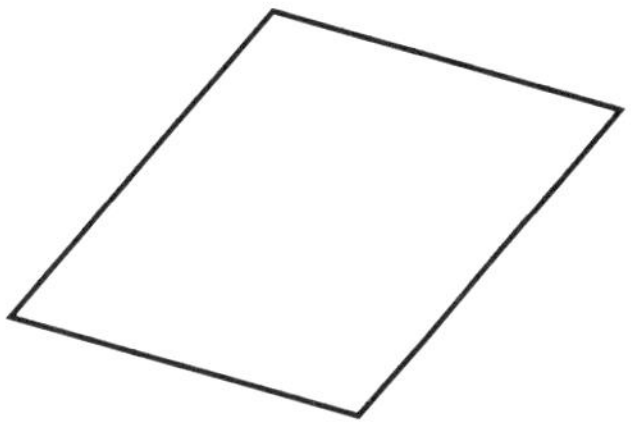

iii)

________________ ________________ ________________

b) Opposite angles in a parallelogram are equal.
Should opposite angles in a rhombus be equal? ________

7. The polygons below are rhombuses.

A.

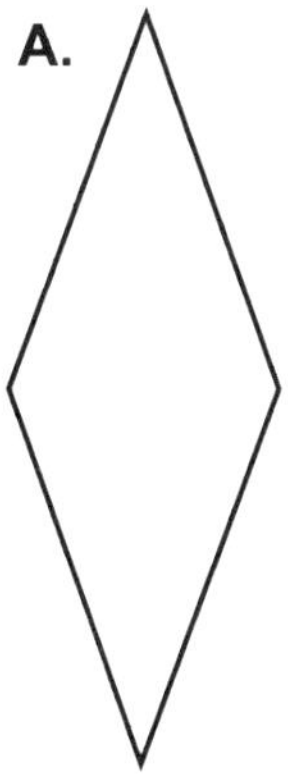

B.

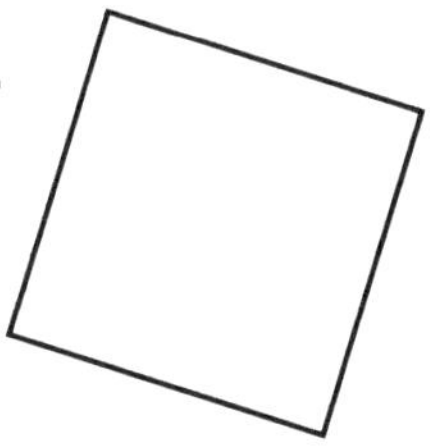

C.

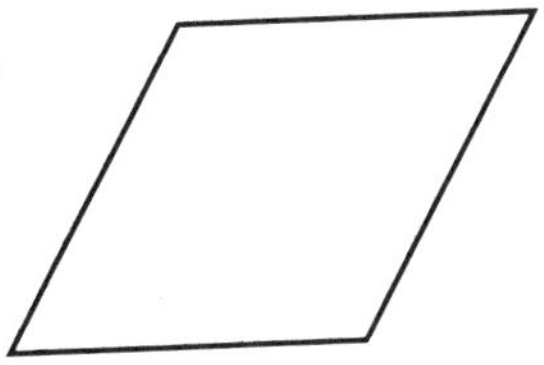

a) Mark the equal sides with hash marks.

b) Mark parallel sides with arrows.

c) Which one of these rhombuses could also be a rectangle? Check your prediction and explain how you know. ____________________________________

8. Use the grid to draw the quadrilateral.

a) a rectangle that is not a rhombus

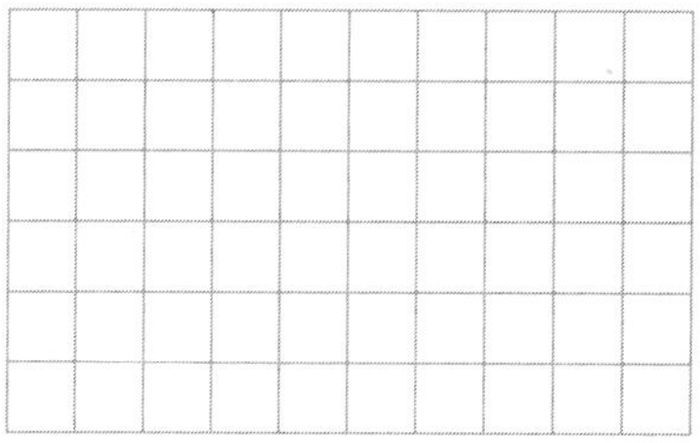

b) a rhombus that is not a rectangle

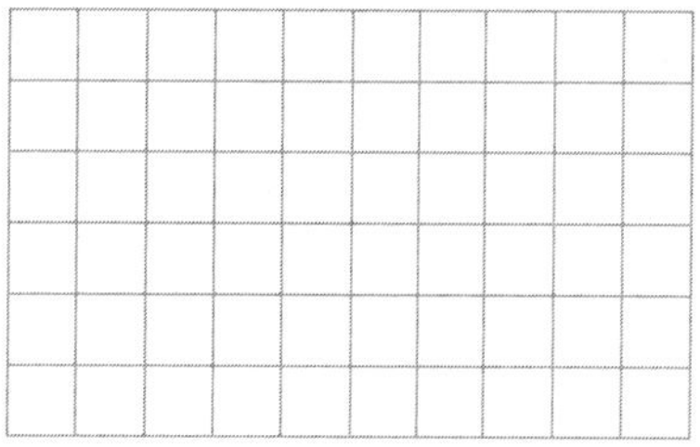

9. a) The equal sides are not marked on some of the shapes below. Mark them. Then mark the right angles.

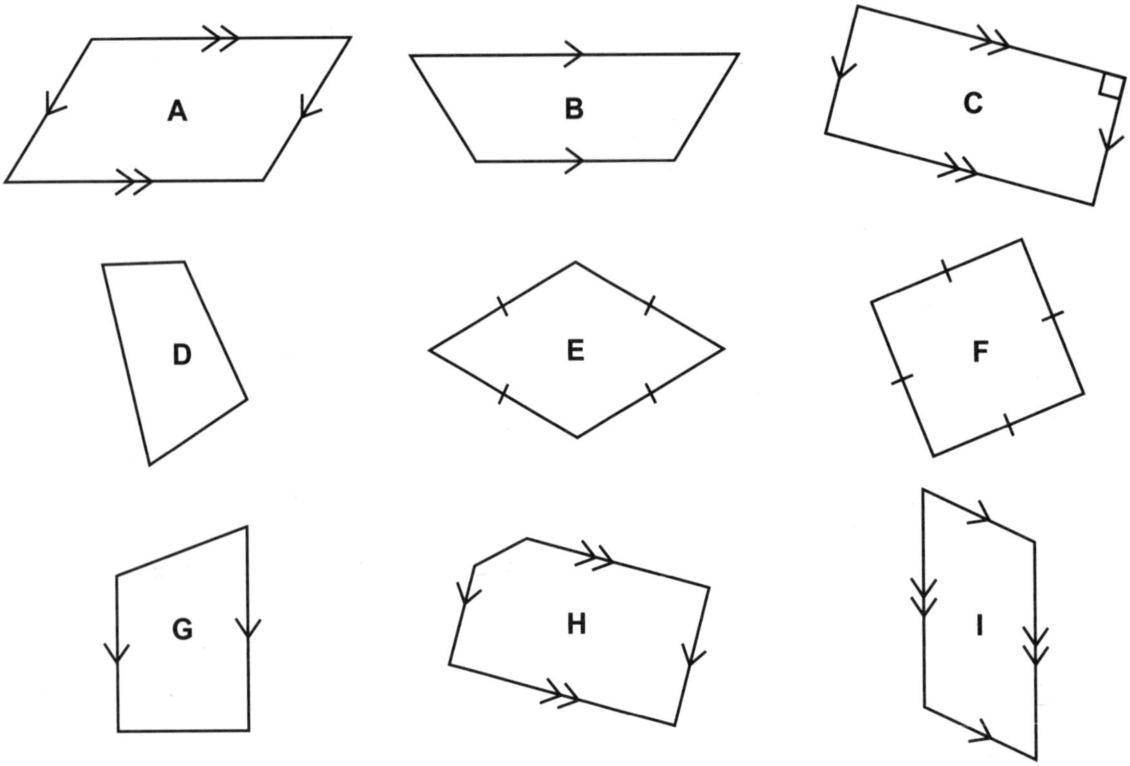

b) Sort the shapes. Some shapes belong in more than one row.

Quadrilaterals	
Trapezoids	
Parallelograms	
Rectangles	
Rhombuses	

A **square** is an equilateral rectangle, or a rectangle with equal sides.

10. a) Is any square also a parallelogram? Explain.

b) Is any square also a rhombus? Explain.

c) Can a square also be a trapezoid? Explain.

d) Shade the region in the Venn diagram where all squares will be.

e) Can there be a polygon that is in the shaded region but is not a square? If yes, sketch it. If no, explain why not.

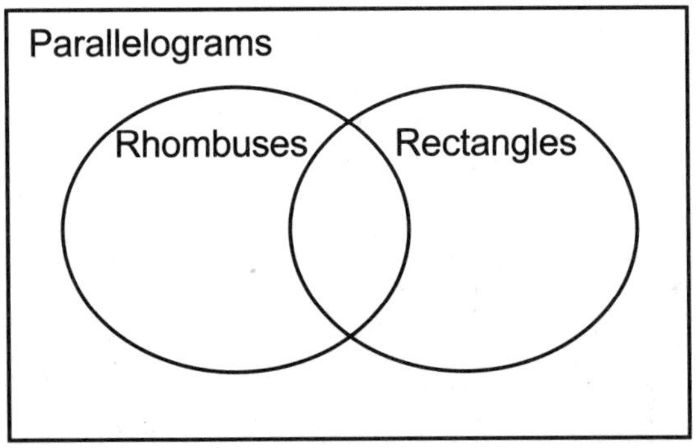

ME4-23 O'Clock, Half, and Quarter Hours

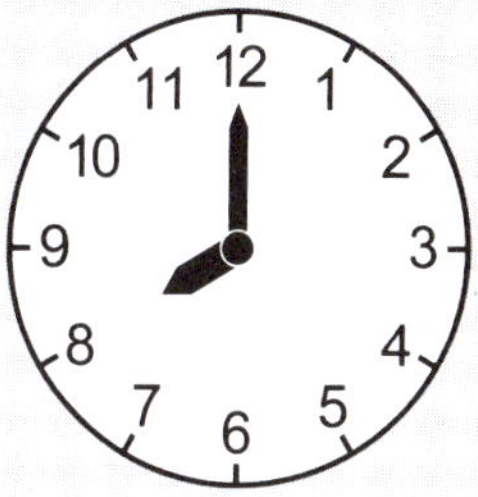

8 o'clock

It is 8 o'clock.
The hour hand is on the 8.
The minute hand is on the 12.

The time is 8:00.

1. Write the time two ways.

a)

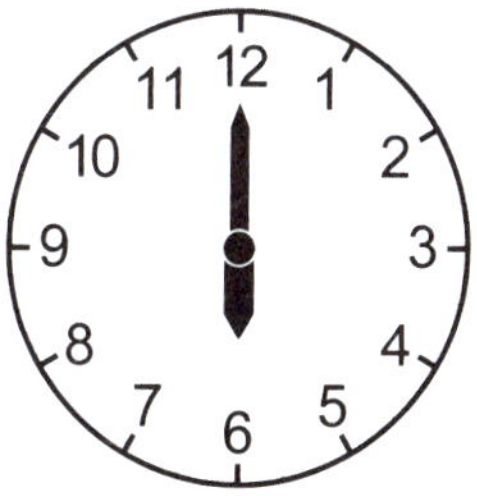

6 o'clock

6 : 00

b)

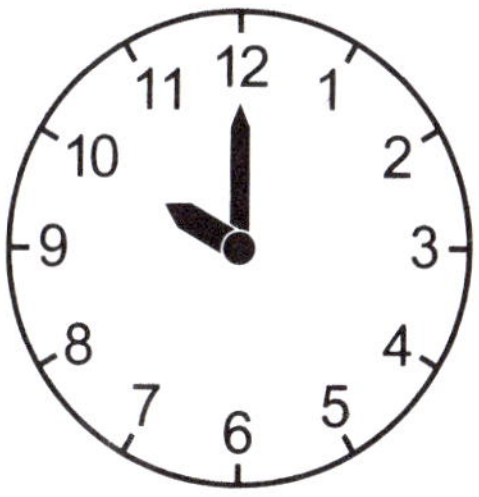

10 o'clock

10 : 00

c)

2 o'clock

2 : 00

d)

12 o'clock

12 : 00

2. Write the time in numbers.

a) 7 o'clock 7:00

b) 5 o'clock 5:00

c) 11 o'clock 11:00

d) 3 o'clock 3:00

3. Draw hands on the clock to show the time.

a)

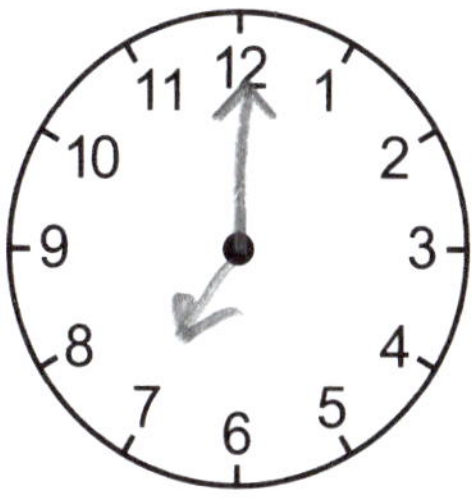

7:00

b)

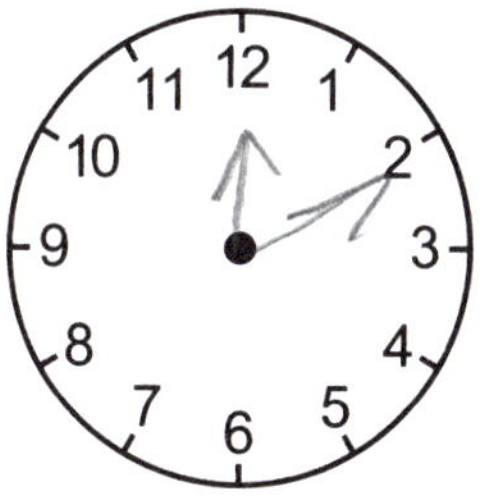

2 o'clock

c)

3 o'clock

d)

4:00

BONUS ▶

e)

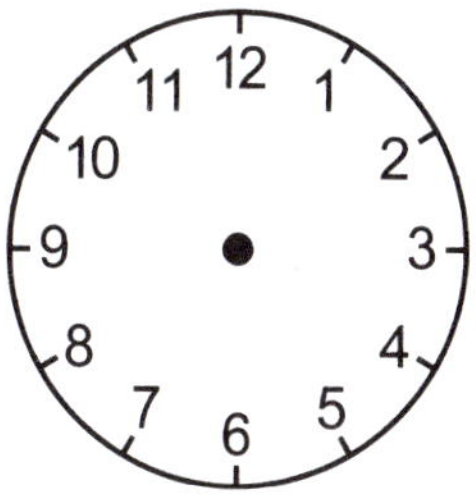

midnight

f)

13:00

g)

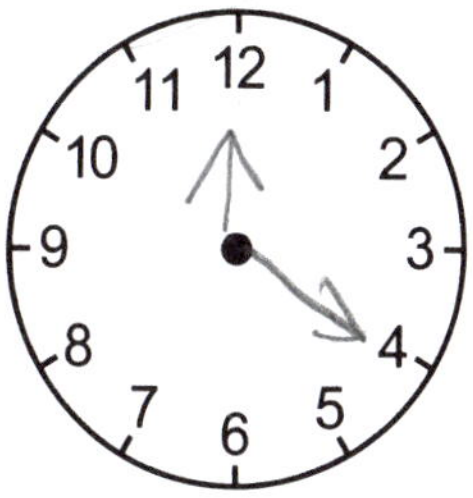

16:00

h)

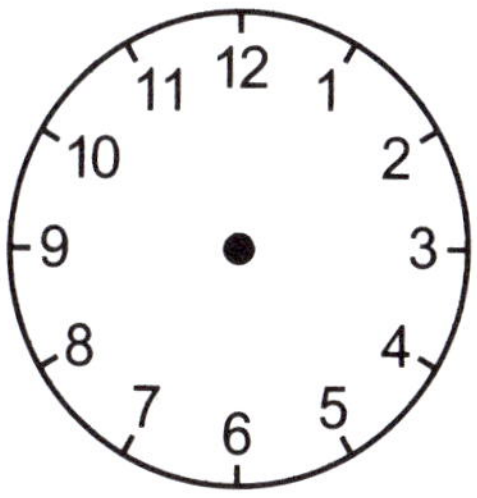

noon

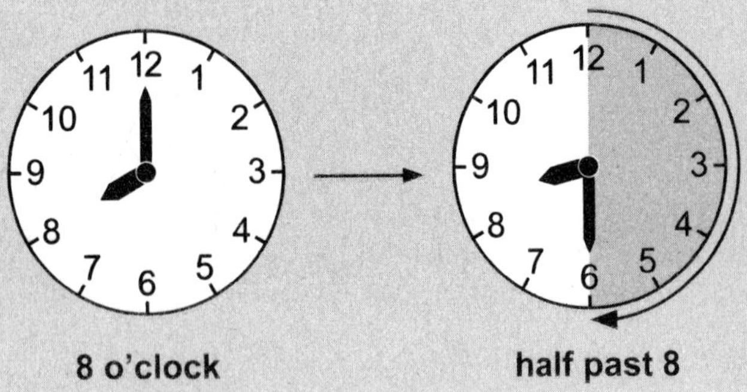

It is half an hour after 8:00.
The hour hand is between 8 and 9.
The time is **half past** 8.

60 ÷ 2 = 30, so the time is 8:30.

4. Write the time two ways.

a) 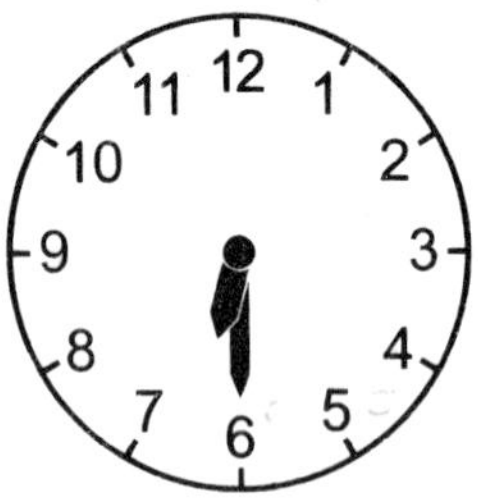

half past 6

6 : 30

b) 

half past 10

10 : 30

c) 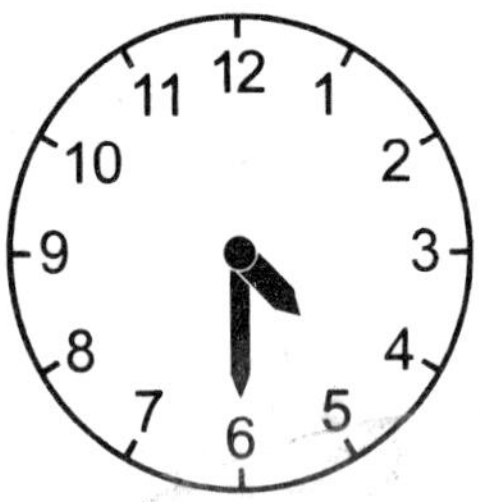

half past 4

4 : 30

d) 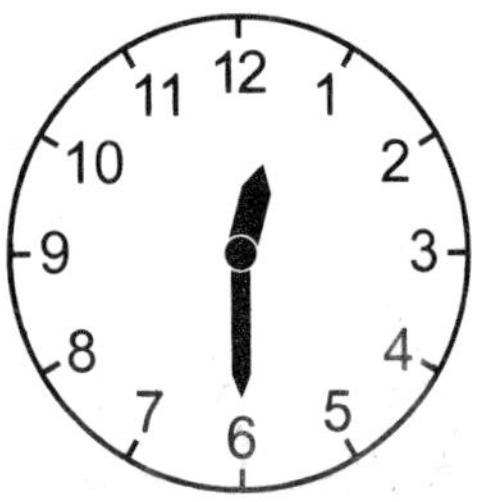

half past 12

12 : 30

5. Write the time in numbers.

a) half past 7 — 7:30

b) half past 5 — 6:30

c) half past 11 — 11:30

d) half past 3 — 3:30

6. Draw hands on the clock to show the time.

a) 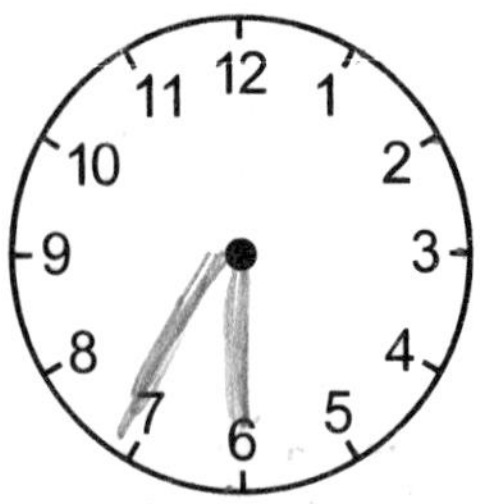

7:30

b) 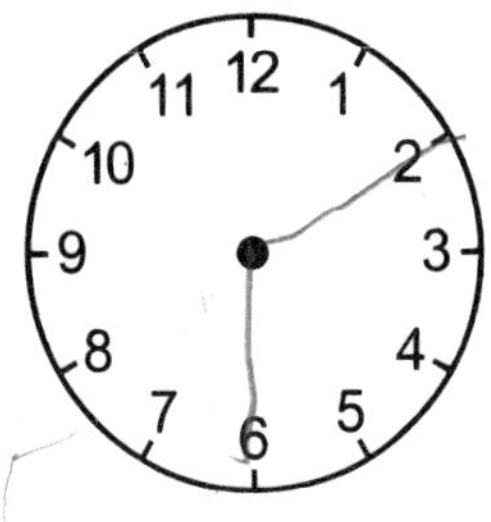

half past 2

c) 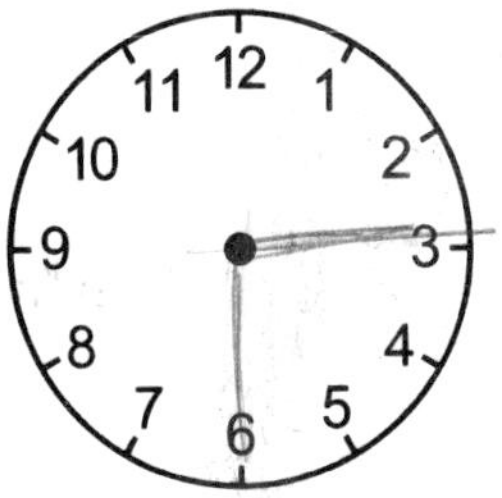

30 minutes after 3

d) 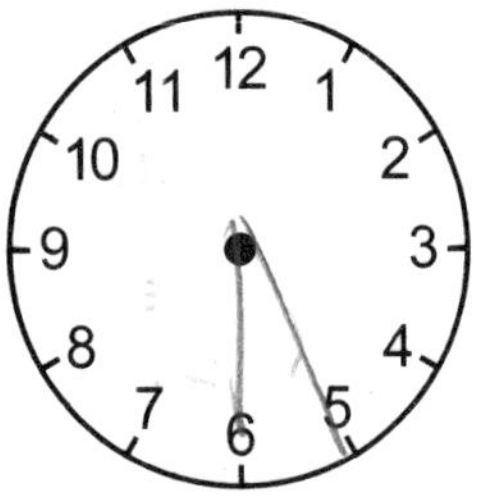

4:30

BONUS ▶

e) 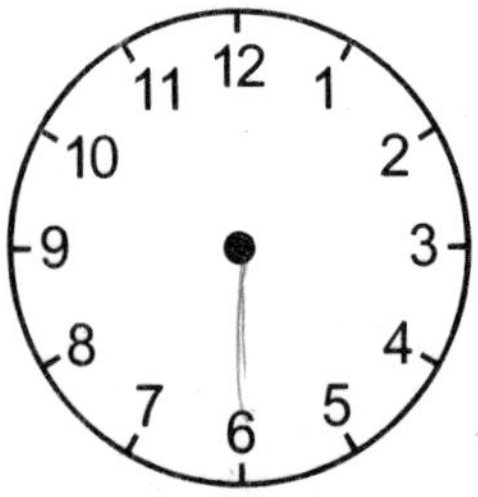

17:30

f) 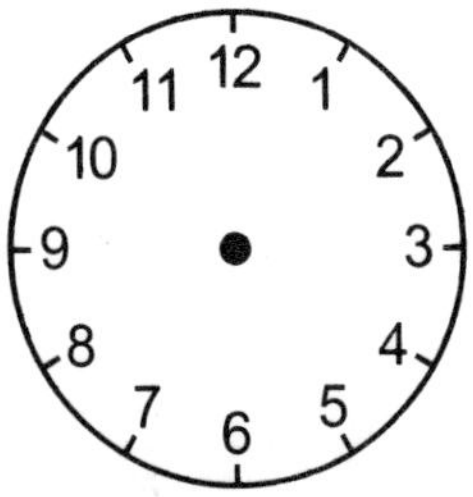

half past noon

g) 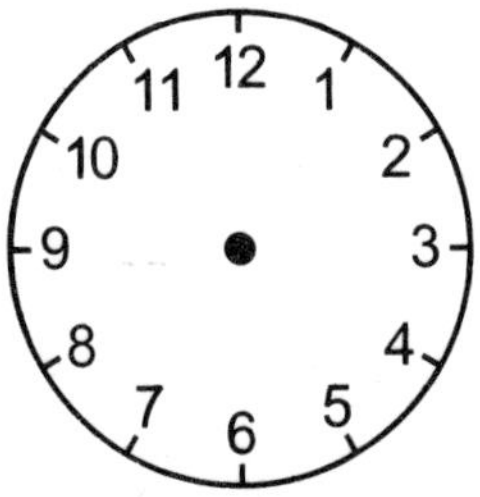

20:30

h) 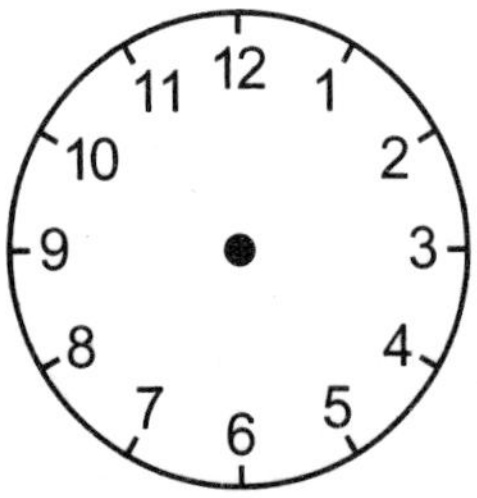

half hour to midnight

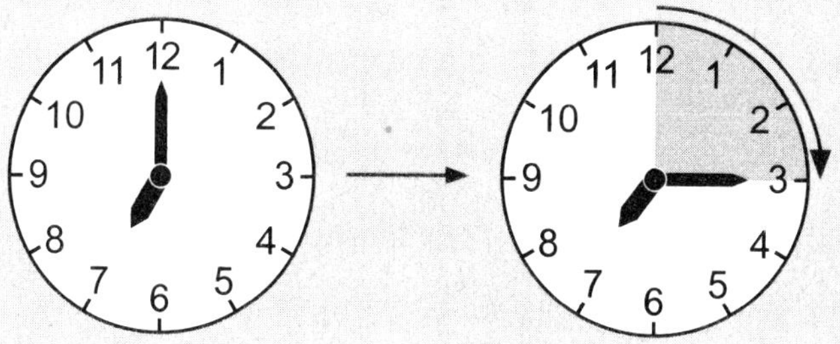

7 o'clock **quarter past 7**

It is a quarter of an hour after 7:00 or **quarter past** 7.

60 ÷ 4 = 15, so the time is 7:15.

7. Write the time in words and numbers. Use "quarter" in your answer.

a) 

____

____

b) 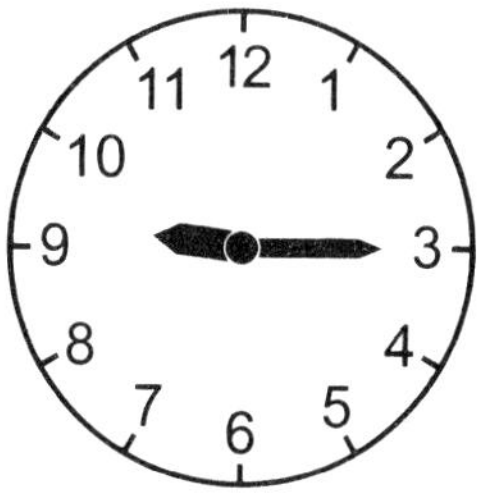

____

____

c) 

____

____

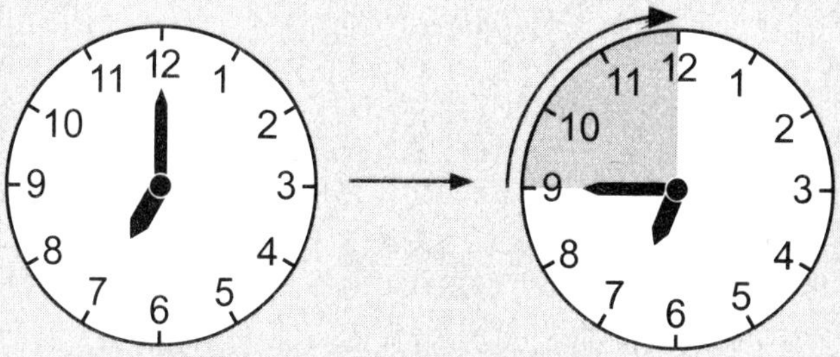

7 o'clock **quarter to 7**

It is a quarter of an hour before 7:00 or **quarter to** 7.

The time is 6:45.

8. Write the time in words and numbers. Use "quarter" in your answer.

a) 

____

____

b) 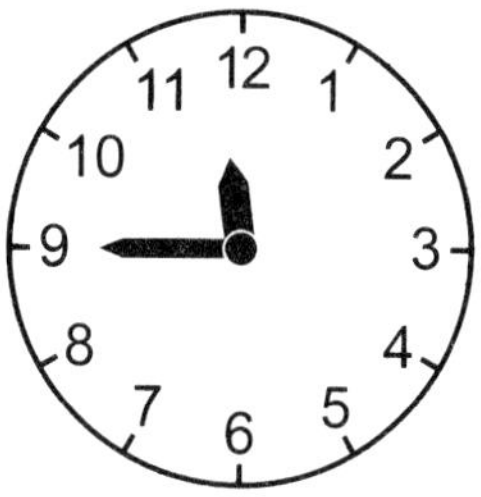

____

____

c) 

____

____

9. Write the time in numbers.

a) quarter past 7 ______

b) quarter to 7 ______

c) quarter past 11 ______

d) quarter to 11 ______

e) quarter past 1 ______

f) quarter to 4 ______

g) quarter to 9 ______

h) quarter past 5 ______

i) half past 9 ______

j) quarter to 12 ______

k) half past 2 ______

l) quarter past 3 ______

10. Draw hands on the clock to show the time.

a) 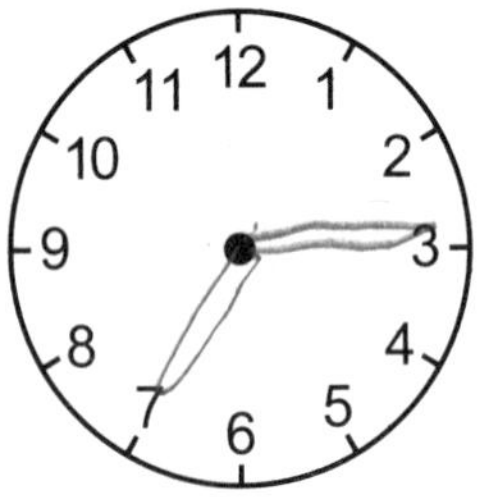

7:15

b) 

9:15

c) 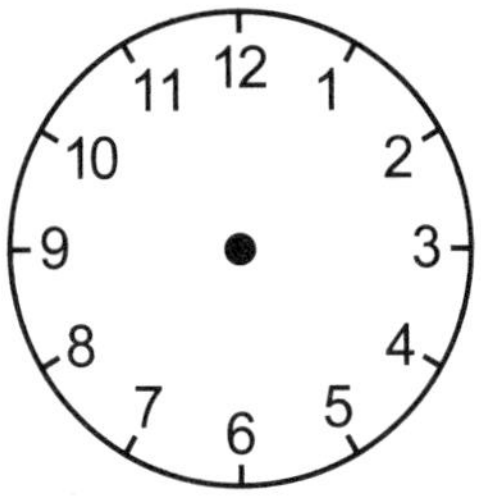

quarter past 4

d) 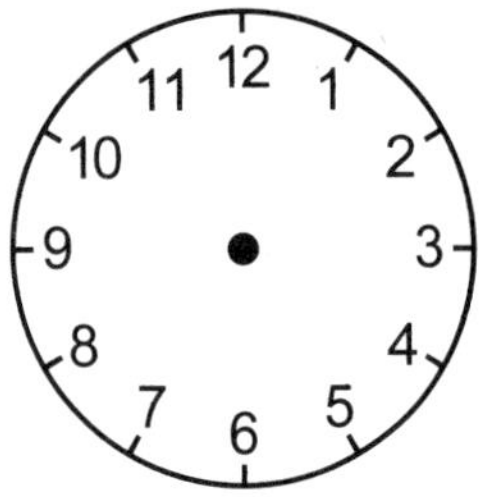

quarter past 6

e) 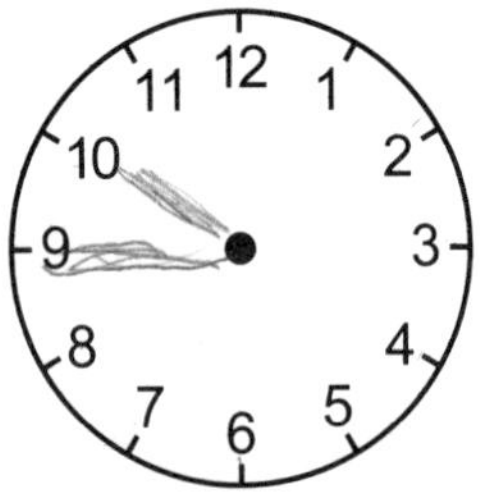

10:45

f) 

8:45

g) 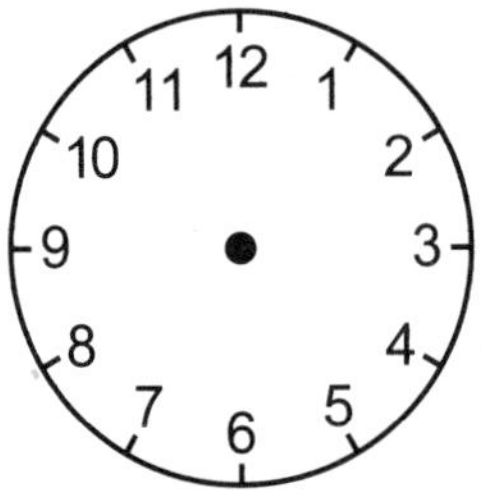

quarter to 4

h) 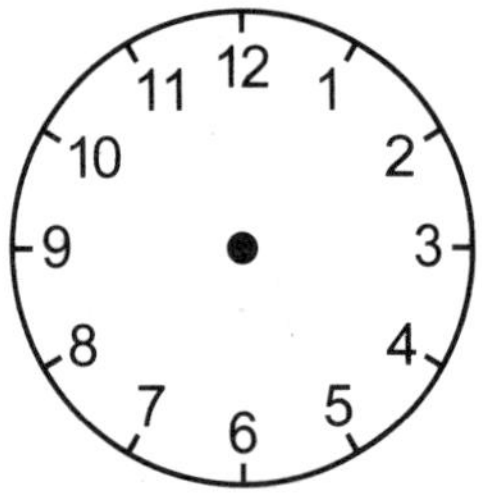

quarter to 6

i) 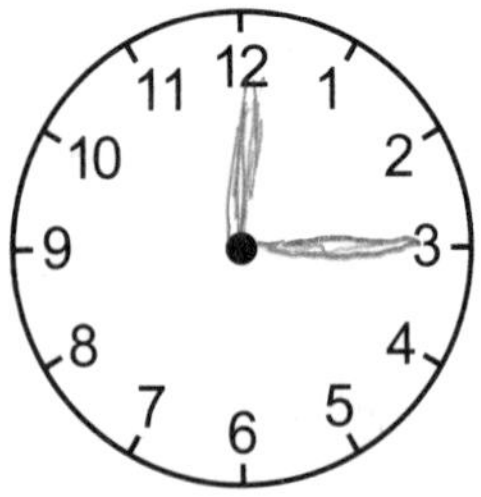

12:15

j) 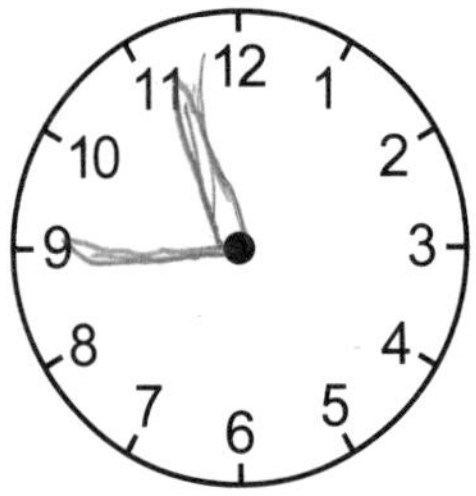

22:45

k) 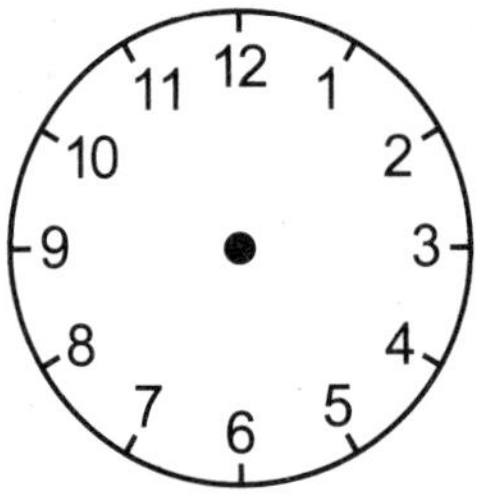

half past 4

l) 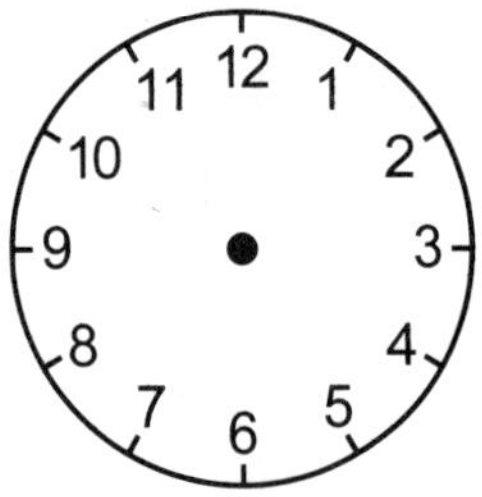

6 o'clock

11. Is the hour hand closer to 4 or to 5 …

a) at 4:15? ______

b) at 4:45? ______

BONUS ▶ at 4:30? ______

Telling Time to Five Minutes

What time is it?

Step 1: Look at the hour hand. It points between 4 and 5. The hour is 4.

Step 2: Look at the minute hand. It points at 2. Skip count by 5s or multiply by 5 to find the minutes: 5, 10, or $2 \times 5 = 10$.

The time is 4:10.

1. What time is it?

a) 

1 : *40*

b) 

___ : ___

c) 

___ : ___

d) 

___ : ___

e) 

___ : ___

f) 

___ : ___

2. Write the time on the digital clock.

a) 

| *0* | *6* | : | *5* | *5* |

b) 

| | | : | | |

c) 

| | | : | | |

d) 

| | | : | | |

e) 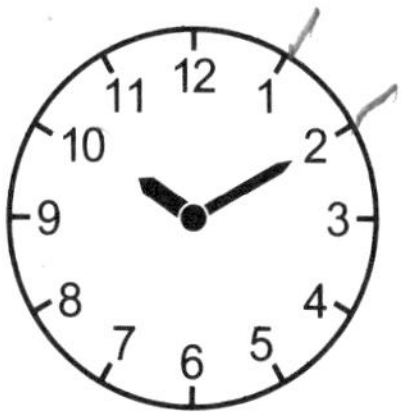

| | | : | | |

f) 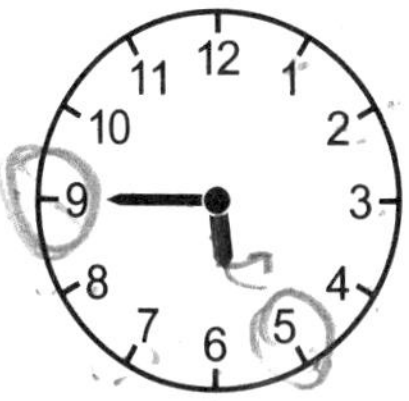

| | | : | | |

3. Write the time two ways.

a) 

6:45

quarter to 7

b) 

c) 

d) 

e) 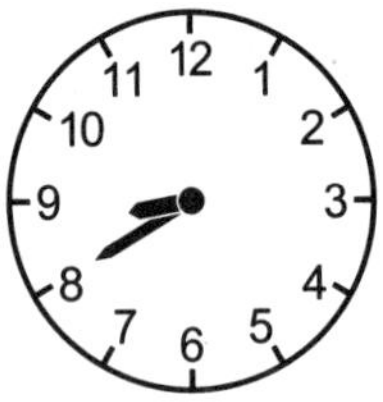

f) 

4. Draw hands on the clock to show the time.

a) 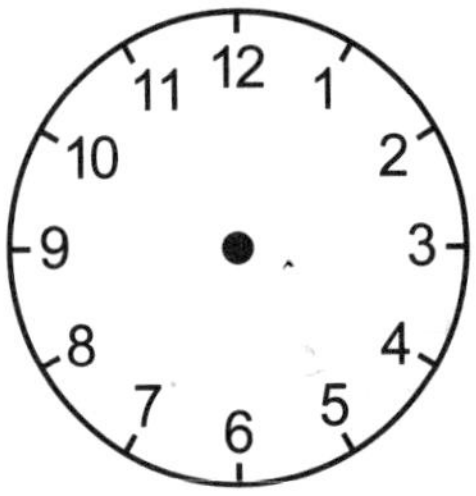

7:10

b) 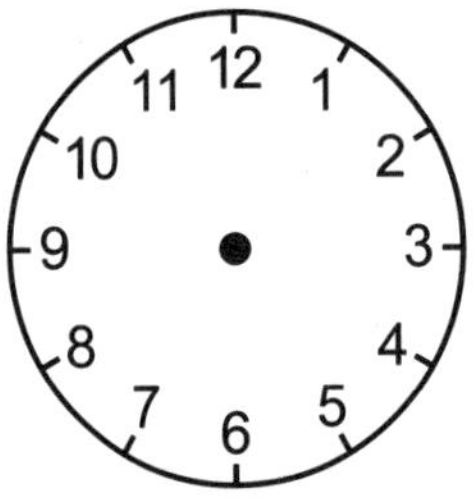

9:40

c) 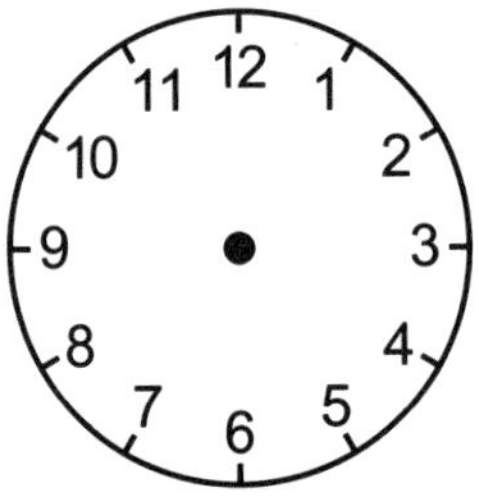

11:05

d) 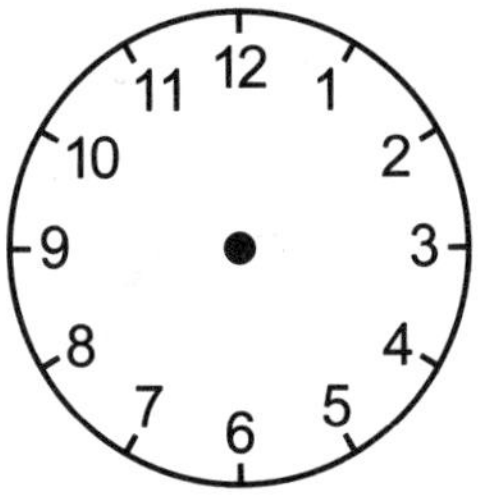

2:45

e) 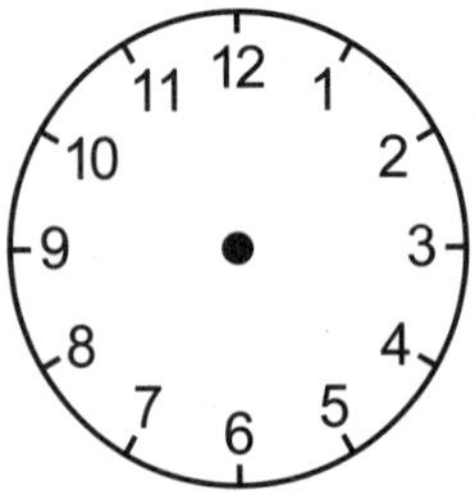

3:35

f) 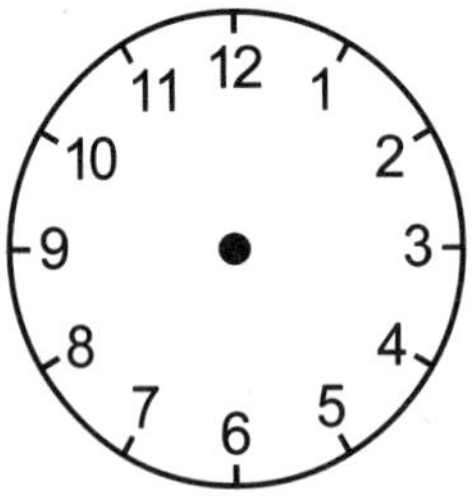

22:35

g) 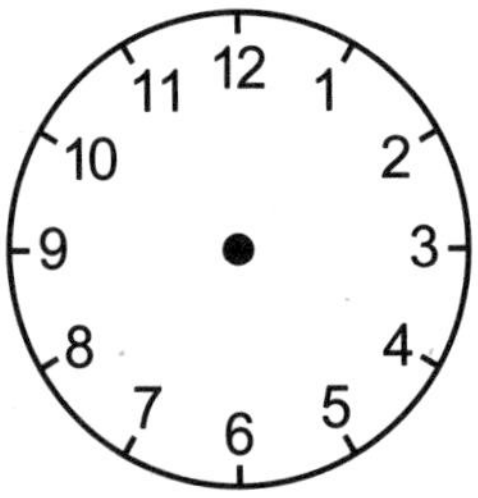

20:20

h) 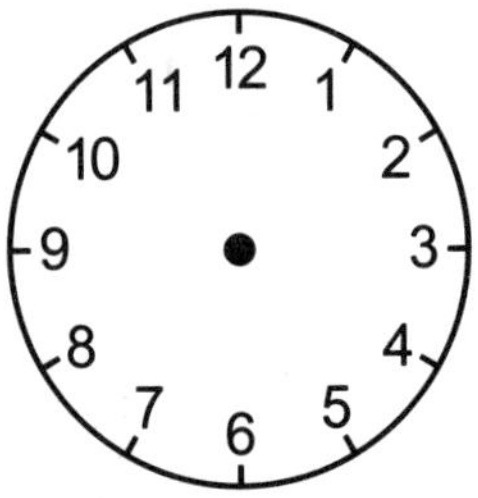

5:25

5. Write the time in Question 4, part f) as many ways as you can.

ME4-25 Telling Time to the Minute

Each division on the clock stands for 1 minute.

The minute hand is pointing between the 4 and the 5.
Count by 5s until you reach the 4: twenty minutes have passed.
Then count on by ones: two minutes have passed.

20 + 2 = 22 minutes have passed

It is **7:22** or **22 minutes after 7**.

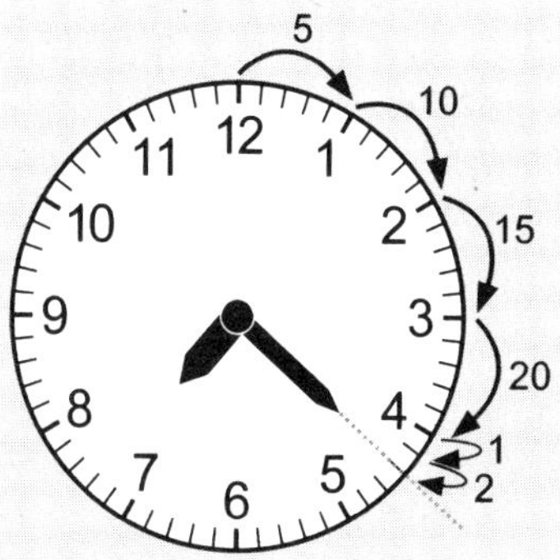

1. How many minutes past the hour is it?

a)

_24_ minutes past

b)
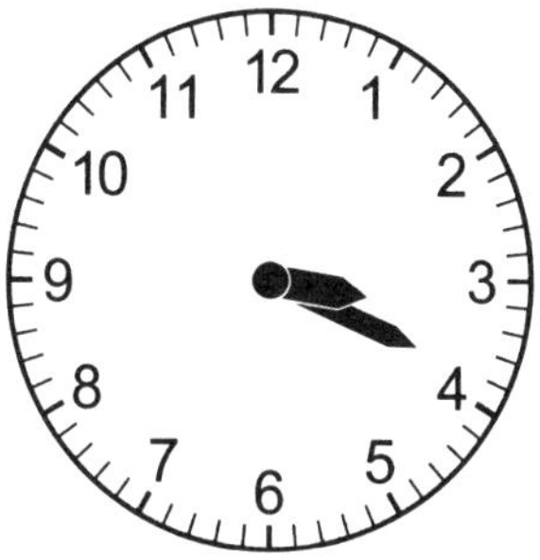

______ minutes past

c)
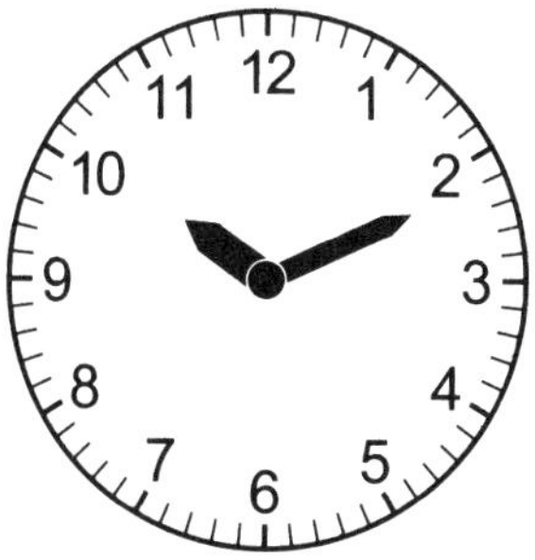

______ minutes past

d)
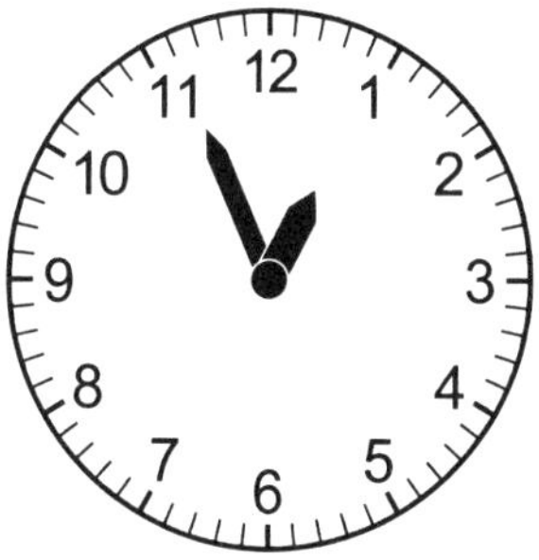

______ minutes past

e)
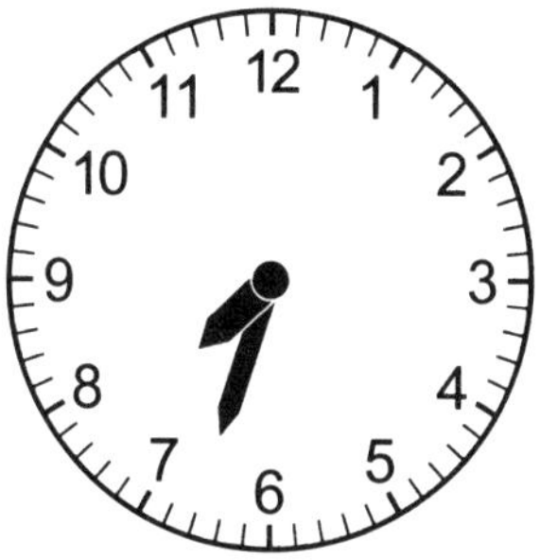

______ minutes past

f)

______ minutes past

2. What time is it?

a)

______ minutes past ______

b)
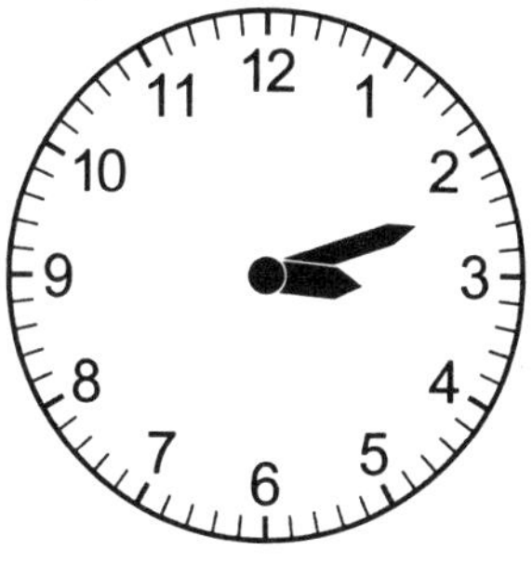

______ minutes past ______

c)

______ minutes past ______

3. Write the exact time.

a) 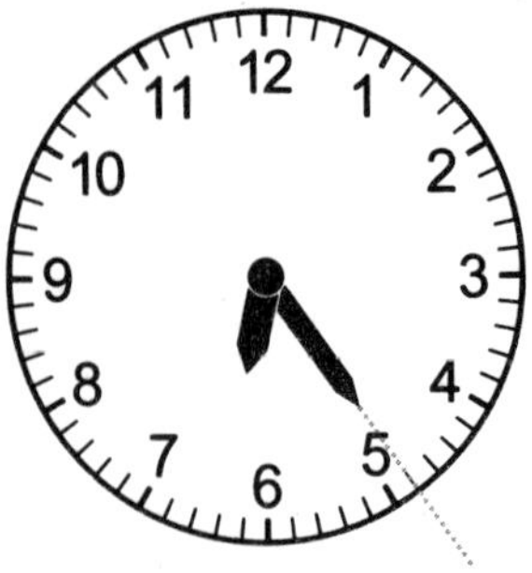

6 : 24

b) 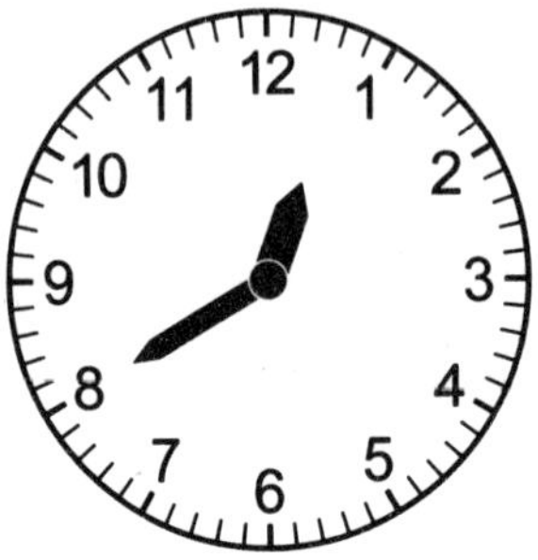

_____ : _____

c) 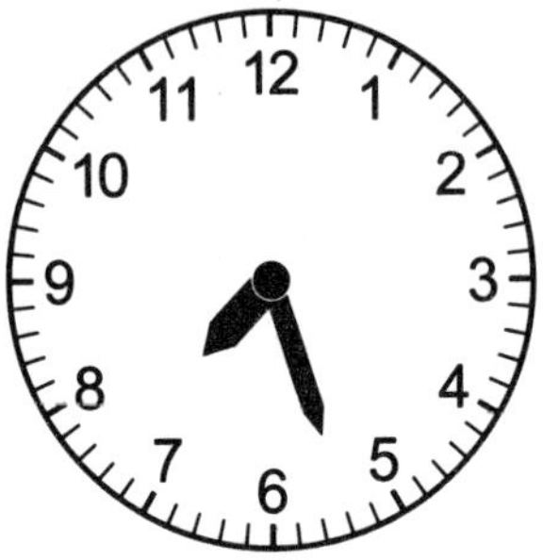

_____ : _____

d) 

_____ : _____

e) 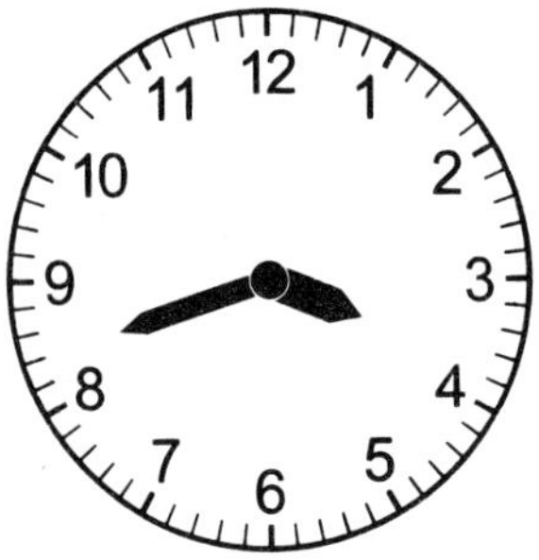

_____ : _____

f) 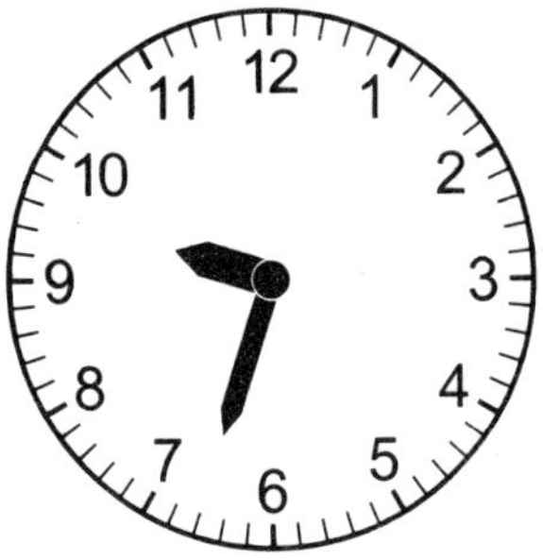

_____ : _____

BONUS ▶

g) 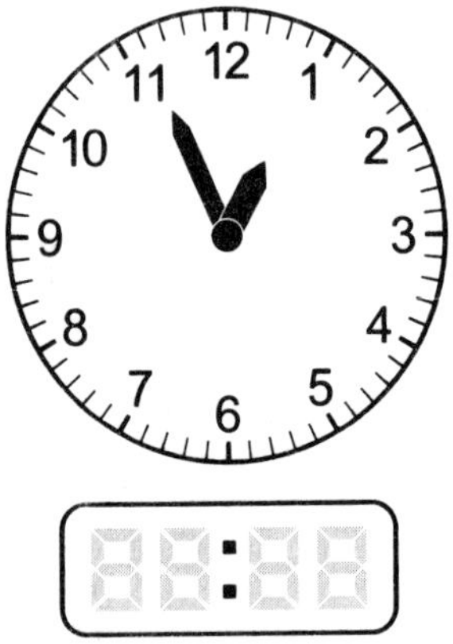

h) 

i) 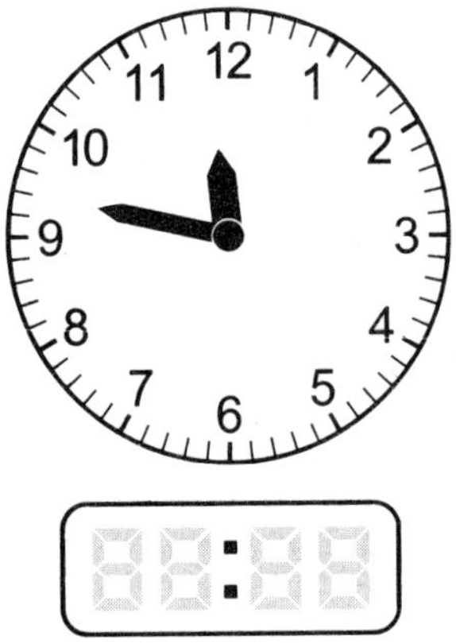

j) 

k) 

l) 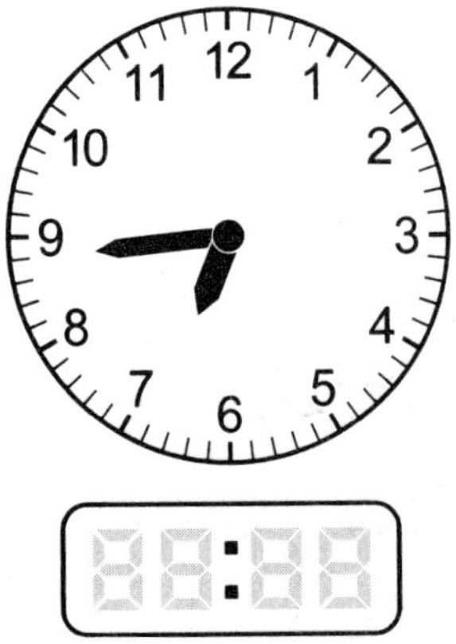

The minute hand is pointing between the 8 and the 9.
To say how many minutes to the hour:

Count by 5s until you reach the 9. Then count on by ones.

15 + 2 = 17 minutes are left before the next hour.

It is **17 minutes to 7**.

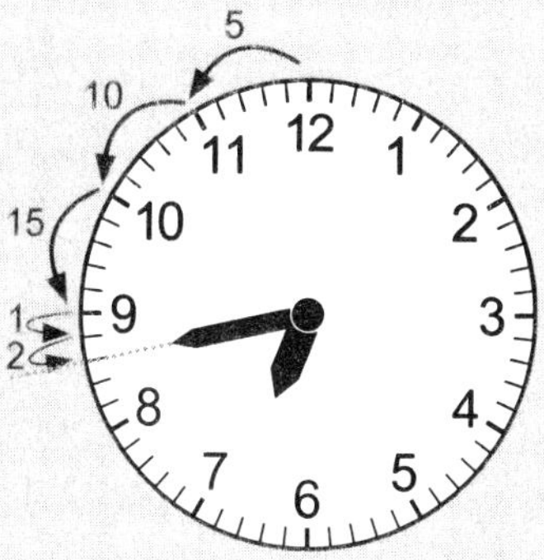

4. How many minutes to the hour is it?

a)

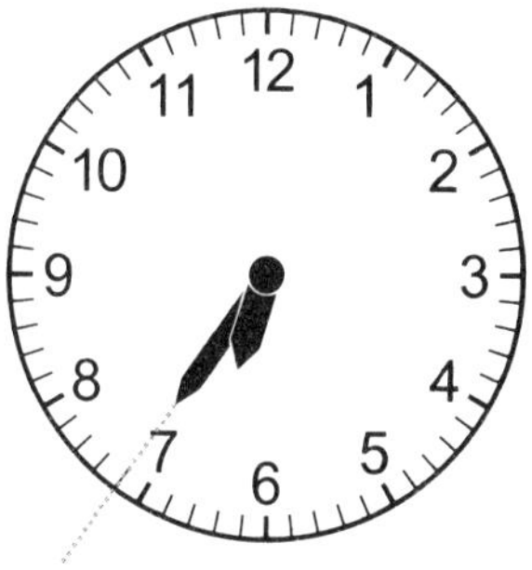

24 minutes to 7

b)

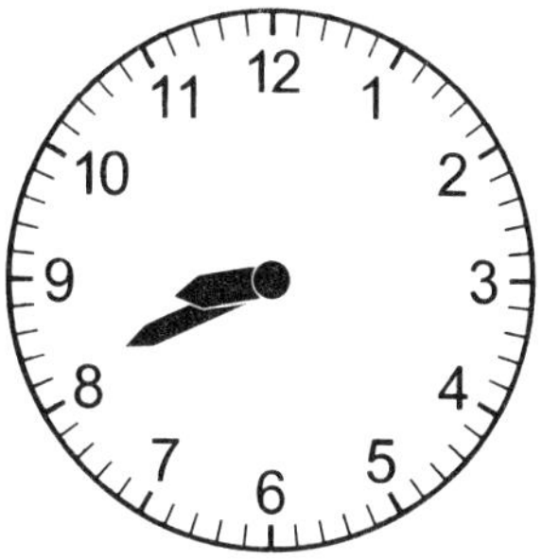

______ minutes to 9

c)

______ minutes to 1

5. What time is it?

a)

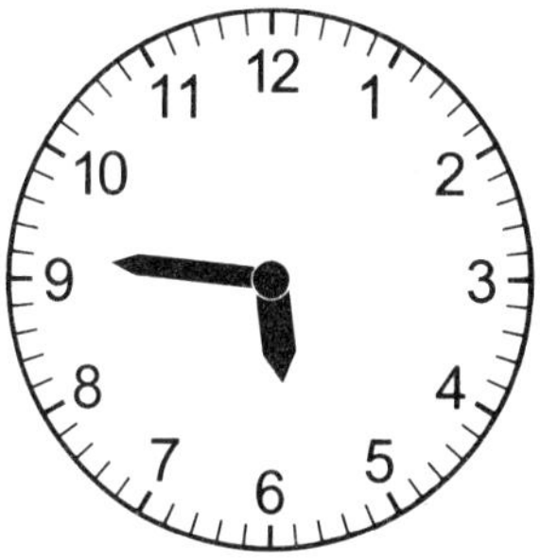

______ minutes to ______

b)

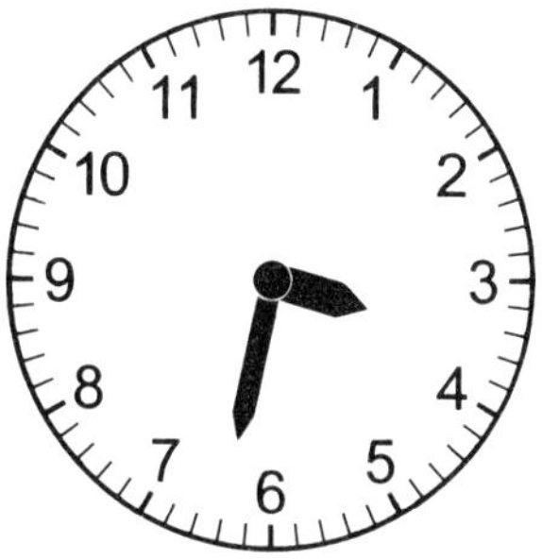

______ minutes to ______

c)

______ minutes to ______

d)

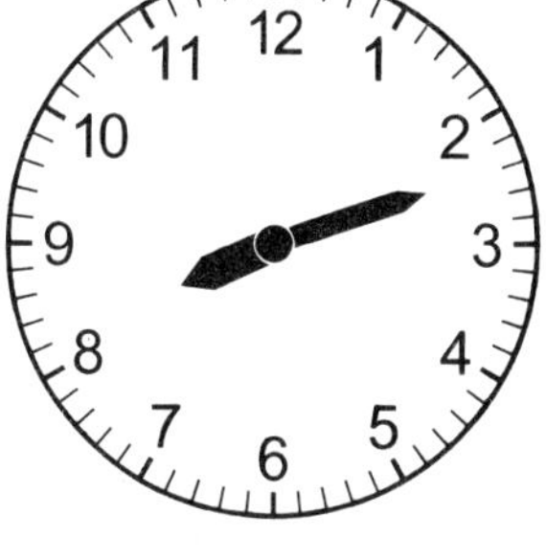

______ minutes past ______

e)

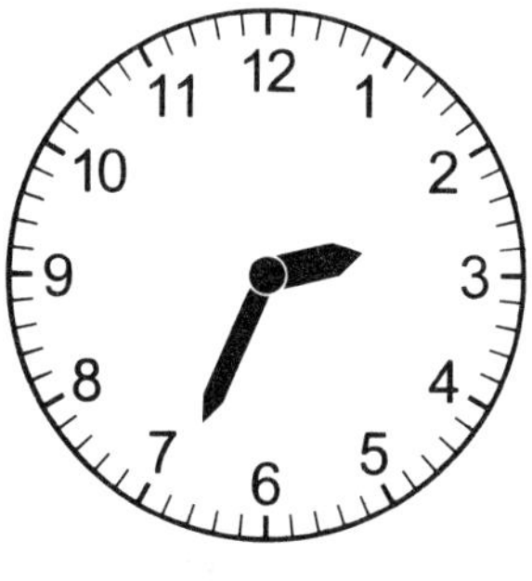

______ minutes to ______

f)

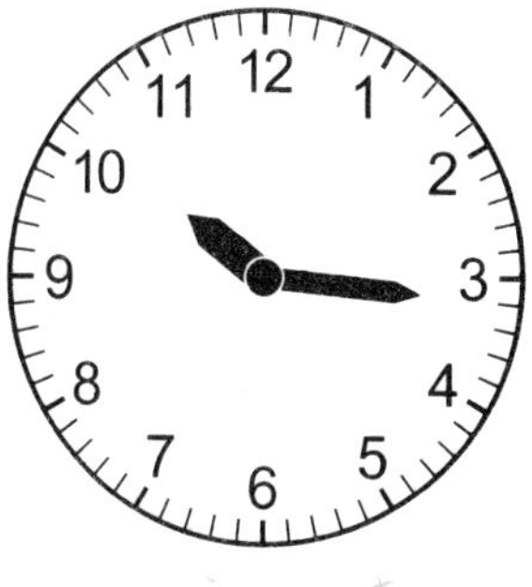

______ minutes past ______

6. Tell the time two ways.

a) 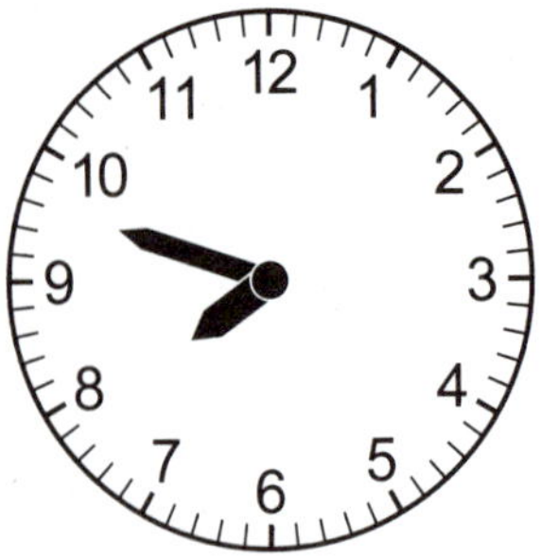

_____ minutes past _____

_____ minutes to _____

b) 

_____ minutes past _____

_____ minutes to _____

c) 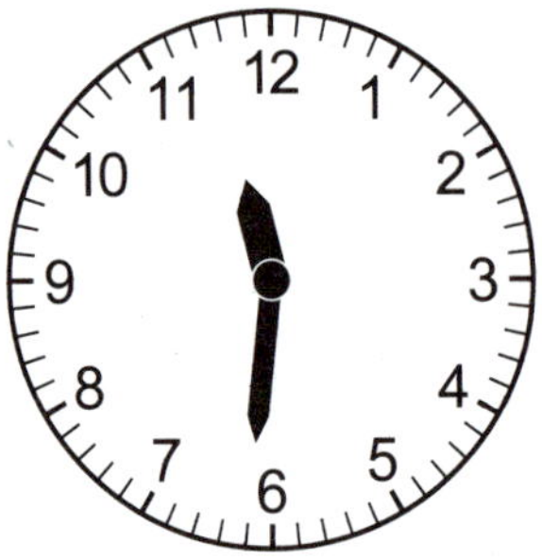

_____ minutes past _____

_____ minutes to _____

REMINDER ▶ 1 hour = 60 minutes.

It is 4:35. This is 35 minutes past 4.

How much time is left till 5 o'clock?

60 − 35 = 25, so it is 25 minutes to 5.

7. Tell the time two ways.

a) 3:40

_____ minutes past _____

_____ minutes to _____

b) 10:51

_____ minutes past _____

_____ minutes to _____

c) 5:39

_____ minutes past _____

_____ minutes to _____

8. Write the time in numbers.

a) twenty minutes after five _5_ : _20_

b) quarter past eleven _____ : _____

c) three fifty-six _____ : _____

d) eight thirty _____ : _____

e) forty-one minutes after seven _____ : _____

f) quarter to nine _____ : _____

BONUS ▶

g) twenty-three minutes to four _____ : _____

h) nineteen minutes to twelve _____ : _____

BONUS ▶ Write the time shown on the clock three different ways.

____

____

____

ME4-26 Time Intervals

1. Count by 5s to find the time interval.

a) 8:10 to 8:25

15 minutes

b) 3:15 to 3:40

c) 10:25 to 11:00

d) 7:35 to 8:00

e) 3:40 to 4:05

f) 9:25 to 10:20

2. Count by 5s and then by 1s to find how much time has elapsed.

a) 8:35 to 8:57

b) 4:30 to 5:04

c) 6:20 to 7:17

d) 4:20 to 4:57

e) 1:15 to 1:31

f) 5:40 to 6:19

3. Count by 5s to find the time interval.

a) 1:12 to 1:52

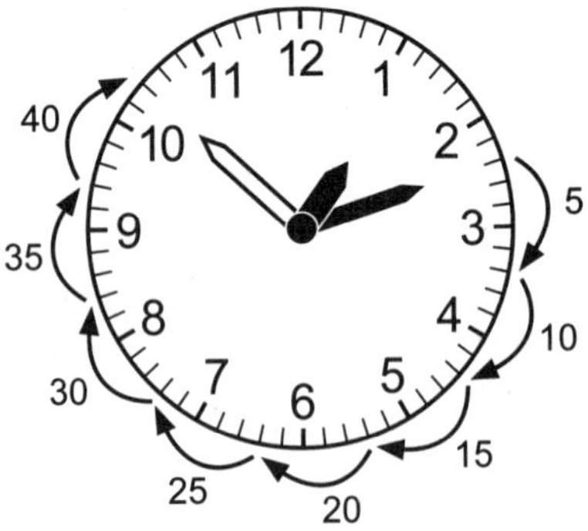

____

b) 6:18 to 6:43

____

c) 7:49 to 8:09

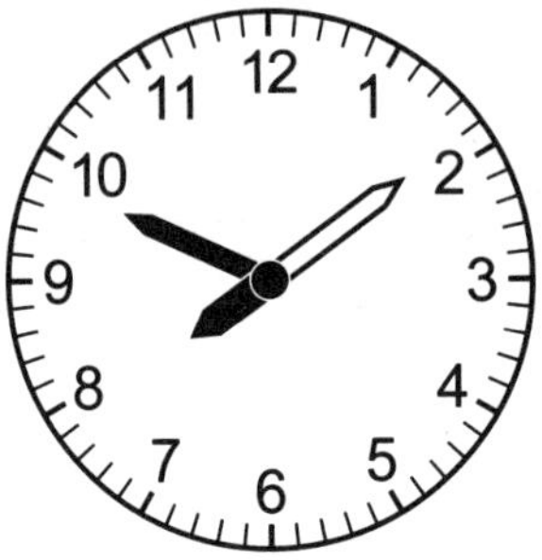

____

4. Count by 5s and then by 1s to find the time interval.

a) 3:14 to 3:47

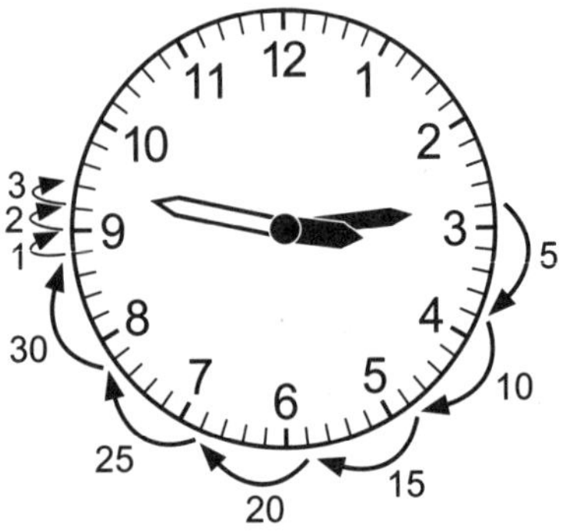

____

b) 11:36 to 11:54

____

c) 4:48 to 5:12

____

5. Count by 5s to estimate the time interval. Then find the actual time interval.

a) 2:47 to 3:15

Estimate: __________________

Actual: __________________

b) 4:33 to 4:59

Estimate: __________________

Actual: __________________

c) 9:21 to 9:38

Estimate: __________________

Actual: __________________

6. It is now 5:13. Matt started playing at 4:21. How long has he been playing?

7. The clock shows the time Kate started reading. At what time did she finish reading? Draw an arrow on the clock to show the time she finished.

a) Kate read for 20 minutes.

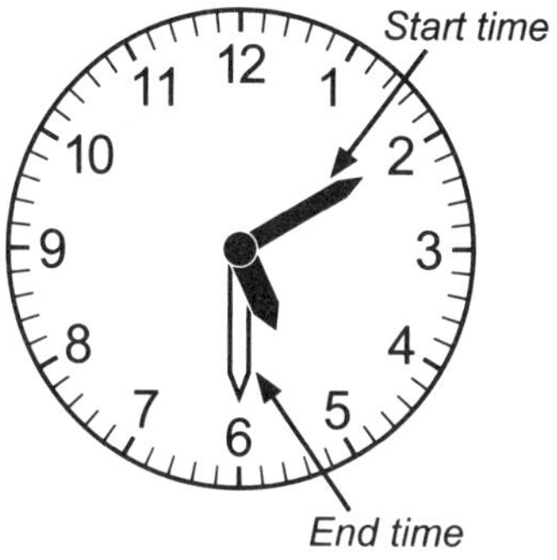

Kate finished at ________.

b) Kate read for 15 minutes.

Kate finished at ________.

c) Kate read for 23 minutes.

Kate finished at ________.

Jake started reading at 1:21. He read for 36 minutes. When did he finish reading?

1:21 ← start time
+ 0:36 ← elapsed time = 36 minutes = 0 hours 36 minutes = 0:36
1:57

Jake finished reading at 1:57.

8. Add to find the end time.

a) 3:23 + 0:20
b) 8:22 + 0:11
c) 1:48 + 5:00
d) 6:37 + 2:15
e) 3:42 + 8:09

9. Regroup 60 minutes as 1 hour.

a) 2:65 *3:05*
b) 7:71
c) 8:80
d) 2:92
e) 1:105

10. Add and regroup to find the end time.

a) 3:23 + 1:40 = *4:63* *5:03*
b) 8:22 + 0:51
c) 9:48 + 1:30
d) 6:43 + 2:25
e) 3:42 + 1:50

11. a) Nina goes to bed at 7:45 p.m. Evan's bedtime is 30 minutes later. What time does Evan go to bed?

b) Tess put chicken in the oven at 4:52 p.m. It should bake for 1 hour and 40 minutes. At what time should she take it out?

12. Cody started reading at 3:33. He finished at 4:27. How long was he reading?

BONUS ▶ Muffins need to bake for 22 minutes. You want them to be ready at 6:00 p.m. When should you put the muffins into the oven?

ME4-27 Elapsed Time

1. Find how much time has passed between the times in bold (intervals are not shown to scale).

a)

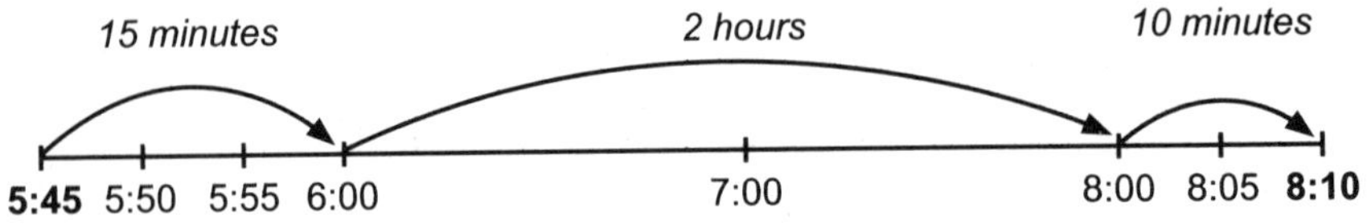

Elapsed time: *2 hours 25 minutes*

b)

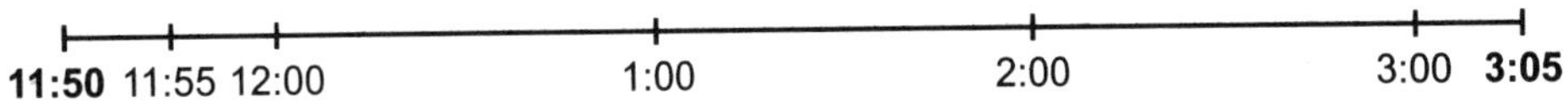

Elapsed time: ____________________

c)

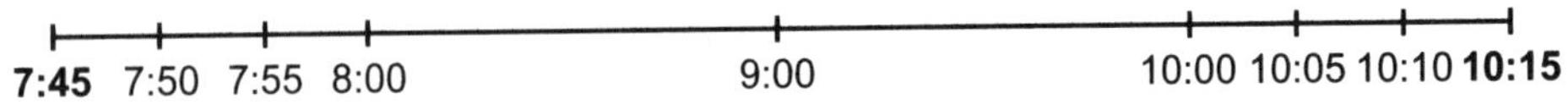

Elapsed time: ____________________

2. Find how much time has passed between the times in bold.
Regroup 60 minutes as 1 hour.

a)

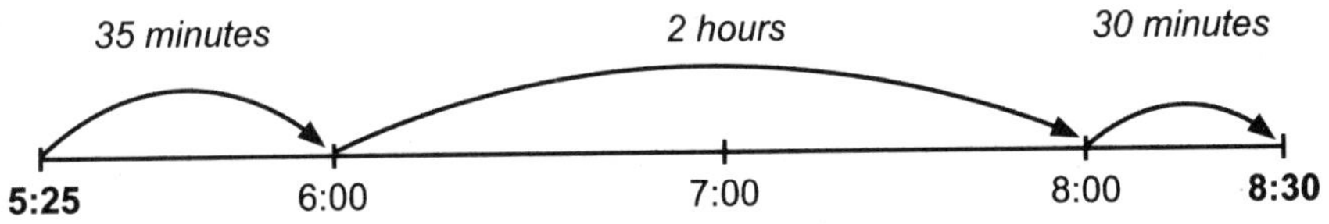

Elapsed time: *2 hours 65 minutes = 3 hours 5 minutes*

b)

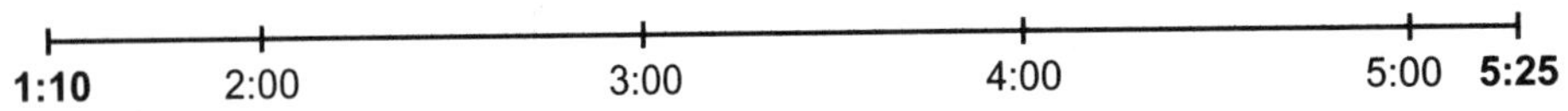

Elapsed time: ____________________

c)

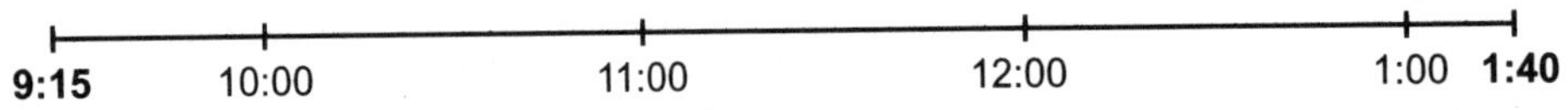

Elapsed time: ____________________

3. Draw a timeline to find out how much time has elapsed between …

a) 7:40 and 10:10 b) 4:35 and 6:05 c) 8:50 and 10:10

4. Draw a timeline to find the arrival time.

a) Sun leaves home at 8:15 a.m. and walks 20 minutes to get to school.

She arrives at ________.

b) Ben leaves home at 8:25 a.m. He walks 10 minutes to the bus. The bus drives 25 minutes to get to school.

Ben arrives at school at ________.

c) Emma wakes up at 6:30 a.m. She takes 15 minutes to eat breakfast, exercises for 1 hour, takes 35 minutes to shower, dress, and brush her teeth, and then takes another 25 minutes to get to school.

Emma gets to school at ________.

5. The movie starts at 7:00 p.m. Will the student be on time? Estimate your answer, then use a timeline or add the times to check.

a) Marla eats dinner at 6:00 p.m. It takes 25 minutes. Then she brushes her teeth for 5 minutes. She walks 5 minutes to the bus stop. She waits 5 minutes for the bus. The bus ride to the movie theatre takes 15 minutes.

b) David leaves his home at 5:45 p.m. and walks 10 minutes to Ken's. Ken takes 5 minutes to get ready. Then they walk together 20 minutes to Hanna's. Hanna is waiting outside when Ken and David arrive. All three walk 10 minutes to a pizzeria. They wait 10 minutes in line and then 5 minutes to get their pizza. They take 15 minutes to eat their pizza. They then walk another 10 minutes to the movie theatre.

c) Mary starts her homework at 11:00 a.m. She studies for 2 hours, then takes a 90 minute break to have lunch and relax. Then she has dance class. Mary is home from dance class after 2 hours. Mary does 1 more hour of schoolwork before stopping for dinner. Helping with dinner, eating, and cleaning up takes 1 hour and 15 minutes. Her father takes 10 minutes to drive her to the movie theatre.

ME3-21 Intervals of Time

I week = 7 days | I day = 24 hours | I hour = 60 minutes

I. Skip count to fill in the table.

a)

Weeks	Days
I	
2	
3	

b)

Days	Hours
I	
2	
3	

c)

Hours	Minutes
I	
2	
3	

2. a) Nina's birthday is in 2 weeks. How many days until Nina's birthday? ______

b) A weekend is 2 days long. How many hours long is one weekend? ______

3. A train ride from Toronto to Vancouver takes 87 hours. How long is the trip? Circle the correct answer.

between 2 and 3 days   between 3 and 4 days   between 4 and 5 days

4. A test is 90 minutes long.

a) Is the test longer than I hour? ________

b) Is the test longer than 2 hours? ________

5. Ronin walks his dog 3 times a day, 20 minutes each time.

a) How many minutes does he walk his dog in one day? ________

b) How many hours does he walk his dog in one day? ________

c) How many hours each week does Ronin spend walking his dog? ________

6. Zara exercises 40 minutes every day.

a) How many minutes does she exercise in one week?

Hint: Skip count by 40. ________________________________

b) A doctor says Zara should exercise at least 3 hours a week.

Does she exercise enough? ________

7. Multiply by 7 to convert weeks to days. Add the leftover days.

a) 2 weeks 3 days

2 weeks = 14 days

2 weeks 3 days

= 14 + 3 days

= 17 days

b) 3 weeks 2 days

3 weeks = ______ days

3 weeks 2 days

= __________ days

= ______ days

c) 4 weeks 5 days

4 weeks = ______ days

4 weeks 5 days

= __________ days

= ______ days

d) I week 5 days

= __________ days

= ______ days

e) 3 weeks 6 days

= __________ days

= ______ days

f) 5 weeks I day

= __________ days

= ______ days

BONUS ▶ Circle the time periods in Question 7 that are longer than I month.

8. Change the hours to minutes. Add the leftover minutes.

a) 2 hours 3 minutes

= 120 + 3 minutes

= 123 minutes

b) 3 hours 20 minutes

= __________ minutes

= ______ minutes

c) 4 hours 15 minutes

= __________ minutes

= ______ minutes

d) I hour 55 minutes

e) 3 hours 30 minutes

f) 5 hours I minute

9. Tom reads a book for I hour 45 minutes. Kathy reads a book for II5 minutes. Who spends more time reading? How much longer does this person read?

10. There are 52 weeks in I year.

a) Iva is exactly 2 years old. How many weeks old is Iva?

b) Lewis is 42 weeks old. Nora is 30 weeks older than Lewis. Who is older, Nora or Iva? Explain.

c) Marcel is 6 weeks younger than Iva. Who is older, Nora or Marcel? Explain.

11. A decade is I0 years long. A century is I00 years long. A millennium is I000 years long. If a ones block represents I year, what do the other base ten blocks represent?

ME3-22 Units of Time

I minute = 60 seconds

I. a) Fill in the table.

Minutes	I	2	3	4	5	6
Seconds	*60*					

b) Ava runs for 3 minutes. How many seconds does she run for? ________

2. Change the minutes to seconds. Add the leftover seconds.

a) 2 minutes 7 seconds
= *I20 + 7* seconds
= *I27* seconds

b) 3 minutes 40 seconds
= __________ seconds
= ______ seconds

c) 4 minutes 23 seconds
= __________ seconds
= ______ seconds

d) I minute 57 seconds
= __________ seconds
= ______ seconds

e) 6 minutes I0 seconds
= __________ seconds
= ______ seconds

f) 5 minutes 5 seconds
= __________ seconds
= ______ seconds

3. Bill can run 500 m in I minute 50 seconds. Ethan can run 500 m in I03 seconds. Who can run 500 m faster? ______________

4. What unit of time would you use in the answer? Choose from seconds, minutes, hours, days, months, and years.

a) How long is your favourite TV show? __________________
b) How old are you? __________________
c) How long is the school day? __________________
d) How long does it take you to run I00 m? __________________
e) How long is March Break? __________________
f) How long is the summer vacation? __________________
g) How long ago did Nunavut become a territory? __________________
h) How long does it take you to do I0 jumping jacks? __________________
i) How long is one half of a soccer game? __________________

5. Does the activity take less than 1 minute or more than 1 minute?

a) eating breakfast ____________

b) blinking 10 times ____________

c) brushing your teeth ____________

d) watering a plant ____________

e) going to school ____________

f) playing a hockey game ____________

6. Does the activity take less than 1 hour or more than 1 hour?

a) eating lunch ____________

b) sleeping at night ____________

c) brushing your teeth ____________

d) making a bed ____________

e) getting dressed ____________

f) the school day ____________

7. Use a calendar to fill in the tables.

Month	Number of Days
January	
February	
March	
April	

Month	Number of Days
May	
June	
July	
August	

Month	Number of Days
September	
October	
November	
December	

8. a) Jennifer's birthday is on July 23. Luc's birthday is 10 days after Jennifer's. When is Luc's birthday?

b) Kate's birthday is on April 20. Glen's birthday is 2 weeks later. When is Glen's birthday?

c) Sandy's birthday is 3 weeks before Kate's. When is Sandy's birthday?

BONUS ▶ It takes about 15 minutes to walk 1 km.

a) Will walking 5 km take less than 1 hour, about 1 hour, or more than 1 hour?

b) About how many kilometres can you walk in 1 hour?

ME5-7 Calculating Elapsed Time

To find the **elapsed time** from 08:10 to 14:25, we can subtract. 6 hours 15 minutes have elapsed.

	1	4	:	2	5	← end time
−	0	8	:	1	0	← start time
		6	:	1	5	← elapsed time

1. Find the elapsed time.

a) 09:12 to 14:18

			:		
−			:		
			:		

b) 05:34 to 18:49

			:		
−			:		
			:		

c) 08:35 to 19:48

			:		
−			:		
			:		

d) 04:18 to 16:44

			:		
−			:		
			:		

e) 06:28 to 09:53

			:		
−			:		
			:		

f) 12:47 to 14:52

			:		
−			:		
			:		

2. Regroup 1 hour as 60 minutes.

a) 4:25 *3:85* b) 3:13 ______ c) 8:08 ______ d) 14:25 ______ e) 13:13 ______ f) 18:39 ______

Example: Find the elapsed time from 07:35 to 14:15.
Jack couldn't subtract 35 min from 15 min, so he regrouped 1 hour as 60 minutes.

Step 1: Regroup 1 hour as 60 minutes.

14:15 → 13:75

Step 2: Subtract.

	1	3	:	7	5
−	0	7	:	3	5
		6	:	4	0

3. Find the elapsed time by regrouping first.

a) 05:35 to 13:24

	1	*2*	:	*8*	*4*
−	*0*	*5*	:	*3*	*5*
			:		

b) 10:47 to 20:35

			:		
−			:		
			:		

c) 8:49 to 14:16

			:		
−			:		
			:		

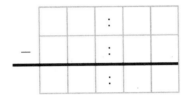

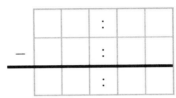

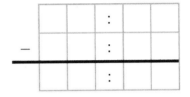

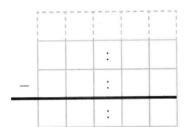

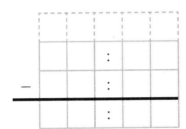

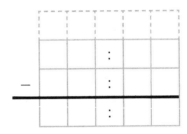

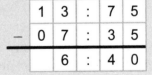

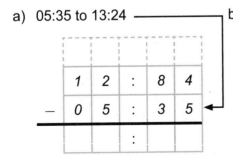

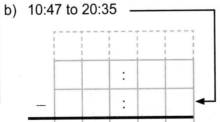

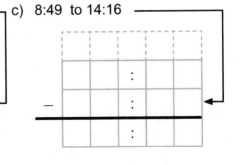

4. Find the elapsed time by first converting to a 24-hour clock. Regroup where necessary.

a) 8:30 a.m. to 2:55 p.m.

	1	4	:	5	5
–		8	:	3	0
		6	:	2	5

b) 7:25 a.m. to 3:45 p.m.

			:		
–			:		
			:		

c) 9:28 a.m. to 1:55 p.m.

			:		
–			:		
			:		

d) 10:45 a.m. to 5:33 p.m.

			:		
–			:		
			:		

A movie ended at 1:45 p.m. and was 2 hours 35 minutes long.
To find the start time of the movie, convert to a 24-hour clock and subtract.

	1	3	:	4	5
–	0	2	:	3	5
	1	1	:	1	0

The movie started at 11:10 a.m.

5. Find the start time. Regroup where necessary.

a) Elapsed time = 3:47
End time = 11:36 a.m.

	1	0	:	9	6
–		3	:	4	7
			:		

b) Elapsed time = 8:27
End time = 11:15 p.m.

			:		
–			:		
			:		

c) Elapsed time = 0:38
End time = 1:25 p.m.

			:		
–			:		
			:		

d) Elapsed time = 12:15
End time = 8:10 p.m.

			:		
–			:		
			:		

6. In Winnipeg, MB, in July, sunset was at 9:20 p.m. There were 15 hours 31 minutes of daylight. What time did the sun rise?

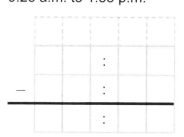

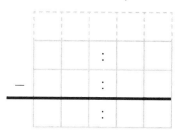

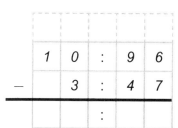

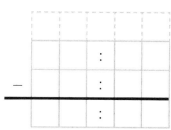

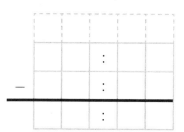

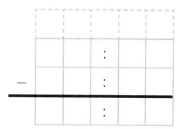

ME5-8 Elapsed Time on Timelines

1. Find how much time has passed between the times in bold (intervals are not shown to scale).

a)

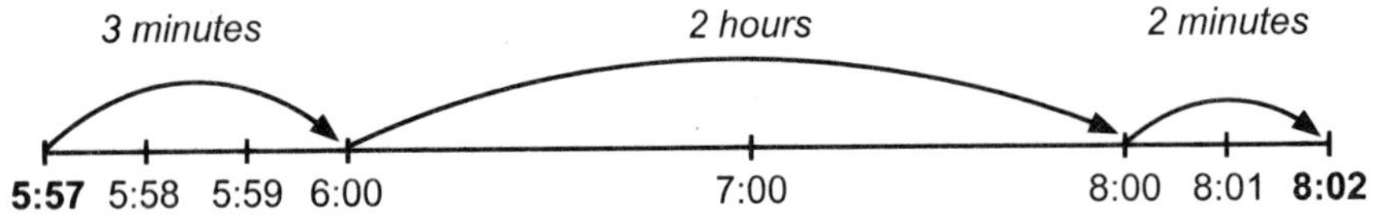

Elapsed time: *2 hours 5 minutes*

b)

Elapsed time: ______________________

c)

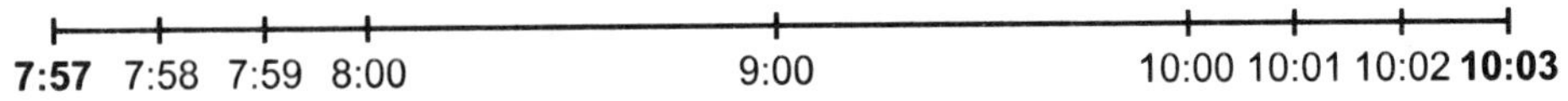

Elapsed time: ______________________

2. Find how much time has passed between the times in bold.

a)

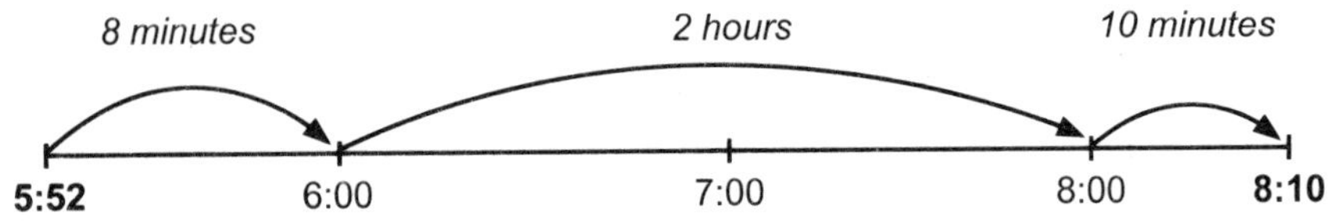

Elapsed time: *2 hours 18 minutes*

b)

Elapsed time: ______________________

BONUS ▸

Elapsed time: ______________________

3. Draw a timeline to find out how much time has elapsed between …

a) 7:50 and 10:12

b) 4:39 and 6:20

c) 8:37 and 10:18

4. Draw a timeline to find the arrival time.

a) Sun leaves home at 8:12 a.m. and walks 25 minutes to get to school.

She arrives at _________.

b) Ben leaves home at 8:03 a.m. He walks 10 minutes to the bus. The bus drives 24 minutes to get to school.

Ben arrives at school at _________.

c) Emma wakes up at 6:30 a.m. She takes 12 minutes to eat breakfast, exercises for 1 hour, takes 27 minutes to shower, dress, and brush her teeth, and then takes another 18 minutes to get to school.

Emma gets to school at _________.

5. The hockey game starts at 8:00 p.m. Will the hockey fans be on time? Estimate your answer, then use a timeline or add the times to check.

a) Marla eats dinner at 7:00 p.m. It takes 22 minutes. Then she brushes her teeth for 4 minutes. She walks 7 minutes to the bus stop. She waits 6 minutes for the bus. The bus ride to the arena takes 19 minutes.

b) David leaves his home at 6:45 p.m. and walks 17 minutes to Ken's. Ken takes 6 minutes to get ready. Then they walk together 9 minutes to Hanna's. Hanna is waiting outside when Ken and David arrive. All three walk 8 minutes to a pizzeria. They wait 7 minutes in line and then 13 minutes to get their pizza. They take 7 minutes to eat their pizza. They then walk another 11 minutes to the arena.

c) Mary starts her homework at 11:00 a.m. She studies for 1 hour and 37 minutes, then takes a 90 minute break to have lunch and relax. Then she has dance class. Mary is home from dance class after 1 hour and 40 minutes. Mary does 45 more minutes of schoolwork before stopping for dinner. Helping with dinner, eating, and cleaning up takes 1 hour and 18 minutes. Her father takes 13 minutes to drive her to the arena.

ME5-10 Periods of Time

1. a) Fill in the table.

weeks	1	2	3	4	5	6	7
days	*7*						

b) What number do you multiply by to get the number of days from the number of weeks? _________

2. A month can have 28, 29, 30, or 31 days. About how many weeks are in 1 month? _______________

3. Change the time expressed in weeks and days to days only.

a) 2 weeks 3 days

= *14* days + *3* days

= *17* days

b) 3 weeks 6 days

= ____ days + ____ days

= ____ days

c) 5 weeks 2 days

= ____ days + ____ days

= ____ days

4. Janice wants to know how long it took her plant to grow a certain height. Help her find the time in days.

Height of Janice's plant	Time After Planting *(in weeks and days)*	Rough Work	Time After Planting *(in days)*
2 cm	0 weeks and 4 days	$0 \times 7 = 0$ $0 + 4 = 4$	*4*
4 cm	1 week and 1 day	$1 \times 7 = 7$ $7 + 1 = 8$	
6 cm	1 week and 5 days		
8 cm	2 weeks and 2 days		
10 cm	2 weeks and 6 days		
12 cm	3 weeks and 3 days		

a) Complete the table.

b) How long did it take the plant to grow 2 cm? _______________

c) How long (in days) did it take the plant to reach 11 cm? _______________ Explain.

____

____

____

d) How long (in days) will it take the plant to reach 14 cm? _______________

5. Convert the multiple-unit measurements to minutes.

a) 3 hours = ___180___ minutes,

so 3 hours 10 minutes = ___190___ minutes

b) 4 hours = _____ minutes,

so 4 hours 25 minutes = _____ minutes

c) 2 minutes = _____ seconds,

so 2 minutes 43 seconds = _____ seconds

d) 10 minutes = _____ seconds,

so 10 minutes 12 seconds = _____ seconds

1 year = 365 days and 1 year = about 52 weeks

There are 366 days in a leap year.

A **decade** is 10 years. A **century** is 100 years.

6. Order the units from smallest (1) to largest (5).

day	minute	week	year	hour
☐	1	☐	☐	☐

7. Fill in the table.

a)

days	hours
1	24
2	
3	

b)

decades	years
1	10
2	
3	

c)

years	weeks
1	52
2	
3	

d)

years	days
1	365
2	
3	

8. Which interval is longer? Explain.

a) 70 minutes OR 1 hour 20 minutes

b) 3 hours 10 minutes OR 170 minutes

c) 4 minutes 24 seconds OR 285 seconds

d) 10 weeks OR 65 days

9. Tom worked for 1 hour 55 minutes. Jo worked 20 minutes longer. How long did Jo work?

10. Fill in the tables.

decades	1	2	3	4
years	10			

centuries	1	2	3	4
years	100			

11. Fill in the blank.

a) 40 years = _____ decades

b) 300 years = _____ centuries

c) 14 decades = _____ years

d) 30 decades = _____ centuries

12. Which interval is longer? Explain.

a) 8 decades OR 75 years

b) 5 centuries OR 47 decades

13. Queen Victoria became queen of the United Kingdom in 1837.

a) About how many centuries ago was this?

b) About how many decades ago was this?

14. A baseball game started at 11:25 a.m. and lasted for 2 hours 45 minutes. What time did it end?

15. Keesha did homework from 3:24 p.m. to 5:43 p.m. For how long was she doing homework?

16. Grace's family drove from Vancouver, BC, to Kamloops. They left at 10:04 a.m. and arrived at 1:58 p.m. For how long did they travel?

17. A bicycle rental company charges per hour for renting a bike. Jayden rents a bike starting at 9:45 a.m. and returns it at 3:45 p.m.

a) For how long did he have the bike?

b) The rental company charges $5 plus $10 per hour. What is the total charge?

18. Nao fills out a timesheet at work. It shows when he starts and ends work.

Day	Start time	End time	Time Worked
Monday	8:25 a.m.	11:40 a.m.	____ h ____ min
Tuesday	12:15 p.m.	2:45 p.m.	____ h ____ min
Wednesday	1:45 p.m.	5:15 p.m.	____ h ____ min
Thursday	9:45 a.m.	5:10 p.m.	____ h ____ min
Friday	8:25 a.m.	4:00 p.m.	____ h ____ min

a) Find the amount of time he worked each day.

b) What is the total time he worked for the week written in hours and minutes?

c) Nao earns $17 per hour. Round the total time Nao worked to the nearest hour and estimate his week's pay using multiplication.

G5-8 Parallel and Perpendicular Sides

Parallel lines are like the long, straight rails on a railroad track.
Parallel lines are:

- Straight
- Always the same distance apart

You can extend lines in both directions as much as you want.
No matter how long they are, parallel lines will never meet.

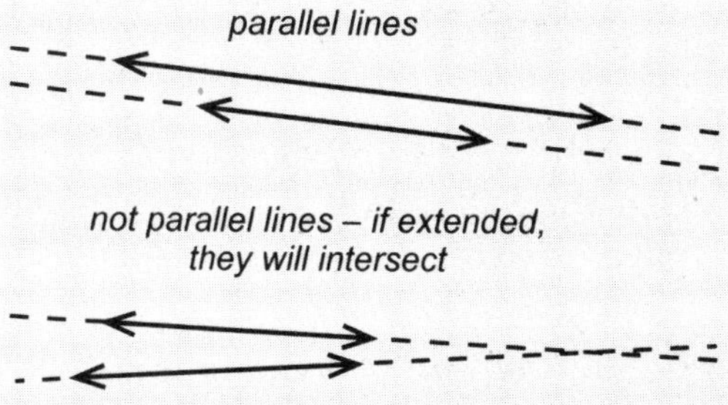

1. Extend the lines to check if they intersect. Then circle parallel lines.

a) 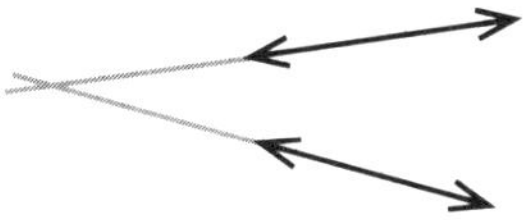 b) 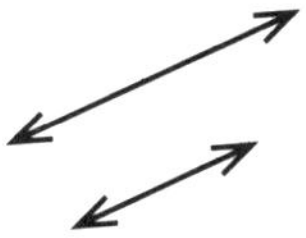 c) 

Mathematicians mark parallel lines with arrows, like this: 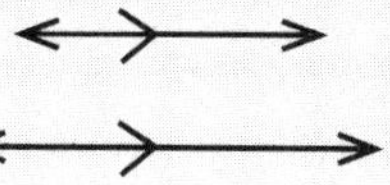

2. Mark any pairs of lines that are parallel with arrows.

a) 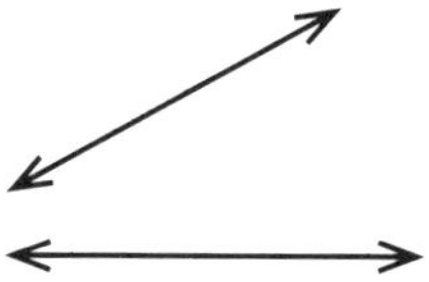 b)  c)  d) 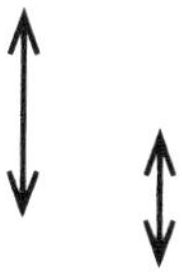

e) 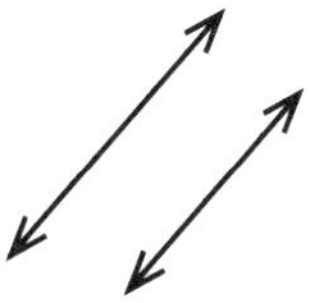 f)  g) 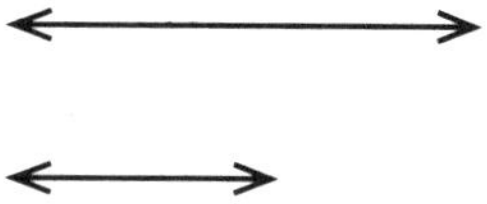 h) 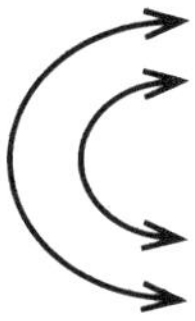

3. The line segments are parallel. Join the end points to make a quadrilateral.
Use a ruler.

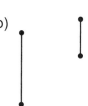

a) 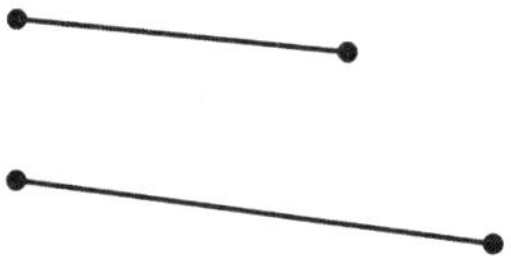 b)  c) 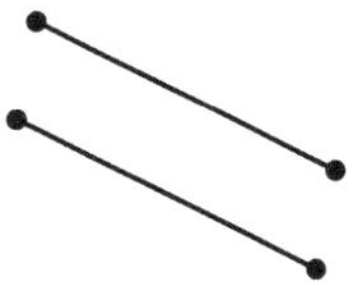 d) 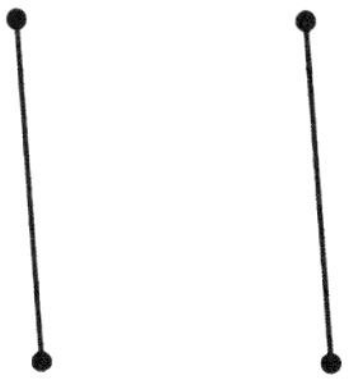

4. Mark the parallel sides with arrows.

a) 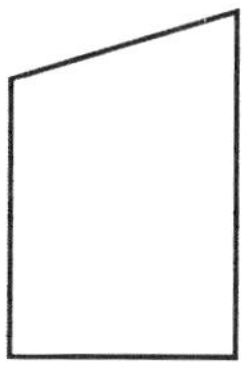 b) 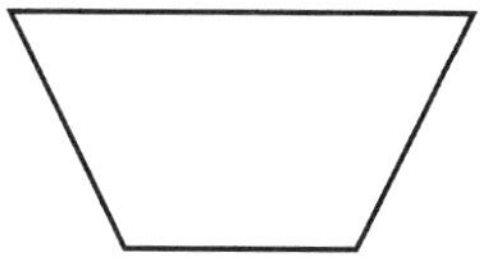 c) 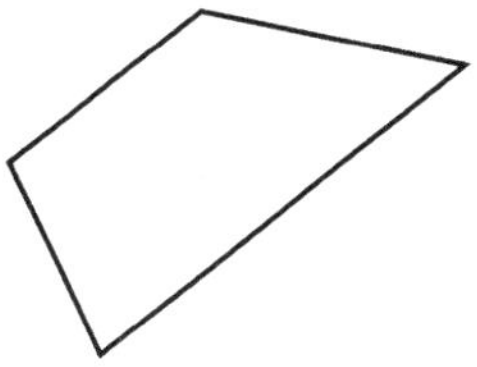 d) 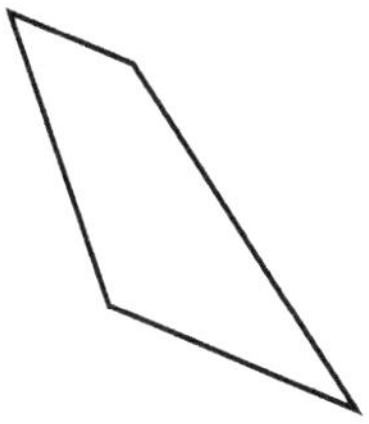

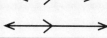

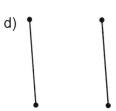

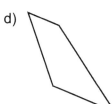

If there is more than one set of parallel sides in a shape, use a different number of arrows to mark each set.

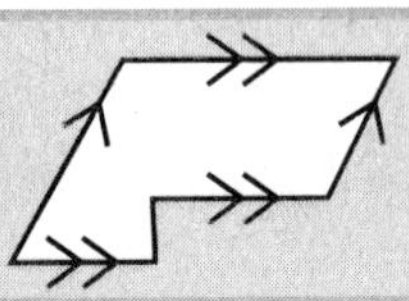

5. Use arrows to mark all the sets of parallel sides. Circle the shapes that have no parallel sides.

a) 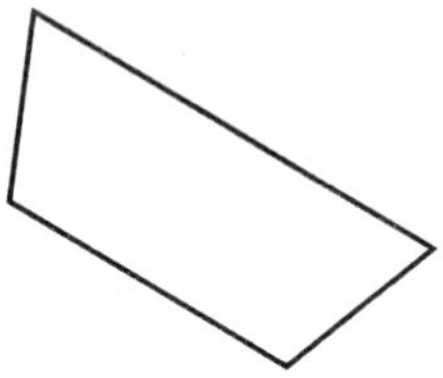

b) 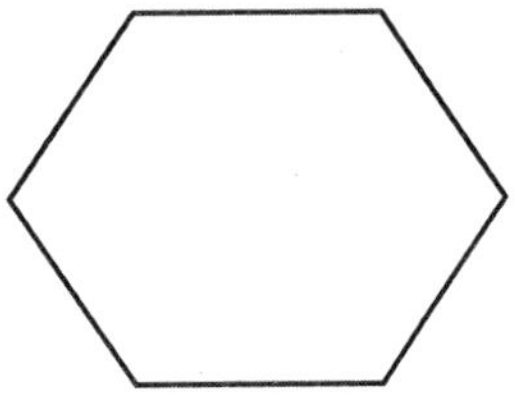

c) 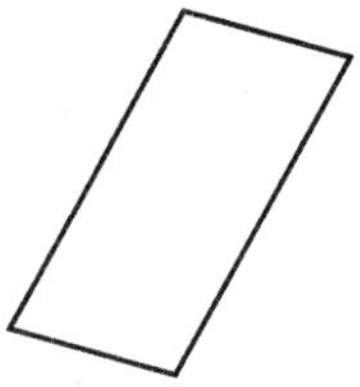

d) 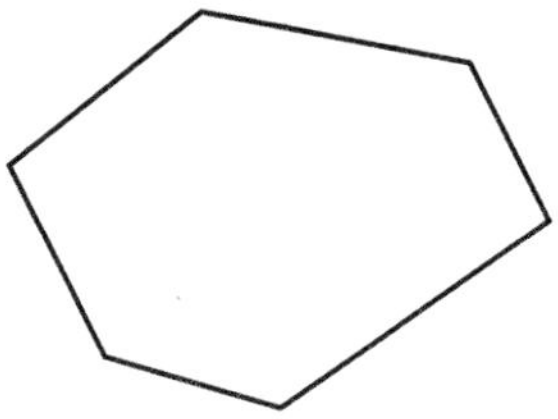

e) 

f) 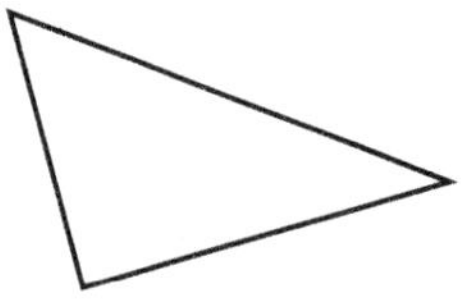

g) 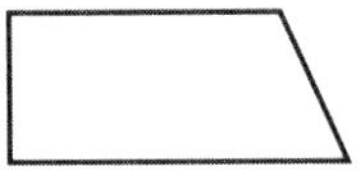

h) 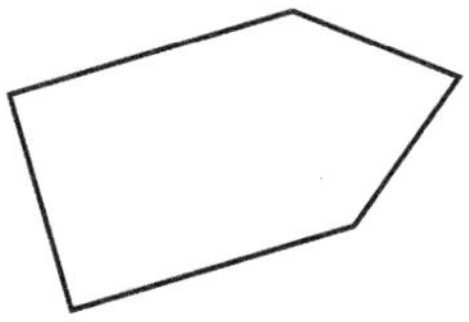

i) 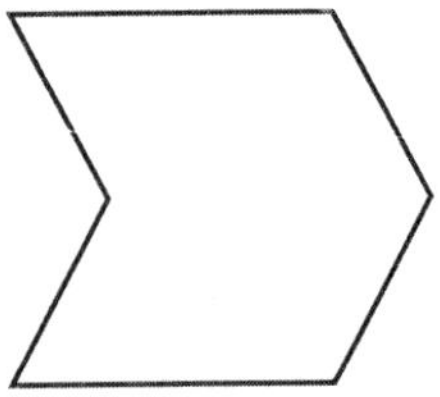

j) 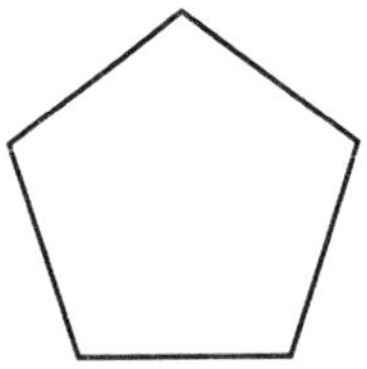

k) 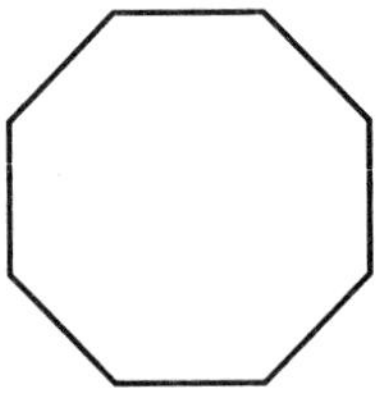

BONUS ▶ 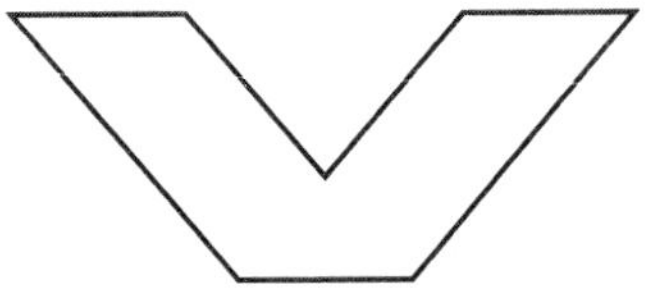

6. a) What is the largest number of **pairs** of parallel sides the polygon can have? Draw a polygon with this number of pairs of parallel sides.

i) quadrilateral ____ 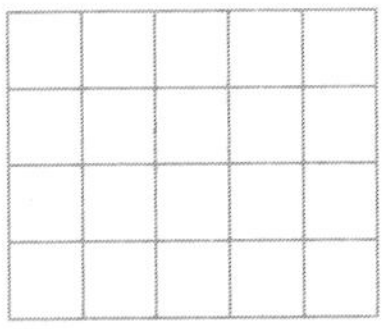

ii) hexagon ____ 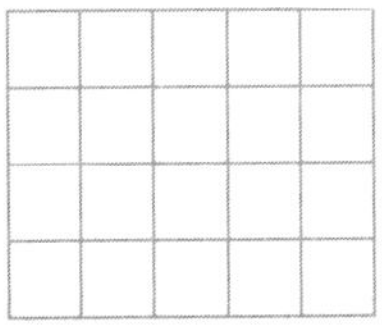

iii) triangle ____ 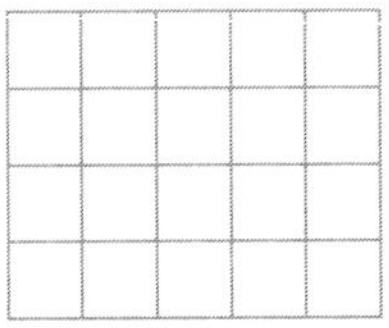

BONUS ▶ pentagon ____ 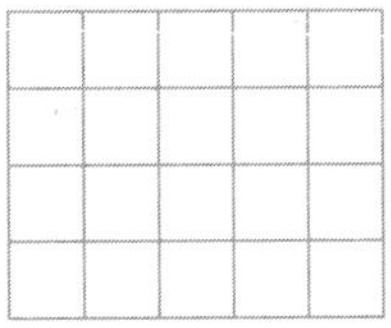

b) On grid paper, draw a quadrilateral and a hexagon that have no parallel sides.

Perpendicular lines are lines that make a right angle.

7. a) Draw a line perpendicular to line *m* that crosses line *n*.

b) The line you drew in part a) and line *n* make a ____________ angle.

c) Draw a new pair of parallel lines *m* and *n* by tracing the opposite sides of a ruler. Repeat parts a) and b) with the lines. What do you notice?

d) How can you use right angles to check if lines are parallel?

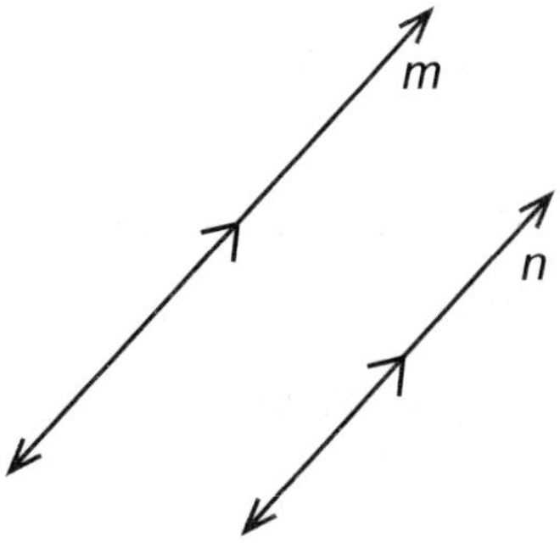

Lines that **intersect** or cross at a point are called intersecting lines.

Two sides of a shape that meet at a vertex are called **intersecting sides**.

Parallel lines and parallel sides never intersect.

8. Circle two sides that are intersecting sides. Draw an X on the vertex where they meet.

a) 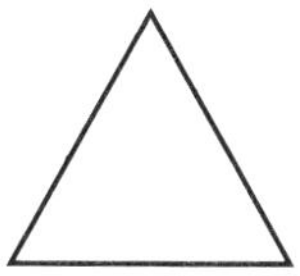

b) 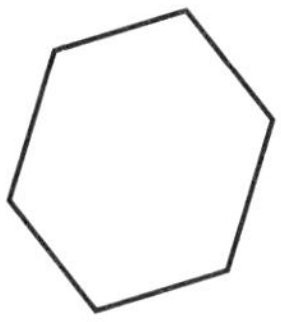

c) 

d) 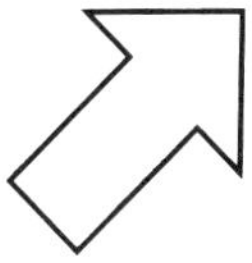

e) 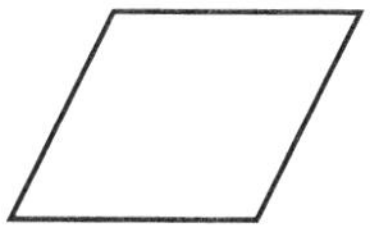

f) 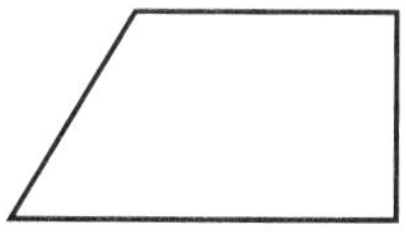

g) 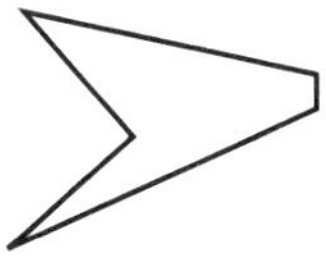

BONUS ▶ 

9. a) Which shapes in Question 8 have perpendicular sides? ____________

b) Which shape in Question 8 has only vertical and horizontal sides? ____________

10. a) Circle two sides that are perpendicular and intersecting. Draw an X on the vertex where they meet.

b) Mark two sides that are parallel with arrows.

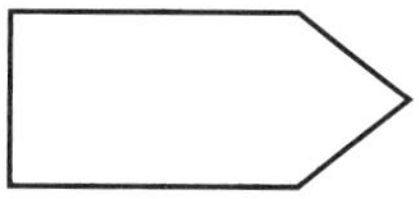

11. The sides of the polygon have been labelled with letters.

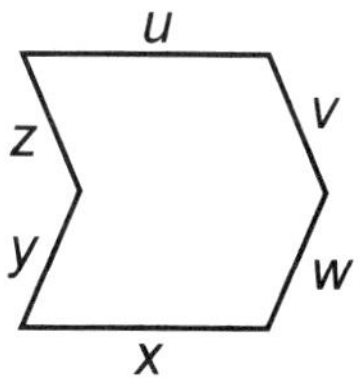

a) Circle all the words that describe sides *y* and *z*.

parallel   intersecting   perpendicular   vertical   horizontal

b) Circle all the words that describe sides *u* and *x*.

parallel   intersecting   perpendicular   vertical   horizontal

c) Circle all the words that describe sides *z* and *v*.

parallel   intersecting   perpendicular   vertical   horizontal

12. On grid paper, draw a polygon that has vertical sides, horizontal sides, at least one pair of parallel sides, and at least one pair of perpendicular sides.

BONUS ▶ Draw a polygon that has the given properties.

a) a pair of parallel sides, a pair of perpendicular sides, and no horizontal or vertical sides

b) no horizontal or vertical sides and any two sides intersect at a vertex

G5-9 Trapezoids and Parallelograms

Follow these steps to check that two lines are parallel:

Step 1: Draw a line perpendicular (at a right angle) to one of the lines.

Step 2: Check the angle the new line makes with the second line.

Step 3: If it is a right angle, the original lines are parallel. If it is not a right angle, the original lines are not parallel.

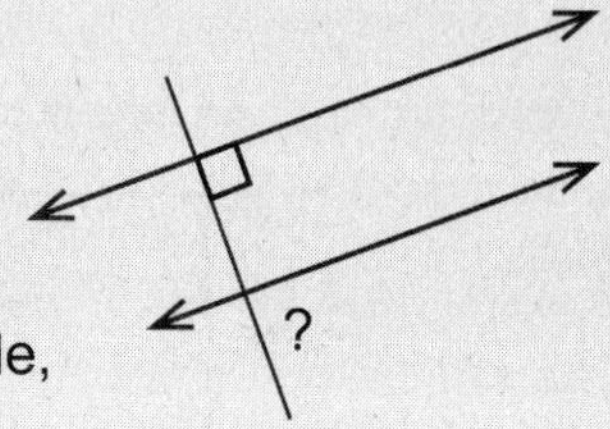

1. Use the steps above to check if the lines are parallel. Mark parallel lines with arrows.

a) 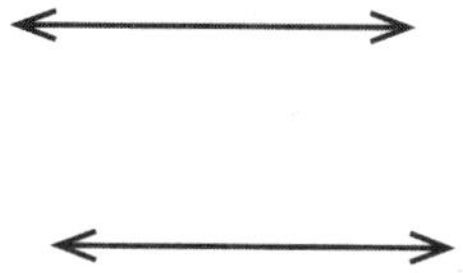

b) 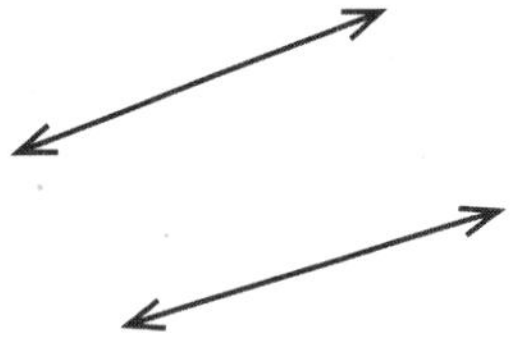

c) 

d) 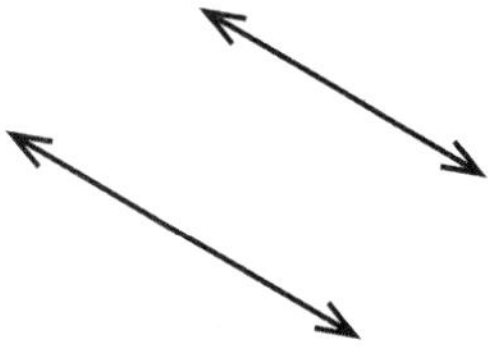

Quadrilaterals with exactly 1 pair of parallel sides are called **trapezoids**.
Quadrilaterals with 2 pairs of parallel sides are called **parallelograms**.

Trapezoids

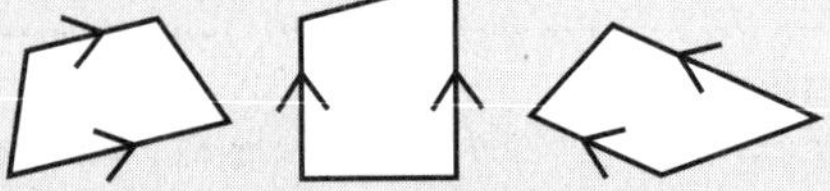

Parallelograms

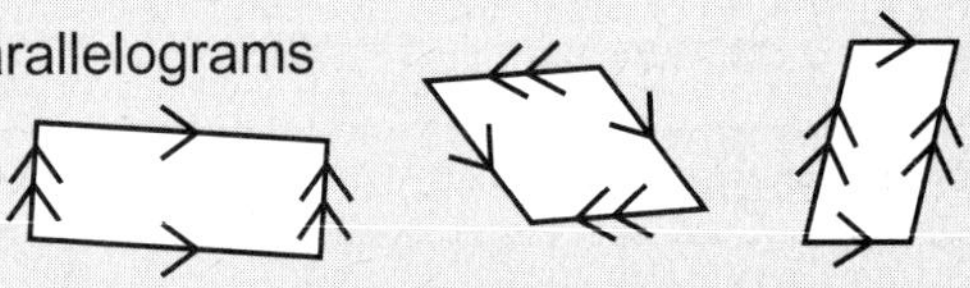

2. Mark the parallel sides with arrows. Then identify the type of quadrilateral.

a) 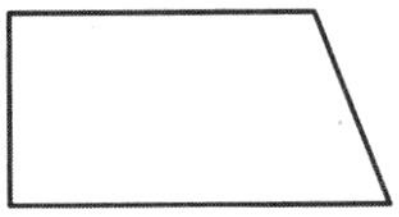

____

b) 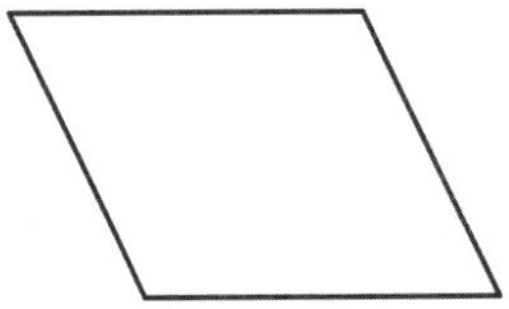

____

c) 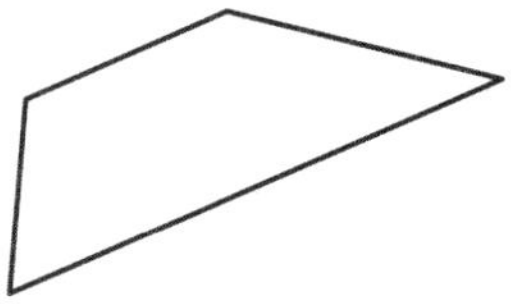

____

d) 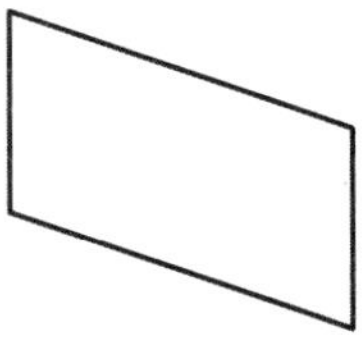

____

3. a) Sort the quadrilaterals to complete the Venn diagram.

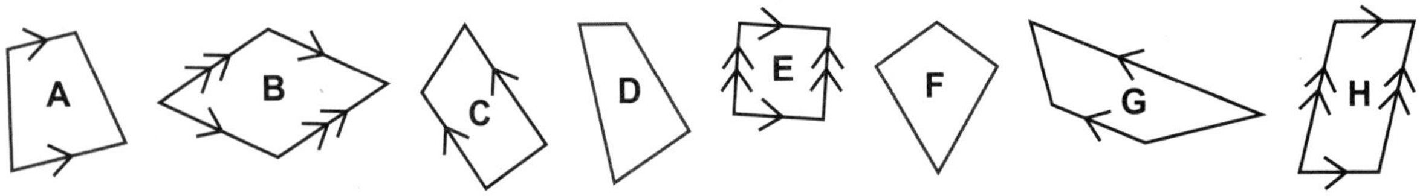

b) Explain why a quadrilateral cannot be a parallelogram and a trapezoid at the same time.

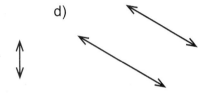

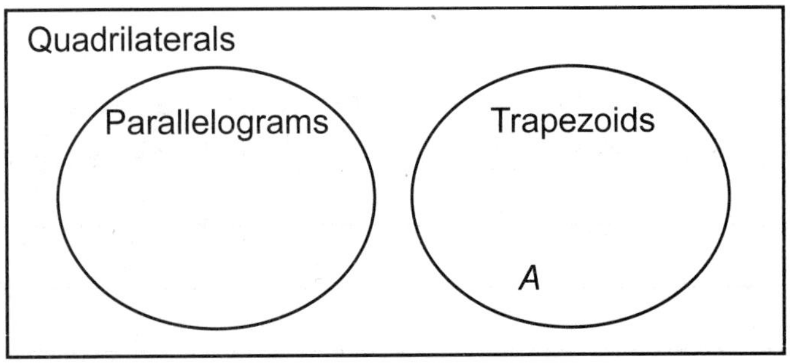

4. a) Measure the parallel sides of the quadrilaterals to the closest millimetre.

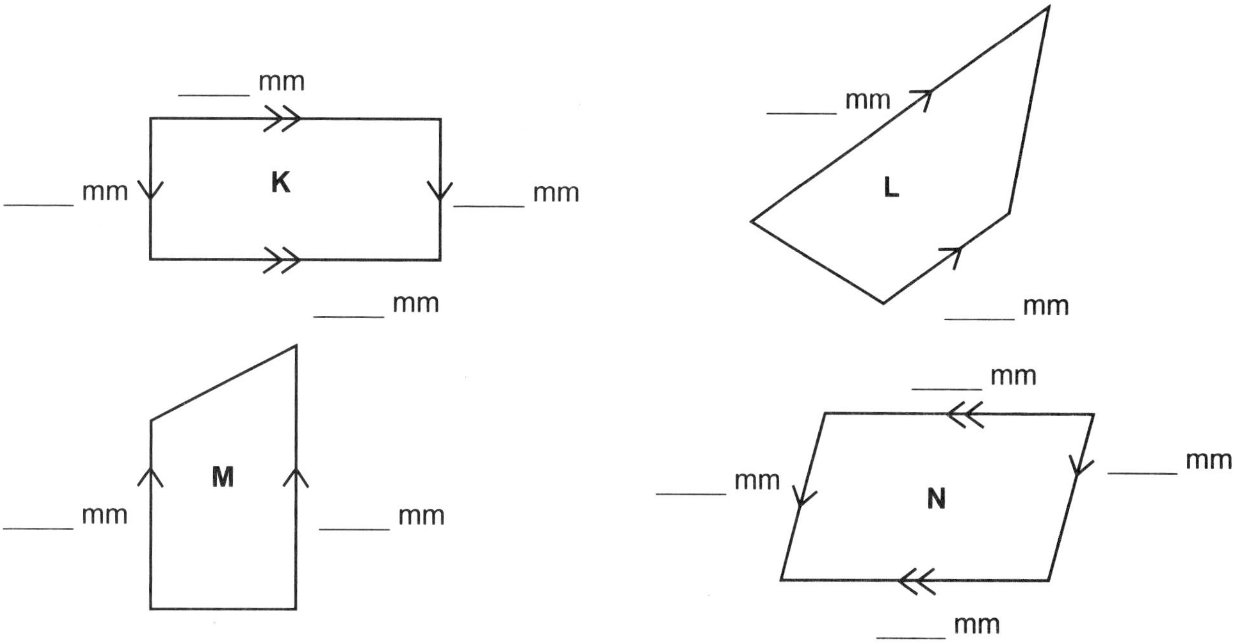

b) Sort the shapes into the tables.

Parallelograms	
Trapezoids	

Parallel Sides are Equal	
Parallel Sides are Not Equal	

c) What do you notice about the tables? ____________________

____

d) One pair of parallel sides is marked. Use your answer in part c) to check if the other pair of sides is parallel. Then identify the type of quadrilateral.

i)

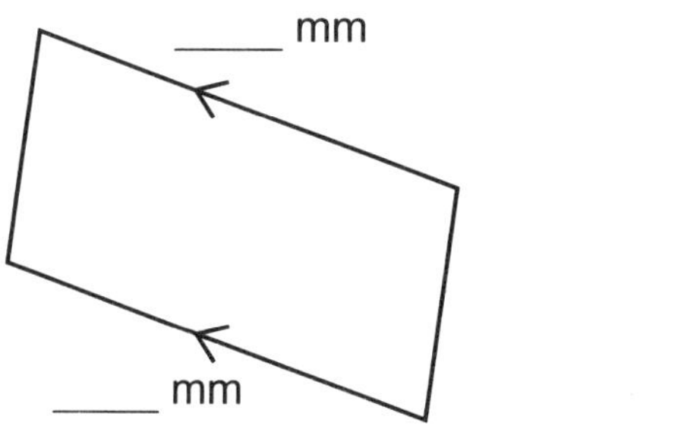

____

ii)

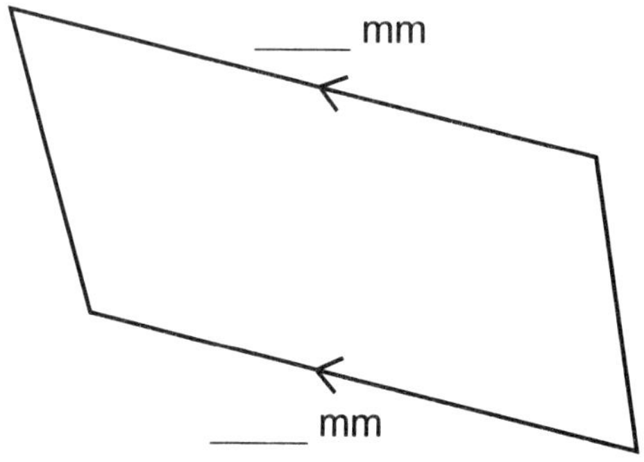

____

5. Ronin thinks that the quadrilateral shown is a parallelogram because the marked opposite sides are equal. Is he correct? Explain.

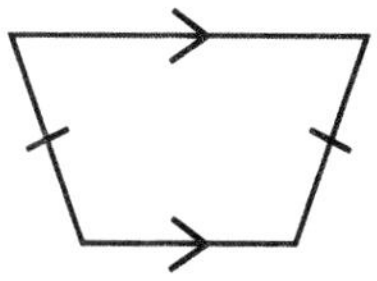

____

____

____

Parallel sides in a parallelogram are always equal. *Parallel* sides of a trapezoid always have different lengths.

6. a) The equal sides are not marked on two of the quadrilaterals below. Mark them.

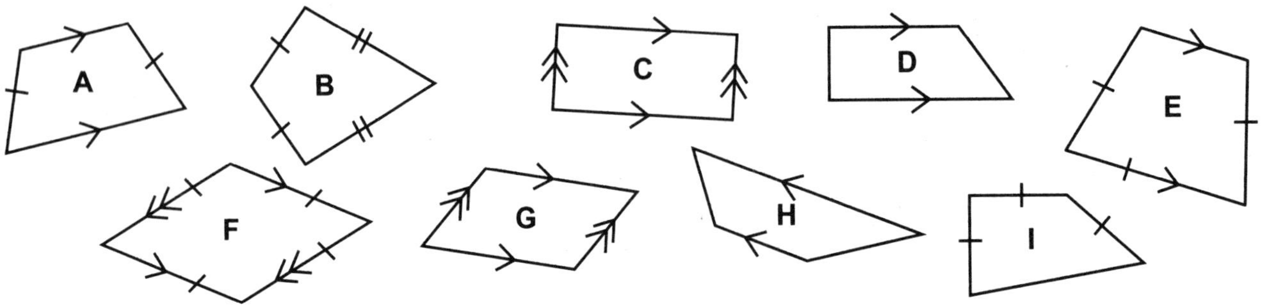

b) Colour the parallelograms red and colour the trapezoids blue.

c) Sort the quadrilaterals.

No Equal Sides	
Exactly 2 Equal Sides	
Exactly 3 Equal Sides	
4 Equal Sides (Equilateral)	
2 Different Pairs of Equal Sides	

d) How many equal sides can a parallelogram have? _________

e) How many equal sides can a trapezoid have? _________

7. A quadrilateral has four equal sides.

a) Can it be a parallelogram? _________ b) Can it be a trapezoid? _________

8. Sort the quadrilaterals in Question 6. Then complete the Venn diagram.

Exactly 1 Pair of Opposite Sides are Parallel	
2 Pairs of Opposite Sides are Parallel	

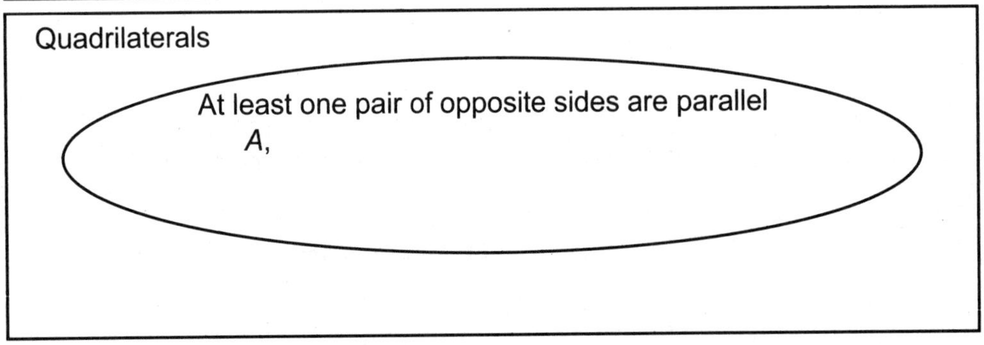

G5-11 Sorting and Classifying Quadrilaterals

1. Mark parallel sides, sides of equal lengths, and right angles.

a) 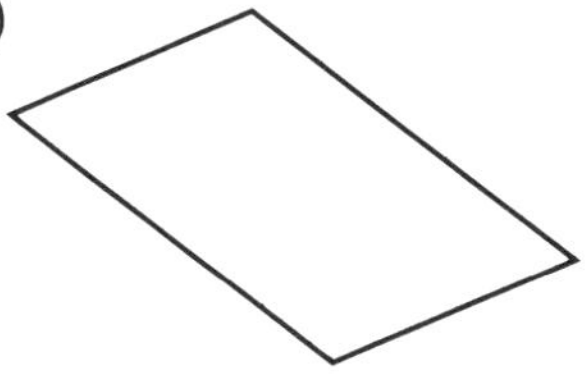

b) 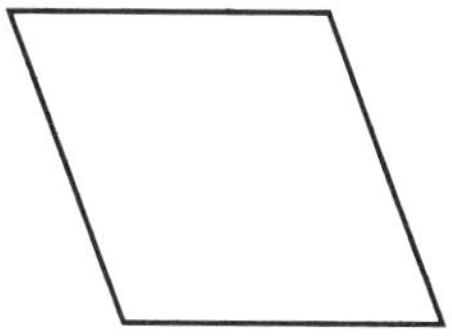

c) 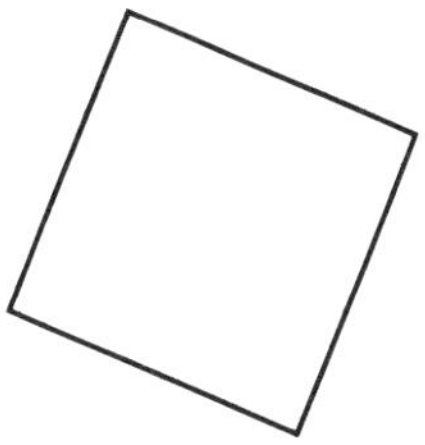

d) 

e) 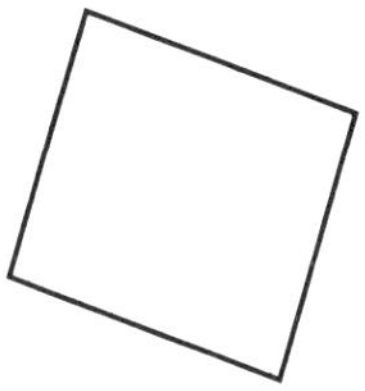

f) 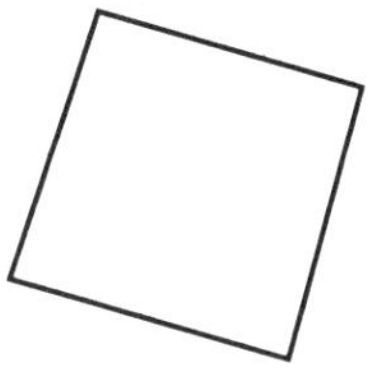

g) 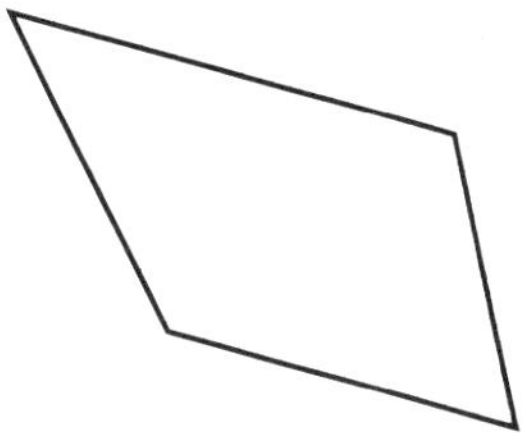

h) 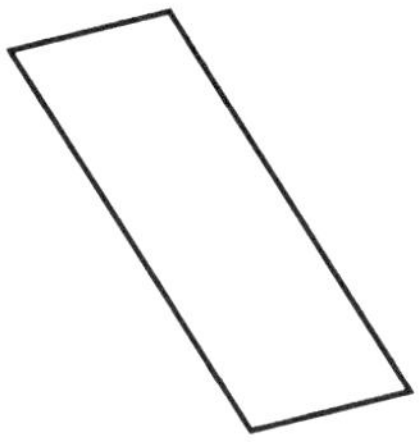

2. Draw a different quadrilateral on each grid. Name the quadrilateral. Be as specific as possible.

a) 

____

b) 

____

c) 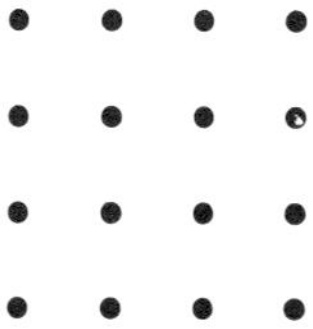

____

d) 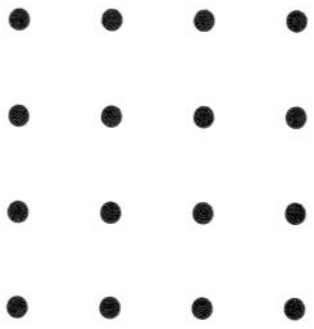

____

e) 

____

f) 

____

g) 

____

h) 

____

3. Write as many different names as you can for the polygon.

a) 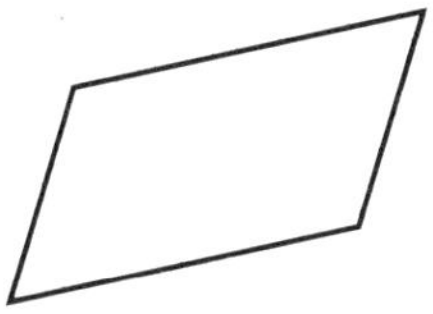

b) 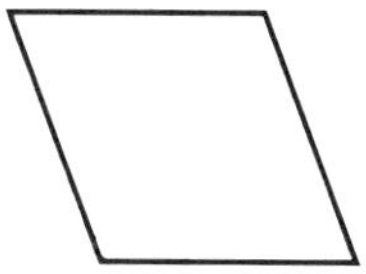

c) 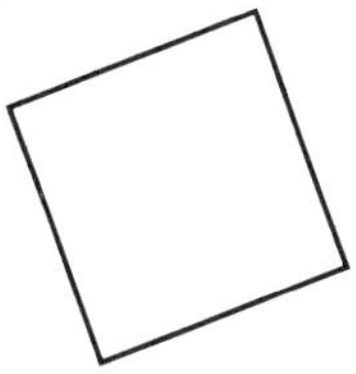

d) 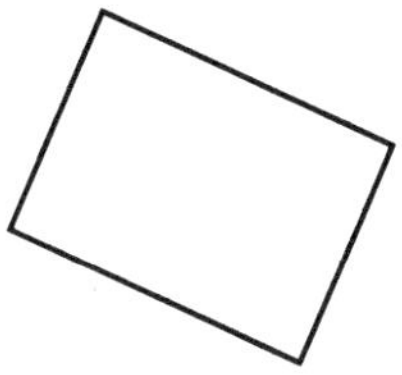

4. Sketch two different quadrilaterals with the given property. Make one quadrilateral of *any type* and try to make the other a *special type* (rectangle, square, parallelogram, rhombus, or trapezoid).

a) exactly 2 right angles

b) exactly 3 equal sides

G5-24 Parallel and Perpendicular in 3-D Shapes

Clara places 3-D shapes on a table.

Edges and faces that run straight up and down are vertical.

Edges and faces that run side to side like the table-top are horizontal.

The bases of the prism are horizontal.

All of the side faces are vertical.

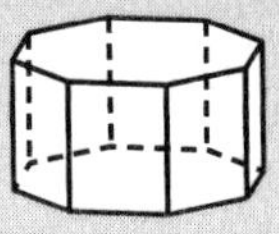

The base of the pyramid is horizontal.

None of the side faces are vertical.

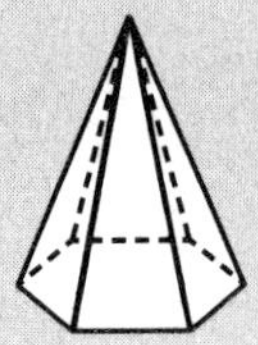

1. Imagine the shape is on a table. One face is shaded or one edge is darkened.
Is it vertical, horizontal, or neither?

a) 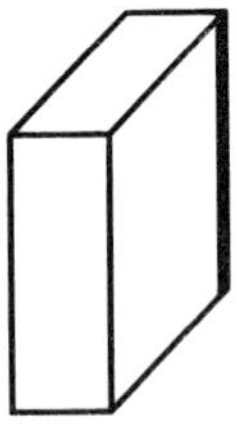

vertical

b) 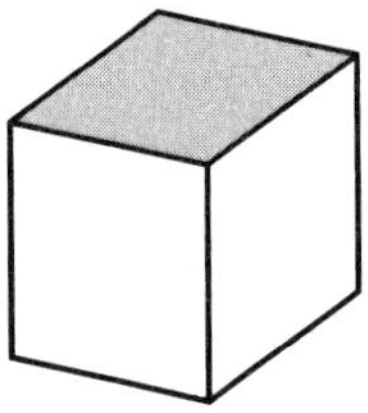

______

c) 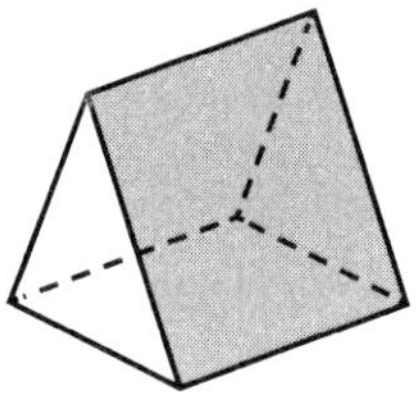

______

d) 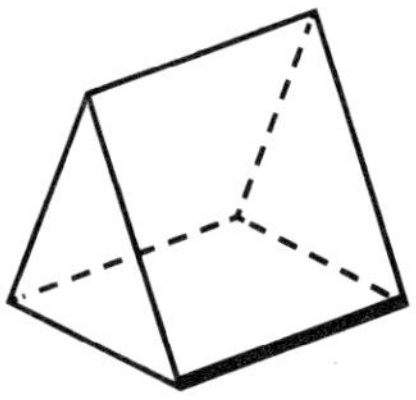

______

Faces that run in the same direction and are always the same distance apart are called **parallel faces**.

To check if two faces are parallel, place one face flat on a table and check if the other face is also horizontal.

In the shape at the right, the shaded faces are parallel.

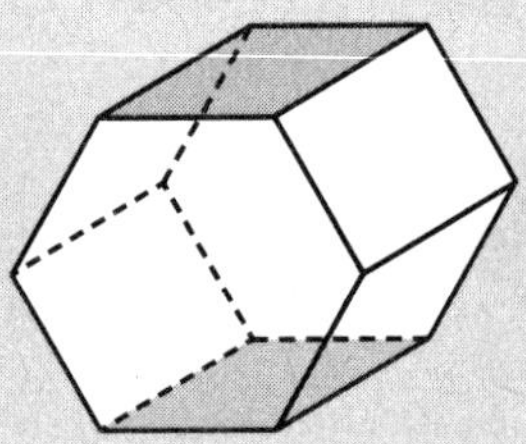

2. Are the shaded faces parallel? Write "yes" or "no." Use actual 3-D shapes if you need to.

a) 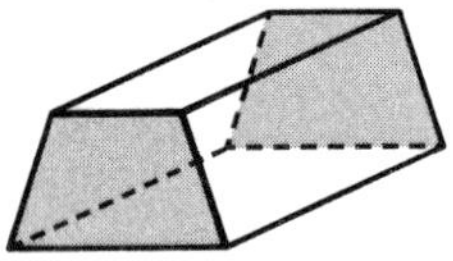

______

b) 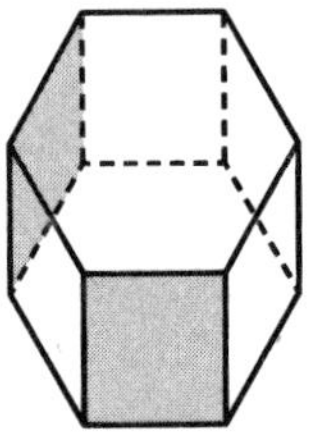

______

c) 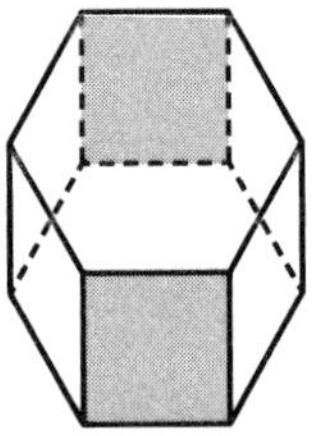

______

BONUS ▶ 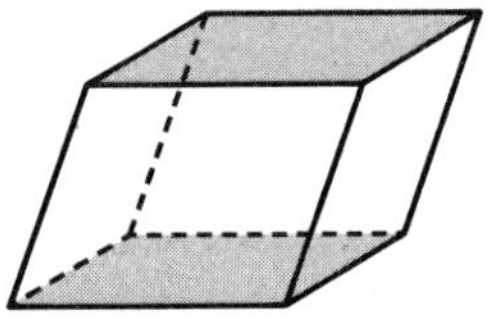

______

d) 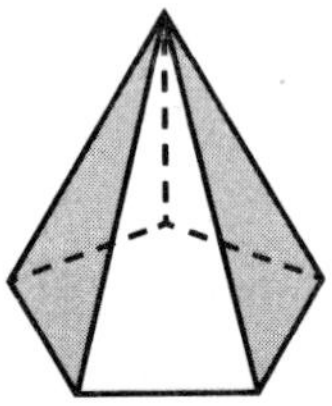

______

e) 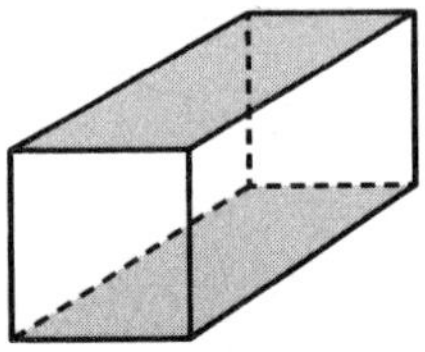

______

f) 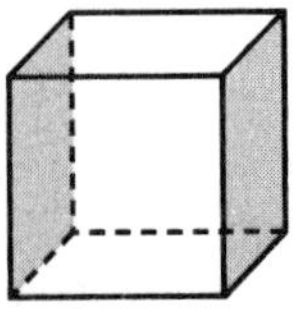

______

BONUS ▶ 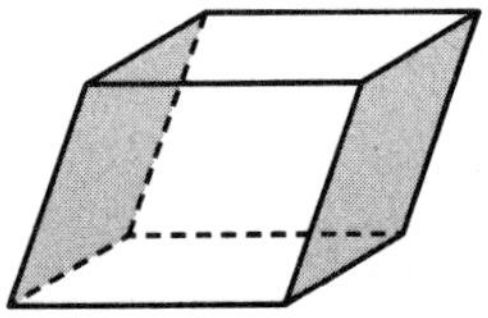

______

Faces that meet at a right angle are **perpendicular faces**. To check if two faces are perpendicular, place one face flat on a table and check if the other face is vertical.

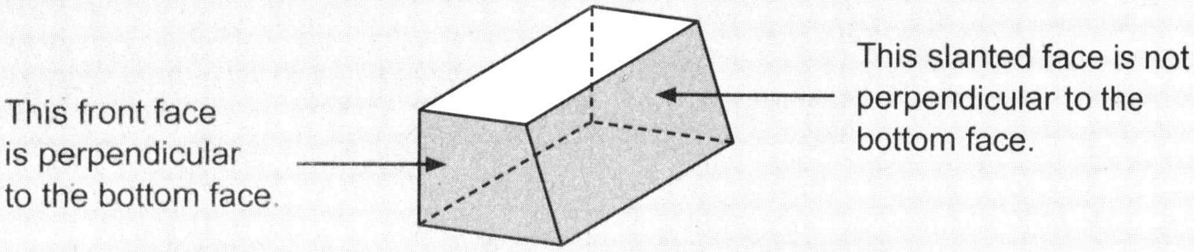

3. Are the shaded faces perpendicular? Write “yes” or “no.” Use actual 3-D shapes if you need to.

a) 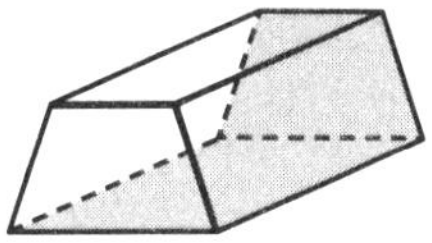 ________

b) 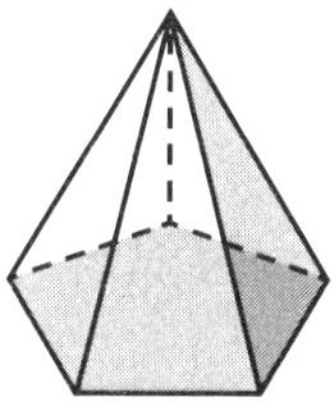 ________

c) 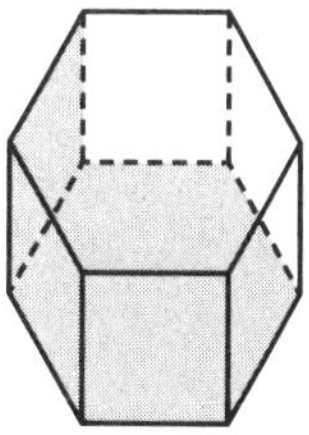 ________

d) 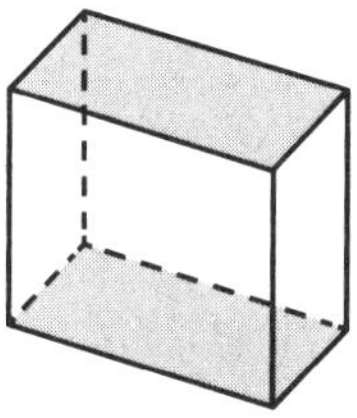 ________

4. Are the darkened edges parallel, perpendicular, or neither?

a) 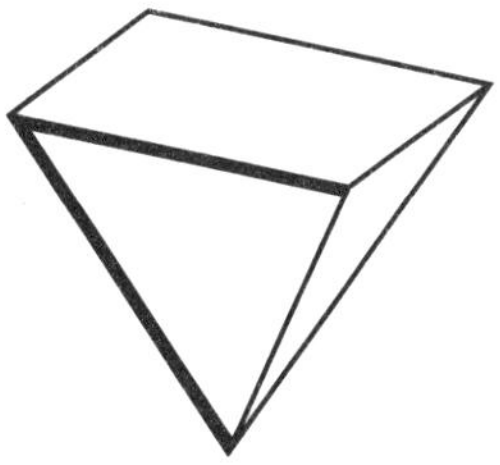 ____________

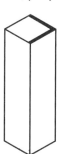

b)  ____________

c) 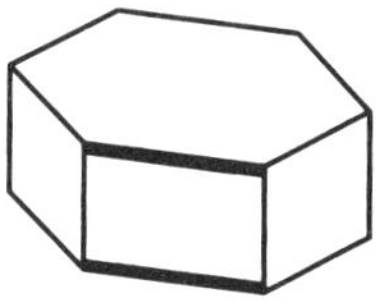 ____________

d) 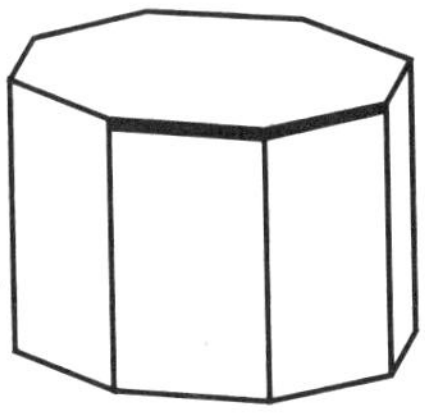 ____________

5. Are the shaded faces parallel, perpendicular, or neither?

a) 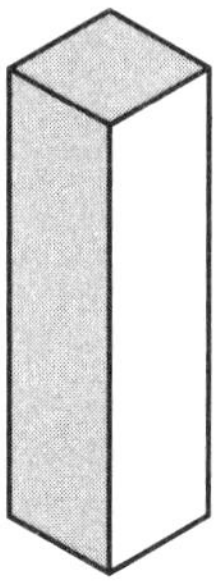 ____________

b) 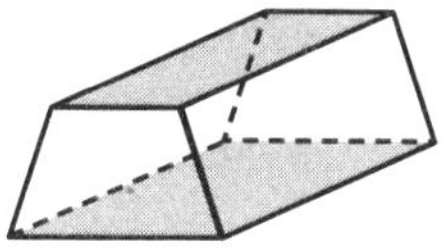 ____________

c) 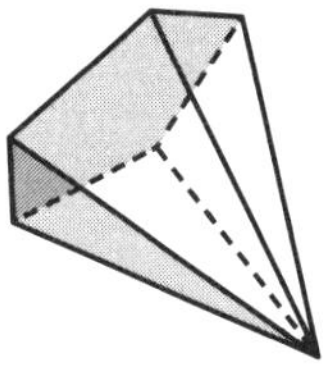 ____________

d) 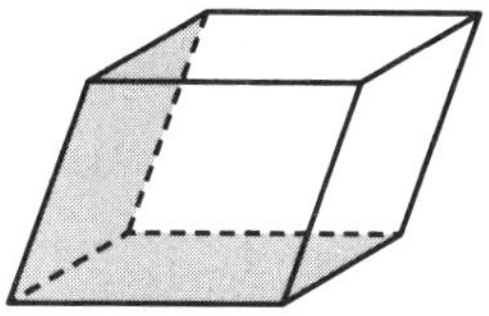 ____________